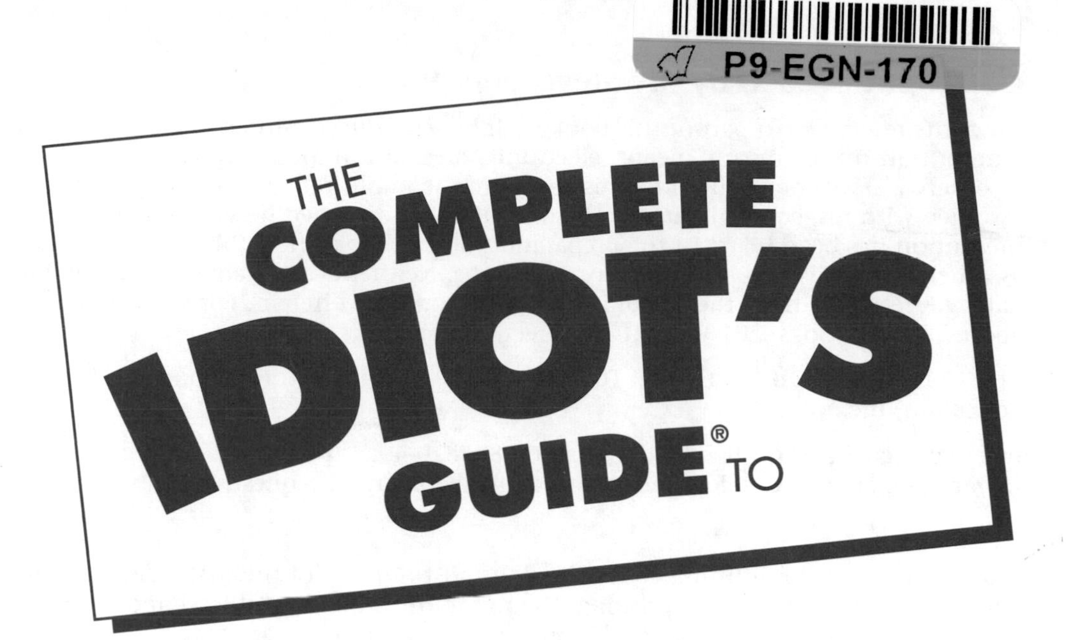

Eastern Philosophy

by Jay Stevenson, Ph.D.

A Pearson Education Company

International Standard Book Number: 0-02-863820-4
Library of Congress Catalog Card Number: Available upon request.

04 03 02 8 7 6 5 4

Interpretation of the printing code: The rightmost number of the first series of numbers is the year of the book's printing; the rightmost number of the second series of numbers is the number of the book's printing. For example, a printing code of 00-1 shows that the first printing occurred in 2000.

Printed in the United States of America

For marketing and publicity, please call: 317-581-3722

The publisher offers discounts on this book when ordered in quantity for bulk purchases and special sales.

For sales within the United States, please contact: Corporate and Government Sales, 1-800-382-3419 or corpsales@pearsontechgroup.com

Outside the United States, please contact: International Sales, 317-581-3793 or international@pearsontechgroup.com

Publisher
Marie Butler-Knight

Product Manager
Phil Kitchel

Associate Managing Editor
Cari Shaw Fischer

Acquisitions Editor
Amy Zavatto

Development Editor
Doris Cross

Production Editor
Christy Wagner

Illustrator
Jody P. Schaeffer

Cover Designers
Mike Freeland
Kevin Spear

Book Designers
Scott Cook and Amy Adams of DesignLab

Indexer
Tonya Heard

Layout/Proofreading
Svetlana Dominquez
Terri Edwards
Ayanna Lacey
Timothy Osborn
Mark Walchle

Contents at a Glance

Appendixes

Contents

Appendixes

Foreword

Don't be put off by the unorthodox title and format of this book. It is a serious and thorough look at Eastern philosophy, but written in an informal and reader-friendly way. Or in the words of the Western sages, "old wine in a new bottle."

While it would certainly be ideal to be able to curl up on a couch with a volume of the Confucian *Analects*, the *Heart Sutra*, or the Gita, today's reader is more likely to be scurrying from place to place and always behind schedule. Even our vacations are hurried, and without the blocks of time we need to read a serious book from cover to cover. So, for the reader interested in Eastern philosophy—who often winds up sandwiched between two other passengers in an overbooked aircraft—this is the book to carry. While it deals with ideas of great complexity, because of the way *The Complete Idiot's Guide to Eastern Philosophy* is organized, it is accessible and rewarding when sampled in chunks of any length.

The author is certainly right when he writes in the introduction that Eastern thought is often noted for its profundity, depth, and elusiveness. Its elusiveness is especially interesting and puzzling at the same time. This elusiveness has to do with several things. First, it has to do with language. How do you understand terms or concepts such as "emptiness" or "nothingness"; "nirvana" or "awareness" that have their origin in another language? Do they mean anything, or are they nonsense? These are terms and concepts we don't know quite what to do with given our Western mindset.

Second, it has to do with the style of presentation or the discourse of Eastern philosophers. Seldom will you find a straight-line argument as in Western-style philosophical texts. Eastern style is more convoluted and circular—not in a bad sense. It is frequently less direct and seems repetitive. The argument will curl back on itself as it were. One can think of an Eastern philosophical text as more like a musical composition or a painting. As in a musical composition, there is a statement of the theme and/or motifs, then a development, variations on the theme, and recapitulation. And if you still don't get it, well.... This is the pattern that an Eastern thinker might employ. And if you still don't get it at the end, the teacher will resort to shock treatment. A Zen master might actually whack you with a stick. The more gentle Taoist thinker will browbeat you intellectually. Read the text of the *Chuang-tzu* to find out.

The third and final point is that Eastern thought attempts to make us use some of our other mental faculties instead of just the critical analysis and chronological historical reasoning that dominate our thinking 95 percent of the time. These are the faculties, or consciousnesses, for lack of a better term, that we can have when we dream, daydream, or meditate. Eastern thought can induce us to employ these faculties more fully and in new ways. How do we experience emptiness or nothingness? How do we perceive the sound of one hand clapping? Eastern thinkers want to take us into another dimension of our being. If you think you are reading a one-dimensional text when you read the Buddhist text, the *Heart Sutra,* think again.

Jay Stevenson's highly reliable and thoroughly engaging guide does a fine job of bringing the Western reader into the intriguing and richly varied world of Eastern philosophy. Take this book along with you on your next trip to Bermuda or China or Japan and explore the mysteries of Eastern thought. If you don't succeed in understanding it all the first time, don't give up; try again.

Peter Li, Ph.D.

Peter Li, born in China and educated in the United States, received his Ph.D. in Chinese literature at the University of Chicago, and teaches at Rutgers, the State University of New Jersey. He has written on a variety of topics on Asia and teaches a course on Classical Chinese and Greek thought.

Introduction

Eastern thought has a well-deserved reputation for profundity, depth, and elusiveness. Rising with the dawn of the great Eastern civilizations and developing over the course of centuries in almost complete isolation from the West, Eastern philosophy holds important secrets that have begun to make sense in the Western world only recently. A typical Westerner, brought up to have a pragmatic, scientific, and individualistic mind set, is likely to feel confused, thick-headed, and intimidated in the face of Eastern wisdom. If you know this feeling, there's no need to feel disoriented anymore.

Deep and mysterious though it may seem, Eastern philosophy makes good sense if you learn to see it in the right way. And, if you stop to think about it, you may realize you're already somewhat familiar with Eastern ideas. You've heard of Confucius, karma, and kung fu; dharma and the Tao; yin, yang, and yoga. These and many other concepts from various branches of Eastern philosophy have been arousing the interest of growing numbers of Westerners. While Eastern ideas remain mysterious and exotic to much of the world, many others are finding that they are not only familiar, but useful, supplying helpful approaches to all aspects of life, from sports to spirituality.

A Note on Spelling

Using the Roman alphabet (the alphabet used to write most Western languages, including English) to write Chinese words is a tricky business. Unlike the Roman alphabet, Chinese characters are not based on sound, so it is Chinese speech—as opposed to Chinese writing—that must be translated. This poses a difficult challenge because Chinese words are pronounced differently in different parts of China. Since there are no hard-and-fast rules for pronunciation, we have to rely on convention. The problem is, convention keeps changing. The two most widely used systems for "Romanizing" Chinese today are the Wade-Giles and the Pinyin systems. The Pinyin system has been gaining in popularity in recent years, but the Wade-Giles system has been in use longer. Except where noted, this book uses the Wade-Giles system to conform to the many important translations of Chinese philosophical works that also use this system.

Here's a breakdown of the sections of this book to make it easier for you to follow your own path:

Part 1, "Orient-ation," where you'll find an overview of the Big Four Eastern philosophies (Hinduism, Buddhism, Taoism, and Confucianism) describing the general character of Eastern thought and sketching its history and influence, including its impact on the West.

Part 2, "Do You Hindu?" discusses the rich philosophical traditions of India from their early beginnings to the Indian Renaissance of the nineteenth and twentieth centuries. You can read about the origins of Hinduism and the ancient Vedas; views of enlightenment, karma, and rebirth; the caste system; and reactions to the new influences of Buddhism and, later, of Western imperialism.

Part 3, "Shake Your Buddha," gives you everything you need to know about Buddhism, one of the world's most important religious philosophies. Since its beginnings in India, Buddhism has spread throughout the world and taken on many new shapes in the process. You can read about the Buddha's teachings, the Theravada and Mahayana traditions, Tantrism, Zen, and other Buddhist spinoffs.

Part 4, "'Way' Cool," focuses on Taoism, one of the most popular and influential strains of Eastern philosophy in the West. Here you can read about the great Taoist sages Lao Tzu and Chuang Tzu, the Taoist principles of wu wei and yin and yang, and the traditional religious approaches to Taoism.

Part 5, "Sages in Service," deals with Confucianism and related branches of Chinese philosophy. In the process, there's a lot to learn here about the role philosophy took in Dynastic China in building and maintaining the imperial Chinese civilization.

Part 6, "Living Wisdom," talks about the many ways Eastern wisdom has been applied to matters of daily life, including many ideas that have become especially influential in the West, such as martial arts and holistic medicine. There are also chapters on food, sex, the arts, business, and government.

And to help you get a good look at Eastern wisdom from front to back, the book concludes with appendixes containing useful information: a glossary, an annotated list of important Eastern thinkers, and a list of books for further reading.

Extras

Meanwhile, as you flip through the book in search of whatever it is you may be looking for, you'll notice lots of boxes containing all kinds of insights, trivia, advice, definitions, and quotations you may find interesting and useful. Here's what they look like:

Lotus Lore

This sidebar, which takes its name from a beautiful and highly revered flower of Asia, includes background explaining what a particular idea or practice "stems from."

Orient Expressions

What you'll find in these boxes is intended to help you on your train ride through Eastern thought by defining the terms you'll encounter along the way. If you don't know what they mean, they can be murder!

Karma Dogma

Even if your karma runs over your dogma, you can still get things sorted out by checking these boxes, which encapsulate famous teachings and quotations from the East.

Not in This Life

Avoid getting reborn into a future life as a warthog by paying attention to these philosophical pitfalls.

Acknowledgments

Many thanks to Takashi Yokoyama for consultation and bibliographic assistance.

Special Thanks to the Technical Reviewers

The Complete Idiot's Guide to Eastern Philosophy was reviewed by two experts who provided insight and guidance to the author and checked the technical accuracy of what is in these pages.

Steven F. Walker, Professor of Comparative Literature at Rutgers University, has been interested in Indian philosophy for a long time. He began the study of Sanskrit as an undergraduate at the University of Wisconsin, and continued at Harvard University, where he got a Ph.D. in Comparative Literature. He has published widely on a number of topics; his most recent book is *Jung and the Jungians on Myth* (Garland Publishers, 1995). He is a member of the Ramakrishna-Vivekananda Vedanta Center of Massachusetts and shares with the author of this book the opinion that Eastern philosophy is as much about experience as it is about ideas.

Michael Hill is a Ph.D. student in Comparative Literature at Rutgers University. His research interests include gender studies in Chinese literature of the Ch'ing Dynasty and early twentieth century, and cultural interactions between China and the West in the nineteenth and twentieth centuries.

Part 1

Orient-ation

Over the course of the past century, growing numbers of Westerners have come to regard Eastern philosophy as a valuable supplement and alternative to Western ways of thinking. As a result, Eastern ideas are becoming increasingly familiar and important in the West. Eastern thought has had such a profound influence on Western popular culture, lifestyle, world view, and spirituality that it's becoming hard to tell East and West apart.

Yet Eastern and Western traditions each have their own history and development that help account for important differences in approach. In fact, the Eastern and Western hemispheres of the planet are as different from one another in their thinking as the right and left hemispheres of the brain. Understanding either from the perspective of the other can be a real challenge.

But once you begin to see the main differences between the two traditions, the many complicated features of each begin to fall into place more easily. So, in this overview, you can orient yourself with the basics: a broad view of the Big Four Eastern philosophies, a general view of how they are related historically as well as conceptually, and an explanation of the main differences between Eastern and Western thought.

Chapter 1

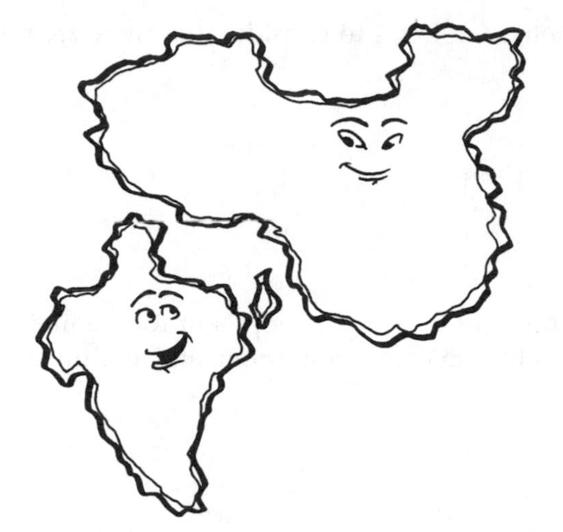

Four Ways to Wisdom

In This Chapter

- The Big Four Eastern philosophies
- Origins, development, and influence
- "Mainstream" Hinduism
- The many ways of Buddhism
- The Tao and Confucian philosophies

Eastern philosophy includes some of the oldest ideas on record about the nature of human beings, the cosmos, and the purpose of existence. After nearly four millennia, during which it has developed and spread all over the world, it remains vitally meaningful in many of its modern-day incarnations. Ideas and traditions stemming from the many schools of Hinduism, Buddhism, Taoism, and Confucianism continue to guide millions of people in their search for wisdom and contentment.

Yet it can be difficult to understand the various traditions of Eastern philosophy in themselves and hard to tell them apart. Philosophical schools branch off and recombine as they spread from place to place and from generation to generation. In the process, they can become transformed almost beyond recognition. Yoga as practiced by gurus in an ashram in ancient India is radically different from yoga practiced by fitness buffs at a workshop in contemporary Indiana.

In sorting out the diversity of Eastern thought, it helps to consider that there are four main traditions:

- Hindu
- Buddhist
- Taoist
- Confucian

These four traditions owe their origins and most of their development to two major civilizations of the East: Hinduism and Buddhism come from India, and Taoism and Confucianism come from China.

The Big Four

The Big Four Eastern philosophies are not, strictly speaking, the only philosophies of the East, just as India and China are not the only Eastern civilizations. But the Big Four have proven most influential in the lives, minds, and histories of people throughout the East. Japan, Korea, Burma, and Nepal all have their own traditions of life and thought. At the same time, they also have much in common. The common features of these distinct traditions reflect the shared influences of the Big Four philosophies, which have made their mark throughout the East and beyond.

Shifting Scenes

In the process of spreading and developing, the Big Four philosophies have been continually modified as new groups of people incorporated them in different ways into their lives and cultures. You might say these philosophies have gone through many incarnations over the years! But despite repeated rebirths and distant travels from place to place, many central ideas have remained intact and are still recognized and applied today.

After reading just a little about the origins, the history, and the basic ideas behind each of the Big Four, you'll be able to tell them apart in your own mind. What's more, you'll probably begin to see how the basic features of each of the four can be combined with one another and with other ideas from other sources to produce new philosophical hybrids.

Lotus Lore

The mixing of ideas and beliefs is common throughout the history of Eastern philosophy. After Buddhism branched off from Hinduism, some Hindus embraced the Buddha as an *avatar,* or incarnation, of the Hindu god Vishnu. In Japan, Buddhism merged with the native Shinto religion, and the Buddha became one of the Kami, or Shinto gods. An astonishing Chinese legend claims that the Buddha is actually the Taoist philosopher Lao Tzu! According to the story, Lao Tzu traveled from China to India to teach and became the Buddha.

In This Corner ...

Here, right off the bat, is a brief overview of each of the Big Four so you'll have an idea of what to expect:

- **Hinduism.** The most influential native philosophy of India. Rather than single, organized belief system, Hinduism encompasses a host of various practices and beliefs recognized for centuries by millions of people. It has its origins in some of the oldest known writings, the Vedas (ca. 1500 B.C.E.), which include hymns to the Hindu gods, as well as philosophical speculation about the nature of ultimate existence. It incorporates Indian ways of life, religion, and scholarship.
- **Buddhism.** Practices and beliefs derived from the teachings of Siddhartha Sautama ("The Buddha" or "Enlightened One," ca. 560 B.C.E.). The Buddha was an Indian prince who attained enlightenment after decades of seeking, fasting, and meditation. He taught that all desire leads to suffering, which can be overcome by renouncing desire. Buddhism spread from India throughout the East, including Tibet, Southeast Asia, Korea, China, and Japan, where it merged with native traditions and changed form. Meanwhile, in India, wherever it wasn't reabsorbed into Hinduism, it died out except on the island of Sri Lanka.
- **Taoism.** Philosophy derived from the writings of ancient Chinese sages, most notably Yang Chu (fourth century B.C.E.), Lao Tzu (sixth or fourth century B.C.E.), and Chuang Tzu (fourth to third centuries B.C.E.). Of these three, Lao Tzu is the most famous for being the attributed author of the *Tao Te Ching* (*The Book of the Way and Its Power*). Philosophical Taoism emphasizes spontaneity, intuitive action, and harmony with nature. In addition, there is a religious, occult strain

of Taoism that emphasizes the search for immortality and the correspondences among human, natural, and cosmic spheres.

- **Confucianism.** Philosophy based on the teachings of K'ung Fu Tzu (ca. 550 B.C.E.), known in the West as Confucius. It stresses social harmony fostered through respect for superiors and benevolence toward subordinates. It became the official philosophy of imperial China starting from around 200 C.E. right up until 1911 and the fall of the Ch'ing Dynasty and founding of the Chinese Republic. Confucian learning formed the basis of the imperial examination system used for selecting public officials and supplied much of the rationale for the administration of the Chinese empire.

Into India

Karma Dogma

My religion is Hinduism, which, for me, is the religion of humanity and includes the best of all religions known to me.

—Mohandas Mahatma Gandhi

The many branches of Hindu thought and religion have developed a reputation in the West for being especially difficult to grasp. There are many reasons for this perception, but none of them necessarily stand in the way of getting a good understanding of the basics of Hinduism.

One major difficulty in getting a grasp of Hinduism stems from the sheer number and diversity of Hindu practices and beliefs. Another difficulty is that many of these beliefs are inherently very different from Western ways of thinking and thus largely unfamiliar to most Westerners. Major difficulties, however, come from having to reckon with the inherent differences between Hinduism in general and the ways of thinking familiar to most Westerners. As a result, explaining Hinduism to someone who knows nothing about it is a little bit like explaining frozen dessert to someone who's never heard of a freezer. There's ice cream (hard and soft) and frozen yogurt, and many different flavors and ways to eat them. And then there are all the different toppings and mix-ins. You could explain it all for hours and still not convince someone who lacks the basic reference points that any of it is worth eating.

In any case, much like different flavors of soft-serve ice cream, different forms of Hinduism are easily blended with one another—sometimes in ways that can seem strange to Westerners. For one thing, much of Hinduism is deeply religious and deeply philosophical at the same time.

Then there are all kinds of ideas about worldly reality and appearance on the one hand and cosmic reality on the other. And in between these two "realities," there's a whole slew of ideas about human reality: What human nature is, what human consciousness is capable of doing, and how human society should function.

Every Which Way but Loose

Just to get a sense of the various forms Hindu thought can take, consider that many Hindus believe in God or in many gods, whereas many do not. Those that do believe in gods adopt all kinds of different attitudes toward them. Some regard God much the way many fundamentalist Christians regard Jesus Christ—as an all-powerful being who cares deeply about them and whom they lovingly adore as a personal savior. Other Hindus believe in many gods and worship each one for different reasons. Still others regard the gods as especially happy, lucky, and blessed beings who should not be worshiped or even imitated, but rather left to themselves. The idea here is that mere human beings should resist the desire for things the gods enjoy so as to concentrate more on their own cosmic destiny.

Not in This Life

If you try to compare Chinese and Indian traditions, you'll find a much greater record of the Chinese. But don't conclude that the Chinese were necessarily more influential. Indian civilization became highly advanced at an extremely early time in the world's history. Yet, unlike China, India did not have its own ancient historians to keep track of who did what and when.

Different beliefs within Hinduism are often hard to tell apart. A single god may be known by various names and be worshiped in different forms. Many gods have numerous incarnations. Krishna, for example, is an incarnation of Vishnu. Some Indians worship Krishna but not Vishnu, whereas others worship Vishnu but not Krishna. Others worship both; still others worship neither. Those who do worship do so in different ways, while those who don't worship disbelieve for different reasons.

While ideas about the relationship between God or the gods and humanity differ from place to place in India, they have continually changed over time in response to changing attitudes and changing social and economic conditions. These changes can be extremely hard to sort out since many ideas that go back to ancient times were transmitted by word of mouth from generation to generation long before being written down. In fact, one of India's important philosophical traditions is that of the guru, who establishes a close and special relationship with his disciple.

The tradition survives because many Indians continue to believe that reading and writing are not adequate substitutes for the personal philosophical instruction that can be supplied by a guru, who is thought to possess knowledge that cannot be expressed in written form. This is not to say, of course, that written sources are not crucial to understanding Hindu thought. In fact, the oldest philosophical writings ever produced come from India and contain the first kernels of Hinduism.

Finding the Center

Just from this brief account so far, you might get the idea that Hinduism is all over the place, with all kinds of different attitudes and beliefs. And this is true in a way. At the same time, however, there are central ideas and central traditions that help make sense of the big picture. Many of these stem from a group of ancient writings called the Vedas. The Vedas include hymns to gods and descriptions of ritual in addition to philosophical speculation. Most of what is now considered the philosophical portion of the Vedas is contained in a group of Vedic writings known as the Upanishads.

The Vedas are the oldest and most important writings in the cultural history of India and are among the most renowned ancient texts in the world. The philosophical ideas in the Vedas, stemming from around 1500 B.C.E. or even before, are profound but somewhat contradictory and undeveloped. They have always been recognized as sacred texts in India, but not by everyone. Those who have recognized their sacred status emphasize different teachings and interpret them in different ways. In fact, in the centuries following the ancient Vedic period, various points of view for and against the Vedas were formed.

As a reaction to the growing confusion and disagreement in regard to the Vedas, an important school of Hindu thought known as Vedanta philosophy emerged around the eighth century C.E. Vedanta means "end of the Vedas," and represents an attempt on the part of Vedic philosophers to restore the authority and recover the original purpose of these ancient texts. The school is called "end of the Vedas" because it bases its thinking on the Upanishads, which were written toward the end of the Vedic period and are thought to represent the culmination of Vedic writing. Vedanta emerged as the most influential school of Indian philosophy. Many have come to regard Vedanta and the Upanishadic teachings stressed by Vedanta philosophy as the backbone of Hindu thought.

Orient Expressions

Maya is the Hindu concept of illusion, used to account for virtually all the problems of worldly existence.

Maya Culpa

One of the key insights found in the Vedas and emphasized by Vedantic philosophy is the idea that the world of apparent reality—the world as we perceive it with our senses—is a world of illusion, or *maya*. Things as they appear are impermanent, misleading, and unreliable. This concept of maya—the problem of illusion—accounts for everything that goes wrong with life. When good things go wrong and when plans and hopes don't pan out, the reason is that the shifting world of appearances cannot be depended upon.

So, to deal with the problem of maya, Vedantic philosophy turns inward in an attempt to find a permanent and reliable answer. This answer, which must be rediscovered on an individual basis by each person who achieves enlightenment, is the merging of the individual consciousness with the divine inner self, called Atman, which is identical with absolute, transcendent being: the ultimate reality known as Brahman. This merger of the finite self with ultimate reality produces perfect clarity of consciousness, so that one is no longer deceived by maya or troubled by the shifting, swirling world of appearances.

For many Hindus, achieving enlightenment is the highest challenge of existence, posing such difficulty that it can take a succession of many lifetimes. In fact, Vedantic philosophy is not the only system of Indian thought that recognizes the problem of maya and promotes the personal quest for enlightenment. Vedanta stands out, however, in linking these ideas with the Vedas and in ascribing the highest authority to Vedic teachings.

School Work

Because Vedanta recognizes the authority of the Vedas as a guide to reliable knowledge, it is considered an orthodox system of Indian philosophy. In fact, it is one of six orthodox schools. Although not all six focus on the Vedas to the same extent or in the same manner as Vedanta, they are all basically in agreement in their view of the world. The names of these six systems or schools are Nyaya, Vaisheshika, Sankhya, Yoga, Mimamsa, and Vedanta.

You can read about these systems in detail in Chapters 7, "Building on Tradition," and 8, "Yogi Bearings," but for now, here's an abbreviated description of each one:

- **Nyaya** focuses on logic and reasoning.
- **Vaisheshika** is known for its theory of atomism.
- **Sankhya** explains the world of appearances with its theory of evolution.
- **Yoga** is a school of philosophy as well as a set of techniques and practices observed within many different philosophies.
- **Mimamsa** is chiefly concerned with action in connection with Vedic teachings.
- **Vedanta** is concerned with the nature of Brahman and its relation to the world as described in the Vedas.

All six orthodox systems formed into schools in response to the rise of philosophies in India that rejected Vedic authority. The most well-known of these unorthodox systems are Carvaka, Jainism, and Buddhism. You can read about Carvaka and Jainism in Chapter 6, "Going to Extremes." Buddhism, of course, gets its own section in this book after the one on Hinduism.

Not in This Life

You won't be able to develop an accurate conception of Carvaka because it died out long ago and is known today mostly from criticisms of it made by adherents of competing schools. It is possible that early Carvaka writings were destroyed at some point in acts of censorship.

For now, here's a thumbnail sketch of each of the three main unorthodox systems of India:

- **Carvaka** denies the existence of transcendent or natural unity. According to Carvaka, existence is limited to what we are capable of perceiving. If you can't tell it's there with any of your five senses, it isn't there! This position corresponds to the Western notion of empiricism. Carvakists were portrayed in a negative light as immoral hedonists by orthodox philosophers.
- **Jainism** teaches rigorous self-denial as the way to enlightenment. The original Jains were among the world's first monks, retreating from ordinary life to devote themselves to fasting and meditation. Some Jaina communities still exist today.
- **Buddhism** deals with the problem that all existence is suffering and teaches a way to rise above this problem—not through mere self denial as with the Jains, but through dissolving the subtle bonds between self and world that feed human desire. Buddhism is also an early monastic sect, or group of sects, since it quickly spread throughout the world. Like Jainism, it denies Vedic authority even while drawing on some Vedic teachings, in attempting to strip Hinduism of unnecessary beliefs and rituals.

Escape from India

Most Jains and Buddhists, of course, don't regard themselves as "unorthodox" Hindus, but as, well, orthodox Jains and Buddhists. Yet both Jainism and Buddhism start with Hindu ideas and take them in new directions. Jainism can be seen as a more severe and rigorous approach to the basic problem of illusion, wanting nothing to do with the many temptations that beset humanity. Buddhism, in contrast, tends to be more relaxed about this problem. Existence is basically illusory, but we can learn to live with the illusions as we work to rise above them. This approach to life turned out to have tremendous appeal outside of India, even though Indian Buddhism eventually faded.

Friends in High Places

This relaxed, accepting approach to the problems of life has helped Buddhism spread throughout the East and into the West. Everywhere it's gone, it has picked up much of the character of its new environment. As a result, even though Buddhists everywhere recognize and accept many of the basic teachings, including the importance of the quest for enlightenment, the notion of what it takes to attain enlightenment varies from place to place.

Orient Expressions

Boddhisattvas, "seekers of enlightenment," are Buddhist adepts who are said to have postponed the attainment of nirvana in order to help others become enlightened. They are legendary figures of Mahayana Buddhism.

For some Buddhists, enlightenment, or nirvana, as Buddhists refer to it, is as difficult to attain as it is for the Jains, requiring years of meditation and yoga and the ceaseless effort to renounce, once and for all, every inclination to feel tempted by the vain pleasures life has to offer. For others, the difference between the state of enlightenment and the state of nonenlightenment is itself illusory. According to this view, everyone is, in a sense, already enlightened, even though they may not realize it. For these people, the challenge of Buddhism is to free the mind of unnecessary and troublesome distinctions.

Still others recognize the challenge of enlightenment as so great that they have no intention of meeting it by themselves. They rely on the help of *Boddhisattvas* in making their spiritual journey. Boddhisattvas are exalted beings who have attained nirvana already, but remain involved with humanity in order to help others. Some Buddhists worship and pray to Boddhisattvas as gods. Others venerate them as teachers and role models.

Different Spins

Buddhism is traditionally broken into two forms. There's Theravada, which means "Doctrine of the Elders." Theravadans believe their brand of Buddhism most closely adheres to original Buddhist teachings. They emphasize the importance of working to attain nirvana on one's own through practice and meditation and without the assistance of Boddhisattvas.

Because of its emphasis on personal inward effort and original teachings, Theravada Buddhism has generally resisted the influence of folk beliefs and other new and alien ideas. In particular, the idea that it is possible to attain nirvana with outside help is contrary to the Theravada attitude. Perhaps as a result of its more rigorous attitude, Theravada has not spread widely, but is concentrated today mainly on the island of Sri Lanka and a few other places in the East.

The other major strand of Buddhism has been more open to new influences and has adopted many different forms as it has spread throughout the East to China, Japan, Korea, Tibet, and elsewhere. This is Mahayana Buddhism, which means "Greater Vehicle." The "vehicle" is the set of teachings that carries your understanding to enlightenment. You could say the Greater Vehicle is a bandwagon, since so many people have climbed on board!

Mahayana Buddhists recognize many different Buddhist teachings in addition to those accepted by Theravada Buddhists. Over the course of time, new ideas became added to Mahayana and incorporated into its many approaches, though some Mahayanans say that all of the teachings, both new and old, represent the original teachings of the Buddha. They explain this variety of teachings by saying that the Buddha recognized that different people have different capacities and are inclined to benefit more from some ideas than others, so he gave different lessons intended for different audiences.

Lotus Lore

Organized Buddhism has spread all over the world. Over a thousand Buddhist meditation centers have started up in North America, most of them within the past thirty years. One Western innovation that has been incorporated into traditional Buddhist practice includes the use of telecommunication lines enabling students to receive instruction from teachers efficiently while meditating! The technology allows greater numbers of students to get individualized guidance while in a meditative state.

In any case, Mahayana Buddhism includes many traditions described later in this book. In Tibet, Buddhist ideas have become the basis for the traditional system of government, run by the Dalai Lama. In China and Japan, Buddhist outgrowths such as the Lotus school and the Pure Land Sect offer salvation to many believers. Also, in China and Japan, Ch'an Buddhism (Zen in Japanese) has become the basis of a naturalistic and spontaneous approach to life, culture, and the arts.

Chinese Minds

Zen, to Westerners, is one of the best-known and most widely appreciated forms of Buddhism. It originated in China, where it derived much of its special character, thanks in part to the influence of the ancient and mystic Chinese philosophy known as Tao, "the Way." Taoism apparently began around 600 B.C.E., almost 800 years before Buddhism came to China. Taoism has existed as a distinct philosophy ever since and, at the same time, has merged with other philosophies, especially Buddhism and Confucianism, putting its mark on the Chinese approach to life and thought.

Finding the Way

Although there is no one single founder of Taoism, the first and most important Taoist writing is the *Tao Te Ching* (*The Book of the Way and Its Power*), which is attributed to the sage Lao Tzu. According to tradition, Lao Tzu lived around 600 B.C.E., although many scholars now say he lived centuries later. In any case, Taoist ideas were clearly in circulation by 600 B.C.E., when Taoists and Confucians first began to discuss their different views of life.

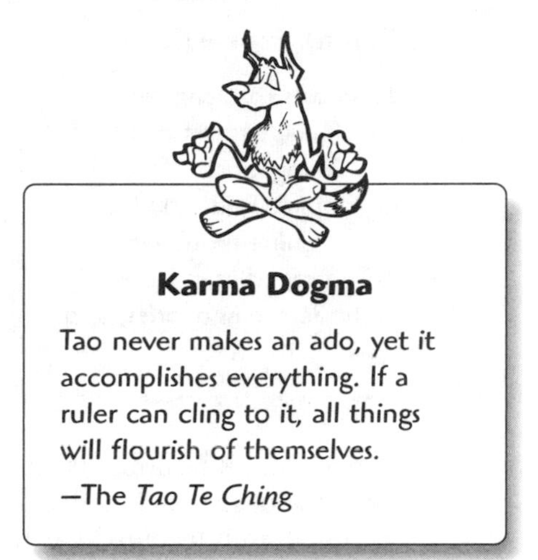

Karma Dogma

Tao never makes an ado, yet it accomplishes everything. If a ruler can cling to it, all things will flourish of themselves.

—The *Tao Te Ching*

The ancient Taoists were recluses who believed that society is based on vain ambitions and hypocrisy. Their approach to life is to avoid conflict with others and to seek harmony with nature. Paradoxically, the wisdom that leads the Taoists to shun society also provides guidance for working effectively within it. Thus the *Tao Te Ching* speaks of the advantages of a solitary lifestyle, but also suggests ways of dealing with people and events so as not to get swept up and carried away by foolish hopes and fears.

By understanding and correcting the temptation to build yourself up and acquire what you don't need, you can detach yourself from the superficial and selfish concerns of society and appreciate the natural, underlying rhythms of life as circumstances develop and change and give rise to new circumstances. This dynamic pattern is produced by the Tao, a mysterious principle that guides the flow of events in such a way as to nourish all beings. By learning to act in harmony with the Tao, it is possible to exert a positive influence on others or, alternatively, to find happiness in solitude.

Many Taoists came to believe that the benefits of the Tao far exceed mere happiness and harmony to include immortality. They believed death is caused by natural imbalance and can be overcome through various techniques of purifying the body. This belief gave rise to many legends about Taoist immortals. It also drew on, and contributed to, China's rich tradition of mind/body health and fitness. This tradition continues today and includes ideas about diet and medicine and the exercise technique known as ch'i kung (qigong).

Orient Expressions

Mandarin was the language used for official written communications during much of the Chinese Empire. Evidently for this reason, Chinese officials came to be called mandarins by Western traders, missionaries, and diplomats.

Confucius Rules

Throughout most of Chinese history, Taoism has coexisted more or less peacefully with China's other major philosophy, Confucianism, which was the official philosophy of the Chinese empire for well over a millennium. Confucian thought formed the basis of the imperial administration in China through a long succession of dynasties, enabling the empire to maintain its rule. Throughout this time, the Confucian scholar-official, or *mandarin* as he became known in the West, represented the ideal of statecraft and civilization.

Although we know very little for certain about his life, Confucius himself was probably an out-of-work public servant who fell back on teaching to get by while looking for a suitable position in government. He had high hopes of working for a benevolent ruler to bring enlightened leadership to one of the many states of the Middle Kingdom, as China was then known. Although he was unable to realize his dream, his students collected and passed along his teachings, which were later adopted and developed as the official ideology of imperial China.

According to Confucian thought, the cultivation of the personal integrity of public ministers is vital for the stability of the government and the prosperity of the state. Those most fit to govern are those with the most wisdom, virtue, and benevolence. These qualities can be acquired through study and practice. Those who can demonstrate these qualities should be employed at high positions in government, regardless of who they are and where they are from.

Confucian virtue is basically a practical matter, geared toward effective leadership, yet Confucian thinking came to be heavily influenced by more spiritual attitudes stemming from Taoist and Buddhist ideas. In fact, with the growth and spread of the major Eastern ways of thought, many hybrids and variations have been formed and continue to be formed as they become adopted by different people and put to use in different ways. This flexibility, enabling new applications under constantly changing circumstances, is one of Eastern philosophy's greatest assets.

Flexibility is also one of the main factors that distinguishes Eastern from Western thinking. It's an important reason Westerners in growing numbers have been turning to Eastern philosophy as a supplement or alternative to Western ideas. You can read more about the distinguishing features of Eastern thought in the following chapter.

The Least You Need to Know

- The four most influential philosophical traditions of the East are Hinduism, Buddhism, Taoism, and Confucianism.
- Hinduism is not a single, organized philosophical system, but includes many diverse philosophical and religious beliefs of India. A concept central to much Hinduism is maya, or illusion, which accounts for the problems of worldly existence.
- Buddhism is an outgrowth of Hinduism that, while disappearing from India, has spread throughout much of the world. Buddhism attempts to provide a solution to the problem that worldly existence is characterized by suffering.
- Taoism originated in China and emphasizes the natural harmony underlying the flux of events. Originally a philosophy for recluses, it can be applied to social challenges as well.
- Confucianism was the official philosophy of imperial China, studied and practiced by government administrators.

Chapter 2

Turning East

In This Chapter

- Wholeness and unity in Eastern thought
- Natural, social, psychic, and cosmic wholeness
- Eastern attitudes toward the self
- Dogma versus rationalism

Volumes and volumes have been written on Eastern philosophy. Ironically, one of the ideas most commonly encountered in them is that true wisdom can't be put into words. But wait! Don't close the book and walk away just yet. It turns out that words are not totally useless. They have their place if you know how to recognize their limitations.

Words—in particular the teachings of the Eastern sages—can provide valuable guidance. They point the way if you know how to follow them. But as many of those sages say, you need to be careful not to confuse the directions with the journey itself. Learning doctrine is not the same as practicing the wisdom the doctrine is intended to teach.

Words come up short in defining reality once and for all because reality includes everything. Words are just a small part of the whole. Although definitions are often useful, they tend to impose unnecessary limitations on things and unnecessary distinctions between them. A great deal of Eastern philosophy has to do with trying to remove these conventional limitations and distinctions.

The Whole Thing

One of the most significant features that distinguishes Eastern from Western thought is the idea that reality is harmonious and unified and that all things are interrelated. This wholeness has important implications for the nature and purpose of Eastern philosophy. Unlike Western thinking, Eastern thought tends not to place itself outside of whatever it is it is thinking about. After all, how can you stand outside of all that exists? Instead, it tends to accept verbal formulations as only partial truths and to recognize and work within the limits of human understanding.

Anything people can say, in other words, is at best only part of the story and, at worst, a false lead on the way to wisdom. In keeping with this attitude, Eastern philosophy is often elusive. What is true under one set of circumstances is no longer true in new situations. More often than not, dogmatic statements are misleading. Knowledge cannot be reduced into words but is a state of mind and an approach to life. The teachings of philosophy can guide, but ultimately, the truth must be experienced and practiced to hold any validity.

Lotus Lore

A story about Taoist philosopher Chuang Tzu tells of a man who destroyed some gourds because they were too big to drink out of. Chuang Tzu reprimanded the man, saying the gourds could have been used in making a raft for traveling on water. The story hints at how we should deal with large philosophical ideas beyond our capacity of understanding. If we have small plans for them, they won't work.

Just as philosophical ideas are only partial and limited in relation to the larger and indescribable unity of reality, so too, the individual self is often considered limited in its ability to know and act on its own. But in connection and in harmony with the whole of reality, the self dissolves—and understanding and action become profound and powerful. This is why Eastern thinking tends to be concerned not so much with defining reality, but in breaking through the boundaries that isolate the self from the whole.

The purpose of much Eastern thought is to provide guidance for experiencing and achieving harmony with this Oneness. Such harmony can be a tricky proposition because existence as we perceive it is in a state of flux. Everything changes, often moving in circles. Eastern philosophy can teach us how to see the changing aspects of our lives as part of a continuous whole, and how to place ourselves outside the ongoing changes of perceived reality or, alternatively, how to achieve a state of equilibrium within them.

Oneness is a major thrust of much Eastern thought, but don't assume all Eastern philosophy goes in for the idea of a unified harmony underlying or transcending visible reality. The unorthodox Indian school known as Carvaka denies the existence of transcendent or natural unity. According to Carvaka, existence is limited to what we are capable of perceiving. If you can't tell it's there with any of your five senses, it isn't there! This position corresponds to the Western notion of empiricism. In addition, Indian philosophy, like Western philosophy, has a long and convoluted tradition of logical analysis.

All for One

Eastern philosophy is often difficult to formulate and analyze because it tends to be holistic—concerned more with the big picture than with sweating the details. According to much Eastern thought, there's a grand totality made up of things that are interconnected in ways we can't always understand. In fact, as soon as you start trying to pin things down, you end up with only part of the picture. Fixating on a small part of the whole can get you in trouble as you start ignoring or taking for granted the rest of reality. As a result, you're no longer living in reality as it is, but in an illusion of your own making.

Many Eastern sages speak of a Oneness that pervades, unites, or transcends all things. The purpose of their teaching is not primarily to prove this Oneness exists or even to explain clearly what it is. In fact, they often say it cannot be proven or explained. It's something that needs to be intuited, experienced, or simply accepted. This is the only choice because it is impossible to stand outside this pervasive unity in order to analyze it objectively. Because we are only a small part of the whole, we can only recognize this in our own way and try to fit in as best and as fully as we can.

Not in This Life

In the sixth century B.C.E., Buddhists thought Hindus placed too much trust in the authority of the Vedic scriptures. Taoist philosopher Lao Tzu is said to have criticized Confucius for spouting hot air about virtue when virtue had disappeared. But don't be put off by the tendency of Eastern philosophers to accuse one another of dogmatism. It reflects the multiplicity of their concepts of reality.

In general, Eastern thought has tremendous respect for the size, scope, and complexity of existence and is careful not to try to boil it all down into easy formulas. Existence is so big that it exceeds the capacity of most ordinary people to understand it. Even so, there are any number of valid approaches to understanding. In fact, Eastern thinkers tend to be more tolerant of inconsistencies and differing points of view than most Western philosophers because the purpose of Eastern thought is not to define the truth, but to live in harmony with it.

Eastern philosophy presents many different depictions of what this pervasive, unified reality is. These depictions can be divided into four interrelated categories:

- Cosmic wholeness
- Natural wholeness
- Social wholeness
- Psychic wholeness

In other words, different philosophies of the East alternatively recognize the cosmos, nature, the psyche, or society as most important.

Four Wholes

Each of the Big Four philosophies of the East has a different focus on the concept of unified reality:

- **Hindu** thought, in general, focuses on cosmic wholeness. The self, nature, and society are only temporary manifestations of transcendent, absolute reality. They must ultimately be left behind as the consciousness develops through the course of successive lifetimes on the way to merging permanently with the absolute. Hindu philosophy supplies guidelines for every step of this process, including rules for social conduct while involved with daily life and techniques for elevating the consciousness in preparation for transcending worldly existence.
- **Buddhism** is most closely concerned with psychic wholeness. The Buddha taught that all life is characterized by suffering. Suffering results from physical pain and hardship, of course, but is more subtly—and dangerously—connected with the mind. Mental suffering is unhappiness resulting from desires, hopes, and fears, which tend to spur the mind into digging itself into a deeper and deeper hole, often without realizing what it's doing. Buddhist teachings are intended to help the mind disentangle itself from all the things it clings to in its restless search for contentment. Once free, it can rest in its own being and appreciate existence for what it is.

- **Taoism** stresses natural wholeness. The workings of the Tao are most clearly evident in the processes of nature. Thus by living in harmony with nature and observing natural change and progression, it is possible to follow the Tao. Just as nature continually balances itself out as the seasons change, so one should strive for balance in living one's life, adjusting to the demands of the time. By acting in accord with the situation, it is possible to accomplish great things in an effortless manner. And by leading a harmonious and carefree life, it is possible to remain healthy in mind and body.
- **Confucianism** is a philosophy of social wholeness. The primary goal of Confucian teaching is to bring about a stable, peaceful, and prosperous society in which all members interact in mutually beneficial ways. This goal can be realized through the efforts of scholar-officials who cultivate personal integrity in order to become effective and benevolent leaders. This self-cultivation is based on the study of classic books of literature, history, ritual, and philosophy.

It's important to stress that these different philosophical visions are not necessarily at odds with one another. In fact, because they tend to be holistic, Eastern philosophies are generally respectful of one another, coexisting and, at times, combining. This is not to say that there haven't been disagreements, debates, conflicts, and even wars stemming from philosophical differences. In fact, there have been many. But the Big Four Eastern philosophies are generally less critical—less concerned with measuring ideas—than Western thought. Although the philosophies have always been used in political arguments, they tend to be tolerant and accepting of one another.

Lotus Lore

You may be familiar with the old parable about the blind men holding onto an elephant at different ends. Each had a hold of something very different from the other—one had the tail, another had the trunk—but it was the same elephant. This parable is a famous Jaina teaching. The elephant stands for truth, which is too big for any one person to grasp entirely. Each individual is only capable of grasping a small portion, and each portion may be different from the others. Thus, the truth can seem very different to different people and still be true.

Who Do You Think You Are?

Often, wholeness has to do with looking at the relationship between the self and the world in fluid terms. Westerners tend to impose a sharp boundary between themselves and the rest of reality. In the East, this boundary is much more permeable. As a result, the distinction between "you" and "not you" is much less hard and fast. This opens up new possibilities for experiencing reality.

Where Am I?

Although much Eastern thinking is deeply concerned with the self, Eastern philosophy generally tends to be much less individualistic than Western thinking. In the West, people tend to take pride in self-reliance and independence. The self, in the East, is rarely thought of as being independent and alone, but is part of something that is greater than the individual. The ties connecting the self to the rest of reality need to be understood and developed in the best possible way.

Of course, you could argue that Westerners recognize God as being far greater than the self, but this God has the overall effect of getting Westerners to focus more on themselves instead of less. They see God as a being who cares about them and judges them as individuals. Their individuality concerns themselves and God, but no one else. As a result, Westerners often erect mental barriers to keep themselves separated from the rest of the world. This way of thinking has encouraged many Westerners to be strong and enterprising. At the same time, however, it has also led to serious emotional problems, including loneliness, alienation, uncertainty, and feelings of guilt.

In contrast, by not isolating the self from the rest of existence, Eastern thought has a way of strengthening the emotional well-being of those who follow it, reducing anxiety and isolation.

In general, Eastern thinking connects the individual to the rest of existence in three basic ways, by seeing the self as defined by—and dissolved by:

- Its place in society
- Its place in nature
- Its place in the cosmos

Lost in Thought

Perhaps the preeminent social philosophy of all time, Eastern or Western, is Confucianism. Confucian teaching looks at the individual in terms of the position he or she occupies in each of the five relationships that hold society together. These are

- Husband and wife
- Parent and child

- Sibling and sibling
- Friend and friend
- Ruler and subject (In Confucius's day, women did not take an active part in public life, so, except for the husband-wife relationship, Confucius was actually thinking of social relationships among men—father and son, brother and brother.)

Confucianism attempts to avoid social problems by defining the appropriate attitude to adopt for each position in society when relating to all other positions. Higher-ups can expect loyalty and obedience from subordinates who, in turn, can expect benevolence from those above.

Taoism, in contrast to Confucianism, denies the importance of social relationships, but emphasizes interconnections between the self and nature. In doing so it focuses on mental, physical, and spiritual health, which is understood as a state of natural balance and harmony. The same unseen forces that enable natural things to grow and change are at work in the human body. In addition, like Zen Buddhism, Taoism teaches that by imposing a separation between the self and experience, your experience becomes less full and spontaneous. Self-consciousness, in other words, stands in the way of authentic action.

Karma Dogma

Grand claims are difficult to live up to.

—The Confucian Analects

Buddhist and Hindu philosophies tend to deny the importance of the self, society, and nature as these things are usually understood in the West. Instead, they are concerned with establishing a profound unity of the individual consciousness with absolute existence, which transcends the appearances of things. The self is not truly separate from transcendent being, but only appears to be so. To perceive this fundamental unity is to be enlightened.

One of the basic teachings of Buddhism is that the self is illusory. This is a challenging idea, especially to Westerners who base their entire sense of reality on the fact that they exist as individuals. One way of understanding the Buddhist concept of the nonself, or empty self, is to think of it as a way of saying that reality doesn't revolve around us. The apparent fact that we are here doesn't mean we can expect to continue to exist in the same form an instant from now.

Another aspect of the concept of the nonself is that we can't rely on our feelings and impressions to give us a reliable sense of existence. For this we have to look deeper—beyond the self—through meditation and the renunciation of self-oriented impulses. Only by getting past our misguided, self-centered impulses can we free ourselves from delusion and suffering.

Hindus recognize a similar process of freeing the consciousness from illusory desires. In Hindu thought, this experience of liberation involves the merging of the individual consciousness with absolute being. On reaching the state of enlightenment, illusions dissolve together with the self, and the consciousness transcends individuality.

Shut My Mouth

Because of its focus on wholeness, Eastern philosophy tends to regard even its own teachings as partial and limited. Much Eastern thought—especially the aspects that Westerners have found most appealing—takes the attitude that it's a waste of time to use words to chop reality up into little pieces. Analysis and proof are not usually the stock-in-trade of the Eastern sages. Instead, the emphasis is often on inner, lived experience, which cannot be defined in words. As a result, silence speaks volumes in the history of Eastern thought.

Silence Is Golden

Silence is often used to convey profound insight. Legend has it that when the Buddha first met with his disciples after attaining enlightenment, he said nothing, but merely held out a flower. Only one disciple named Kashyapa understood the say-it-with-flowers approach and responded with a smile. He went on to become a great Buddhist patriarch. The others failed to grasp the message and continued their search for truth along different paths.

Similarly, in the Chinese tradition of Taoism, words are often thought to obscure, rather than illuminate the truth. The ancient Taoist classic *Tao Te Ching* begins with the words, "The Tao [the Way] that can be talked about is not the true Tao." Often in Eastern philosophy, true wisdom is not so much a doctrine that can be explained in words, but an experience, a state of mind, or a way of life. Actions, attitudes, and experiences are frequently valued over arguments and reasoning. Words can point out the right direction, but they are not the end in themselves.

Even the Confucians, who devote themselves to the study of books, generally recognize the wisdom of being cautious in speech. Confucius himself was averse to explaining his ideas at length to his disciples. He was willing to explain only one corner of a topic and expected his students to figure out the rest.

Inner Quiet

Perhaps the most profound use of silence in Eastern philosophy occurs in Hindu and Buddhist meditation. Meditation is generally practiced in silence, enabling intensified concentration and clarity. In many cases, the silence is of the mind as well as of the ears. With all thoughts dissolved into nothingness, there is nothing to stand in the way of absolute being.

Silence is important even when meditation is accompanied by chanting. Since ancient times, Hindus of India have meditated on the cosmic and spiritual absolute while chanting the syllable *OM*. OM is what is known as a *mantra*—a word or syllable chanted or silently repeated in meditation to help clear and focus the mind. OM is the best-known mantra. They say the syllable contains three sounds: ah, oo, and mm, each of which represents a different state of consciousness. The syllable is concluded by silence, which is the most important aspect of the chanting because it represents a transcendent state of being, the fourth and highest state. Silence, in other words, is a way of concentrating on, and even merging with, the absolute.

Orient Expressions

In many schools of Hinduism and Buddhism, a **mantra** is a word or syllable chanted or repeated silently in meditation in order to clear and focus the mind. A mantra may be commonly known, such as the syllable **OM,** or it may be a personal matter known only to the one who uses it.

All this goes to show that what often passes for "understanding" in the West—fixing on a concept and analyzing it to see what it is and how it works—tends to look like so much obsessive bean-counting from the perspective of much Eastern philosophy. You're only taking a small part of an enormous changing picture and trying to turn it into something it's not. Instead of attaining knowledge, you only end up deluding yourself. Or, what's worse, you end up being deluded by others. All too often, people who earnestly seek wisdom are taken in by charlatans and demagogues. Of course, Eastern philosophy hasn't developed a permanent solution to this problem, but silence helps keep the focus on inward experience rather than dogmatic formulations.

So to Speak

Eastern philosophers tend to avoid dogma, but this doesn't mean they don't claim to have direct knowledge of cosmic unity, psychic clarity, natural balance, or social harmony and attempt to describe these things. In fact, many ancient writings provide testimony and accounts of the higher truths that lie beyond the reaches of the ordinary self. These accounts are often visionary and poetic as much as philosophical. Eastern sages tend to rely on parables, riddles, analogies, and myths to convey their teachings. In this way, Eastern thinking points the way to personal insight indirectly.

Mind and Spirit

This approach to teaching by analogy, parable, riddle, and myth often makes it difficult to distinguish philosophy from religion and folk belief. In fact, Hinduism and Buddhism are religions as well as philosophies. Taoism has a religious and a philosophical branch. In Confucianism, ritual is crucial as an expression of feelings and as the symbolic fulfillment of interpersonal obligations. While many Eastern thinkers recognize a difference between religion and philosophy, others do not.

Eastern thinking often unifies religious and philosophical concerns. In the East, speculation and inquiry (associated with "mind" in the West) often have devotional and ritual aspects, while devotion and ritual (associated with spirit in the West) may lead to discovery. Eastern knowledge is not organized into the same categories. Knowledge is often the result of mind and spirit working together.

In Hindu philosophy, devotion and study are sometimes seen as complementary aspects of the pursuit of enlightenment. Neither will fully succeed without the other. Many Buddhist beliefs that appear naive or even superstitious are said to point the way for those who are not yet ready to understand more difficult teachings. Thus praying to the Buddha and offering flowers at a Buddhist shrine, though not consistent with the teachings of the Buddha himself, are often considered an acceptable way for many to begin the long journey to nirvana.

Buddhists, Hindus, and Taoists all tend to regard enlightenment as a kind of religious experience that, instead of stemming from a heavenly vision, results from the stripping away of conventional attitudes in order to perceive ordinary reality as miraculous. A well-known Zen poem describes the moment at which a monk attained enlightenment when he experienced his ordinary daily activities—chopping wood and carrying water—as miraculous events.

Karma Dogma

When those above are inclined to observe the rites, the common people will be easy to govern.

—*The Confucian Analects*

Even in Confucianism, a philosophy of China that stresses practical, rather than spiritual knowledge, religious devotion plays an integral part. Ritual and devotion are important for practical reasons; they help establish and preserve social harmony and personal virtue. The ability to take a leading part in religious rites was often an important criterion for becoming a minister of state. Confucius himself was famous for his knowledge of ritual observance.

In Confucianism, religious ritual is also considered a natural expression of human feelings. The deep feelings expressed through ritual are regarded as the basis of sincerity, which is a necessary attitude in any successful enterprise. Without this sincerity, you can go through the motions of whatever you're doing, but you won't exert a favorable influence on others.

Spirit and Mind

Westerners often describe the difference between religion and philosophy in terms of devotional and intellectual practice. These two kinds of activity have been separated for centuries in the West, thanks to the phenomenal success of Western science. In the East, however, the two are often thought to complement one another. Spirituality and intellect are better able to work together in Eastern thinking because of the Eastern tendency to avoid dogmatism.

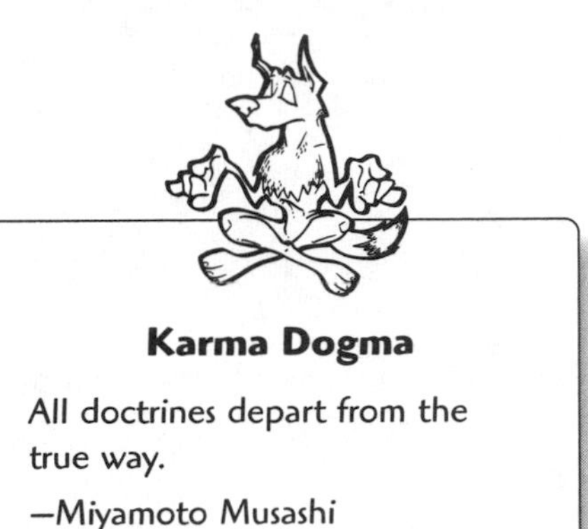

Karma Dogma

All doctrines depart from the true way.

—Miyamoto Musashi (1584–1645) in *The Book of Five Rings*, a book of strategy for martial artists

While avoiding spiritual dogma, Eastern philosophy often provides a rational understanding of spiritual ideas. Many Buddhists recognize the psychological significance of religious thinking. Taoists understand spirituality as an important aspect of human nature. Confucians regard spirituality as a way of harmonizing personal feelings with society.

Thus Eastern philosophy tends to be less at odds with religious belief than Western. Because it is often nondogmatic and highly rational, many find Eastern spirituality easier to accept than Western religion. This is part of what has made it so appealing to Westerners over the course of the twentieth century and helps explain why many Westerners in search of spiritual fulfillment have turned East.

The Least You Need to Know

- In general, Eastern philosophy is holistic, looking at reality as a unified oneness in a constant state of flux. The purpose of its teaching is to promote harmony within the unified whole.
- Eastern thought recognizes many paths to enlightenment, including both personal and communal approaches.
- Eastern philosophy tends to be less individualistic than Western thought, regarding the self as closely interconnected with the cosmos and with society.
- In general, Hinduism is concerned with cosmic unity, Buddhism with psychic purity, Taoism with natural harmony, and Confucianism with social stability.
- Much Eastern philosophy recognizes devotional practice and intellectual learning as two aspects of the search for enlightenment.

Chapter 3

East Meets West

In This Chapter

- Western science, technology, and industry
- The ideal of progress
- Western colonialism in the East
- The Enlightenment and Romanticism
- New Age, the collective unconscious, and synchronicity

There has been a great surge of interest in Eastern thought on the part of Westerners over the course of the twentieth century. The fascination is due in part simply to the fact that lines of communication have opened up considerably, so it is increasingly easy to learn about ideas and practices that, not long before, were shrouded in mystery. All the most important books of Eastern thinking are available in good translations, and Western scholars, often with the help of scholars from the East, have had a chance to chew the translations over and see what they're like.

Yet there's much more than mere academic interest behind the Western fascination with Eastern thought. Eastern thinking serves special needs in the West that homegrown Western thinking can't always satisfy. In serving these Western needs, Eastern ideas have permutated a good deal but continue to retain much of their original character.

Eastern philosophy holds a unique appeal for many Westerners in search of a way to square personal spirituality with intellectual understanding. Often in the West, spirit and intellect seem at odds. At the level of society, this split leads to religious and political disputes. At the psychological level, it can result in confusion and malaise. For many Westerners, the merging of spirit and intellect that takes place in Eastern thinking is just the solution.

Worlds Apart

The emphasis on oneness, harmony, and adapting to changes that are common to much Eastern thought contrasts with traditional Western scientific thinking. Instead of starting with a pervasive oneness, Western science makes sharp distinctions between things. It tries to understand reality, not in order to adapt to and achieve harmony with it, but to master and control it. Although the scientific world view has led to the phenomenal triumph of Western technology and fostered an ideal of rational progress, it has left many Westerners in search of something more.

Lotus Lore

Traditional Newtonian physics has been supplemented and revised in the twentieth century by new developments, such as the theory of relativity and the study of quantum mechanics. Several popular "New Age" books have claimed that the findings of these new approaches to physics are consistent with much traditional wisdom from the East. Among these books are *The Tao of Physics,* by Fritjof Capra and *The Dancing Wu Li Masters,* by Gary Zukav.

Proof of the Pudding

A distinguishing feature of Western science is its objectivity. Scientific ideas are verified by controlled, observable, replicable experiments. Because scientific experiments are designed to be replicable, anyone conducting the same experiment under the same controlled circumstances should obtain the same results. This enables all scientists to develop a common understanding of things, regardless of what language they speak or what background they come from.

Experimental verification also ensures that scientific findings are true independently of the feelings, beliefs, and attitudes of those involved. This effectively eliminates wishful thinking, delusion, hype, and spin-doctoring from the field of pure science. The knowledge gained through scientific experimentation doesn't depend on anyone's moral, spiritual, or emotional state of mind. It depends instead on the predictable, observable characteristics of things.

This approach to knowledge-seeking has proved phenomenally productive. As science developed, increased experimentation led to increased knowledge of the world, which led, in turn, to astonishing advances in technology. Over the course of the past two and a half centuries, this technology has made drastic changes in human society. Although not everyone is happy with all of them, many people swear by them, insisting that the quality of life on Earth has been—and continues to be—dramatically improved as a result.

Getting Somewhere

Although science has transformed our world, it cannot tell us everything we need to know about life and how it should be lived. Even so, the success of Western science and technology has deeply influenced the thinking and lifestyles of most Westerners. During the eighteenth century (often referred to as "the Age of Reason"), science and technology contributed to a strong intellectual current known as *the Enlightenment*. Science was regarded as a triumph of human reason, which many people hoped would yield advances not only in technology, but in human morality and happiness as well.

Orient Expressions

The Enlightenment is the broad movement in Western intellectual history beginning late in the seventeenth century and extending through the eighteenth, when many hoped that human life could be perfected through reason. At this time, many traditional notions were rejected or revised, including divine right monarchy.

The growing importance of "reason" during the Enlightenment period has to do with the fact that the social order, previously based on aristocratic privilege and divine-right monarchy, was becoming increasingly centered on trade, which radically increased social mobility in Europe and America. Because social status was no longer solely dependent on birth, new ideas about human nature were advanced to explain how individuals are able to regulate their own behavior independently of their social relationships. Reason provided the perfect explanation since it could be understood as an interior faculty governing behavior.

Many subscribed to an ideal of rational progress, blaming everything bad about life on ignorance and superstition stemming from outmoded ways of doing things. Eager to do away with harmful traditions, including corruption stemming from divine right monarchy, Westerners set out in large numbers to modernize their way of life. Many hoped reason would make it possible to build a just and carefree society. Thus Westerners have been less inclined than the Eastern sages to think of human history as cyclical. Existence doesn't go round and round, but onward and upward as we learn more about the physical world and develop new and better ways of doing things.

Tied in with this trend was the separation of church and state in most Western countries and an increasing movement toward democracy. The idea behind democracy was that each individual can make better choices guided by reason than by tradition or by religious teachings. Therefore, individual citizens should be able to have an equal say in government and exercise as much personal freedom as possible.

During the Enlightenment, religious belief lost its powerful hold over the minds of many Westerners. Although many looked at the slew of new scientific discoveries as mounting evidence of the existence of an intelligent creator, these same people also increasingly regarded this creator as remote from human affairs. God was thought of as a kind of "watch-maker in the sky" who designed and built the mechanism of nature but took no active part in its working.

I'll Buy That

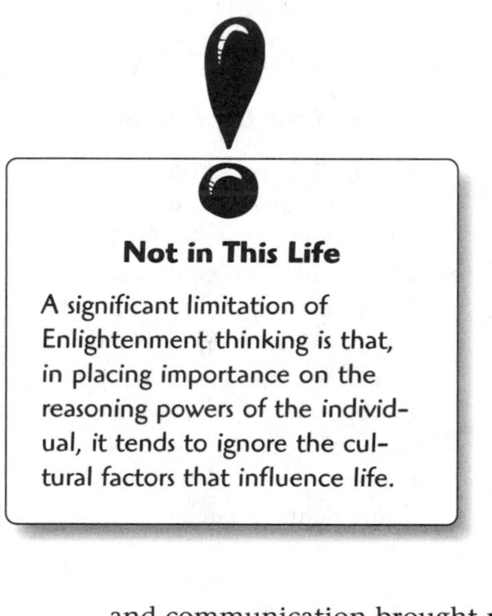

The legacy of Enlightenment thinking is still with us today. The United States Constitution was largely inspired by Enlightenment ideals. And the Enlightenment faith in progress continues to fuel the search for new technology. Many Westerners consider tradition quaint and backward, and many have come to rely unquestioningly on science and technology, trusting it over traditional approaches to life and its problems.

The Enlightenment ideal of progress has had a strong influence not only on Western government, but on Western industry and economy. As the wheels of time kept turning, the Industrial Revolution built up steam and fed people's faith in progress and reason. Technological breakthroughs in medicine, transportation, and communication brought major changes to the West. Optimism grew that human ingenuity could overcome all obstacles to happiness.

The fact that so many Westerners became eager for new things was a tremendous spur to industrial development and open trade. The industrial countries of Europe and, later, America vied intensely with one another, not only to industrialize themselves, but to colonize other undeveloped countries in order to gain cheap raw materials and exploit new markets for finished goods. Many believed the ripest markets could be found in India and China, which already possessed highly developed civilizations.

Blinded with Science

Behind a big political, economic, and technological head of steam, in the eighteenth and nineteenth centuries scores of Westerners converged on the venerable empires of India and China. These Westerners were confident in their technology, proud of their scientific and religious beliefs, and eager for trade and conquest. They encountered Easterners who were, in contrast, deeply respectful of tradition, suspicious of innovation, yet largely flexible in their religious and philosophical views.

India-pendence

In general, Western colonialists in India and China were not as interested in learning about Eastern philosophy as they were in trading for Eastern goods, gaining political power over Eastern subjects, or converting Eastern souls to Christianity. All too often, they dismissed Eastern wisdom as empty superstition. This arrogant attitude—and Western influence in general—actually prompted new developments in Eastern philosophy.

For many Indians of the nineteenth and twentieth centuries who resented Western arrogance and cultural domination, the native philosophical tradition became a source of nationalistic pride. They organized societies that promoted Indian philosophy as a way of resisting Western rule and Western thinking. Others in India sought common ground between Indian and Western thought. Thus national and political tensions stimulated interest in traditional and new Indian philosophies.

Karma Dogma

We are in and of the great Hindu community, and it devolves upon us by example and precept to hold up as a beacon the highest truths of the Hindu shastras [scriptures]. In their light, we must purify our heritage of customs, usages, rites, and ceremonies and adapt them to the needs of our conscience and community.

—Devendanath Tagore on the Brahmo Samaj reform movement

This period in the history of Eastern thought is often referred to as the Indian Renaissance. The Indian Renaissance culminated in the work and thought of Mahatma Gandhi, who led peaceful resistance movements that helped India win independence from British rule in 1949. India's first and most famous president was the well-known philosopher, Sarvepalli Radhakrishnan. So, by drawing on and adapting its philosophical traditions, India has managed to retain its identity and national character while making the difficult adjustment to democracy and industrialization.

Breaking the Mold

In China, Western colonialism eventually triggered a peasant revolution as the efforts of the Chinese empire to fend off Western encroachment weakened it to the point of collapse. In the waning years of the empire, a reform movement that adapted Confucianism to a planned constitutional monarchy failed. The empire fell and a power struggle ensued, out of which a military regime led by Sun Yat Sen emerged. Sun's efforts to lead China through a gradual adjustment into a democratic republic were cut short by the successful communist revolution led by Mao Tse-tung.

Mao became the first Chairman of the People's Republic of China and is looked to by loyal Chinese communists as a great teacher and philosopher, as well as a politician and military hero. His philosophy combines many traditional Chinese ideas with Marxism, adapting the Marxist idea of a call to revolution and directing it not, as Marx intended, to the industrial proletariat, but to the Chinese agrarian peasant.

As these tumultuous events were taking place in India and China, Indian and Chinese philosophy gradually took greater hold in the West. Of course, Westerners did not use Eastern ideas in the same way or for all of the same reasons as Eastern philosophers. Yet just as Indian and Chinese nationalists were reacting, indirectly, to the Enlightenment ideal of rational progress that lay behind much Western colonial arrogance, many Westerners back home were also becoming disillusioned with this ideal.

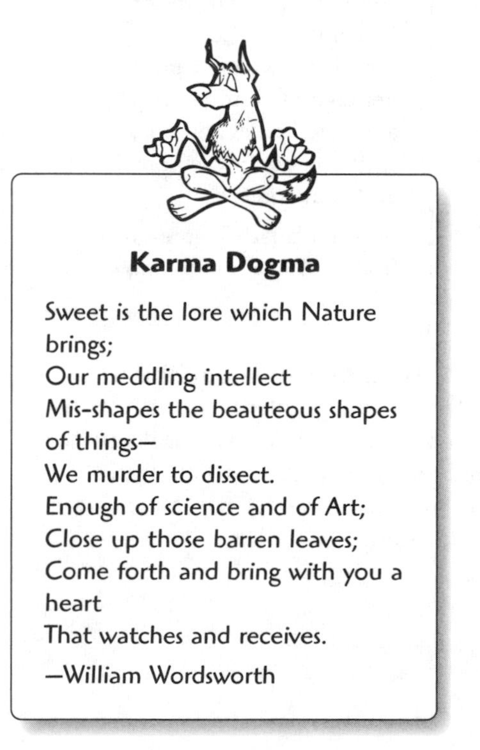

Karma Dogma

Sweet is the lore which Nature brings;
Our meddling intellect
Mis-shapes the beauteous shapes of things—
We murder to dissect.
Enough of science and of Art;
Close up those barren leaves;
Come forth and bring with you a heart
That watches and receives.

—William Wordsworth

Grinding Gears

At various times in the history of the West, people have turned sour on the hope of progress held out by science and technology and, as a result, have become attracted to Eastern thought. Two intellectual movements loom especially large in Western history as times when people turned East in large numbers. The first is the Romantic movement of the nineteenth century. The second is the New Age movement of the twentieth century.

A Little Romance

In the wake of the Enlightenment period around the turn of the nineteenth century, many Westerners came to see science and reason as increasingly cold, calculating, and soulless. As the Enlightenment began to wear itself out, the excitement over the potential of human reason began to take a toll on human feelings. Many grew unhappy without realizing why. Gradually, they began to yearn openly for emotional fulfillment and longed to experience the beauty and mystery of life.

Out of this desire, shared by growing numbers of Westerners, the Romantic movement was born. At this time, many poets and philosophers of Europe and America turned East for inspiration and drew on the ancient wisdom of India in forming a revised perspective. The notion that human existence is somehow continuous with a mysteriously changing, harmonious universe supplied relief from the pressures of trying to maintain rational control over everything.

But despite the wide appeal of the Romantic movement, the ideal of scientific progress didn't die out completely. Instead, the industrial revolution got into full swing, and Western society grew increasingly dependent on technology. As the twentieth century dawned in the West, practical, progressive, scientific thinking existed side by side with dreamy romantic attitudes, each finding expression in different ways in society and culture.

Rat Race

The allied victory of World War II provided a big boost for the ideal of progress. Democracy and technology formed a successful partnership in defeating the Nazi and fascist threats. Post-war prosperity fed optimism and pride in the American way of life. The ranks of the middle class grew as increasing numbers of people began earning more and spending their money on high-tech entertainment and labor-saving appliances.

Not in This Life

Don't count on so-called "labor-saving" devices to free up more of your time for recreation and relaxation. Chances are, if you're like most people, you'll just use the time to do more work!

In recent decades, however, large numbers have soured on the ideal of progress once again. Despite the many conveniences it has brought, many feel that industrial technology has exerted a harmful influence on Western lifestyles.

While "convenience" and "time-saving" devices provide extra time for people in technological societies, the extra time is almost always devoted to more work rather than socializing, relaxation, and self-expression. As a result, people commonly feel dissatisfied, stressed out, and alienated.

And industrial technology presented far worse threats as a result of the Cold War and the shattering experience of Vietnam. Warfare and violence—never desirable—have become unconscionably devastating, thanks to more powerful guns, mines, and missiles, and chemical, biological, and nuclear weapons. And the destructive potential of technology and industry are not limited to warfare. The careless use of natural resources has taken a tremendous toll on the environment, threatening the well-being of the planet itself.

In search of a solution to these problems, many have turned once again to Eastern thought in hopes of spiritual renewal and reintegration. These days, Eastern wisdom often comes West in the form of "New Age" philosophy. New Age is an amalgam of all sorts of practices, ideas, and beliefs, including Eastern philosophy. So, once again, the East seems to be supplying a philosophical antidote for Western woes.

Feeling Your Age

Although not all Eastern philosophy in the West is necessarily "New Age," the New Age movement has helped fuel surging Western interest in the East. This movement is not centrally organized, but includes all sorts of approaches to alternative spirituality, such as shamanism, paganism, witchcraft and other occult practices, channeling, crystals, pyramid power, biofeedback, and many different spins on Eastern philosophy. In fact, New Age draws heavily on Eastern thought, adding to it and changing it significantly in the process.

New Heights

New Age is the recent movement of popular philosophy and spirituality that supplies an alternative to organized religion on one hand and academic knowledge on the other. It is originally based on the belief that, within the past few decades, human consciousness has begun reaching a new state of awareness and improvement around the world. Forgotten spiritual truths are being recovered while new ones are being discovered. The human mind is turning out to possess a heightened spiritual capacity, which will help people all over the world come together, find peace, respect and nurture the environment, and realize their inner potential.

This idea does not come from Eastern philosophy, but was first suggested by Marilyn Ferguson in her best-selling book, *The Aquarian Conspiracy* (1970). It impelled many Westerners toward Eastern teachings in search of ways to cultivate and express their heightened consciousness. Of course, not all those who are interested in Eastern thought associate themselves with the New Age movement, but it has been a big part of the West's enthusiasm for Eastern thought and has strongly influenced Western attitudes toward it.

Today, while Eastern thought and other alternative spiritual approaches are as popular as ever in the West, many distance themselves from the New Age label, which has come to be associated with soft-headed, flaky idealism and off-the-wall beliefs and practices. Yet, whether they think of themselves as New Agers or not, millions of Westerners accept many beliefs that are not wholly consistent with science or organized religion, including, especially, ideas borrowed from Eastern thought.

Lotus Lore

As an alternative to the New Age label, the term **metaphysical** is often used to describe ideas and beliefs that cannot be confirmed by science. The term metaphysics comes from the writings of the ancient Greek philosopher Aristotle, who used it to refer to the area of philosophical inquiry "beyond physics." So metaphysics applies to anything spiritual, supernatural, and outside the field of physical science.

Covering the Spread

Today, much of Eastern thought makes a lot of sense to many people in the West. Many ideas from Eastern philosophy have seeped into Western consciousness and are widely familiar. This familiarity results from gradual and repeated exposure through many sources. In addition to New Age, organized Eastern religious groups have spread West. Many Buddhists and Hindus have immigrated to the West from Asia. And many Westerners have joined Eastern religious and philosophical groups.

Among Westerners, the most popular religious groups have been Buddhism and the Hindu offshoot, Hare Krishna. In addition, Transcendental Meditation, an organization with roots in Hindu thought that claims not to have religious status, has been successful in the West. Membership in Hare Krishna and TM have declined since the 1970s and 1980s, but Buddhist groups continue to attract Western followers.

Another important avenue of exposure for Eastern thought is academic scholarship. Scholars from Europe, America, India, and China have done a great deal to share ideas and knowledge. Although scholarship tends to be technical and specialized and, as a result, often fails to make a popular impact, some scholars have succeeded not only in discovering and sharing new ideas but in popularizing them.

Forever Jung

Psychologist Carl Jung generated a lot of interest in Eastern thought, and his work has had a profound influence on the way many Westerners approach Eastern philosophy. Jung draws on the study of Eastern traditions in developing his famous theory of the collective unconscious. According to this theory, all people share a common set of images, called archetypes, that represent universal aspects of the human psyche. Jung's work suggests that much Eastern and Western thinking meet at the psychological level. The theory of the collective unconscious can be understood as a Western interpretation of the Hindu concept of *Atman,* the absolute universal self that exists as pure, transcendent, undifferentiated consciousness.

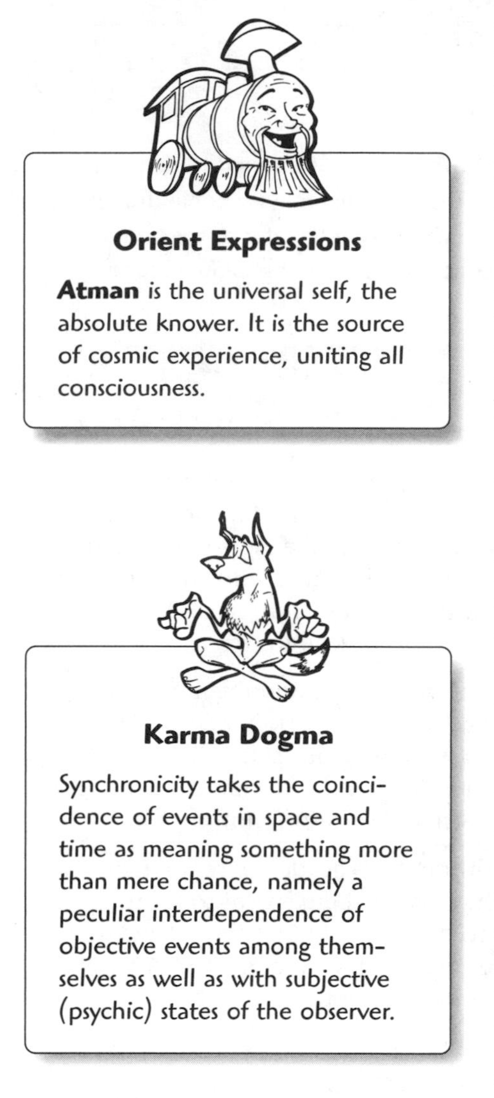

Orient Expressions

Atman is the universal self, the absolute knower. It is the source of cosmic experience, uniting all consciousness.

Karma Dogma

Synchronicity takes the coincidence of events in space and time as meaning something more than mere chance, namely a peculiar interdependence of objective events among themselves as well as with subjective (psychic) states of the observer.

Another of Jung's famous ideas is the concept of synchronicity. Synchronicity accounts for the coincidence of an individual's state of mind and an outside event. For example, Jung found in examining patients that they sometimes had dreams that seemed to anticipate and predict future events in their lives. Rational explanations failed to account for these dreams.

Synchronicity suggests that there is some deeper, metaphysical connection between the mind and physical reality. It ties in with the Chinese concept of the Tao, a principle that underlies the workings of nature. Jung refers to synchronicity in order to explain the uncanny ability of the Chinese *I Ching* (*Book of Changes*) to resonate with psychic energy that can provide accurate predictions of the future.

Jung's ideas continue to be popular with New Agers, perhaps because they suggest that Western science is not the last word in reality. Jung manages to capture and translate much of the spirit of Eastern thought in a way that is provocative and intellectually challenging, but not entirely alien.

Setting Trends

Of course, many ideas from the East are familiar even to Westerners who don't study them in books. They can be picked up through exposure to the many aspects of Eastern culture that have been influenced by philosophy. Eastern business, holistic medicine, martial arts, cooking, gardening, interior decorating, and yoga are just some of the activities that reflect the profound influence of Eastern philosophy and that have made a big impact on the West.

Today, ideas and practices from Eastern philosophy can be found in restaurants, in computer games, in the backyard, in the boardroom, and in the bedroom. Of course, the original ideas set forth by the ancient sages often get radically distorted as they make their way from place to place and time to time. But change is completely in keeping with the spirit of most Eastern thought. It has remained meaningful over many centuries and across many thousands of miles by virtue both of its profundity and its adaptability.

The Least You Need to Know

- Western science, technology, and industry have fostered ideals of progress and independence that contrast with the Eastern ideals of interconnectedness and respect for tradition.
- Technological and economic success fueled the arrogance of Western colonialism in the East which, in turn, influenced developments in Eastern ideas and politics.
- Disillusionment with the ideal of progress spurred interest in Eastern thought among Westerners, especially during the Romantic movement of the nineteenth century and the New Age movement of the twentieth century.
- Carl Jung's famous theories of the collective unconscious and synchronicity draw on Eastern philosophy.

Part 2

Do You Hindu?

Hinduism is not a uniformly organized system of philosophy or religion, but a rich and multifaceted set of traditions from one of the oldest civilizations on the planet (India, that is). It is a diverse and complex amalgam of myths and mystic practices, exotic beliefs, spiritual discipline, and ancient wisdom. If you're looking for insight into existence that penetrates worldly appearances, or for a better grasp of the ongoing connection between karma and the cycle of death and rebirth, or if you just want to get some background on vegetarianism, meditation, or the caste system, Hinduism is the philosophy for you.

Hindu philosophy is often said to be the oldest known philosophy. Since its origins in the ancient Vedic writings, its influence has spread throughout the globe. The Vedas consist of ancient hymns, ritual rules, and mystic teachings that have been expanded, explained, revised, and reinterpreted across the ages.

These ancient texts are considered by many to contain the essence of Hindu thought. Yet ideas about their significance have changed dramatically over the centuries. These ideas, in turn, have elicited conflict and controversy, even while showing the way to transcendent awareness. Historically speaking, the road to enlightenment hasn't been a smooth one! Even so, Hindu philosophy points consistently beyond the struggles, to inner peace and absolute consciousness.

Chapter 4

Beyond the Gods

In This Chapter

- Basics of Hinduism
- The origins of Hindu philosophy
- The Vedas and the Upanishads
- The Brahmin priesthood
- The principles of Brahman and Atman
- Moksha, maya, and karma

Indian philosophy developed over millennia in close connection to religious beliefs. In fact, there is, at best, a blurry line separating Hinduism the philosophy from Hinduism the religion. Hinduism cannot simply be defined as a systematized set of ideas. Many conflicting beliefs, practices, and concepts have developed side by side in India. Despite the conflicts, however, there are several central important points of Hinduism that give Hindu thought its distinct character.

Perhaps the most challenging aspect of Hindu philosophy is its emphasis on renouncing the world in the attempt to achieve a transcendent state of being. This can be understood as a practical matter and as deeply spiritual, a way of understanding reality and a mystical act of devotion. The point of this transcendent state is not simply to gain knowledge but to experience higher consciousness. It is this focus on consciousness that sets Hindu philosophy apart. In Hinduism, the truth is literally a state of mind.

In the last half of the twentieth century, large numbers of people in the West came to appreciate the significance of consciousness. In India, however, the idea stretches back almost 4,000 years. It is not simply the main idea behind a philosophy or a religion, but the focus of many distinct, but interrelated, philosophies and religions, all of which approach the concept in different ways. This chapter talks about the thinking behind higher consciousness as the concept first developed in ancient India.

Blast from the Past

Hindu philosophy had its beginnings in a collection of ancient lore known as the Vedas. The Vedas included a diverse collection of magical, religious, and philosophical teachings—mostly hymns, prayers, incantations, and ritual instructions—that were passed down from generation to generation by word of mouth, long before they were written down. According to some estimates, the Vedas go back as far as 2000 B.C.E. Most scholars, however, place them somewhere between 1000 and 1500 B.C.E., and everyone agrees that the Vedas are old—even older than the earliest philosophies of ancient Greece.

Lotus Lore

In the 1920s, excavations of the ancient cities of Mohenjo-Daro and Harappa in what is now Pakistan revealed the existence of a thriving and advanced civilization stretching back beyond 3,000 years B.C.E. These cities were apparently sacked and destroyed around 2000 B.C.E. by invading barbarian tribes from the North known as Aryans. The Aryans originated in the region of the Caucasus Mountains in what is now Russia. Some migrated to Northern Europe. (The Nazis, claiming to be "the master race," traced their lineage to these European Aryans.) Others migrated to Northern India where they mixed with the Indus people.

The Vedas laid the groundwork for most of Hindu philosophy, introducing concepts that have been developed and reworked ever since. It is because of these influential ancient Vedic concepts that Indian philosophy can be seen as a coherent, unified tradition. This tradition, however, has grown and changed throughout the centuries as new points of view have emerged in response to the old ideas. Different schools of Hindu philosophy emphasize different aspects of Vedic teaching. Even so, there are several central points found in the Vedas that most later philosophy draws on. These points include the concepts known as

- Brahman
- Atman
- Moksha
- Maya
- Karma

Not in This Life

Don't look for consistency in the many different Vedic hymns. They say conflicting things about which gods did what, and even whether or not they existed. The conflicts show that the ancient Hindus—and the Brahmins in particular—were struggling to get a handle on some very deep questions.

Keep in mind that while these points are introduced in the ancient Vedas, their significance changes over the centuries, depending on how they are interpreted by later thinkers. In fact, even within the Vedas there is disagreement about the specific significance of these things. Thus, what is often referred to as "Vedic philosophy"—the basics of Hindu thought outlined in this chapter—is not exactly the philosophy formulated in the Vedas. After all, the Vedas themselves don't amount to a systematic philosophy. Instead, when people talk about Vedic philosophy, they usually mean the ideas that originated in the Vedas and have turned out to be especially important in retrospect. These basic concepts, then, lay the groundwork for Indian philosophy.

High Priests

The Vedas were compiled, guarded, and preserved by a class of priests known as Brahmins. The Brahmins enjoyed high status in ancient Indian society. They alone were privy to the sacred teachings contained in the Vedas. They presided at sacrifices and other ceremonies and were well paid for their services. They devised many complicated procedures for worship, prayer, and sacrifice that enabled them to jack up the cost of the ceremonies they performed! Ritual, in other words, was good business, and the Brahmins maintained a kind of spiritual monopoly.

The Brahmins evidently competed among themselves and with non-Brahmins in developing religious and philosophical ideas. Signs of dissatisfaction and jealousy from both inside and outside the priesthood are apparent in the fact that the Vedas set forth a variety of beliefs and attitudes regarding the many Hindu gods.

Lotus Lore

One of the most important ritual sacrifices performed during the Vedic period involved libations to the gods of the juice of the soma plant, which, according to the Vedas, has tremendous divine power. In fact, Soma is both a plant and a god. Scholars believe the ancient soma plant is the fly agaric mushroom, which causes hallucinations. In any case, the Vedas associate the effects of the soma plant with higher states of consciousness. The link between hallucinogenic drugs and heightened states of consciousness is explored in the works of English essayist and novelist Aldous Huxley. Huxley's best-known novel, *Brave New World* (1932), concerns a modern version of the soma drug.

Old-Time Religions

Here's a list of some of the conflicting religious beliefs expressed in the ancient Hindu Vedas, together with some of the fancy labels Westerners often use to describe these beliefs:

- Many Vedic hymns refer to numerous gods with different functions, including Indra, the God of thunder, Agni, the god of fire, and Yama, the god of the dead. In the West, this form of belief is known as *polytheism,* worship of more than one god.
- Sometimes many gods are recognized, but only one is worshiped as the god of the particular group of worshipers. This is called *henotheism* in the West.
- Other hymns say only a single god exists. Westerners call this *monotheism.*
- Some hymns express doubt as to whether the gods exist at all. In the West this is called *agnosticism.*
- Other hymns say that there is an absolute reality that goes even beyond the gods and that includes or transcends everything that exists. (This belief is called *monism.*)

As you can see from this list, the Brahmins didn't have a single, tightly organized point of view, but were kicking lots of big ideas around. The last idea, monism, eventually emerged as a mainstay of Hindu thought. The idea of a transcendent, absolute reality, subordinating the gods themselves, became central to the systematic thinking of later periods.

Higher Ground

Hindu monism probably developed as a reaction against the elaborate ritualism of the Brahmins, as people attempted to cut through the ceremonial rules and regulations in order to find a deeper meaning. In fact, some of the Vedas seem critical of ritual sacrifice, portraying the Brahmins not as holy, but as greedy and self-serving. Even so, the term *Brahmin* means divine and is closely related to the Hindu concept of ultimate reality known as *Brahman*.

Orient Expressions

Brahman is the name of transcendent, absolute reality in Hindu thought. The word Brahman, meaning "absolute reality," and **Brahmin,** meaning "priest," are really the same word, meaning "divine." They are spelled differently in order to prevent confusion.

The Whole Truth

The concept of Brahman went a long way toward unifying Hinduism, both religiously and philosophically. This idea was developed in an important group of writings called the Upanishads that were added to the Vedas starting around 900 or 800 B.C.E. The name comes from a term that means "to sit near" someone, as a pupil sits near a teacher. The Upanishads further the tradition of sacred wisdom begun in the Vedas, but with much less emphasis on ceremony and ritual and more focus on the nature of existence and consciousness.

There are over 200 Upanishads of various lengths. Of these, 108 are recognized as sacred, with 10 of these considered particularly important. In these writings, Brahman appears in various ways. It is a cosmic force containing all things, a unifying natural force that makes all things what they are. It is without qualities. It is present everywhere and beyond all things. It is where all things reside. It is a state of bliss. It is indescribable.

Centuries later, different Hindu philosophers, attempting to systemize the ideas of the Upanishads, emphasized different interpretations of Brahman. Some would view Brahman as a force that constituted reality and manifested itself in all things. Others would see it as a causal principle and transcendent force that did not make up the world as we perceive it. Competing theories were

Karma Dogma

Hymn 164 from *Book I of the Rig Veda,* a collection of sacred lore thought to date back to 1500 B.C.E., contains a verse to which some scholars point as the oldest known example of Indian philosophy. The hymn refers to various nature gods as different names for a single, unified higher reality.

> *Reality is One, although the*
> *sages give it different names*
> *Calling it Agni, Yama,*
> *Matarisvan.*

set forward about how transcendent unchanging Brahman related to the perceived and changing world. But this happened many years after the Upanishads were composed.

Despite differences in how the concept was originally understood, Brahman was an important development that shifted emphasis away from gods, worship, and sacrifice, and toward ultimate reality, contemplation, and experience. Ritual lost much of its earlier significance and was replaced by the search for knowledge and understanding. The ancient gods were not necessarily rejected, but were subordinated. They too were contained and transcended by Brahman.

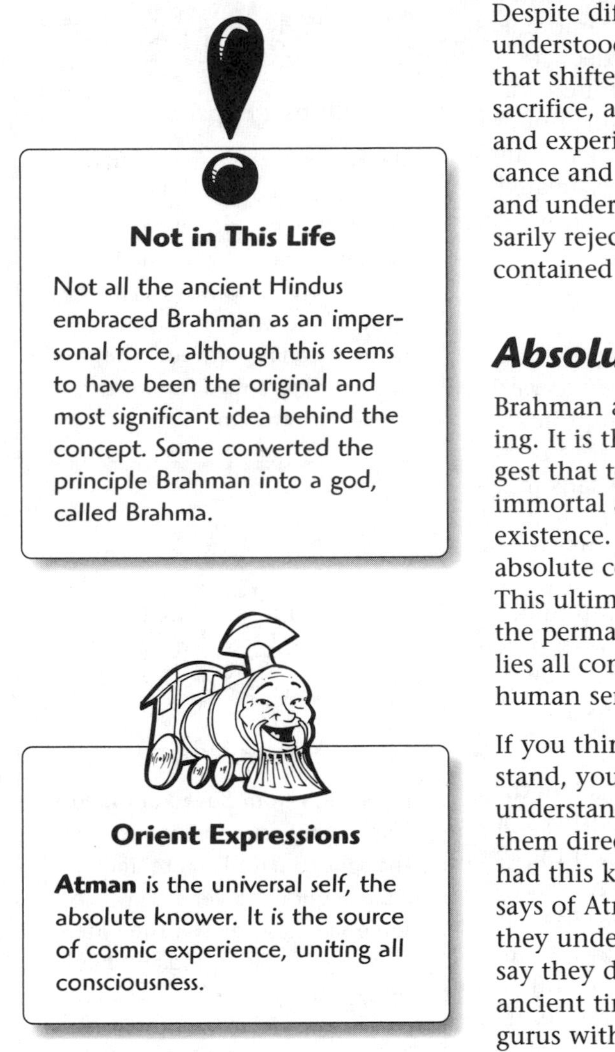

Not in This Life

Not all the ancient Hindus embraced Brahman as an impersonal force, although this seems to have been the original and most significant idea behind the concept. Some converted the principle Brahman into a god, called Brahma.

Orient Expressions

Atman is the universal self, the absolute knower. It is the source of cosmic experience, uniting all consciousness.

Absolute Awareness

Brahman alone of all things is timeless and unchanging. It is thus a source of peace. The Upanishads suggest that to understand Brahman is to become immortal and free forever from the cares of ordinary existence. They describe a transcendent self, an absolute consciousness capable of knowing Brahman. This ultimate, universal self is called *Atman*. Atman is the permanent, unchanging, universal self that underlies all consciousness. It is not known through the five human senses, but it enables knowledge to take place.

If you think Atman and Brahman are hard to understand, you're not alone. The only sure-fire way to understand Atman and Brahman is to experience them directly. Sources differ as to who has actually had this kind of experience. One of the Upanishads says of Atman, "It is not understood by those who say they understand it, and is understood by those who say they do not." You get the idea that even back in ancient times, people took the pronouncements of the gurus with a grain of salt!

Yet, as difficult as Brahman and Atman are to understand, the Upanishads offer an explanation for both that has inspired and intrigued philosophers for millennia: Brahman is Atman. Atman is Brahman. This discovery stands as perhaps the single greatest cosmic and timeless truth of Hinduism. The ultimate self is the ultimate reality. Transcendent consciousness pervades transcendent existence.

Because it is absolute, Brahman does not depend on awareness to exist. Even without anyone to notice it, there will always be absolute existence. Brahman, in other words, can be described as an objective absolute. This means it exists independently of point of view. Atman is a corresponding subjective absolute. It is consciousness that takes place independently of physical reality. Even without anything to be aware of, there is absolute awareness, called Atman. Though seemingly different, Brahman and Atman are the same, transcending temporal being and awareness.

Karma Dogma

One of the most famous phrases from the Upanishads is *Tat tvam asi,* which is Sanskrit for "That art thou" and refers to the idea that Brahman is Atman. The insight is ascribed to an ancient Hindu sage named Aruni.

Getting Over It

Brahman and Atman are timeless and eternal. They are the reconciliation of opposites, including life and death, male and female, all and nothing, and the condition of knowing and the condition of being known. They are the powers behind the forces of nature and divinity. Every individual creature is a reflection of Brahman and Atman, even though they may not realize it. Thus, the good news is that everyone has a chance to come to eternal rest by merging with Brahman and Atman. The bad news is that, to do so, we have to renounce everything we care about in this life.

Bliss and Bondage

According to Vedic philosophy, human beings can experience Brahman and Atman directly. In fact, this direct experience is the only way to fully understand them. Unless you've had this experience, you won't know what they are. The Vedas describe it as a state of bliss and of cosmic oneness. The history of Indian philosophy includes many different approaches to attaining this state. Among the more important are meditation, study, virtuous living, and religious devotion.

The Vedas suggest it is necessary to become free of the human condition that stands between each individual and cosmic unity. The Vedic term for this freedom is *moksha,* which means "release." Moksha is sometimes translated into English as "enlightenment." It is the state of experiencing Brahman and Atman and can be compared to being let out of prison or seeing the truth after a lifetime of delusion. Some say moksha is a blissful experience; others say it is completely empty of both good and bad. Some believe moksha can be achieved during one's lifetime; others say it can happen only after death. In either case, it is said to be the ultimate goal of all human life. Like Brahman and Atman, you have to experience moksha in order to understand it fully.

Lotus Lore

A concept and symbol that may have originated as a representation of Brahman is the number zero. Like Brahman, zero is said to provide a reconciliation of all opposites, standing both within and outside all known reality. The zero soon traveled west from India to become an essential feature of the Arabic number system, used by most people in the world today. The Arabic system, which has all but completely replaced Roman numerals, is based on the idea of using digits to represent multiples of 10. This idea, like zero, originated in India to become indispensable to mathematics.

Orient Expressions

Moksha is release from the human condition that prevents union with Brahman and Atman. It is what happens to you when you experience enlightenment. **Maya** is the illusory condition of everyday experience. Belief that maya has permanence prevents us from experiencing unity with Brahman and Atman.

Moksha is ultimate release from illusory thoughts, perceptions, and desires—from the shifting, impermanent world of impressions, feelings, and beliefs that tie us down to physical reality. This illusory world is known as *maya*. Maya makes people think that what is impermanent—including physical reality, desires, and beliefs—is the most reality has to offer. Thus maya makes it harder to merge with Brahman and Atman.

Although maya appears to be real, its illusory nature is evident in the fact that it is always shifting and changing. Nothing about it is permanent. As a result, life within the world of maya leads only to pain and disappointment. To take pleasure in the things of this world is to set yourself up for a letdown. Only Brahman and Atman are permanent. They alone can provide release from the suffering and disappointment that always come as part of the human condition. In order to merge with Brahman and Atman, it is necessary to renounce all attachments to maya.

Making Progress

From the perspective of most Westerners, renouncing the world is a radical idea that amounts to a rejection of life itself. Even within Hinduism, it is not a simple thing to renounce maya in order to strive for unity with the absolute. Only the most serious and dedicated seekers take the difficult path of renouncing the world. Taking this path can be understood as a kind of voluntary death, in which you reject all holds life has on you. In doing so, you are eventually born again into the absolute.

While maya prevents us from experiencing moksha and uniting with Brahman and Atman, it is not simply bad or false, but is a manifestation of the power of Brahman and Atman. Some see the gods as maya—part of the world of appearances that stands between human consciousness and the absolute reality. The Vedas say it is not wrong to be devoted to maya and to worship the gods, since to do so is, indirectly, to worship Brahman and Atman, which exist beyond them.

Some say that the entire world of maya traces an important process of liberation and that, eventually, all individuals will attain enlightenment, and maya—the world as we know it—will cease to exist. Thus existence is undergoing a process of self-purification. As people come to reject the shifting, undependable forms of appearance, these forms disappear forever until there is nothing left but pure, absolute existence.

Play It Again, Samsara

Maya remains a barrier to unity with Brahman and Atman, which is the highest possible goal people can have. Working through this barrier is a process that can take lifetimes. The Upanishads put forward the idea that when people die, they are reborn into new lives. This is called *samsara*. Samsara is the ongoing cycle of birth, death, and rebirth into the physical world. This cycle is understood as a form of bondage from which we can be released by merging with Brahman and Atman. Once merged, we will no longer experience samsara, and will be reborn.

Orient Expressions

Samsara is the cycle of birth and death that accounts for our physical existence. It is the idea of reincarnation as explained in the Upanishads.

According to the theory of samsara, we are bound to earthly existence by our desires and emotional attachments. We can break these bonds only after experiencing the pain that goes along with all pleasures. With this experience, we can gradually gain the wisdom to forego worldly attachments. As we grow in wisdom, we are reborn into higher and higher states of existence, culminating in final release from the bondage of maya and samsara.

Wheel of Fortune

It is not simply our deluded thoughts that keep us bound to worldly existence, but our actions as well. These actions influence what sort of lives we will be reborn into after death. This influence is known as *karma*. The idea behind karma is that our past actions account for our present situation and, to a degree, our future situation as well.

In addition, our present actions will influence our future situation. This influence continues even after we die because we will be born again into a new life determined by the karma established in previous lives.

Karma has become a widely influential concept since it was first expressed in the Vedas centuries ago. Many people use it to account for unpredictable twists of fate, including unexpected good fortune and undeserved bad luck. For many, it also serves as a reminder to remain on their best behavior so as to avoid future unwanted repercussions from present actions.

The Vedas speak of three kinds of karma, *prarabdha-karma, sanchita-karma,* and *agami-karma:*

- **Prarabdha-karma** is karma built up from your past, including previous lives, that influences your present life.
- **Sanchita-karma** also carries over from the past, but will not take effect until a future life.
- **Agami-karma** is built up in your present life and will take effect in future lives.

Orient Expressions

Karma is the ongoing influence of past actions on the future. It carries over from past lives into present and future incarnations. **Prarabdha-karma** is the influence of past actions on your present life; **sanchita-karma** is the influence of past actions on future lives; **agami-karma** is the influence of present actions on future lives.

Both prarabdha-karma and sanchita-karma are irreversible. The course of agami-karma may be altered by actions taken in the future. Prarabdha-karma may be symbolized by an arrow which has been shot from a bow but has not yet reached the target. It is inevitable. Sanchita-karma can be compared to an arrow that is still in the quiver. It is likely to be shot at some point, but this isn't certain. Agami-karma is like an arrow that is in the archer's hand. It is almost certainly about to be shot, but there's still a chance it will not be. In other words, it's still possible to do something about sanchita- and agami-karma if you act fast.

The Bad with the Good

The idea of karma has appealed to lots of people all over the world. It's reassuring to think that we'll get another chance in life to make up for mistakes we've made. It's also exciting to imagine past lives for ourselves in which we may have acted out our natures very differently from the way we do today. Maybe you were once a great ruler, a warrior, priest, or magician. Who knows, maybe you were even the dog who played Lassie on TV!

It's also satisfying to think that good deeds will be rewarded and bad deeds will be punished. And it only seems fair that people who have it easy in this life should get a taste of hardship in other existences. If you're having a tough time now, just hang in there 'til the next go-round, and everything may fall into place for you. Everyone should get what they've got coming to them, and karmic reincarnation can seem like a perfect way of ensuring cosmic retribution.

Yet the idea behind karma is not simply the belief that everyone should get an equal taste of the hardships and enjoyments of life. It also has to do with cosmic punishment and reward for good and evil actions—but even this isn't the main point. A deeper purpose of karma is to give people the opportunity to develop spiritual mastery of the pains and pleasures involved with life. Once you come to terms with what life has to offer and grow to see things as they are, then you're ready to move on to a higher level of existence.

In addition to its broad appeal all around the world, the idea of karma plays a more specific role in helping to regulate traditional Hindu society. In the context of traditional Hinduism, the idea of karma has encouraged people to behave in accordance with an elaborate social code that sets down rules for how all different sorts of people should live. To avoid bad karma, people live according to their station in life, determined by their social caste, their age, and their sex. This traditional centuries-old system of social stratification has been a continual source of controversy in India.

In some ways, Vedic philosophy reinforces the caste system. The law of karma is just one way. It encourages people to accept caste distinctions, both to avoid bad karma in future lives and to atone for misdeeds committed in past lives. In addition, the whole idea of renouncing the world and pursuing spiritual enlightenment tends to encourage people simply to put up with social injustice rather than work to change it. Liberation obtained through moksha does not mean social liberation. Thus the Upanishads do not teach that we should strive to solve our problems by working things out with others. Instead, they teach that problems should be transcended. The solution to these problems is to refuse to let them bother us.

This attitude toward life and its problems seems wrong to many in the West—and to many in India, for that matter. At the same time, Hindu philosophy has a tremendous appeal and importance that is recognized all over the world. It helps millions put things in perspective and get in touch with deeper priorities. The continuing challenge, of course, is to apply this philosophy in the best way. The following chapter talks about some of the more famous recommendations for how Vedic philosophy should be applied to everyday life.

The Least You Need to Know

- Hindu philosophy had its beginnings centuries before it began to be written down, perhaps as early as 1500 B.C.E.
- Ancient philosophy in India stems from the teachings of the Brahmins, priests in charge of the ritual and wisdom contained in the Vedas.
- Hindu philosophy comes into its own in the Upanishads, that assert a central tenet of Hindu thought: Brahman and Atman are one.
- The goal of humankind is the attainment of moksha—liberation or enlightenment. The chief barrier to achieving this goal is maya, the illusory, changing, impermanent world.
- Karma is the cosmic law that determines people's future lives based on their past actions.

Chapter 5

Life Goes On

In This Chapter

- Traditional ethical philosophy in India
- The Epic period of Indian philosophy
- Bhakti and the Bhagavad-Gita
- Dharma and the *Code of Manu*
- The caste system

One of the major points of Vedic philosophy says that we should renounce life in order to unite with the absolute. This view poses a major challenge to anyone who takes it seriously. Renouncing life doesn't mean your life is over. What are you supposed to do with yourself in the meantime? What about going to work, paying the bills, walking the dog, and all that sort of thing? Obviously, there's a huge gap between ordinary life as it presents itself to us and cosmic absolute being as described in the Vedas. How can we bridge this gap?

Some famous answers are offered in ancient writings produced in India in the wake of the Vedic period. These include the Bhagavad-Gita, which contains words of inspiration that generations of Hindus have turned to for comfort and guidance much as many Westerners have turned to the Bible. A very different work from about the same time period is the *Code of Manu*, a kind of lawbook with specific recommendations for how to live. Both these works start with Vedic philosophy and apply it to the problem of daily living.

One result of these attempts to square Vedic philosophy with ordinary existence has been an approach to life that has inspired generations and has spread far beyond India itself. At the same time, however, these very attempts helped perpetuate a system of social stratification—the caste system—that has been widely denounced as oppressive and unjust. The social and philosophical conflicts over the Vedas and their legacy ultimately gave rise to many new philosophical schools.

Epic Struggle

Many ancient cultures have produced literary works known as epics that set forth the cultures' most important ideals and achievements in the form of a story, usually a story about a great battle. The most famous epics of Western literature are the *Iliad* and *Odyssey* of Homer (ca. 700–800 B.C.E.) and Virgil's *Aeneid* (ca. 20 B.C.E.). There are two great epics of Indian literature, the *Ramayana* and the *Mahabharata* (ca. 400 B.C.E.). Of these, the *Mahabharata* has special philosophical significance because it takes on the question of action in the world of impermanent forms.

The question of how to deal with the problem of action is taken up in the most important and widely read section of the *Mahabharata,* known as the Bhagavad-Gita, the "song of the adorable one." The Bhagavad-Gita tells the story of a prince, Arjuna, who is on the verge of leading troops into battle. He is reluctant to do so, however, since the enemy forces are those of his uncle, so that, win or lose, large numbers of his relatives will be slain.

Orient Expressions

An **avatar** is an appearance on Earth of a deity, usually Vishnu, in human or animal form. Vishnu is often said to have 10 avatars, including Krishna. The avatars appear on Earth to restore righteousness during times when evil predominates.

Arjuna asks his charioteer, Krishna, to drive him out to the front lines so he can look at the armies on both sides. There he sees his family and friends, all preparing to slaughter one another for the sake of the kingdom. He confides in Krishna that he has no desire for the kingdom if it means so many people who are close to him must die. He would prefer not to take action rather than go through with the battle. The Bhagavad-Gita consists mostly of the words Krishna offers in response.

Avatar in Action

Arjuna's problem is easy to relate to for those who go along with the basics of Vedic philosophy, which suggests that the things of this world have no real value, and participation in life is pointless and may even make things worse. Krishna's words are therefore full of significance for many Hindus. This is especially the case because Krishna is a divine figure. A god in human form, Krishna is an *avatar,* or incarnation, of the god Vishnu.

Krishna explains that it is not wrong to take action in the world. In fact, it is often appropriate to do so, given the situations we encounter in life. It's true that the "fruits of action," the results of our efforts (represented in the Bhagavad-Gita by the kingdom for which Arjuna will fight), are unimportant in the grand scheme of things, but this doesn't mean that it's pointless to act. Action is the working out of karma. This process will culminate in the reabsorption of all things into absolute being.

Lotus Lore

The god Vishnu originated during the Vedic period as a minor solar deity but rose in importance in the following centuries. Vishnu is a key member of the divine Hindu triad, the trimurti, including Brahma and Shiva. Vishnu is good and merciful and preserves the universe. Shiva is vengeful and destructive. Brahma balances these two opposing principles. Vishnu is regarded by Vishnuists as Isvara, the Lord of All Being. The universe is his breath that he will re-assimilate by inhaling. Then he will exhale again and re-create the world. In the Bhagavad-Gita, as well as in other sources, Vishnu is associated with Brahman, or absolute being.

Krishna reminds Arjuna that no one killed in battle, including himself, will be permanently destroyed, but will be reborn again and again into new forms as they work out their karma. Thus Arjuna need not fear for his family or himself. It is right that he fight in battle since he is the son of a king, and the kingdom is rightfully his. He simply needs to recognize that the kingdom, like life itself, is transitory. Thus it is right to take action but also to remain detached to avoid becoming too involved with worldly things.

Keep on Truckin'

This somewhat paradoxical idea of detached involvement has provided inspiration for millions who have sensed a gap between spiritual and ordinary concerns. Lots of people have wondered what the events and actions of daily life have to do with the ultimate purpose of the universe in general. Mundane things can seem pointless and, as a result, it can be tempting to say, "To heck with it. Nothing really matters. I don't care what happens. It's all basically meaningless." The message of the Bhagavad-Gita is that, despite the insignificance of worldly affairs, it's important to go through the process of living your life anyway since this process will lead you through to higher things.

Mundane responsibilities that seem painful, tedious, or trivial may thus have significance for personal spiritual growth. What matters is not the outcome of our actions in and of themselves, but the process of following out the path of life to the end. Of course, everyone is different, so everyone has a different path to follow. All paths can lead to enlightenment and release from worldly things.

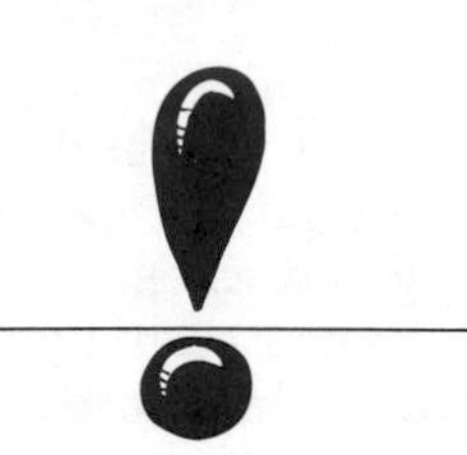

Not in This Life

He who withdraws from the world of action while imagining the fruits of action in his heart is deluded and follows the wrong path. But great is he who is free from attachments and harmonious in spirit and follows the path of righteous and holy action.

—The Bhagavad-Gita, 3:6–7

Three Yogas

The infinite number of individual paths are broken down in the Bhagavad-Gita into three *yogas,* or disciplines. These are the three yogas of knowledge (*jnana-yoga*), action (*karma-yoga*), and devotion (*bhakti-yoga*). (You can read more about yoga, the gunas, and their place in Indian philosophy in Chapter 8, "Yogi Bearings".)

Karma Dogma

Most westerners are familiar with yoga as a set of techniques for exercise and relaxation, but this is only a small part of what yoga is within Hindu philosophy. **Yoga** is a Hindu term that can be translated as "discipline" or "path." In fact, yoga can refer to many different kinds of practices, including magic. In addition, yoga is the name for a philosophical school developed by Patanjali sometime between 500 and 200 B.C.E.

Bhakti Basics

The Bhagavad-Gita, in saying that it is right for different people to follow different paths, has become perhaps the most influential inspirational work of Hinduism. It has been revered, studied, and even memorized in India in much the same way as the Bible among Christians and Jews. And while the Bhagavad-Gita inspires, it also helps to reconcile conflicting points of view. An important question it raises is, "Which is the best way to attain enlightenment?" The answer is, "It depends on the person." For some, it is searching for knowledge, for others, it is performing acts of kindness and justice, and for others, it is worshiping God.

Worship of God is known as *bhakti,* which means "devotion." The concept goes back to the Vedas, but the importance of bhakti emerged and developed in the Bhagavad-Gita, where Krishna tells Arjuna to worship him. (In fact, the word *bhagavat,* "adored one," stems from the same root as bhakti.) By worshiping Vishnu in the form of Krishna, Arjuna joins in a kind of partnership with God and comes closer to actually merging with God.

The relative importance of bhakti versus karma as alternative paths to enlightenment corresponds to the old question among Christians of whether "faith" or "good works" leads to salvation. Those who practice bhakti believe that devotion to God can override negative effects of karma, much as Christians believe that prayer can atone for sin. At the same time, constructive karmic activity is in keeping with devotion to God, since it imitates Vishnu's creation and perpetuation of the universe.

Orient Expressions

Bhakti is devotion. It represents the pursuit of enlightenment through the adoration of God. The importance of bhakti within Hinduism was galvanized through the Bhagavad-Gita.

All Roads Lead to Enlightenment

The idea that there are many possible paths to enlightenment is important in part because it implies that everyone can follow an enlightened path. No matter who you are, you can undertake your own spiritual journey. This point of view was especially important at the time the Bhagavad-Gita was first written because Indian society was so highly stratified—divided into various classes with each class having different privileges and responsibilities. In effect, the Bhagavad-Gita is saying that spiritual pursuits cut across class lines.

No matter what you do and no matter what path you follow, it's possible to proceed without regard for the worldly fruits of your actions. It's still important to do your best, but this is not so you will get money and recognition, but so you will learn from your experiences and become prepared to move beyond them. If instead you get carried away by the pursuit of worldly gain, you'll end up losing your path, no matter how far along it you may have come.

Manu's Manual

The Bhagavad-Gita and the Mahabharata, of which it is a part, supply not only spiritual insight, but practical advice on how to go about the business of living. These practical recommendations are similar to those found in a group of writings from about the same time period known as *Dharmashastras*. These are lawbooks specifying the duties of all members of society. They contain the rules of traditional ethical philosophy in India. The most famous of the *Dharmashastras* is the *Code of Manu*.

Laying Down the Law

The *Code of Manu* is an ancient compilation of rules for behavior traditionally ascribed to a legendary sage. Legend has it that the code was developed by Manu, the first man, though it actually draws on the Vedas and on established custom for its ideas. The code sets forth what is expected of people in all the different walks of life within Indian society.

Lotus Lore

Many legends surround the mythical sage, Manu, said to be the first human and to have descended from the gods. He performed the first sacrifice to Vishnu and was rewarded with a gift of a bride, whom Vishnu fashioned out of the sacrificial food. She tried to escape Manu's embraces by transforming herself into various animals, but Manu transformed himself into a male of each of the same species in order to procreate with her. In this way, all the animals were born. Another legend tells how Manu saved all the creatures from a great flood by herding them onto a large boat. Thus Manu bears resemblances to the Biblical figures Adam and Noah.

The Code of Manu says that *moksha* (enlightenment or spiritual liberation) is only one of four goals of humankind. The other three are *dharma* (righteousness and duty), *artha* (wealth), and *kama* (pleasure).

These four goals are known as *purusarthas* (human goals). The purusarthas suggest that it's good to pursue those things that make life enjoyable, including food, sex, material belongings, and status, just as long as you don't get carried away with any of them.

What It's All About

Here's a list to make it easier to peruse the purusarthas:

- **Purusarthas** are the four goals of human life according to the ancient lawbooks known as *Dharmashastras*, including the *Code of Manu*.
- **Moksha** is the highest goal—that of enlightenment and spiritual liberation. To attain it is to merge with absolute being.

- **Dharma** has a wide range of meanings but generally refers to duty. According to Manu, your duties depend on your station in life.
- **Artha** is wealth or, more broadly, purpose. It refers to any form of secular advancement.
- **Kama** (not to be confused with karma) is pleasure, including sexual pleasure, as in the famous sex manual, the *Kama Sutra*.

The four purusarthas cover the major aspects of human existence. Moksha is spiritual, dharma is moral, artha is economic, and kama is mental and physical. Moksha remains the highest goal of life, with the other three goals as means to an end. Fixating on any of these other three for their own sake is a mistake. As in the Bhagavad-Gita, the *Code of Manu* suggests that the proper attitude toward life is one of detached involvement.

A detached attitude makes it easier to achieve a balance among the various aspects of life. Pursuing wealth so obsessively that you sacrifice pleasure or justice is a mistake. Pursuing duty to the exclusion of wealth and pleasure is also wrong. Of course, this contradicts all those who say that you must completely renounce the world and its pleasures. But Manu's rules, like the Bhagavad-Gita, help to reconcile the notion of a transcendent, absolute being with the process of living an everyday life.

Karma Dogma

The *Code of Manu* says, "Some say that dharma [duty] and artha [wealth] are the most important things in life. Others say kama [pleasure] and artha [wealth] are best. Some say that only dharma [duty] is best .... But the fact is that the three go together."

Setting the Stages

Although there should be a balance among the goals of life, Manu says that we should pursue different goals at different stages. The stages are called *ashrama,* or "resting places." These are studying, householding, forest-dwelling, and renouncing. While moving through each successive stage, you can acquire the knowledge and experience necessary for attaining enlightenment.

Orient Expressions

The **ashrama** are the four stages of life—studying, householding, forest-dwelling, and renouncing—recommended by Manu's *Dharmashastra.* An ashram is also the retreat or hermitage of a guru or spiritual seeker.

Pay-Back Time

Each stage enables you to fulfill your dharma, or duty. The first major duty is to study the Vedas, which is accomplished in the first stage of life. The next duty is to have children, which is accomplished as a householder. The third duty is to focus on living a purely religious life, and this can be accomplished by being a forest-dweller. Each of these duties involves repaying a debt to those who made the practical and spiritual aspects of life possible. Studying the Vedas fulfills a debt to the teachers and seers; having children fulfills a debt to your parents; and offering sacrifices fulfills a debt to the gods.

Finally, when the debts have been paid, you are ready to renounce the world and prepare for enlightenment. This involves leading the austere life of an ascetic—fasting and meditating while traveling from place to place and living frugally on whatever you can beg. This is a voluntary life of poverty entered upon in old age, ideally at the height of wisdom and experience when mind and body have been purged of passions and worldly attachments.

This scheme for living suggests that everyone can obtain enlightenment in a single lifetime, but the *Code of Manu* acknowledges that it doesn't usually work this way. After all, it's not easy to give up the prosperous life of a householder with a family to go off into the woods by yourself to perform sacrifices and from there to give up all worldly comforts just as you reach old age. Not everyone is willing or able to do these things. This is okay. The idea is to go as far as you can in fulfilling your dharma. By making as much progress as possible, you'll be better situated to go even further in your next life.

Lotus Lore

Different Hindu scriptures are traditionally regarded as having varying degrees of authority. Most authoritative are those texts designated as *sruti,* which means "heard." These texts were thought to stem from the divine inspiration of seers known as *rishis*. They were then passed along by word of mouth for generations before being written down. This designation was applied originally to the portions of the Veda known as the *Mantras* and the *Brahmanas,* and later applied to the Upanishads. Of secondary authority are writings known as *smriti,* which means "remembered." Smriti texts are of a later period and include the Bhagavad-Gita and other epic writings, as well as the *Code of Manu* and the other *Dharmashastras*.

Class Action

You may be under the impression that, as far as the *Code of Manu* is concerned, making progress on the path to enlightenment is all a matter of personal choice. This is true, however, only for those referred to as "twice-born." Traditionally, the twice-born are those who have read the Vedas—a privilege reserved exclusively for male members of the three upper castes of society. Women and members of the servant caste simply have to wait to be reincarnated into higher social status!

Castes are stratified groups within society that have different rights, privileges, and duties. For centuries, the caste system has determined social status for many in India, assigning a life of servitude to some and a life filled with special privileges to others. To many people today, both inside and outside India, the caste system seems inherently unfair, and, although it continues to influence social life in many areas of the country, it has been officially abandoned.

The *Code of Manu* describes four main castes, or *varnas*. These are the *brahmins* (priestly caste), the *kshatriyas* (warrior caste), the *vaisyas* (merchant caste), and the *shudras* (servant caste). In addition to these, which are the most widely known, hundreds of other castes have been recognized at various times and places in India. Those who do not belong to a caste were traditionally recognized as social outcasts, the pariahs, or "untouchables."

According to the *Code of Manu*, each of the four main castes fills a necessary function within society. Each person is born into one or another caste as a result of karma carried over from previous lives. In addition, your caste supposedly reflects your personality as determined by your gunas, your personal characteristics. Thus someone born into servitude could be said to belong in his or her caste, deserve his or her lot in life, and be expected to bear his or her misfortunes in a spirit of detachment.

Orient Expressions

The **varnas** are the four castes in India's traditional caste system. They are the brahmins, kshatriyas, vaisyas, and shudras. Varna also means color, reinforcing the theory that the original caste system reflects racial differences between white Aryans from the North and the brown city dwellers they invaded. The word "caste" is not originally Indian, but comes from the Portuguese *casta*, meaning race or breed.

The *Code of Manu* even suggests that shudras cannot achieve enlightenment before being reborn into a higher caste. In contrast, Manu describes the brahmins as divine and infallible authorities. Thus, Brahmanism has played a big part in preserving the caste system.

This problem lies at the heart of the major social and philosophical controversies of Hinduism. What connection, if any, exists between social status and readiness for enlightenment? Many believe concern with status only stands in the way of enlightenment. As a result, many of India's teachers have argued that caste and sex have no bearing on spiritual matters. Whoever wrote and compiled the *Code of Manu*, however, was not one of these teachers.

In fact, the *Code of Manu* was probably written as a conservative reaction against progressive ideas that were threatening the caste system and other features of India's highly stratified traditional society. It defends the caste system by suggesting that it is all part of the natural karmic process. In contrast, many others attacked the caste system more or less indirectly, by proposing alternate views of what it means to attain enlightenment, who can obtain it how, and whether enlightenment is even possible. In this climate of disagreement, many philosophical schools and systems took shape. You can read about the most important of these in the following two chapters.

The Least You Need to Know

- The Bhagavad-Gita encourages worldly activity without concern for worldly results. Instead, action has a transcendent spiritual purpose.
- The three paths to enlightenment described in the Bhagavad-Gita are jnana (knowledge), karma (action), and bhakti (devotion).
- The *Code of Manu* describes four goals of human life: moksha (enlightenment), dharma (duty), artha (wealth), and kama (pleasure).
- The *Code of Manu,* which provides philosophical support for the caste system, was probably a conservative reaction against newer ideas that posed a threat to the traditional social order.

Chapter 6

Going to Extremes

In This Chapter

- Unorthodox schools of Indian philosophy
- Carvaka and Jaina philosophy
- The materialist reaction to Vedic philosophy
- The idealist reaction
- Scholastic logic in India

Two of the more interesting branches of Indian philosophy are known as Carvaka and Jainism, which came on the scene around 600 B.C.E. and went on to shake up the tranquil meditations of the Brahmin philosophers. These schools set forth ideas that challenged the traditional social order and questioned the authority of the sacred Vedas. Although they caused a backlash, they also helped define a new, more systematic approach to philosophy in general.

Despite the fact they are often lumped together as two unorthodox schools of Indian philosophy, Carvaka and Jainism could hardly be more different. Jainism is extremely idealistic, interested in moral, spiritual, and intellectual purity. Carvaka, in contrast, is thoroughly materialist, refusing to accept spiritual beliefs of any sort. Jainism is essentially a religious philosophy, whereas devotion has no place in Carvaka.

Yet both emphasized reason as a means of proving assertions, helping to start a whole tradition of argumentation and analysis in India. Together they presented a threat to Brahminism from two opposing sides. The only possible defense for the old way of thinking was to change and adapt to the more rational approaches of the new schools.

Orient Expressions

Darsanas are the main philosophical schools in India. They include six orthodox systems and three unorthodox schools. The term comes from a word meaning "sight."

School Work

As Indian philosophers continued to express their opinions on the old traditions—and to air their disagreements—several distinct philosophical systems emerged. These systems were not content to spin out divine-sounding pronouncements about how things are, as the ancient Vedas had done. The newer systems were more systematic, developing carefully worked out answers to some basic philosophical questions, questions like what is reality as a whole, and how do its parts all work together? What are we capable of knowing, and how do we know what we know? What is the purpose of human existence, and what's the best way to act in accordance with this purpose? These systems are known as *darsanas,* from a word meaning "sight." These are the main schools of philosophy in India.

Branching Out

As the darsanas developed, they proposed different views in response to these big questions. Of course, many of these views had been in the wind already for quite a while, but they had never truly been explained, elaborated, and defended on rational grounds. Instead, people took them on faith or left them alone. Gradually, however, Indian philosophy grew more systematic and coherent. The schools emerged complete with elaborate logical distinctions between kinds of things and ways of looking at them.

Although the points of view were multiplying, these various schools were all drawing on, and responding to, the Vedas—the earliest of India's philosophical teachings—and to one another. The schools gradually separated in the process of dispute that went on between rival positions. In all, there are nine main darsanas. In this chapter, you can read about two of them—Carvaka and Jainism.

Off-Beat Beliefs

The major darsanas traditionally get sorted out into orthodox and unorthodox systems, depending on whether they accept the Vedas as authoritative. This distinction, however, is somewhat misleading since some of the so-called unorthodox schools share important ideas in common with Vedic teachings while most of the orthodox schools put forward ideas that contradict the Vedas. It may be more accurate to say that the unorthodox systems are labeled unorthodox because they ultimately failed to gain acceptance by the Brahmin priesthood. In contrast, the orthodox systems were accepted by the Brahmins, even though many of their ideas are critical of Brahmanism.

The fact is, all the darsanas represent aspects of an ongoing adjustment within Indian philosophy, moving away from dogmatic acceptance of Vedic pronouncements and toward reasoned, logical, and systematic points of view. Thus, even the more conservative schools became more systematic in the way they set forth and defended the old ideas—and they had to be to keep pace with the more progressive philosophies.

Not in This Life

Be careful not to confuse the distinction between unorthodox and orthodox schools of Indian philosophy with the distinction—so important in the West—between atheism and belief in God. In fact, several orthodox systems—Sankhya, Vaisheshika, and Nyaya, as well as early Mimamsa—deny the existence of a personal God.

There are three main unorthodox schools of Indian philosophy:

- ➤ A materialist school known as Jainism Carvaka.
- ➤ An ascetic and religiously oriented school called Jainism.
- ➤ Buddhism, an ethical philosophy that practically disappeared from India soon after it was founded. (It quickly spread all over the world, however, to become one of the most widespread belief systems on the planet. You can find the section on Buddhism following this one.)

What You See Is What You Get

Among the first of the darsanas to emerge and the most radical was Carvaka, a philosophy that posed a head-on challenge to the most cherished teachings of the Vedas. Carvaka is the preeminent materialist philosophy of India, categorically stating that all existence is made up of matter. Whereas the Vedas taught that the world of appearances is illusory, the Carvaka system is based on the idea that nothing exists that cannot be observed. Physical reality, in other words, is all that exists.

Accidents Happen

This means that, in Carvaka, there is no Brahman, no Atman, no gods, no afterlife, no reincarnation, and no immortal soul. There's just a lot of material stuff that combines temporarily into forms and dissolves again into its basic components. According to the Carvaka system, this means the world and everything in it occurred by accident. The four elements (earth, air, fire, and water) happened to come together in such a way as to make reality as we know it, including living and even thinking things.

Even the human soul is thus a physical conglomeration of elements, combined in the right way to enable us to think and feel. Carvaka philosophy explains this by pointing out some of the things that can happen when different materials get mixed together. Chemicals that are inert can become potent drugs when mixed together in the right combinations. Similarly, some dull-colored substances can be combined to form brightly colored dyes. The point is that many physical things have characteristics that appear to be more than the sum of their parts. This is true of the human soul, which is simply an aspect of our physical bodies.

Karma Dogma

The essential teaching of Carvaka is this: There is no other world than this one. There is no heaven and no hell. The realm of Shiva and other such regions have been invented by stupid and false teachers. To experience heaven is to eat delicious food, enjoy the company of young women, wear fine clothes, perfume, flowers, and sandal paste.

Spiritual Baggage

Given the Carvaka idea that there is no immortal soul, it only makes sense that the pervasive concern in India with Atman, Brahman, and enlightenment are misguided. In fact, the Carvaka system teaches that karma does not exist, so it's pointless to attempt to lead a virtuous life in hopes of becoming reborn in a better state, or enlightened and "released from bondage to the physical world." Since the physical world is all there is, there is nothing to be released into!

What's more, says Carvaka, there's no point in seeking personal purity through yoga and meditation, since desire, fear, joy, and suffering are inescapable. They are simply a natural part of being a person. The best we can do in life is try to derive as much enjoyment out of it as we can by pursuing things that give pleasure—especially good food, nice clothes, and the pleasing company of the opposite sex!

And, of course, Carvaka says religious sacrifice and ritual are a waste of time since there are no gods to appease. In fact, Carvaka philosophy suggests that the so-called holy actions of monks and yogis are signs of weakness and stupidity. People cling to religion because they can't face reality, because they can't understand what is right in front of them, and because they want a way to make a living without having to exert themselves in any practical fashion. Carvaka, then, presents a searing indictment of India's religious practices.

Censored System

Clearly, Carvaka flies in the face of the most cherished notions of Brahmanism. This may help explain why the original texts containing the first Carvaka teachings have been lost. They may have been destroyed by priests or other authorities who saw them as a threat. In fact, we know about Carvaka only indirectly through the writings of those who have criticized it. These critical sources present a somewhat distorted and negative picture of Carvaka, portraying it as immoral, reckless, shallow, and selfish.

Yet despite its possible suppression and misrepresentation by others, Carvaka evidently had a stimulating influence on Indian philosophy in general. It was, after all, a powerful way of thinking that holds together on its own, without appealing to higher sources. According to Carvaka, the only reliable knowledge we can have is based on what can be observed and experienced. Thus Carvaka is consistent and systematic in saying what exists and how we know about it.

Carvaka's systematic quality challenged other schools to develop more systematic approaches as well. Thanks in part to Carvaka, material reality became a more important concern within other schools of thought, which devoted more attention to the question of how the material world relates to divine and spiritual things. In addition, the question of how we know what we think became more important. The traditional attitude regarding Vedas as a source of infallible truth did not disappear, but Vedic philosophers stepped up their efforts to defend the ancient teachings with rational arguments.

Lotus Lore

Conflicting views exist about the origin of the term "Carvaka" for India's materialist school of philosophy. Some say the term combines the word *charu*, meaning "beautiful," with *vak*, meaning "word," so Carvaka stands for "beautiful word," or "beautiful teaching." (This may actually have been intended as a put-down of the system, suggesting that it looks good but is really deceptive.) Others say that Carvaka is the name of a philosopher who lived around 600 B.C.E., the founder of the school. Some say the school was founded by a sage named Brihaspati. Another name for Carvaka philosophy is Lokayata, which means "things of this world."

Jaina's Addiction

Those who continued to recognize the authority of the Vedas had to have felt threatened by the Carvaka philosophy, which suggested that Brahmanism was based on hypocrisy and delusions. But they had a fairly clear and obvious means of defense—they could discredit Carvaka as immoral. In rejecting the spiritual beliefs of Brahmanism, Carvaka also rejected the ethical teachings that go along with them. So Carvaka could be—and was—branded as an evil way of thinking.

Conservative Vedic philosophers had to be careful, however, since morality, though important in Brahmanism, was not the essential thing. As you may have noticed from reading the previous chapters, moral action is just one of several ways to enlightenment. In contrast—and in reaction against the Vedic emphasis on ritual and worship of the gods—the religious philosophy known as Jainism emphasized moral conduct as crucial to enlightenment.

Unlike Carvaka, Jaina philosophy has a prominent moral and spiritual emphasis. To a degree, this emphasis is consistent with Vedic beliefs. Jains believe in reincarnation, in the value of transcending worldly desires, and in spiritual enlightenment. Yet Jaina philosophy rejects the Vedas as infallible authorities, seeing them instead as valuable guides that should be supplemented with logic, experience, and personal discipline.

In fact, like Buddhism, Jainism is both an outgrowth of Vedic philosophy and a reaction to it. Much as Protestantism in the West reacted against Catholicism without abandoning traditional Christianity, both Buddhism and Jainism attempt to revise Brahmanism while preserving many of its essential features. Jainism tends to be more rigorous, morally and intellectually, than Brahmanism, placing more emphasis on conduct and understanding than belief.

Orient Expressions

Tirthankaras are legendary teachers of Jainism who have attained liberation for themselves and have taught it to others. The word means "ford maker."

Starved for Knowledge

Jainism was founded by a teacher and religious leader named Mahavira (ca. 600 B.C.E.) who lived around the same time as the Buddha. Old as Jainism is, the Jains trace their origins even further back, regarding Mahavira as the last of 24 *tirthankaras*—legendary teachers said to have achieved complete freedom from worldly desires. In fact, the word Jaina comes from the title "Jina," or victorious one, referring to those who have achieved victory over their own passions. At least a few of these teachers seem to have been actual historical figures, and some are mentioned in the Vedas, despite the fact that Jainism rejects the Vedas as an infallible authority in developing its own view of reality.

Jaina philosophy emerged only gradually out of the religious teachings of Mahavira, who taught *asceticism*—acts of self-discipline, self-deprivation, and self-denial—as a means of purifying the self. Asceticism is an element in much Hindu thinking, but the Jains went especially far in this direction. A Jaina sect known as "sky clad" would not even wear clothes! (Other Jaina monks and nuns wore white robes.) Legend has it that Mahavira's parents were hard-core ascetics who denied themselves food for so long they starved to death!

Let It Be

Jaina nuns and monks take five vows in confirming themselves:

- Devotion to the truth
- Aversion to material possessions
- Celibacy
- Aversion to stealing
- Nonviolence

All these things are thought to make them pure and better prepared for enlightenment. The commitment to nonviolence is especially important, however, since it has become an important Jaina contribution to Hindu philosophy in general. This commitment is known as *ahimsa* and reflects a deep respect for all life.

Orient Expressions

Asceticism is the practice of self-denial, usually for the sake of spiritual development, and can be found as part of many religious and philosophical traditions. Ascetic practices include celibacy, fasting, self-induced sleep deprivation, and the rejection of material comforts in general. **Ahimsa** is the moral principle of respect for life. This principle has been practiced in many forms, including vegetarianism and nonviolent resistance.

Jains see living things as profoundly interconnected. To hurt something that is alive amounts to hurting life itself. Some Jains held this belief so strongly that they would not take a step without sweeping the ground in front of them so as to avoid stepping on any hapless insects in their way! Of course, the idea of ahimsa ties in with belief in karma and reincarnation. Since souls may be reborn as people or animals, there is obviously a spiritual connection between them. Jains believe that, in being respectful of all living things, they become wiser and more pure as individuals. Hindus of other sects have since come to accept this belief as well. Most notably, it was embraced and made famous in the twentieth century by Mahatma Gandhi.

Lotus Lore

The Jains practiced ahimsa, or nonviolence, in part by refusing to eat meat. Jaina vegetarianism spread to other Hindu sects and eventually led to the tradition of revering "sacred cows"—animals that were permitted to wander free throughout Indian villages without fear of being slaughtered and eaten. This has baffled many Westerners who can't understand why so many Indians would rather go hungry than turn their sacred cows into holy hamburger.

Jaina's Logic

Jainism has continued as a tradition for centuries and was alive and well during the Middle Ages in India. During this time, in addition to living ascetic monastic lifestyles and concentrating on morality, the Jains were also scholars who produced many writings on the nature of reality and of understanding. Thus, together with the Jaina philosophy of morals, an influential system of logic and metaphysics developed, complete with categories for breaking down reality into its component parts.

Any Way You Cut It

At first glance, it may seem that the scholastic, logic-chopping aspect of Jaina philosophy doesn't have a whole lot to do with its monastic, devotional aspect. Jaina monks, however, were scholars throughout the Middle Ages much as many Christian monks were. The complicated scholastic philosophy they came up with can seem to lead around in logical circles, much like the scholastic philosophy of the Middle Ages in Europe! Evidently, coming up with convoluted logical relationships for everything was a good way for the monks to keep out of trouble.

In fact, Jaina philosophy was not the only Indian philosophical school to have a highly developed scholastic, logical component. All the schools discussed in the following chapter, like Jainism, chopped reality up into categories, known as *padarthas,* in order to examine, analyze, define, classify, and debate all manner of things and ideas in all kinds of ways. You might say the padarthas are quasiscientific terms for organizing and describing the world. They are supposedly based on experience and observation, but they often seem more like arbitrary conceptual kitchen sinks.

They can get pretty complicated, especially since the different schools all have more-or-less different padarthas. What's more, though I hate to say it, they're not terribly useful for much of anything these days since Western science has pretty much taken over the job of investigating reality. Even so, you may get a kick out of looking into the padarthas of Jainism. Who knows, maybe Hindu scholasticism will make a comeback. If so, read on; you're on the cutting edge!

Orient Expressions

Padarthas are analytical categories describing objects of experience. Different philosophical schools recognize different groups of padarthas and sometimes interpret the same padarthas differently.

Categorically Speaking

In Jainism, observable reality is made up of substance, called dravya, which includes these items:

- Physical reality, or matter, is called pudgala. This is the only physical substance within dravya. The rest are immaterial.
- Temporal reality (time) is called kala. This is the only substance within dravya that does not exist within the three dimensions.
- The principle, medium, or mode of motion is dharma (note that this is the word for "duty" in ethical philosophy). Somehow it exists independently of matter and of space.
- The principle, medium, or mode of rest is adharma. This, along with motion, or dharma, may seem like a pretty strange category. For some reason, the Jain scholastic philosophers thought of rest and motion not as states of material objects, but as immaterial substances in their own right.
- Spacial reality is akasha. For some reason, it is considered a separate substance from rest and motion, rather than the place where motion and rest take place.
- Living souls are called jiva. Each soul is conscious, alive, immaterial, and—somehow—three-dimensional. The category of jiva is further broken down into liberated (mukta) and bound (baddha) souls. Bound souls are broken down according to the number of senses they possess. Plants have only one, worms have two, human beings have five senses.

Mental Breakdowns

... and these are just the padarthas! We still have the *pramanas,* which are a set of criteria for determining whether a proposition is true and valid. To give you a basic idea, there are two main pramanas: direct knowledge and indirect knowledge. Direct knowledge is divided into worldly (sensed) knowledge and spiritual (extrasensory) knowledge. Worldly knowledge may be verbal or perceptual. Spiritual knowledge may be absolute or limited. Many of these subdivided pramanas are divided even further. Indirect knowledge, by the way, is further divided into five more kinds of knowledge.

... and these are just the categories for how we know things in themselves! In addition, there's a set of classifications for how things relate to other things. These are the Nayas (not to be confused with Nyaya, which is a whole other school of Indian philosophy discussed in the following chapter). Nayas are standpoints, or points of view, and there's a whole slew of them.

Orient Expressions

Pramanas are criteria or proofs for the validity of knowledge, important for the logical aspects of Indian philosophy. Different philosophical schools recognize different pramanas and emphasize similar pramanas to varying degrees.

Syad-vada is the "maybe theory" of Jaina philosophy that says reality is too complex to be described adequately by any single statement. Thus, conflicting statements can be valid simultaneously, provided they are made from distinct points of view.

The nayas give rise to the idea that knowledge is partial and relative. This view is called *syad-vada,* the "maybe theory," that says that what you know depends on your point of view and that there are always many points of view. According to syad-vada, reality is so complex that a mere statement about something is not capable of explaining the thing in its entirety. The best we can do is say that the statement may be true from where we stand. From another point of view, a contradictory statement may be true. What is true, for example, at one point in time, may not be true at another point.

All this goes to show that it's probably a good idea to avoid intellectual debates with scholastic Jaina philosophers whenever possible. The good news is that most Jains consider knowledge to be pointless unless it is used in connection with good moral conduct and spiritual faith as a means to enlightenment. These three priorities—knowledge, faith, and conduct—are known as the "three jewels" of Jainism. Each of the three reinforces the other two, and all three work together in helping the individual transcend worldly reality.

The Least You Need to Know

- The three unorthodox systems of Indian philosophy are Carvaka, Jainism, and Buddhism. They are unorthodox because they rejected the Vedas as infallible authority and challenged Brahmanist ritualism.
- Carvaka is materialist, rejecting the ideas of god, spirit, immortal soul, and reincarnation.
- Carvaka posed a severe threat to traditional Vedic philosophy and may have been censored. In any case, it was severely criticized as an immoral way of life and thought.
- Jainism is an ascetic and monastic religious philosophy that developed an elaborate system of logic and metaphysics.
- The influential principle of ahimsa, including respect for life and nonviolence, stems from Jaina teachings.

Chapter 7

Building on Tradition

In This Chapter

- The orthodox philosophical systems
- Defense of tradition
- Nyaya and Vaisheshika
- Mimamsa and Vedanta

By around 600 B.C.E., when Jainism and Buddhism got started, the ancient and venerable teachings of the Vedas were already starting to look outdated. Although they contained the seeds of many important philosophical ideas that were still current in India—including ideas shared by Buddhists and Jains—they also remained fixated on ritual and sacrifice, the gods, and ideas about existence and devotion, all of which came to seem increasingly irrelevant to the all-important task of attaining enlightenment. Many of these notions had served to bolster the reputation and the authority of the Brahmanic priesthood so, when the ideas came under fire, the Brahmins were deeply implicated.

But the Brahmins and other Vedic philosophers did not simply accept criticism lying down. They took a new look at the Vedas in light of the more important recent developments in Indian philosophy. Buddhist skepticism, Jaina logic and morality, and Carvaka materialism were scrutinized, assimilated, adapted, and tied in with traditional Vedic ideas. The philosophical lines were not only redrawn, they were delineated more clearly.

This philosophical overhaul didn't happen all at once and did not represent the official consensus of a single governing philosophical body, but took place over the course of centuries as different thinkers responded in different ways to new ideas and criticisms. The result, ultimately, was the rise of six orthodox schools of Hindu philosophy. These schools are very different from one another but share the common thread of respect for traditional Vedic authority.

School Work

The six orthodox darsanas, or schools of Indian philosophy, developed in the wake of materialist and skeptical attacks on Vedic authority stemming from the rise of Carvaka, Jainism, and Buddhism. They took on the difficult job of defending the old Vedic ideas and of extending them into logical and rational ways of thinking. In the process, they worked out a kind of philosophical compromise between tradition, faith, and revelatory inspiration on the one hand, and logical, rational, and critical thought on the other.

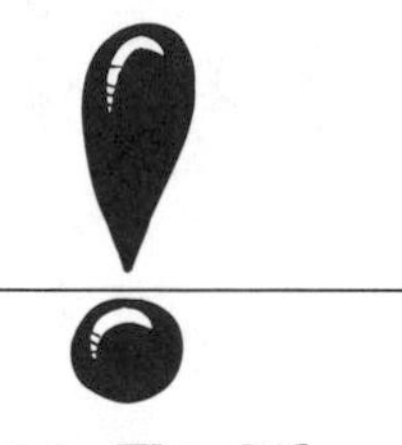

Not in This Life

You probably won't want to turn to the writings of the Vaisheshika, Nyaya, and Mimamsa schools for light, diverting reading. In fact, they tend to be highly specialized and technical.

Mix and Match

To some extent, the different systems share a common Brahmanist point of view on how the world works and what life is all about. Broadly, each system has its own separate area of interest and doesn't interfere too much with the other schools. But points of contention and conflict among the orthodox schools continue to crop up.

A legendary account of a debate between leaders of two of the orthodox schools, Vedanta and Mimamsa, gives some flavor of the philosophical rivalry of the time. Mandana Mishra, of the Mimamsa school, challenged Shankara of the Vedanta school to a debate. He appointed his wife, who was secretly none other than Sarasvati, the Goddess of Learning, as judge. Yet Shankara won the debate, whereupon Sarasvati challenged him to a second debate on the topic of sexuality. Now Shankara lived an ascetic, celibate lifestyle and had no experience in the matter, so he asked for some time to bone up on the topic, so to speak. He went off in search of experience and soon found the dead body of a rich king. Using his yogic powers, he entered the body, brought it back to life, and returned to the palace as the king himself. In this way, he gained complete access to the king's harem, where he stayed for many days, learning all he could about sex. At last, he let the king die once more (so to speak) and returned to Sarasvati for their debate. Full of new-found knowledge and experience, Shankara triumphed, and Sarasvati's husband became his disciple.

In general, there are three main sources of disagreement within the orthodox schools:

- First, while all the orthodox systems recognize the authority of the Vedas, not all ascribe equal importance to them.
- Second, different schools look in different directions for enlightenment. Some say knowledge is best, others positive action, and others devotion to God.
- Finally, the question of whether God exists is answered in different ways by different schools. Though all have a strong metaphysical bent, not all see God as a key player in the reality business.

The differences and contradictions among the six orthodox Hindu darsanas—points of view—reflect the idea that each different system, while accepting the authority of the Vedas, takes its own perspective on reality. Contradictions do not necessarily disprove the validity of opposed ideas, but stem from the fact that all teachings are partial truths. Reality includes many levels, and no single point of view is capable of comprehending them all at once. What is most important is the usefulness of the teachings in helping people find their own way to enlightenment. Thus the different approaches of the different schools may be more or less useful to different people.

Six Pack

Here's an overview of the six orthodox Hindu schools:

- **Nyaya,** which focuses on logic and reasoning, was founded by Gautama, possibly around 150 B.C.E. Some scholars place him even earlier, around 400 B.C.E., and suggest his work may have influenced Aristotle. Gautama is nicknamed Aksapada, which means "foot-eyed." This name suggests logic was not always highly esteemed by all Indians, since it could be equated with staring at one's feet!
- **Vaisheshika** focuses on the nature of physical existence and is known for its theory of atomism. It was founded by a sage named Kanada, or "atom eater," possibly around 300 C.E. The name Vaisheshika stems from *vishesa,* the Sanskrit term for difference, referring to the difference of all atoms from one another.

Not in This Life

Don't assume that because Indian philosophy has made an impact on Western thinking that the reverse is also true. Nyaya and Vaisheshika, the Indian schools that most closely resemble mainstream Western philosophy in that they focus on logic and physical existence, are among the least influential in India's intellectual history.

- **Sankhya** talks about human nature and describes the means of attaining enlightenment. It also explains the world of appearances in terms of its theory of the evolution of existence and consciousness. It is said to have been founded by the legendary sage Kapila. The word Sankhya means "exact knowledge."
- **Yoga** is a school of philosophy as well as a set of techniques and practices observed within many different philosophies. The school was founded by Patanjali, perhaps around 300 B.C.E., although the practice of yoga is much older. The word yoga means "united" and refers to the unity of mind and body and to the unity of the individual consciousness with the absolute.
- **Mimamsa** means "reflection or profound thought" and is said to have been founded by the sage Jaimini, possibly around 300 C.E. It is chiefly concerned with explaining and organizing the Vedic teachings on ritual and sacrifice.
- **Vedanta** is concerned with the nature of Brahman and its relation to the world as described in the Vedas. It was supposedly founded by the sage Vyasa. The word vedanta means "end of the Vedas."

This chapter focuses on Nyaya, Vaisheshika, Vedanta, and Mimamsa. You can read about Yoga and Sankhya in the following chapter.

Lotus Lore

The basic teachings of the major philosophical systems in India were originally written down in short, terse statements called **sutras**. They are very brief observations offering little explanation or detail, so they are often hard to understand and require interpretation. As a result, the sutras have elicited a great deal of commentary that provides contradictory notions of what they mean. One reason the sutras are so brief and cryptic may be that they were intended, not as explanations of philosophical ideas, but only as notes or reminders of concepts that were meant to be communicated orally from teacher to student. Thus the sutras may not provide a complete picture of the early philosophical systems.

Testing, Testing

Nyaya is the philosophical school most closely concerned with logic and standards for testing the validity of knowledge. It emphasizes rational inquiry and argumentation in order to determine whether what we believe is, in fact, true, developing an elaborate system of concepts to carry out these activities. The concepts describe various ways of knowing and of testing knowledge—in general by weighing ideas against observed reality and logical inference.

Nyaya is often linked to the Vaisheshika school of Indian philosophy. In general, Nyaya and Vaisheshika agree in their basic principles but differ in their philosophical emphasis. Whereas Nyaya focuses on logic and reasoning, Vaisheshika describes physical and metaphysical reality. Each takes the other system more or less into account.

Whattaya Know?

According to Nyaya philosophy, correct knowledge eliminates confusion and ignorance, which are sources of suffering and unhappiness. Nyaya identifies four sources of potentially valid knowledge, namely perception, inference, comparison, and verbal testimony. Of these four, inference is especially important, since, by inferring things, we can greatly increase what we know from other sources. At the same time, inference often leads to mistaken ideas rather than valid knowledge.

Not in This Life

Expressing an idea in the form of a syllogism may make it seem more logical, but it doesn't make it true. For the conclusion of a syllogism to be true, the premises have to be true as well.

To fix this problem, Nyaya proposes a method known as syllogism to produce and test inferences. As you may know, if you are familiar with Western logic, syllogism was also taught by Aristotle as a way of generating valid inference. The classic Aristotelian syllogism has a major premise (to take the most famous example, "Socrates is a man"), a minor premise ("All men are mortal"), and a conclusion ("Therefore, Socrates is mortal"). The syllogism is constructed so that as long as the premises are true, the conclusion will be true as well. Thus syllogism helps us say what can be known based on whatever it is we know already.

Nyaya syllogism is strikingly similar to that of Aristotle, but instead of three parts (major premise, minor premise, and conclusion), it has five (proposition, reason, example, application, and conclusion). This difference is only in the way the syllogism is set up. It accomplishes essentially the same logical inference as Aristotle's. Here is a classic Nyaya syllogism:

Proposition: The hill is on fire.

Reason: It is smoking.

Example: Things like firewood smoke when they're on fire.

Application: The hill is smoking.

Conclusion: The hill is on fire.

Syllogism is just one of many Nyaya tools for framing and debating philosophical questions. Because Nyaya emphasized logic rather than metaphysics, it could be (and was) used by other philosophical systems without creating disagreement. Nyaya, in other words, is more important for its methods than for its conclusions. It was most closely associated with Vaisheshika philosophy.

Karma Dogma

Certainty is the elimination of doubt and the settling of a question by considering two opposing sides.

—Nyaya sutra

Up and Atom

Vaisheshika is notable for its theory of atomism, which may have developed from early Jaina ideas. According to Vaisheshika, all material things are made up of four kinds of atoms: earth, air, water, and fire. These were originally said to be eternal (and therefore not created by god), indestructible, and indivisible. In addition, different atoms have the attributes of smell, taste, touch, and shape. In a striking anticipation of scientific molecular theory, Vaisheshika says that atoms tend to combine into groups of two or three. A group made up of a cluster of three paired atoms is said to be the smallest that can be seen by the human eye.

Lotus Lore

Scholars have suggested that atomism in India spread to the Mediterranean where it was reformulated by the ancient Greek philosopher, Democritus, during the fifth century B.C.E. This view—that atomism originated in India—revises the idea that Democritus was the first to propose an atomic structure of the universe. According to Democritus's theory, free-falling atoms collided by accident, initiating the random movements that resulted in the formation of the universe. In contrast, the Vaisheshika school holds that atoms are not inert specks of matter but are capable of change and self-movement.

Important as they are, atoms are not all there is to reality according to the Vaisheshika system. The four kinds of atoms make up four of nine substances. The other five are ether, time, space, mind, and soul. Thus Vaisheshika is a dualist philosophy, recognizing material and immaterial substances. These substances are the causes of all things, including human life and knowledge.

As a result, despite the fact that Vaisheshika philosophy has developed a way of understanding reality in material terms, it doesn't overturn the traditional teachings. Vaisheshika follows Vedic philosophy in attributing observable events to the workings of karma. Karma, in Vaisheshika, is a substantial force that influences the nature of individual souls. Each soul becomes a unique individual as it becomes shaped, through karma, by its actions in life. Karma, in turn, is governed by a principle called *adrishta,* an unseen power that directs the course of existence. Some Vaisheshika philosophers associate adrishta with God.

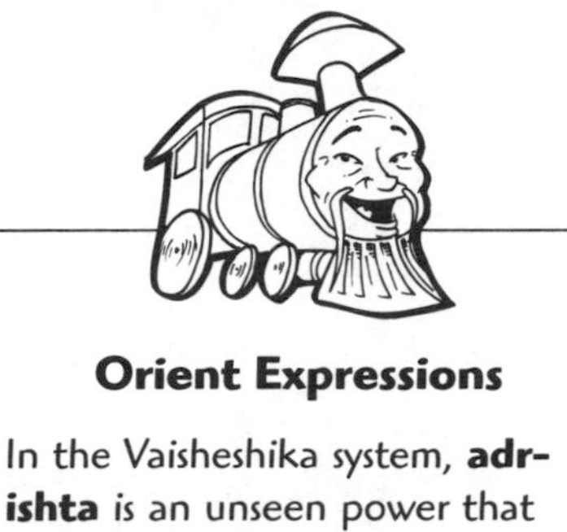

Orient Expressions

In the Vaisheshika system, **adrishta** is an unseen power that causes and directs the course of existence. It is closely related to the principle of karma and associated with God by some philosophers.

The Vaisheshika system suggests alternative explanations for existence as we know it—to an extent it was formed by self-moving atoms and to an extent it was caused by adrishta. The relation between these two explanations doesn't get fully explained. It may be that the early Vaisheshika philosophers were primarily interested in accounting for the observable, physical world, and that the metaphysical features of the system were added later. In any case, a more carefully integrated account of the relationship between material and spiritual reality is provided by another school, known as Sankhya, which is described in the following chapter.

Vedas Revisited

Two additional orthodox schools of Indian philosophy are the most orthodox of all in the sense that they are set up to defend and explicate the Vedas. These are Mimamsa, which means "reflection," or "inquiry," and Vedanta, which means "end of the Vedas." Mimamsa focuses on the actions and duties recommended by the Vedas. Vedanta deals with the nature of Brahman, the ultimate principle of being.

Best Behavior

Mimamsa explains those portions of the Vedas that apply to religious responsibilities, including sacrifice. The Vedas suggest that sacrifice is a way of influencing karma in positive ways. Sacrifice is even said to give human beings an advantage over the gods. Since the gods don't perform sacrifices, they can't improve their karma the way people can.

This traditional view has come under attack from several other philosophical systems since Vedic times. Buddhists and Jains, in particular, opposed Brahmanic sacrifice as irrelevant to enlightenment. Mimamsa defends the idea of sacrifice not primarily as a way of propitiating divine powers—in fact, the original Mimamsa sutras deny the existence of God. Instead, Mimamsa says the purpose of sacrifice is to purify the soul.

Lotus Lore

While much Indian philosophy deemphasizes the importance of worldly action, Mimamsa has been used to counteract this tendency. The Indian nationalist scholar and politician B. G. Tilak (1856–1920) drew on Mimamsa teachings in an attempt to inspire Indians to defend their rights against British colonialists. Tilak conveyed his ideas to a student of his named Mohandas Gandhi, who combined the call for action with a commitment to *ahimsa*—nonviolence. Gandhi, of course, went on to be a leader in the movement for Indian independence in the 1940s. Both Gandhi and Tilak drew much of their inspiration from the Bhagavad-Gita, one of the foundational writings behind Mimamsa philosophy, which teaches the value of worldly action.

This understanding of sacrifice helps bring it in line with the other aspects of personal discipline in Hindu philosophy, such as yoga. By explaining Vedic sacrifice in terms of personal purity, Mimamsa helps rationalize and organize the many Vedic ritual teachings which, in and of themselves, can seem like a lot of mumbo-jumbo. Thus Mimamsa, in effect, updates the Vedic rituals.

Sacred Sound

Since Mimamsa doesn't recognize God, it elevates the Vedas themselves to the highest metaphysical level. One traditional means of defending the divine status of the Vedas was to say they were created by the gods. But since Mimamsa says the gods don't exist, it came up with a different approach—that of saying that the Vedas were uncreated. They have always existed. The point is not exactly that the word imparted by the Vedas is God, but that the Vedas are an eternal expression of the cosmic absolute. Their meaning, contained in the sound of their words, has existed for all time.

The idea is that the Vedas are a manifestation, in sound, of absolute being. This absolute status of the Vedas accounts for their sacred power, which can be tapped by human beings when they chant Vedic passages in ritual or as mantras while meditating.

In keeping with its exaltation of the Vedas to such lofty heights, Mimamsa philosophy is especially concerned with verbal testimony as one of the pramanas, or means of reliable knowledge. Because Mimamsa focuses on the portions of the Vedas concerned with action, it sees action as the essence of all meaningful ideas. The significance of any piece of information lies in its relationship to some form of human action. This means that knowledge of the world is important insofar as it teaches people to behave. As the uncreated, eternal, and infallible guide for behavior, the Vedas are the most important source of knowledge.

Back to Brahman

Vedanta philosophy focuses on Brahman and the relation of Brahman to the world of things and individuals. In doing so, it continues and completes the project begun by Mimamsa philosophy of explaining and justifying the Vedas in philosophical terms. Within Vedanta, there are different ways of understanding Brahman. The most famous of these are known as nondualism, qualified nondualism, and dualism. Each of these terms refers to a different conception of Brahman, the self, and the world.

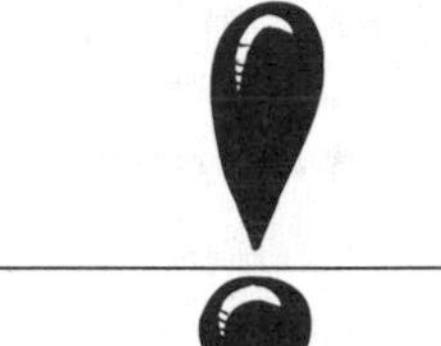

Not in This Life

Don't confuse dualism as applied to Indian philosophy with dualism in Western philosophy. Western dualism usually refers to the idea of a metaphysical distinction between matter and spirit. (Descartes was an influential dualist who said that the mind includes a spiritual aspect capable of rational thought.) Indian dualism, in contrast, refers to the idea of a distinction between Brahman and Atman, or Being and Consciousness.

Only One

Best-known among all Vedanta philosophers is Shankara, who commented on the Vedas during the eighth century C.E. He advanced the Vedanta philosophy of nondualism, which says that all distinctions are finally illusory. This means that everything that exists is a unity of Brahman and Atman. The world of things and people only appears to be different from absolute reality.

Actually, this last statement isn't quite as simple as it sounds, at least not the way Shankara means it. On the one hand, there is absolute existence, which the Vedas call Brahman. On the other hand, there's the world of physical things known in the Vedas as maya. What everyone back in the eighth century wanted to know was whether Brahman and maya are the same or different. If the appearance of difference is false, they must be the same. Right? And if the appearance is true, they must be different. Right?

Not exactly, according to Shankara. He explains the relationship between Brahman and maya by saying, in effect, that the idea of a relationship is an illusory idea, belonging to maya and the world of distinctions. Such distinctions don't exist in Brahman. They are themselves illusory. In Brahman, the very idea of a relationship is misleading. Thus the world of appearances neither is, nor is not, Brahman. It is an appearance of Brahman, depends on Brahman, and is conditioned by Brahman, yet Brahman is independent of it and is not conditioned in any way, but is eternal, unchanging, and self-sufficient. Brahman is all that truly exists. As a result of this oneness that characterizes Brahman, Shankara's philosophy is called nondualism.

Orient Expressions

Ishvara, which means "Lord," is used to refer to a concept that resembles the Judeo-Christian and Islamic idea of God—that is, an all-powerful being who cares about human beings in a more-or-less personal way. In India, those who believe in the supremacy of Brahma, Vishnu, or Shiva may address their particular god as Ishvara.

Of course, it's difficult to understand Brahman accurately, since most people rely on distinctions in their thinking. People tend to see Brahman as different from themselves and from their experience. According to Shankara, when Brahman is considered from this perspective—from the point of view of the world of distinctions—he appears as God, or *Ishvara*. Belief in God is not exactly wrong, but is something of a misconception, since it implies a distinction between God and humanity.

Brahman includes God, but includes humanity as well. For Shankara, bhakti, or devotion to God, is by no means a bad thing, but it is not the most direct path to enlightenment.

Enlightenment among all Vedanta philosophers is a matter of recognizing the unity of Brahman (absolute being) and Atman (absolute self), and recognizing at the same time the unity of the universal Atman with your own individual atman, or soul. In fact, Shankara makes the same nondistinction between your personal atman and the universal Atman that he makes between Brahman and maya. Both exist, but the universal Atman *really* exists. If you're like most people, you can say "I am," meaning you (or atman, your soul) exist. If you have attained enlightenment and recognize the unity of atman and Atman, you can say "I am," meaning that you exist as Atman, the absolute self.

Only One, Sort Of

A few centuries after Shankara, a Vedanta philosopher named Ramanuja came along and put a few wrinkles in Shankara's nondualism. The result is known as qualified nondualism. Whereas Shankara said that Brahman has no qualities, but simply exists, Ramanuja said that all physical appearances are qualities of Brahman. Brahman, in other words, is still a unity, but is qualified.

Unlike Shankara, Ramanuja explains the relationship between Brahman and maya in physical terms. He says that the physical world, along with the world of individual souls, is like the body of Brahman, and Brahman is like the soul of the world. Neither body nor soul can exist without the other. In fact, the souls of individuals have existed in later form from time immemorial as the body of Brahman.

This close relationship, and partial distinction, between Brahman and individual souls is significant for Ramanuja because, according to him, Brahman and Ishvara (God) are the same. Ishvara, in fact, is a personal God, and people can merge with him through devotion (bhakti). Devotion is thus more important for Ramanuja than for Shankara.

Two for One

Still another version of Vedanta—dualism—was put forward by the philosopher Madhva during the thirteenth century. Madhva's system is dualist because it regards Brahman and Atman as separate. Atman, moreover, is not unified, but divided into all the individual living creatures. According to Madhva, individuals can never fully merge with Brahman but can be released from bondage to the world through devotion and adoration of Brahman, understood as a personal God.

Although Madvha's philosophy is described as dualist, it actually recognizes five distinctions between kinds of things: Atman and Brahman are distinct; each individual Atman is also distinct from every other Atman; matter and Brahman are distinct; atmans are distinct from matter; different material beings are distinct from one another. Although these things are different, they are not all independent. Everything depends on Brahman, which controls the whole show.

The Least You Need to Know

- There are six orthodox schools of Indian philosophy—Nyaya, Vaisheshika, Sankhya, Yoga, Mimamsa, and Vedanta.
- Nyaya focuses on logic and reasoning.
- Vaisheshika is known for its theory of atomism.
- Mimamsa is chiefly concerned with action in connection with Vedic teachings.
- Vedanta is concerned with the nature of Brahman and its relation to the world.

Chapter 8

Yogi Bearings

In This Chapter

- The Sankhya and Yoga schools
- Emanation and evolution of reality
- Purusa, *prakriti*, and the gunas
- The eight limbs of classic yoga
- Kinds of yoga

Although many Westerners think of yoga as little more than a set of positions that contort the body into various pretzel shapes, yoga is of crucial importance to Hindu philosophy. Doing philosophy without yoga in India is a little like building a house without a foundation. It may stand on its own for a little while, but it won't last long, and you wouldn't want to live in it!

Yoga originated in the distant past, possibly before Indian philosophy really got started. Although it has roots and branches in many religious and philosophical traditions, it came to be recognized as its own philosophical school. And, about the same time, it was paired with another complementary school known as Sankhya. Together, the Sankhya and Yoga systems put a whole new spin on Vedic teachings.

While yoga does things with the body that you may not have thought possible, Sankhya performs amazing contortions on reality itself, turning it inside-out and backward in order to show how consciousness evolves from absolute being, into physical matter, and back into the absolute self. So in order to get the most out of yoga and sankhya, you need both a limber body and a limber mind!

Theory and Practice

Although the Sankhya and Yoga schools are recognized as two of the six orthodox branches of Hindu philosophy (the six that accept the authority of the Vedas), they did not have their origins in the Vedas, but emerged out of a parallel tradition. Actually, Yoga and Sankhya ideas are extremely old and were originally opposed to the Vedas. They were later incorporated into the Vedic tradition during the classical period of Indian philosophy following the advent of Buddhism and Jainism.

Yoga and Sankhya are often linked and said to be two aspects of the same path. Sankhya represents the theoretical side, as opposed to the practical applications of yoga. Many sources stress that both theory and practice are necessary for successfully freeing the consciousness from its limited, worldly perspective. Yet, as with most Hindu thought and practice, neither yoga nor Sankyha prescribes rigid rules; each person must work them out on an individual basis in his or her own way.

Sankhya provides an elaborate and sophisticated account of the human predicament in relation to the cosmos. It differs in its view of the cosmos from Vedanta philosophy in that it regards the natural world of appearances as real, though separate, from absolute being, and in that it says all atmans—individual souls—are finally distinct from one another. Thus, whereas Vedanta is usually nondualistic, seeing the cosmos as a grand unity, Sankhya is pluralistic, regarding the cosmos as made up of distinct entities. Despite their differences, Sankhya philosophy was accepted as an orthodox Vedic school around the fifteenth century.

Knowing the Difference

The word "Sankhya" means discrimination. The purpose of Sankhya philosophy is to discriminate between the two major principles of existence—matter or physical nature, called *prakriti,* and pure, absolute being called *purusa*. (The concept of purusa is basically similar to the Vedantic concept of Atman.) To confuse purusa and prakriti is not only a philosophical error, it is the cause of bondage of the spirit within the physical world. Telling them apart is thus the first step to realizing the truth and achieving spiritual liberation.

According to the Sankhya system, the physical universe originated as a cosmic intelligence, which reflects and responds to timeless, unchanging, absolute being. The cosmic intelligence/material world

Orient Expressions

Prakriti, according to Sankhya philosophy, is physical nature, including the world of things and the finite intelligence. **Purusa** is pure, absolute being. Prakriti is the constantly changing reflection of purusa.

is called prakriti. It is not absolute, and its existence and the changes it undergoes have no effect on the absolute ground of being, called purusa. Yet prakriti revolves around purusa, confusing itself with what it isn't and, ironically, seeking to realize itself in order to disappear! How prakriti and purusa were first formed is not known, but together they form the basis of existence.

Both principles are considered real, but are completely separate. Purusa—consciousness—is tranquil and inert, unchanging and eternal. It has no necessary relation to anything else that exists. It does not act and is fully sufficient unto itself. Prakriti is the reflection of purusa in finite, cosmic intellect. Out of this finite intellect, the world of nature evolved. Included in the world of nature are the physical bodies of human beings, together with their minds. Yet living creatures are more than merely minds and bodies constituted by prakriti. In addition, they are atmans—individual components of purusa, struggling to realize their true nature.

Lopsided Pair

Although the existence of prakriti depends completely on purusa, purusa did nothing to create prakriti or give it its shape. And although prakriti is real, it is constantly changing, and is thus unreliable. Yet human experience is bound up with prakriti. In fact, the human mind evolves out of prakriti as a further emanation of purusa. Beyond the mind, however, resides the individual atman of each person. The atman is not bound up with prakriti, but is a constituent—in an elaborated, evolved form of purusa.

Sankhya teaches that we should look beyond our personal affinities with prakriti and realize the timeless, unchanging nature of our true selves, or atmans, which reside beyond prakriti as aspects of purusa. This realization can be understood as the culmination of the process of evolution out of, and back into, purusa, much as a plant sprouts out of a seed before flowering and putting forth new seed.

Sankhya explains the human situation essentially by saying that human consciousness evolves out of purusa into and through the material world and then evolves back into purusa as an individual atman. The goal for each individual is to recognize him or herself as an eternal, unchanging atman instead of confusing the self with the material mind and body, which are bound up in prakriti.

Because purusa is perfect, unchanging, and complete unto itself, there is no reason for it to have taken an active role in the creation of prakriti. Thus the concept of purusa is entirely unlike the idea of God as a creator of the world, and, although some versions of Sankhya recognize the existence of God, most Sankhya is atheistic. Many Sankhya philosophers argue that a perfect, unchanging God could not have created the world, since, to do so, this God would have had to change. Prakriti, on the other hand, is merely a reflection or emanation of purusa; therefore, purusa remains unchanging and perfect. Sankhya philosophers further argue that since the world of prakriti is filled with evil, a benevolent God would not have created it.

Sankhya philosophy bears strong affinities with Gnosticism, a heretical Christian sect that regards the Christian God as an evil emanation from a perfectly good realm of existence. According to Gnosticism, God created the world in the vain attempt to compensate for his feelings of inadequacy. Individual human souls contain sparks that have become separated out from the good realm. Those who recognize their status as sparks of divine goodness may return to the good realm. Others remain stranded in the material world.

Lotus Lore

Sankhya and Gnostic traditions have similar myths telling of a king's son who grows up in ignorance of his true status before eventually learning of his birthright and attaining the kingdom. The Greek word *gnosis,* which means "wisdom," is etymologically related to *jnana,* the Sanskrit word for "wisdom." Both words are related to the English word *knowledge.* Many religious historians believe gnosticism was influenced by Indian philosophy, but just when or how the influence took place is not known.

Theory of Evolution

Although the human mind represents a separate stage of evolution from the rest of prakriti, it is made up of the same stuff. The close relationship between the inner world of thoughts and feelings and the outer world of things shows that they evolved from the same material. Yet it appears to most ordinary people that there is a profound difference between the inner and outer worlds: This appearance is illusory. The illusion, like the evolution of the world, results from the reflection of purusa in prakriti.

Loose Threads

All of prakriti, including the finite mind, is formed of three qualities, or characteristics, called *gunas*. The gunas are sometimes said to be woven together in all things like the strands of a rope. They define the things of the world, as well as individual personality. They constitute the variety in things in the world and in human nature by combining in different proportions. In fact, according to Sankhya philosophy, disproportion among the gunas is generated when purusa is reflected in prakriti. This reflection creates tension among the gunas. The bad thing about this is that all the evil things involved with material existence, such as pain and suffering, are formed. But this is how material reality gets its shape.

Originally, existence was not developed into a universe of separate forms. The three gunas were perfectly blended within it, so no differentiation had taken place. As the gunas combined in differing proportions, they gave rise to the world of differently formed things. It is tension between the three gunas that gives the changing world its shape and appearance. The gunas are *sattva,* or purity, *rajas,* or passion, and *tamas,* or inertia. Sattva is the guna of illumination, purity, and stability. This guna predominates in unselfish people and in the gods. Rajas is the guna of activity, energy, and passion. This guna predominates in those who lack self-control. Tamas is the guna of darkness and inertia. It predominates in sluggish people and in plants, animals, and nonliving things.

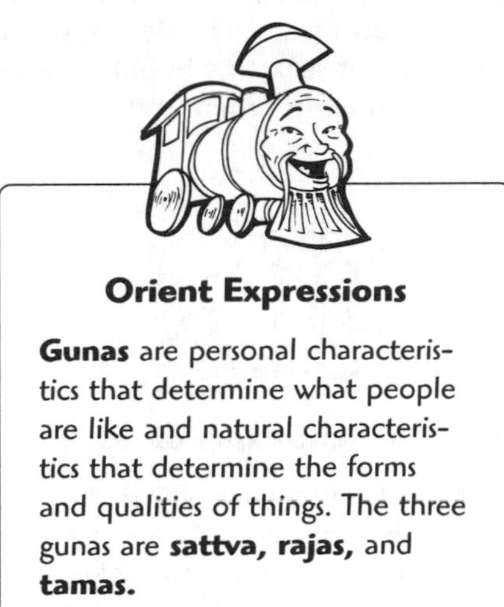

Orient Expressions

Gunas are personal characteristics that determine what people are like and natural characteristics that determine the forms and qualities of things. The three gunas are **sattva, rajas,** and **tamas.**

The gunas produce the impressions of pain and pleasure and allow us to feel and even think about the world of things. They are thus responsible for human psychology, with its passions, hopes, and fears. And they determine the inclinations and attitudes of individual people.

People who are predominantly characterized by sattva, for example, like mild and solid foods, which also consist mostly of sattva. The same people also engage in ritual and acts of charity in an unselfish spirit.

People who are predominately characterized by rajas like pungent, spicy food. They tend to be motivated by ambition in whatever they do. When they worship gods, they do so in the hope of gaining rewards or blessings or in order to display their piety to others or themselves.

Finally, people characterized by tamas like bland food, stale food, spoiled food, and leftovers. They are averse to action and involvement, not out of spiritual purity, but out of laziness.

Missing Links

Sankhya philosophy recognizes several separate stages in the evolution of consciousness. Out of the gunas evolves *mahat*—the great one, or mind—which is endowed with *buddhi*—intelligence. This gives rise to the five senses as well as the five elements of the physical world.

Next to evolve is *ahankara,* the ego. The ego and intelligence see purusa reflected in themselves and mistake themselves for purusa. The ego thinks it is eternal and immortal and cannot see how it is only a changing, impermanent cluster of desires and fears. The delusion is what keeps purusa bound to prakriti. Purusa, however, does not seek this bondage or do anything other than passively provoke tensions within prakriti where it is reflected.

Orient Expressions

Mahat, in Sankhya philosophy, is cosmic intellect, which is the first aspect of nature to evolve. **Buddhi** is this intelligence as it exists in individuals. **Ahankara** is consciousness of individuality, which evolves from buddhi and gives rise to the senses.

Notice that it is this very bondage of purusa to prakriti that causes prakriti to evolve. In this way, the illusion perpetuates itself. The world is real, but it exists as a result of the fact that eternal consciousness is mistakenly bound up with temporal, changing nature. Physical and psychological existence are real, but they exist as displays and projections of purusa before it has been accurately realized within the individual.

As pure consciousness realizes its true nature and separates itself from prakriti, the gunas regain their equilibrium and lapse into inactivity. The evolution of the world subsides. Sankhya philosophers compare the world of prakriti to a dancing girl who withdraws when people stop paying attention to her. When we look beyond the world, it will go away. This happens within individual souls as they separate themselves from hopes, fears, desires, and passions, renouncing the guna aspects of the intellect to realize their true nature as pure consciousness.

Pretzel Logic

Sankhya seeks metaphysical knowledge in the form of pure consciousness as a release from bondage. Such knowledge, however, is only one of many approaches recommended by Indian philosophy. A whole range of techniques for spiritual liberation are described by the Yoga school. Yoga, of course, is widely known in the West in the form of hatha-yoga, a set of positions and exercises that promote health and relaxation, increase flexibility, and stimulate energy and awareness. In India, Yoga is also a school of philosophy that draws on the theoretical underpinnings of the Sankhya school, adding techniques of physical and psychological discipline. The idea is to achieve physical and psychological mastery over the bonds connecting the atman, or soul, to the world and, thus, to attain freedom for the soul.

Into Position

The idea of yogic self-discipline in Indian philosophy goes way back, possibly predating the Vedas. As far as we know, yoga has always been an important aspect of Indian culture. Certainly it has profoundly shaped the character of Indian philosophy in general. Whatever its origins, it produced a rich and unique tradition of introspective discipline.

Lotus Lore

Archeological evidence suggests that yogic practices originated long before the Vedic period, perhaps as far back as 3000 B.C.E. The nature of its origins, however, remains speculative. It may have emerged out of shamanistic techniques in which adepts sought out-of-body experiences by entering a state of trance. Or ancient yogis may have sought spiritual benefits from the practice of devoting their inner consciousness to acts of ritual observance, even without the outward show of ritual. Since its beginnings, yoga has become not only a school of Indian philosophy, but a set of techniques practiced within Jaina, Buddhist, Sankhya, and Vedanta systems. Dozens of different kinds of yoga have evolved, all with overlapping techniques and aims.

Eventually, yoga came to be understood as a means of attaining spiritual liberation from the bonds of appearances. Thus yoga includes all the various techniques for attaining mastery over one's own psychic processes, including many disciplines concerned with quieting the mind, bringing the self into a state of equilibrium, and renouncing all desire for worldly things. These disciplines can include fasting, meditation, physical postures, and controlled breathing, as well as intellectual study, devotion to God, and forms of social involvement, such as selfless acts of charity.

Yoga is such an important concept in Hindu culture that almost any practice can be described as a kind of yoga. Thus the practice of being a guru can be described as guru-yoga, meditation is dhyana-yoga, chanting a mantra is mantra-yoga, and so forth. In fact, there's no reason why you couldn't practice taking-out-the-trash yoga and vegging-out-in-front-of-the-TV yoga, as long as you recognized that these are not traditional Hindu undertakings! Of course, these various yogas are practices, but do not constitute philosophical schools. Yet the basic idea behind them is philosophical: Work toward spiritual liberation. This is the main idea behind Hindu yoga, as well as Buddhist and Jaina yoga.

Orient Expressions

Siddhi are magical powers said to be acquired by yoga adepts who have achieved mastery over the powers of nature in the process of attaining mastery over their own psyches.

Siddhi Slickers

While yoga in general has the aim of achieving spiritual liberation, it has also been used as a magic art. Some yogis are said to be able to develop occult powers, known as *siddhi*. These include the ability to fly, the ability to enter in spirit into another's body, the ability to assume different physical shapes, and many other powers. The use of these powers, however, has nothing to do with achieving spiritual release. In fact, they represent another stage of temptation binding the individual to the world. Wise yogis are said to possess these powers but refrain from using them, since they have renounced the world.

The siddhi can be explained in terms of Sankhya philosophy, which understands reality as a manifestation of consciousness. Because prakriti, the natural world, takes shape according to the same principles that organize human consciousness, achieving mastery over one's own consciousness presupposes mastery over the natural world as well. So watch out for flying yogis!

A Classic Twist

Yoga was formulated as a philosophical school around 300 B.C.E., centuries after its earliest beginnings, by a sage named Patanjali. Patanjali succeeded in giving yoga a theoretical underpinning by linking it with Sankhya philosophy and by elaborating the steps to attaining spiritual release. While Patanjali provided yogic practice with a carefully worked-out philosophical rationale, he was not dogmatic about applying his ideas, but said that yoga could be effective in conjunction with a variety of philosophical and religious approaches.

Out on the Limbs

Patanjali describes eight steps (called eight limbs) of yoga that lead to realization of ultimate consciousness. Together, the eight limbs constitute an entire way of life. The first two of these steps involve following the proper way of life as preparation for the more specific yogic disciplines of the last five steps.

- **Restraint.** Abstinence from violence, falsehood, theft, sex, and accepting gifts.
- **Observance.** Commitment to purity, austerity, contentment, study, and devotion.
- **Good posture.** Balance, stability, and effortless relaxation.
- **Breath control.** Breathing slowly and rhythmically.

- **Withdrawal.** Of the mind from the senses and objects of sense.
- **Concentrating the mind.** Focusing on a single object, such as a word, sound, or visible thing.
- **Meditation.** This is not simply concentration as in the previous step, but attainment of a heightened state of consciousness.
- **Superconsciousness.** A state beyond the human condition attainable only by adepts in yoga.

Karma Dogma

To him who sees the difference between consciousness and pure existence comes mastery over all the states of being, as well as omniscience [total knowledge].

—The *Yoga Sutras* of Patanjali

Hold That Pose

Hindu tradition includes various yogic techniques for achieving the desired state of union with absolute consciousness. Specific postures and disciplines are intended to break down specific psychological and physical barriers. Different aspects of the psychological and physical world—the gunas, that is—stand in people's ways to different degrees depending on the individual. This means you need to find your own particular techniques that will best help you address your own problems.

Yoga techniques may focus on attaining oneness with God, freedom from delusion, transcendence of mind, or self-realization. Different approaches to yoga may also reflect differences in the philosophy behind them. For example, various ways of understanding the goal of enlightenment can result in different approaches to yoga.

Thus different kinds of yoga have proliferated. Hindu scriptures refer to many distinct varieties, the most important of which are raja-yoga, hatha-yoga, jnana-yoga, karma-yoga, and bhakti-yoga. All five of these approaches can be taken to represent an entire way of life in themselves or as a set of practices incorporated into one's life.

Yoga Party

Here's a brief sketch of each of the five major varieties of yoga:

- **Raja-yoga.** This means "kingly yoga" and refers to the classic approach developed by Patanjali. The term may allude to the idea that the yoga is intended to help the practitioner realize the unchanging, kingly state of the atman.
- **Hatha-yoga.** This means "forceful yoga" and is intended to strengthen the body. The idea behind hatha-yoga is that mind and body form a single system, so what is good for the body is also good for the mind. Hatha-yoga includes the

many challenging postures most often practiced in the West as relaxation and fitness exercises.

- **Jnana-yoga.** This means "knowledge yoga." It refers to the intellectual and theoretical aspects of the path to enlightenment. It includes study and introspection and enables the intellectual discernment of what is permanent and absolute from what is transient and delusory.
- **Karma-yoga.** This is "action yoga," the practice of improving one's karma through righteous behavior and a selfless attitude in one's actions. Good actions and refraining from bad actions are a time-honored approach to spiritual release.
- **Bhakti-yoga.** This is "devotion yoga," the practice of attaining release through the adoration of God. This approach is strongly emotional and religious. Some yogis regard submission to God or identification with God as a form of release in itself. For others, adoration of God is a bridge that leads to other paths that seek transcendence, even of God.

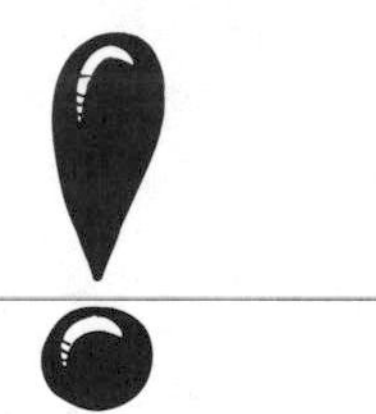

Not in This Life

Many books on yoga for Western readers imply that they contain all the reader needs to learn. This may be true only if you accept "yoga" to refer merely to a set of physical techniques and postures. Yogic adepts stress that in order to learn the spiritual aspects of yoga, one needs personal training and guidance, and for this, you need a guru.

Many other approaches to yoga have developed in response to changing ideas and new traditions. You can read about one of these, kundalini-yoga, in Chapter 13, "The Diamond Path." Kundalini is a tantric practice that has taken hold in Tibet as well as other parts of the world. Yoga has had a profound, influence in India and a wide, though less profound influence in other parts of the world. It has affected the development of meditation and martial arts in China and Japan. It has also become popular in the West, sometimes as a spiritual discipline, but more often as an approach to physical fitness.

In general, all the traditional yogic disciplines, including postures and meditation techniques, are designed to free the self from the effects of pain and pleasure by placing the mind beyond their influence. This process is understood as a mastering of desires, aversions, and inclinations. Through discipline and meditation, the yogi merges in spirit with the source of the problem, taking possession of it and overcoming it. In so doing, the yogi is said to acquire direct knowledge of reality. For example, yogis can gain complete awareness of the human condition—of human emotions and their causes. They can also gain recollection of previous lives.

The Least You Need to Know

- Sankhya and Yoga are often said to be complementary aspects of a single approach to enlightenment with Sankhya representing theory and yoga representing the practice.
- Sankhya originated as a separate tradition from Vedic philosophy but was incorporated into the Vedic tradition in the fifteenth century.
- Sankhya explains the world of appearances with its theory of evolution. It bears strong affinities with Christian Gnosticism.
- Yoga is a school of philosophy as well as a set of techniques and practices observed within many different philosophies.
- Some yogis, known as siddhis, are said to develop magical powers such as flight and invisibility together with spiritual mastery.

Chapter 9

Culture Clash

In This Chapter

- Muslim and Christian influence
- Sufism and Sikhism
- India's philosophical Renaissance
- Roy, Sarasvati, Ramakrishna, Vivekananda, Aurobindo
- Gandhi and Radhakrishnan

There has always been a certain amount of conflict and disagreement within the age-old traditions of Indian philosophy. Many philosophical differences reflect class disputes between members of the powerful upper castes and reformers seeking to make enlightenment available to everyone. This situation has continued down to the present time but has also changed in response to new cultural and political tensions caused by the invasion and subjugation of India by outsiders.

India was invaded and conquered by Muslims who established the Mogul Empire, which lasted from 1526 to 1707. As Hindu thought encountered Islam, new hybrids developed, drawing on aspects of both traditions. Despite the development of many shared ideas between Hindus and Muslims, conflict between the two groups has continued, resulting in the separation of Muslim Pakistan from India.

Big changes in Indian philosophy also resulted from the British conquest that followed the period of Muslim rule. British rule and the influx of Western ideas prompted a drastic reaction, reassessment, reform, and revival of traditional Indian thinking. Indian nationalists combined philosophy, religion, and politics to achieve Indian independence.

Islam in India

Islamic domination lasted for centuries, enabling the Muslim faith to get a firm foothold in India. In addition to those Muslims who came into India from Arabia, many Hindus converted. Meanwhile, Islam in India was influenced by Hinduism. In fact, many Mogul rulers and officials adapted to the caste system since it helped them wield power more easily. In general, the Islamic regime did little to disrupt the feudal system of government and economics already in place.

Sufi's Choice

But not all Muslims in India belonged to the ruling class. Some had more in common with those who followed India's reform religions, Buddhism and Jainism, in opposing caste distinctions and the ritualism practiced both by Hindu Brahmins and the Islamic priesthood. In fact, one of the Moslem sects that prospered in India under the Mogul empire was Sufism, which, like Jainism and Buddhism, opposed ritualism and the caste system and promoted asceticism and meditation.

Lotus Lore

Scholars are unsure as to where, precisely, Sufism originated. Some suggest that it was brought into the Arab world from gnostic hermits. In any case, it shares much in common with other forms of mysticism, including the bhakti-yoga tradition of India. Sufis practice chanting, meditation, and physical discipline that closely resembles yogic practice and, in fact, merged with yoga during the Islamic occupation of India. Through stilling the mind, emptying the heart, and controlling the breath, Sufis, like yogis, hoped to attain unity with God.

Sufism is a mystic sect that teaches unity with God through meditation and ecstatic experience. Sufi mysticism is modeled in part on the supernatural experiences of the prophet Muhammad, who is said to have been transported to heaven by angels. At the same time, many Sufis in India adopted many of the teachings of the Upanishads, combining them with the lessons of the Muslim Koran.

Sikh and Ye Shall Find

Another religious sect strongly influenced both by Hindu and Muslim thought, but belonging entirely to neither, is Sikhism. Sikhism was founded by a teacher and holy man known as Guru Nanak (1469–1533). Nanak was originally Hindu, but was influenced by Islam before developing his own beliefs. Guru Nanak emphasized devotion to God, but taught that God is unknowable. Yet God is immanent in all things—inside them and part of them. Creation is God's way of revealing himself. People can experience mystical union with God—in effect, becoming one with God—through inner devotion. In emphasizing devotion to God, Sikhism dovetailed with India's bhakti movement, serving the practical purpose of reducing the power and authority of the priesthood.

Sikhs oppose idolatry—idol worship—and the ritualism of Brahmins. They also oppose ascetics who renounce the world and beg for their food, believing it is better to work for a living. Sikhism in India proliferated and branched off into many sects, often coming into conflict with Mogul rule. As a result, Sikhs became increasingly militant in the later years of the Mogul empire.

Karma Dogma

Not all Moguls were intolerant of Sikhs and Hindus. A powerful sixteenth-century Mogul ruler, Akbar, abolished taxes imposed on Hindus on account of their religion and employed Sikh and Hindu officials. He even attempted to found a new religion drawing on Hinduism, Islam, and another faith popular at the time in the Middle East, Zoroastrianism.

Spiritual Rebirth

The Mogul empire was a part of the larger Islamic empire that extended into Europe, Africa, and Asia throughout the Middle Ages. The Islamic empire receded in the sixteenth and seventeenth centuries as the sea-faring nations of Europe—especially Spain, Portugal, France, England, and Holland—began competing aggressively for trade and colonies all over the world. India became increasingly important to British traders and the British economy in general and fell under British rule in the eighteenth century.

The British maintained power in India by controlling trade and industry. They also spread Western ideas by setting up schools and missions. British administrators, teachers, and missionaries tended to regard India as a "backward" country because it lacked Western technology and a highly organized system of government—and for racist reasons, too. They also tended to regard Hinduism in a negative light, failing to appreciate its philosophical principles and condemning many Hindu practices as superstitious and primitive.

British rule in India prompted various reactions from Indian thinkers. Many Indians became westernized, since, by adopting British ways, they stood to gain economic rewards. Others rejected foreign influence as evil. But whether they accepted British rule or not, most Indian thinkers came to reassess Indian philosophy in light of western values. The result was a period of intellectual activity that is often referred to as the Indian Renaissance, in which Indians sought out new significance for ancient ideas and found renewed national pride in philosophy and religion.

Seeing to Reason

One of the earliest movements within the Indian Renaissance was the *Brahmo Samaj,* or "Brahma Society," which was founded by the Indian nationalist Ram Mohun Roy (1772–1833). The society combined a religious, philosophical, and political outlook in promoting Indian independence and in justifying Hinduism in the face of criticism from outsiders, especially Christian missionaries. Yet Roy's ideas were strongly influenced by Islam and Christianity.

The Indian Renaissance involved, simultaneously, a revival and reformation of Indian thought. On the one hand, many Indians wanted to return to Indian ideas in reaction to westernization. On the other hand, many came to see certain traditional ideas and practices as wrong, outmoded, or at odds with the essence of Indian philosophy. These included the caste system, the worship of idols, and a gruesome custom known as *sati,* in which widows were burned alive on the funeral pyres of their dead husbands. Nationalist leader Ram Mohun Roy witnessed the burning of his sister-in-law in a sati ritual and came to condemn the practice. Roy was committed to monotheism (belief in a single God) and so rejected the polytheistic beliefs and practices of many Hindus. He regarded the worship of idols and avatars of the gods as a symptom of intellectual weakness, which he condemned in many fellow Hindus. Reason, according to Roy, indicates that there is only one supreme spirit who cannot be represented by words and images.

Roy's monotheism led him to reject not only Hindu polytheism, but Christianity as well, which teaches that God takes three forms—the Father, the Son, and the Holy Ghost. God does not become incarnated either as an avatar or as Christ. Roy felt that many religious beliefs stand in the way of universal cooperation and shared spirituality and wanted to espouse religious ideas that recognized a universal spirit. In doing so, he came into conflict with conservative thinkers among his own countrymen and among the British, yet he succeeded in attracting a large following as the Brahmo Samaj movement spread.

Lotus Lore

Ram Mohun Roy worked with the Indian civil service and traveled widely in the West, speaking fluent English. Wanting to persuade Westerners that Hindu monotheism is a rational religion, he wrote translations in English of Vedic and Upanishadic writings. In addition, he wrote commentaries on the teachings of Jesus in which he refuted the idea of the Christian Trinity. He was hailed as a fellow Unitarian by members of the Unitarian faith in America, but attacked by Christian missionaries in India. He defended his point of view by arguing that there is no real difference between the Christian Trinity and polytheism, and even succeeded in converting a missionary to his way of thinking!

Old-Time Answers

Another political, religious, and philosophical movement of the Indian Renaissance was the *Arya Samaj* (Society of Aryans), founded by Dayananada Sarasvati (1824–1883), a Brahmin who believed that the Vedas held the answer for India's problems. He wrote commentaries on the Vedas that attempted to show that many Hindu practices most criticized by Westerners were actually not condoned by the Vedas. These practices included child marriages and forbidding widows to remarry.

Through a careful amassing of scriptural evidence, Sarasvati tried to show that the Vedas opposed the marriage of girls who had not yet reached puberty and condoned second marriages for widows. He also used the Vedas to defend the idea that the caste system should be based on occupational distinctions rather than birth. Thus, in many ways, the Arya Samaj was a conservative voice of Indian nationalism.

Social Service

While Dayananda Sarasvati advocated purifying Hinduism through a return to the Vedas, others favored combining diverse philosophical and religious influences as a means of working for progress in India. Among these are Sri Ramakrishna (1836–1886), who is widely regarded as a Hindu saint, and his follower, Swami Vivekananda (1863–1902). Ramakrishna taught that all religions are acceptable paths to the truth. Vivekananda spread Ramakrishna's teachings in India and the West.

Karma Dogma

If one rightly follows spiritual discipline, one will see God directly. Discipline can be followed only by plunging in. What will you gain merely by reasoning about the words of scripture? What fools they are who reason themselves to death over information about the spiritual path. They never take the plunge!

—Words of Sri Ramakrishna recorded by a disciple

Vivekananda advocated social service as part of the religious life. Whereas the monks of many sects retreat from the world to lead a life of contemplation, Vivekananda argued that the holy life should involve practical work, especially for the benefit of the poor. He also said that religion should be consistent with rational principles. The best religious teachings are the most general and apply to everyone. They are not based on dogma, but on the idea of universal spirit.

In his view, it is wrong to take a dogmatic attitude toward religion. He says that all religions point in a universal direction and are therefore valid, whatever particular form they take. The right thing to do is look past the dogmatic pronouncements.

Vivekananda studied Christian and Muslim belief, as well as Hinduism, in developing his position, which he shared with Westerners as well as Hindus. In fact, he attended the World Parliament of Religions held at the World's Fair in Chicago in 1893 as a representative of the Hindu faith. His grasp of the similarities and differences between Christianity and Hinduism, as well as his passionate commitment to Indian religion, made him an especially popular speaker at the congress.

Super Yogi

Many interested in philosophy in India were increasingly interested in Western philosophy. Among these was Aurobindo Ghose (1892–1959), who drew on the ideas of Friedrich Nietzsche in explaining his own. Early in life, Aurobindo was a militant activist, fighting against British rule. He was arrested in 1908 in connection with a bombing and spent a year in prison before being acquitted. While in prison, he underwent a transformation and renounced his militant stance to devote himself to yoga and metaphysical philosophy.

Aurobindo developed the view that creation is circular. All things come into being by descending out of Brahman. This descent takes place in five steps he calls supermind, overmind, mind, life, and matter. The three lowest levels of reality—matter, life, and mind, can be investigated through the principles of Western science. The upper levels cannot; they can, however, be realized through yoga.

Yoga is important as a means of retracing the steps of descent back toward Brahman. It also enables the individual to become a "Superman"—a superior human being with a uniquely actualized life. Aurobindo's Superman has features in common with the

Superman as described by Friedrich Nietzsche. Both are above the common crowd of ordinary people and both are specially aware of the possibilities existence holds. But the two Supermen differ in important ways.

Nietzsche's Superman (or *Übermensche,* as he is known in German) sets himself above others by obeying his will rather than convention. In contrast, Aurobindo's Superman surrenders his ego. This, of course, is in keeping with the tendency in Indian philosophy to associate the ego with maya, or delusion.

Lotus Lore

Much Indian thinking has a great deal in common with Western existentialism. Both emphasize the importance of the individual as opposed to group process, saying that truth and reality need to be understood in individual terms. In other words, you have to experience reality for yourself; you can't simply have it explained to you. Both focus on "being" as primary and attempt to strip away false impressions that interfere with a heightened state of being or an "authentic" existence. A crucial difference between most versions of existentialism and the ideas in Indian philosophy that can be compared to them is that Indian philosophy often recommends renouncing the worldly self while existentialism tends to be self-affirming.

Gandhi but Not Forgotten

The best-known and most widely admired figure in the Indian nationalist movement is Mohandas Mahatma Gandhi (1869–1948), who galvanized his countrymen into nonviolent resistance of British rule, helping India achieve independence. Gandhi stands out as a committed leader and organizer who taught ordinary Indians to assert their rights against British authority. His activism, however, is based on the philosophical ideals he developed.

Getting Organized

Like many prominent figures in the Indian Renaissance, Gandhi was educated in England, so he understood Western ideals and biases. He received training as a lawyer, so he had an intimate knowledge of the practical and theoretical basis of English society. Though he came to admire many Western ideals, he could not ignore the discrimination and exploitation he saw practiced against Indians—often in violation of ideals Westerners claimed to hold.

Gandhi began his career as an activist in South Africa where he worked as a legal representative for a business firm. There were many Indians living in South Africa who were victims of discrimination—denied rights and opportunities available to white South Africans. So Gandhi organized the Indian South Africans and, in so doing, made a name for himself back home in India, where his work made an impression.

He returned to India in 1915 after nearly 20 years in South Africa and quickly emerged as a nationalist leader. He taught Indians to organize and to carry out demonstrations, boycotts, and tax protests. He promoted programs for adult education and village industry in order to improve economic conditions. Indians responded in great numbers to the economic and civil policies Gandhi suggested and, as a result, the resistance movement spread and drew international attention.

Orient Expressions

Satyagraha is the philosophy of adhering to the truth, advanced by Mahatma Gandhi. Truth-adherence underlies Gandhi's commitment to nonviolent resistance, as well as to his belief that all people contain aspects of divinity.

Nothing but the Truth

Underlying Gandhi's practical measures for improving conditions for Indians was his philosophy of *satyagraha,* which means "adhering to the truth." Gandhi's notion of truth lies behind what has become the most famous aspect of his thinking—the commitment to nonviolence (ahimsa) in his activism. In fact, Gandhi associated truth with moral action, the spiritual unity of people, and with God.

Gandhi believed that all people are capable of understanding and acting in accord with truth and that this is what we must do in order to improve the world. At the same time, he recognized that people make mistakes and suffer from delusions. To avoid delusions and the negative consequences that go along with them, Gandhi recommended two things. First, people should purify themselves spiritually in order to free themselves from evil motives. This will allow them to understand the truth more easily. Second, they should avoid doing harm to others.

Inevitably, people's convictions lead them into conflict with other people. Gandhi saw this as natural and right. But rather than say people should renounce their convictions, he said they should uphold them as much as possible—but draw the line at doing violence to others. Truth, for Gandhi, is not something that prompts people to do harm.

Like many other thinkers of the time, Gandhi set forth ideas that had broad applications. They could be adopted by people of different beliefs and backgrounds. In fact, Gandhi cautioned against looking for eternal truth in books, saying that these truths applied only to the time in which they were written. New times require us to identify new truths.

In keeping with his flexible conception of truth, Gandhi believed in peaceful relations among people of different religions. In particular, he favored unity between Muslims and Hindus, who were often bitterly opposed in India. His stance in regard to Islam made him unpopular with many Hindus, and he was finally assassinated by a fanatic Hindu nationalist.

Not in This Life

Don't assume that just because Gandhi recognized divine qualities in all people and faiths, he wanted to abolish social and ethnic distinctions. He is said to have discouraged Hindus from eating with other people, regarding eating as a private, bodily function, not an occasion for self-indulgence.

Philosopher for President

Gandhi represents grass-roots philosophizing in India. More academically oriented is the philosophy of Sarvepalli Radhakrishnan (1888–1975), a scholar who studied Eastern and Western philosophy. He taught philosophy at the University of Mysore, the University of Calcutta, and Oxford. This is not to say that Radhakrishnan avoided politics. In fact, he was President of India from 1962 to 1967. His philosophy, however, stands on its own as a system of thought, making him perhaps the most eminent philosophical thinker in twentieth-century India.

Brahman's Intuition

One important thrust of Radhakrishnan's philosophy is his emphasis on intuition. He says that intuition as a way of knowing is not opposed to reason, judgement, or other ways of knowing, but is the basis of all knowledge. Intuition, in other words, is a factor in all knowledge, including logical judgements. At the same time, intuition can go beyond reason to tell us things that we otherwise couldn't know. For example, Radhakrishnan's ideas about enlightenment, God, and metaphysics are intuited rather than simply reasoned.

Radhakrishnan recognizes degrees of spiritual existence, including individual atmans (souls), Ishvara (the personal God) and Brahman (the cosmic absolute). Over the course of time, individual atmans may merge with Ishvara. When that happens, Ishvara will merge with Brahman and the universe will attain perfection. Maya, the phenomenal world, will cease to exist.

We're All in This Together

Karma Dogma

To be saved is not to be moved from the world. Salvation is not escape from life .... If the saved individuals escape literally from the cosmic process, the world would be forever unredeemed.

—Sarvepalli Radhakrishnan

In keeping with Vedic teaching, Radhakrishnan says that individual atmans must first become enlightened before they can merge with Ishvara. But even on attaining enlightenment, they cannot experience unity with Ishvara until all other atmans become enlightened as well. Only then will all atmans merge with Ishvara together at the same time. Meanwhile, enlightened souls will not just sit there twiddling their thumbs. They have the job of helping other souls attain enlightenment. In fact, they want to do this job since the sooner everyone gets enlightened, the sooner they can experience unity with Ishvara and Brahman.

If you think about it, this is a good philosophy for a teacher and political leader to have. It offers a metaphysical basis for the project of helping others help themselves. In fact, Radhakrishnan is remembered in India as a great teacher and exemplary leader. Teacher's day is celebrated on his birthday.

The Least You Need to Know

- A blending of ideas took place amid ongoing conflicts throughout the period when India was ruled by Muslims.
- The Indian Renaissance was a revival and reformation of Indian religion and philosophy in reaction to British rule.
- Many philosophers of the Indian Renaissance emphasized the universal tendencies of religion and philosophy.
- Gandhi's philosophy of satyagraha provided a basis for nonviolent resistance by linking God to the idea of truth.
- Sarvepalli Radhakrishnan was India's leading philosopher in the wake of the Indian Renaissance and served as President of India.

Chapter 10

Go West, Young Brahmin

In This Chapter

- The influence of Indian philosophy in the West
- Indian philosophy and the ancient Greeks
- Indian philosophy and Western Romanticism
- Religious and philosophical movements: Theosophy, Hare Krishna, and TM

Since ancient times, Indian philosophy has exerted an ongoing influence outside India. The biggest influence has been on the Far East where Buddhism (the subject of the next section) has spread, settled in, and adapted to its new surroundings. But apart from Buddhism, Indian thinking has made a big impression on the West, providing a valuable supplement and alternative to Western ideas. Disillusionment with worn-out Western ways, the desire for something different, and the inherent appeal of Indian spirituality have enabled various forms of Indian thought to take hold in the West.

Some say that traces of Indian thought showed up millennia ago in the philosophy of the ancient Greeks. Since then, Indian thinking has influenced certain Middle Eastern religious sects. But it wasn't until the nineteenth century that Indian philosophy really dawned on Western consciousness. At this time, it was incorporated into the work of prominent Western thinkers, as well as adopted wholesale by Westerners looking for a new form of spirituality.

For many Westerners, Indian thought has become an aspect of spiritual and philosophical belief that includes and supplements Western ideas. For others, it has provided an alternative. Yet even in its most radical forms, Indian spirituality in the West has made its mark on popular consciousness.

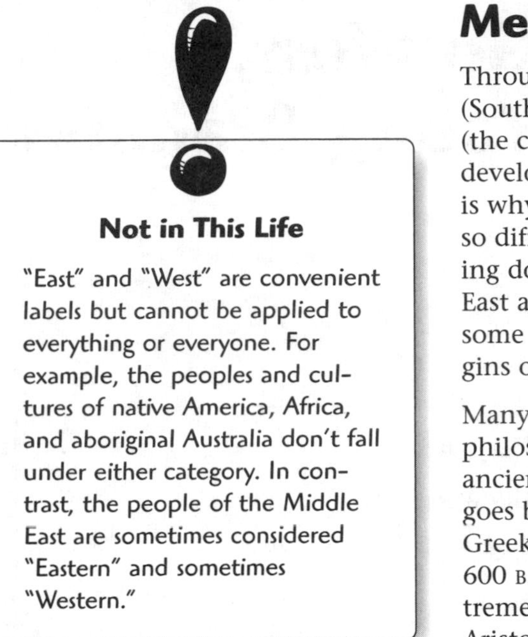

Not in This Life

"East" and "West" are convenient labels but cannot be applied to everything or everyone. For example, the peoples and cultures of native America, Africa, and aboriginal Australia don't fall under either category. In contrast, the people of the Middle East are sometimes considered "Eastern" and sometimes "Western."

Meeting of the Minds

Throughout most of human history, "the East" (Southeast and Far East Asia, that is) and "the West" (the countries of Europe and their colonies) have developed largely in isolation from one another. This is why Eastern and Western thought and culture are so different. This difference, however, has been breaking down gradually as contact and exchange between East and West has increased. It may be that at least some exchange of ideas has taken place since the origins of philosophy itself.

Many Indian philosophy buffs like to point out that philosophy in India is older than the philosophy of ancient Greece. They often say philosophy in India goes back as far as 1500 B.C.E.—or earlier—whereas Greek philosophy didn't get started until around 600 B.C.E. Ancient Greek philosophy, of course, enjoys tremendous prestige in the West, where Plato and Aristotle have always been venerated as the wisest of the wise. But, since the Greek philosophical tradition got started so many years after Indian philosophy, is it possible that the Greeks were merely imitating the Indian sages?

Some say yes—especially those who think the Western intellectual tradition has become carried away with its accomplishments. The idea that Western philosophy actually began in India rather than Greece puts things into a different perspective. It suggests the West doesn't have a monopoly on philosophy and even owes its very existence to the East. So far, there's little hard evidence that the ancient Greeks were influenced by Indian philosophy. There are, however, many intriguing similarities and parallels.

In fact, the traditional distinction between East and West is being eroded by many factors. It is based on cultural differences reflecting the geographical separation, throughout most of the world's history, of people from Southeast and Far Eastern Asia and people from Europe and European colonies. In recent times, though, many people from the East have moved to the West and vice versa. For another thing, the world includes millions of people who belong neither to the East nor to the West, including Africans, Native Americans, Aboriginal Australians, and Middle Easterners—who can be classified either way.

Gurus Go Greek

One of the earliest and most important of the ancient Greek philosophers was Pythagoras (famous for the mathematical theorem named after him). In addition to being a brilliant mathematician, Pythagoras was one of the first in the West to teach that human life is intimately connected to other kinds of life. He believed that living souls are reincarnated and may be reborn as animals or as humans. In connection with this belief, he taught that it is wrong to eat meat.

Pythagoras was known to have traveled widely and may have picked up his ideas about reincarnation and vegetarianism through contact with other travelers who brought these ideas from India. Some scholars have gone so far as to claim that Pythagorean philosophy is based on the Sankhya system of Indian thought.

Among the parallels that some claim to find between ancient Greek and Indian philosophy are portions of the writings of Plato, including the *Parmenides* and the *Phaedo*. The *Phaedo,* in fact, seems to be indebted to Pythagoras. This dialog talks about the relationship between the body and the soul, saying that the soul tends to be confused when it is imprisoned in the body. It is the job of the philosopher to see past this confusion.

Lotus Lore

Scholars have speculated that the ancient Greek school of philosophy known as Cynicism was transplanted to the Hellenistic world from India during the life of Alexander the Great, who conquered part of India. The Cynics condemned ease and luxury, together with virtually everything about civilized life, much as many Indian ascetics. The most famous cynic was Diogenes who is said to have lived in a tub and criticized nearly everything.

The idea of the soul being imprisoned and blinded by physical reality resembles the Vedic notion of maya, the principle of worldly delusion. More broadly, Plato's idealism—his belief that things of the mind have a higher reality than the world of appearances—has been said by some to hearken back to Indian thinking.

Orient Expressions

Manicheism is a Gnostic sect combining ideas taken from Christian, Zoroastrian, and Buddhist teachings. It spread throughout much of the East and West during the Roman Empire but has since disappeared.

Mixed Blessings

Although the influence of Indian thinking on ancient Western philosophy remains conjectural, there is direct evidence that Indian ideas influenced Western religion. In fact, there was quite a lot of blending of religious ideas in the centuries following the death of Christ. One religious mixture that drew on Indian ideas, Christianity, and the Persian (Iranian) religion Zoroastrianism, was founded by the Middle Eastern sage and visionary Mani, who lived during the third century. This religion is *Manicheism* and is sometimes described as a branch of the Christian sect known as Gnosticism.

Mani taught that all religions had an incomplete and fragmentary grasp of the truth but were corrupted by worldly considerations. He taught that the physical world is the creation of evil spirits, and that good human souls are trapped in this corrupt world and must free themselves by acquiring knowledge of their true, divine nature. This knowledge can be gained in part through ascetic discipline, much as the Hindu yogi attains knowledge of the Atman through meditation and fasting. A significant difference between Manicheism and Hindu thinking is that Mani believed that Jesus Christ paved the way to enlightenment through his wisdom and suffering! Manicheism continues as a religion in some parts of the world, despite continued persecution from more mainstream faiths. Mani was condemned as a heretic and died in prison.

Romantic Notions

Indian thought went largely disregarded by the West throughout the Middle Ages and the Renaissance, despite the growing importance to Europe of the spice trade with India. India was regarded as an exotic place full of wondrous things and strange ways, and, together with Arabia, provided the setting for popular tales by Western writers, but there wasn't much serious assessment of Indian ideas. This changed during what is known as Europe's Romantic period, which began late in the eighteenth century and continued well into the nineteenth. During this time, scholars, poets, and philosophers of Europe and America developed an appreciation for Eastern thought.

Lotus Lore

The intellectual interest in the East exhibited by Westerners during the seventeenth, eighteenth, and nineteenth centuries was due more to its exoticism than to any respect and appreciation for Eastern philosophy. In fact, according to a now famous study by cultural studies scholar Edward Said, the Western literary and artistic fascination with the East, which Said calls "Orientalism," served the purpose of rationalizing colonial enterprise. The idea is that, by portraying the East as an exotic "Other" in art and literature, Westerners could alternately justify and ignore the harm they were doing to non-Western people in the effort to colonize the East.

Where There's a Will, There's a Veda

One of the first philosophers of Europe to draw on Indian thinking was Germany's Arthur Schopenhauer (1788–1860). Schopenhauer was interested in will as a driving force behind human action and recognized that the will and the desires that are bound up with will can lead to conflict and suffering. He believed that desires can be transcended through contemplation.

Even so, he had a rather pessimistic view of life. He was drawn toward the Vedas and the Upanishads because of their recognition of the suffering that pervades existence. He entertained but rejected the idea that the Atman is finally one with absolute being. Instead, he claimed that will alone has absolute existence.

Karma Dogma

In *The World as Will and Representation,* Schopenhauer said, "In India our religions will never take root; the ancient wisdom of the human race will not be supplanted by the events in Galilee. On the contrary, Indian wisdom flows back to Europe and will produce a basic change in our knowledge and thought."

Yankee Sages

Appreciation for Eastern thinking grew especially strong in America during the second half of the nineteenth century, thanks in part to an intellectual movement based in New England known as Transcendentalism. This movement was spearheaded by

Ralph Waldo Emerson and Henry David Thoreau, two of America's most admired essayists. The Transcendentalists believed that reality itself is spiritual and that all human beings are united with nature in expressing this spirituality.

Emerson and Thoreau were both enthusiastic readers of Indian philosophy, especially the Bhagavad-Gita, which they often quoted and referred to in their essays. In addition to citations of Indian writings, they adapted many Indian concepts to their own ways of thinking.

Karma Dogma

Emerson, a noted Unitarian, once defined God in terms reminiscent of Brahmanism as "that Unity, that Over-Soul, within which every man's particular being is contained and made one with all other."

American Know-How

Many terms pop up in Emerson's writings that correspond closely to important concepts found in Indian philosophy. Here's a list:

- **Over-Soul.** Universal consciousness corresponding to the Hindu concept of Brahman.
- **Higher Self.** Ideal selfhood corresponding to Atman.
- **Illusion.** Mistaken notions about reality corresponding to maya.
- **Fate.** Emerson sometimes used this term the way it is usually used in the West, but also used it in a way that corresponds to the Hindu notion of karma.

Living Like a Yogi

Henry David Thoreau's best-known work is *Walden; or Life in the Woods*, which tells of his thoughts and experiences while living by himself in a one-room shack on Walden Pond from 1845 to 1847. In this work, he occasionally compares his simple, secluded lifestyle to that of an Indian yogi.

Thoreau was not trying to replicate a yogi's existence exactly, but to adapt aspects of Indian life and thought to his own life and world. He was deeply inspired by the Bhagavad-Gita and its philosophy of detachment. Interestingly, Thoreau's writings on civil disobedience later supplied a source of inspiration in turn for Mahatma Gandhi in the struggle for Indian independence.

Dark Secrets

Of the many forms Eastern thought has taken in the West, one of the most remarkable is Theosophy. Theosophy played a role in the Indian Renaissance—the time when Indians were turning to philosophy as a way of asserting nationalist pride. The Theosophy movement supported Indian teachings as viable religious and philosophical alternatives to Western science and religion, leading many in the West to embrace them.

But although the Theosophy movement played an important role in helping to spread Indian philosophy, the motives, techniques, and conclusions of its practitioners have been looked at with suspicion by Easterners and Westerners alike.

Feeling the Spirit

Theosophy began in New York City in the late nineteenth century as a spiritualist society. Spiritualism was a popular pastime involving attempts to communicate with the dead through seances. Gradually, the interest in ghosts and seances expanded to include exotic beliefs of all kinds, including hypnotic techniques and ancient religions. Theosophy's unique blend of Eastern religion and occultism became popular with many Westerners, including such renowned figures as W. B. Yeats, Thomas Edison, and Abner Doubleday, reputed as the father of American baseball.

Theosophy was founded in 1875 by a Russian-American named Helena Blavatsky, who wrote volumes expounding Theosophical beliefs. The genius of Blavatsky's writings lay in her ability to combine elements from a wide range of religious and philosophical sources into a single more-or-less coherent system. She claimed this system—Theosophy—was a "secret doctrine" that originated millennia ago in the East, predating all the world's major religious and philosophical ideas, which stem from—you guessed it—Theosophical teachings.

Thus Theosophy combines Indian thought with Christianity and Judaism, occultism, Kabbalah, and Gnosticism, claiming to be a universal religion based on the most ancient wisdom. Blavatsky and other early Theosophists traveled to India where they adjusted their doctrine to suit the circumstances. Sometimes, for example, they would emphasize the Hindu component of Theosophy in order to appeal to Indian nationalists; at other times they would emphasize the occult aspects to appeal to Westerners in search of exotic beliefs!

Which Way Is Up?

Blavatsky claimed to be in touch with mystic sages called *Mahatmas* who had attained enlightenment and possessed super-human powers. These powers, including telepathic communication, were put on display in front of admiring observers until it was discovered that Blavatsky's rooms were rigged to enable her to pass concealed letters to the Mahatmas! Despite continued accusations of fraud, the movement retained a dedicated following for many years.

Orient Expressions

Mahatma is a term of honor and respect accorded a great person in India, most notably Mahatma Gandhi. It is also a title given by Theosophists to spiritual adepts who are supposed to have enlightenment and superhuman powers.

More harmful to Theosophy than its stigma of chicanery were the internal quarrels that divided its leadership. Ironically, these quarrels stemmed from the teachings of the movement. According to Theosophical teachings, all conscious beings are in the process of evolving to a higher level of being. In fact, there are supposedly many beings—known as ascended masters—who have outgrown the need of a physical body. These superhuman beings remain on Earth in physical form in order to help others make their spiritual journey more easily.

In time, those who took over the reins of the Theosophy movement claimed to be ascended masters. The problem was that there were too many of them. They quarreled among themselves and refused to recognize one another's "ascended" status! As a result, Theosophy is no longer a single organized group but has given rise to many small, splinter organizations.

World Spirit

Theosophy was the first, but by no means the only, organization for bringing Indian thought and spirituality to the West. In fact, not long after the Theosophy movement got under way, the Vedanta Society opened up centers in the United States in order to spread Hinduism in this country. The Vedanta Society grew out of the work of Swami Vivekananda, who you may remember from the previous chapter. Vivekanada was a follower of Sri Ramakrishna, and the Vedanta Society was the main exponent of the Ramakrishna movement in the United States.

The first Vedanta Centers in the U.S. opened in New York and San Francisco around the turn of the century in the wake of Swami Vivekananda's appearance at the World Parliament of Religions in Chicago in 1893. The American Vedanta Society began as a Western extension of the teachings of Sri Ramakrishna in India, emphasizing Ramakrishna's view that all religions are valid approaches to spiritual truth. This broad view caught on with many Americans, especially since the Indian leaders of the American movement were willing to adjust to American ways and tastes, tolerating, for example, eating meat and wearing Western-style clothes.

Vedanta Society activities included spiritual ceremonies, philosophical lectures, and training in meditation and deep breathing. Adherents of the movement stressed its spiritual as well as psychological value, claiming that Vedanta philosophy and practice was more spiritually beneficial and more in tune with science and reason than traditional Christianity. In particular, Vedanta Society adherents criticized the Christian reliance on blind faith and the Christian concepts of sin and damnation.

Currently there are 12 or so Vedanta Society groups active in the U.S. The movement has influenced a number of prominent Western writers, including Aldous Huxley, Joseph Campbell, J.D. Salinger, and Christopher Isherwood. In addition, many Indian-American immigrants make up Vedanta Society membership.

Not in This Life

The Ramakrishna movement has been active in social services in India and other parts of the world, working to support hospitals, orphanages, and charitable organizations. Social service is not an important thrust of the Vedanta Society in America, however. Here members focus more on personal spiritual enlightenment.

Merry Krishnas

Another well-known—and controversial—group is ISKCON, the International Society for Krishna Consciousness, better known as Hare Krishna, which began in New York City in the mid-1960s. Hare Krishna is a separatist cult based on devotion to Krishna. (Whereas many Hindus recognize Krishna as an avatar of the god Vishnu, Hare Krishnas, as well as the followers of the Krishna-bhakti movement in India, accept Krishna as God.) Hare Krishna members live a monastic existence, eating a strictly vegetarian diet and chanting the famous Hare Krishna mantra. Male initiates have their heads shaved.

Chants Meetings

Hare Krishna was founded by an Indian devotee of Krishna named A.C. Bhaktivedanta Swami Prabhupada. While in India during the 1930s, Bhaktivedanta studied Krishna consciousness with a guru who, in turn, studied with a guru before him. The line of Krishna consciousness gurus evidently stems back to Caitanya (sixteenth century), a bhakti revivalist leader who spread Krishna worship throughout Eastern India. Caitanya taught that Krishna is both transcendent and personal—a timeless, absolute being that still has personal qualities and characteristics. Thus Krishna can—and should be—loved in a direct, personal way. Caitanya also taught that the best way to worship Krishna is by chanting, a practice revived by Hare Krishnas in America.

Karma Dogma

Hare Krishna Hare Krishna
Krishna Krishna Hare Hare
Hare Rama Hare Rama
Rama Rama Hare Hare

This is the Mahamantra ("great mantra") of Hare Krishna. "Hare" is the supreme power of God to experience pleasure. "Krishna" is God in his adored, beloved aspect. "Rama" is God in the aspect of enjoyer of existence. Existence is thought to give God pleasure. Human beings can experience pleasure only through the pleasure of God.

Caitanya himself was actually worshiped as an avatar of Krishna. He is also one of many gurus in a long line that includes both legendary and historical figures, originating with the god Krishna and culminating, according to Hare Krishnas, with A.C. Bhaktivedanta Swami, who brought the message of Krishna worship to America. The Hare Krishnas venerated Bhaktivedanta not exactly as an incarnation of Krishna, but as the most pure living devotee of Krishna consciousness. Because Bhaktivedanta learned from a spiritual master of Krishna consciousness, he became a spiritual master himself. Bhaktivedanta is also a Vedic scholar who has translated many Hindu scriptures into English, including one of the most widely read English translations of the Bhagavad-Gita, a central text of the Hare Krishna movement.

Lotus Lore

In many branches of Indian philosophy and religion, the relationship between a guru and his disciple has special importance—so much so, that without it, true learning is considered impossible. A guru is often considered the spiritual parent of his disciples and may preside over a spiritual rebirth at an initiation ritual of some kind. This helps explain why so much Indian philosophy was not written down until many years after being passed along by word of mouth from guru to disciple. Swami Bhativedanta traces his gurus back in an unbroken line to Krishna himself.

Cult Following

Bhaktivedanta came to America in the 1960s to spread Krishna consciousness at the age of 70, bringing with him only seven dollars in cash and some books of Vedic scripture. He supported himself by begging on the street while acquiring followers by speaking and chanting. Before long, he attracted many devotees in New York and San Francisco, and ISKCON was officially incorporated in 1966.

Despite its message of Krishna's love, which resonated well with the counterculture movement of the sixties, Hare Krishna has been harshly condemned by conservative and mainstream America for a variety of reasons. One is the fear that ISKCON brainwashes its converts into accepting an austere and regimented lifestyle of seclusion from society. In fact, Hare Krishnas largely cut themselves off from the outside in order to practice their devotions more fully. Members are discouraged from communicating with family and friends outside the group. Meanwhile, they are taught a world-renouncing philosophy that requires them to live a frugal lifestyle of total submission. In other words, it takes some serious sacrifices to become a Hare Krishna. And, of course, the spiritual rewards members stand to gain are intangible.

Another aspect of the Hare Krishna movement that rubs many Westerners the wrong way is the practice of begging. Many Hare Krishnas support themselves and the movement by asking for donations in public places, including parks and airports. Hare Krishna solicitors have been known to resort to deception in order to raise money. For example, rather than say the money goes to the Hare Krishnas, they may suggest the money is intended for some other cause. An especially outrageous example of this sort of deception occurred when Hare Krishna members dressed up in Santa Claus outfits during Christmas time like the Salvation Army! But begging is not the only means of support for the Hare Krishna movement. ISKCON runs many vegetarian restaurants and also markets Spiritual Sky incense.

Sitting and Thinking

Because the Hare Krishna movement rejects the values and structure of mainstream Western society, it has been targeted as the embodiment of everything that can go wrong with cult movements. Another prominent movement with roots in India is Transcendental Meditation, founded by Maharishi Mahesh Yogi. Unlike Bhaktivedanta, Maharishi has worked hard to tailor his message to Westerners in hopes of appealing to mainstream society.

Maharishi began his career as a spiritual teacher when he joined a monastery in Badarinath, India to study under a famous holy man named Guru Dev. From Guru Dev, Maharishi learned a technique of meditation he believed could expand the "cosmic consciousness" of the entire world. So, beginning in the mid-1950s, he traveled around the globe teaching people to meditate and to teach his method of meditation to others.

Change My World

The TM (Transcendental Meditation) movement grew slowly, but got a big lift in 1967 when The Beatles became involved. George Harrison had been studying the sitar with the famous Indian musician Ravi Shankar and learned about TM from Shankar. Soon afterward, the whole rock group went off on retreat to India with TM's founder. Thanks to The Beatles, the movement gained international exposure in the media and became popular with young people in Europe and America, especially on college campuses.

Lotus Lore

The Beatles song "Across the Universe" was inspired in part by Maharishi and TM. The refrain of the song is "Jai Guru Dev," which means "Thank you Guru Dev." (Guru Dev was Maharishi's spiritual teacher.) George Harrison, who introduced The Beatles to TM, later became interested in Hare Krishna and wrote "My Sweet Lord," which has as its refrain the Mahamantra of Hare Krishna. Other celebrities besides The Beatles to become involved with TM include Mia Farrow, Joe Namath, and Efrem Zimbalist Jr.

Although TM is based on spiritual and religious ideas from India, its proponents tend to talk about its value in practical and scientific, rather than religious, terms. Advocates of the movement have made lofty claims about the physiological benefits of meditation. They say it can increase intelligence by helping draw on untapped creative resources in their brains. This can make them more productive at work, more successful in school, and healthier both physically and emotionally. In addition, meditators become free from stress and, in general, happier than they would be otherwise.

And TM advocates say the benefits of TM go beyond the individual level. As more and more people around the world come to practice TM, people will find better solutions to our most serious social, economic, and environmental problems, including war, drugs, crime, poverty, and pollution. In fact, in 1978, Maharishi sent a team of more than 100 TM instructors to five of the world's biggest trouble spots of the time: Zimbabwe, Central America, Thailand, Lebanon, and Iran. The idea was to rebuild the spiritual fabric of these war-torn regions from the ground up. This was the most ambitious feature of TM's World Plan, established in 1972, for bringing meditation to the world.

Meditate on This

TM's opponents have attempted to debunk the movement both on scientific and religious grounds. Some have seen TM as a religious cult disguised as a practical meditation technique. They point to the spiritual underpinnings of the movement evident in Maharishi's writings and to a ceremony for initiating new meditators in which the line of gurus stretching back through Maharishi and Guru Dev is honored and in which Hindu gods are briefly invoked.

During much of the 1970s, TM instruction was subsidized in many areas with public funds. Public officials took its social claims seriously, hoping that TM could reduce crime and drug addiction, so they were willing to help fund TM centers with tax money. In 1978, however, subsidies for TM were attacked in a New Jersey court on the grounds that TM was a religious practice. The court upheld the view that TM is essentially religious, thus making public funding a violation of the Constitutional separation of Church and State.

When others argued that TM's health benefits were exaggerated, TM encouraged studies conducted by scientists that showed that it could be beneficial in reducing stress. Subsequent studies have shown that such beneficial results are not unique to TM but can be obtained through other kinds of relaxation exercises. In addition, it seems that studies showing the benefits of TM were based on specially selected samples of meditators. The percentage of those who benefit from TM, in other words, is not as high as some of the early studies indicated.

Finally, the broader, social benefits of TM have failed to materialize. Of course, this could be because its popularity peaked and faded before it attracted enough followers to make a noticeable difference. Even so, it's been estimated that over a million people have taken the basic course required for learning TM. Of these, many thousands have continued to meditate regularly.

The Least You Need to Know

- Some scholars have speculated that ancient Greek philosophy was influenced by Indian thought, which predates it.
- Famous Western thinkers who have drawn on Indian philosophy in their writings include Arthur Schopenhauer and Ralph Waldo Emerson.
- The Theosophy movement was embraced by Indian nationalists as well as many Westerners, but came under suspicion of fraud.
- Ramakrishna Vedanta Centers in the U.S. emphasize the spiritual validity of all religious beliefs.
- The Hare Krishna movement traces its line of spiritual teachers all the way back to Krishna.
- Transcendental Meditation emphasizes the practical emotional and physiological benefits derived from meditating.

Part 3

Shake Your Buddha

Buddha, "the Awakened One," is the honorary title of a man who lived long ago in India and changed the world simply by sitting and meditating. He understood how deeply the human condition is characterized by suffering and came to see a way out—a way beyond the ego and its desires and fears. This turned out to be just what much of the world had been looking for.

The Buddha's teachings have spread practically all over and, in the process, have influenced peoples' lives as philosophy, as religion, and as the basis of social and political organizations. As it spread, Buddhism has been absorbed into many different cultures, and aspects of these cultures have been absorbed into Buddhism. From the austere, unembellished Buddhism practiced in Sri Lanka to the highly symbolic tantric Buddhism of Tibet to the unpredictable, intuitive Zen Buddhism of China and Japan (to name just a few), the ancient teachings have been taken up in a variety of fascinating ways.

Chapter 11

News from Nirvana

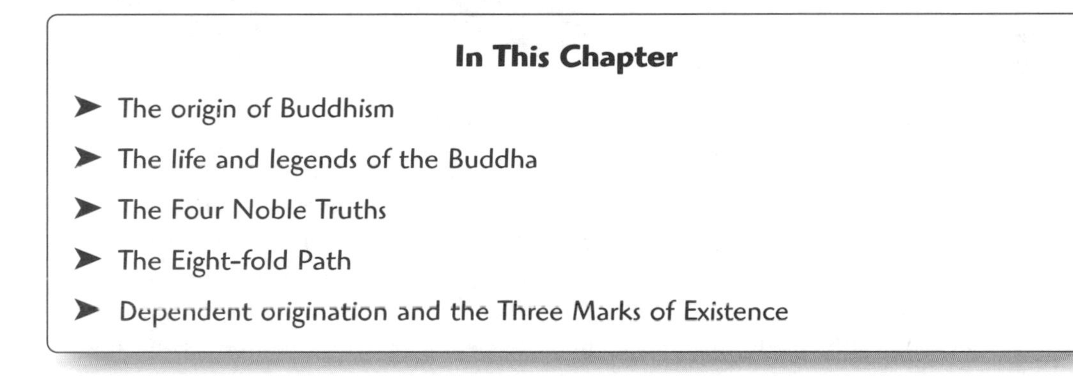

In This Chapter

- The origin of Buddhism
- The life and legends of the Buddha
- The Four Noble Truths
- The Eight-fold Path
- Dependent origination and the Three Marks of Existence

Buddhism began in India as one of many religious philosophies during a period in which many new ways of thinking were being developed—the sixth century B.C.E. Like numerous other philosophies of India, Buddhism advanced ideas about the nature of reality, the problem of impermanence, and the way to attain enlightenment. Unlike the many other philosophies of India, Buddhism spread all over the world, changing and developing in the process and emerging as one of the most influential religious philosophies on the planet.

Many factors help explain the phenomenal success of Buddhism. When it first emerged, it supplied a timely alternative to the ways of life practiced in India. While abandoning the harsh asceticism that characterized other Indian sects, it has remained deeply moral, pointing out a "Middle Way" between the acceptance and rejection of life and worldly things. It was soon embraced by a powerful emperor named Asoka, who sent Buddhist missionaries throughout India and into other parts of the world.

Adding to the appeal of Buddhism is its flexible attitude toward questions of dogma, belief, and practice. This attitude has helped it catch on in many countries, where it has assimilated with local ways of thinking and behaving. Buddhism has become one of the most widespread religious philosophies in the world, and it all began with the experience and teachings of a man named Siddhartha Gotama.

The Birth of a Legend

Buddha is both a historical and a legendary figure. In fact, there are a number of legendary Buddhas, some of whom even predate the historical founder of Buddhism. But it is this historical founder, Siddhartha Gotama, who is usually meant by "the Buddha," which means "the enlightened one." He is often called Sakyamuni, "the sage of the Sakyas," after the clan of rulers into which he was born.

Lotus Lore

Buddhist legend tells that, when she conceived the future Buddha, Siddhartha's mother, Queen Maya, dreamed that a beautiful white elephant descended into her womb. During her pregnancy, she was so deeply content that she inspired everyone who came in contact with her. King Suddhodana, her husband, gave up worrying about the problems of government and devoted himself to spiritual practices. Years later, King Suddhodana beheld Siddhartha meditating under a tree. He meditated all day, yet the shadow of the tree did not move from the spot. By this, the king realized his son was special. Yet, not wanting the child to leave home, he sheltered him within the palace, apart from the outside world, surrounded by luxuries and pleasures.

From Prince to Pauper

Siddhartha was born a prince whose father provided everything he desired. Yet he was not satisfied with the worldly delights he enjoyed as a prince and occasionally took secret trips outside the palace with his chariot driver, Chandaka, to see what was going on in the world. During these trips, he witnessed the famous Four Signs that spurred him to renounce his life as a prince and seek enlightenment.

On the first trip, he encountered a very old man, alone and so weak with age he could hardly move. Chandaka told him that everyone who outlives youth must suffer old age. On another trip, he encountered a man afflicted with disease, sick and in pain. Chandaka told Siddhartha that all people are subject to sickness. On a third trip, he saw a dead man being carried away to be buried. Chandaka told him that death overtakes all living things. The young Siddhartha was upset by the suffering he had witnessed outside the palace. No one could give him a satisfactory explanation of what should be done about it.

Siddhartha set forth on another trip, and this time, he came upon a wandering ascetic who, despite his difficult existence, radiated peace and serenity. He appeared to be detached from the problems and suffering of life. The encounter gave Siddhartha hope that there was a solution to the seemingly inescapable suffering of life, and he became determined to go out and seek it for himself. So he renounced his kingdom, his luxuries, his beautiful wife and child, and shaved his head and took up an alms bowl to go out into the world as a traveling ascetic.

Though it may seem odd that Siddhartha Gotama would choose to forsake his comfortable existence to lead the life of a wandering ascetic, it was not unusual for wealthy men of his time to make this choice. What set him apart from other householders-turned-ascetics was his age. Siddhartha left home in his early 20s rather than later in life, as was more common.

Wake-Up Call

Siddhartha met with and learned from many great sages who were skilled in mental and physical discipline and asceticism. He learned to master his physical and emotional desires, subjecting himself to rigorous hardships and deprivations. He nearly starved himself to death, subsisting on as little as a grain of rice a day. He exposed his body to extremes of heat and cold. He also humiliated himself by lying down in burning grounds among the remains of the dead, where people came to ridicule and abuse him. All of these things were part of the path he had chosen as an ascetic.

He continued on in this way for a period of six years, during which time he had attracted five followers who joined him in his search for enlightenment. He spent his days meditating and keeping his mind, body, and emotions perfectly steady. Finally, he came to an important realization. Asceticism was not the answer.

Physical self-denial, he concluded, does not necessarily lead to enlightenment. In fact, practices that harm the body can actually stand in the way of knowledge. Although the ascetics learned to master their desire for worldly things, they still suffered from a desire for heavenly experience, and this, too, led to suffering and disappointment.

So, to the surprise of his followers, he gave up his asceticism and accepted a bowl of food offered him by a young woman named Sujata. His followers became convinced that Siddhartha had abandoned himself to worldly pleasures, so they deserted him. Siddhartha, however, remained committed to his pursuit of enlightenment, believing that the answer lay neither in ascetic practices nor in luxurious living. Instead, there was a "Middle Way" that avoided the excesses both of the pursuit of pleasure and of renunciation.

Orient Expressions

Nirvana is the Buddhist state of enlightenment roughly equivalent to the Hindu concept of moksha. Whereas moksha means release, nirvana means extinguishing and refers to the extinguishing of desires and the ego.

Siddhartha continued meditating for another 49 days under the fig tree, or "boddhi" tree, where he sat. At that point, he found what he had been looking for. He experienced enlightenment, known to Buddhists as *nirvana*. This is a state of indescribable peace in which desires and the ego are extinguished.

Have Wisdom, Will Travel

Different Buddhist traditions have since provided different interpretations of the nature of Buddha's enlightenment. In general, Buddhists say that he attained a perfect understanding of all of his past lives, as well as of how all things come into being and disappear again. And he transcended desire and conquered ignorance.

Buddhists tend to agree on what this enlightenment was not. Many seekers before Siddhartha claimed to have had mystic experiences in which they became aware of the influence on their consciousness of a higher spiritual power, such as God. The Buddha's enlightenment was not like this. Instead, it resulted from his own efforts to attain an accurate, undeluded awareness of reality. He was certain he had found the answer and believed he could help others find the answer for themselves.

Lotus Lore

Buddhist legend says that, while Buddha was on the verge of experiencing nirvana, he was visited by Mara, the god of illusion, who tried to prevent Buddha from attaining enlightenment through threats and enticements. When these failed, Mara demanded to know what made him worthy to become enlightened. Buddha responded by referring to the countless deeds of goodness and compassion he had performed over the course of his previous lives. He called the Earth itself as witness to the truth of his statements. In reference to this legend, statues of the Buddha sometimes show him seated with one hand gesturing toward the Earth.

To spread his message, he traveled to a Deer Park in Benares, a place near the Ganges River known today as Varanasi. There he met with his five former disciples, who had previously abandoned him for renouncing his ascetic self-discipline. To them, he imparted the basic teachings of Buddhism, including the Four Noble Truths, the Eightfold Path, the Three Marks of Existence, the Four Laws of Dharma, and the principle of Interdependent Origination.

Deep Dukkha

The chief problem Buddhism sets about dealing with is suffering. Even as a boy leading a sheltered and pampered existence, Siddhartha observed that suffering was everywhere and was unavoidable. The existence of suffering is the first and most central of the Four Noble Truths, which make up the first teaching of Buddhism. The other three are the origin of suffering, the termination of suffering, and the path that leads to the termination of suffering.

The first Noble Truth is that suffering exists. The point here is not simply that there is such a thing as suffering, but that suffering comes with the territory of being a living human being. People often tend to think that suffering is an unusual state of affairs, caused by social factors, such as cruelty and oppression, or psychological factors, such as phobias, fixations, or compulsions. The Buddha taught that suffering was more basic than this. It has its roots in birth, sickness, old age, and death. Neither social nor psychological change can alleviate these problems. There will be suffering.

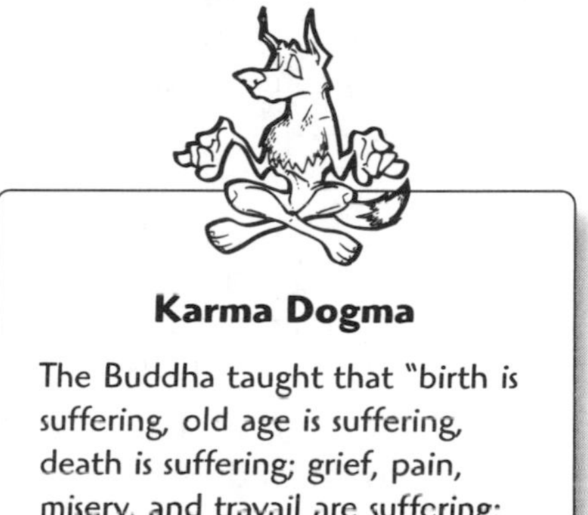

Karma Dogma

The Buddha taught that "birth is suffering, old age is suffering, death is suffering; grief, pain, misery, and travail are suffering; not getting what is desired is suffering and, in short, all things subject to the five senses are suffering."

There are additional causes of suffering: the presence of unpleasant things, separation from pleasant ones, and not getting what we want. Yet all these various kinds of suffering have a common origin. This is the Second Noble Truth. Suffering is caused by ignorance. Suffering amounts to a general failure to see reality for what it is. This ignorance leads people to react emotionally when things go wrong. Our emotional reactions, instead of alleviating our suffering, only dig us deeper into the problem, making us more heavily involved in suffering. This deeper involvement confuses us further, leading to still more suffering. Thus, suffering and ignorance form a kind of feedback loop, reinforcing one another.

The Buddha and his followers understood this vicious cycle of ignorance and suffering as being bound up with the traditional Indian ideas of karma and samsara—successive reincarnation into earthly existence. The cycle of suffering driven by ignorance includes the other causes of suffering, such as birth, old age, and death. These elements help make up what is known as the *Wheel of Becoming*.

Lotus Lore

The **Wheel of Becoming** is an ancient Buddhist symbol representing the process of existence. At its center are desires, hatred, and ignorance. The rim of the wheel is divided into 12 sections that, together, represent human existence in the continuous process of birth, death, and reincarnation. These sections are: becoming, birth, death, ignorance, impulses, consciousness, mind and body, the six senses (mind counts as one of the six senses), predisposition, perception, desire, and attachment. Each stage of the wheel depends on the next stage. The interdependence of all the stages perpetuates the movement of the wheel through the successive lives of the individual. In popular depictions, the wheel is often shown held in the grasp of the fearsome god of the underworld, Yama.

Noble Truth number three is that ignorance and suffering can be conquered. The fourth and final Noble Truth is the means to do so—the way out of the ignorance and suffering that characterize ordinary human existence. This is the path of the termination of suffering, also known as the Eight-fold Path.

The Buddha is known both for his compassion for all living creatures and for his philosophy of detachment, which enables people to deal with suffering. In the West, compassion and detachment are often regarded as contrasting traits, but Buddhists teach that the two are closely related and illustrate this point with a parable. The parable tells of a woman whose only child had died, leaving her distracted with grief. Hearing that the Buddha could work miracles, she brought the child's body to him and asked him to restore her child to life. Buddha said he would grant her wish if she would bring him a mustard seed from a house where no one had ever died. She hurried off to bring the seed, but found, after asking at every house in the village, that death had come to them all. This enabled her to put her child's death into perspective. She buried the body and returned to Buddha to become a Buddhist nun.

Eight Is Enough

The Eight-fold Path is a list of rules for behavior for those who want to achieve Buddhist enlightenment. The Eight-fold Path is simultaneously the outline of a code of ethics and a set of pointers for how to live in such a way as to maximize your potential for enlightenment. It centers on the right, perfect, or pure way of doing things.

The elements of the Eight-fold Path are ...

1. **Right outlook or right understanding.** This means having an accurate view of what the problem is—ignorance—and the passions that get people harmfully attached to their suffering.
2. **Right purpose or right intent.** This means deciding that you can and should deal with the problem of suffering and ignorance.
3. **Right speech.** This means you should speak in such a way as to minimize harmful attachments.
4. **Right conduct.** You should behave so as to minimize harmful attachments.
5. **Right livelihood.** However you make your living, it should not stand in the way of your goal of enlightenment.
6. **Right effort.** You should be prepared to make sustained progress in becoming enlightened since it may not happen right away.
7. **Right awareness.** You should keep in mind—continually—the importance of what you're trying to do.
8. **Right concentration.** Meditation is important in order to understand and control your thoughts, feelings, and emotions.

The Eight-fold Path sketches a program for personal development on three fronts: social ethics and lifestyle, personal health and discipline, and intellectual knowledge. All three are helpful in completing the path.

Stop Asking Silly Questions!

Philosophy, of course, forms the basis for Buddhist knowledge and teachings, but, in fact, philosophical teaching has played an ambiguous role in Buddhism. It conveys the essential approach to attaining enlightenment, as well as the rationale for trying, yet many Buddhists stress that enlightenment is a personal thing that each person must figure out for themselves and that too many complicated instructions or a misguided fixation on dogma can stand in the way of the process.

One way to understand the role of Buddhist teachings in the path to enlightenment is in terms of an ancient Buddhist parable that tells of a man who uses a raft to cross a river. When he reaches the other side he doesn't take the raft with him and continues on his way. Similarly, a person who follows Buddhist teachings to achieve nirvana no longer needs those teachings once nirvana is achieved. The point is that the teachings are not a goal in themselves, but a means to an end.

The Buddha is said to have been vague and evasive in answering certain philosophical questions. Various explanations for this have been put forward. Some say he was not well-versed in philosophical matters. Others say that while he understood the philosophical debates of his day, he wanted to reach a wide following, including those who were uneducated, so he often stayed away from abstract philosophical arguments. Still others say that questions Buddha avoided are questions that have no bearing on the individual's actual attainment of enlightenment.

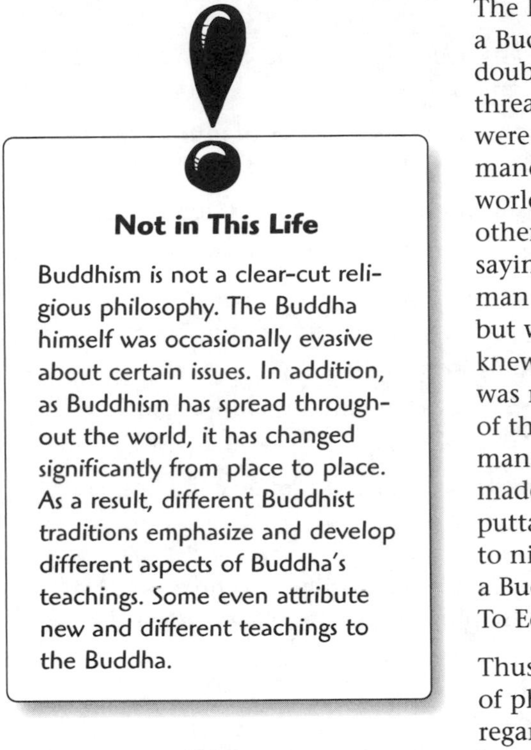

Not in This Life

Buddhism is not a clear-cut religious philosophy. The Buddha himself was occasionally evasive about certain issues. In addition, as Buddhism has spread throughout the world, it has changed significantly from place to place. As a result, different Buddhist traditions emphasize and develop different aspects of Buddha's teachings. Some even attribute new and different teachings to the Buddha.

The Buddha is said to have had a famous debate with a Buddhist monk named Malunkyaputta who had doubts about the Buddha's knowledge and who threatened to renounce Buddhism unless his doubts were resolved. He went to the Buddha himself, demanding categorical answers to questions about the world, eternity, infinity, the soul, reincarnation, and other metaphysical issues. The Buddha responded by saying Malunkyaputta's situation was like that of a man who had just been shot with a poisoned arrow but who refused to have the arrow pulled out until he knew all about who shot it and why, what the arrow was made out of, and in what style it was made. None of this information, of course, would alleviate the man's suffering or prevent his dying. The point is made that, in any case, no answers to Malunkyaputta's questions would have brought him any closer to nirvana. An account of this exchange is provided in a Buddhist sermon called "Questions Which Tend Not To Edification."

Thus, within Buddhism, there is both a rich tradition of philosophical teachings and a healthy skepticism in regard to the effectiveness of dogma. This helps explain why Buddhism has spread so successfully throughout so much of the world. People have been free to take from it what they find useful, leave aside what seems unimportant, and retain what they want to from their own cultures and mindsets.

It All Depends

Although some Buddhists do not attach much importance to metaphysical questions, many feel that Buddhist ideas about existence—what it is and how it works—help explain enlightenment. The most significant thing Buddha taught about existence is that it is conditioned. In other words, everything that exists depends on everything else. What's more, everything is made up of other things. Therefore, nothing has its own independent existence.

Three Marks Against You

Everything is interconnected and constantly flowing and changing, like water in a stream. Everything that happens has an effect on everything else, so it's impossible to isolate separate elements and say, "These aren't part of the rest of it all." This is the Buddhist theory of causality, an idea called *pratityasamutpada,* which has been translated many ways, including "dependent arising," "conditioned arising," "dependent origination," and "interdependent cooperation." The idea is that everything is caused, or conditioned, by everything else. You can't separate cause from effect.

Orient Expressions

Pratityasamutpada has been translated as "dependent arising," "conditioned arising," "dependent origination," and "interdependent cooperation." It is the Buddhist principle of causality and explains why all things are conditioned by other things and are impermanent.

The conditioned nature of existence accounts for what Buddhists call the Three Marks of Existence. First, nothing is permanent. Everything is constantly changing, coming into being and disappearing again. Second, existence is characterized by suffering. Third, what most people think of as "the self" doesn't exist. Suffering, impermanence, and selflessness all result from the conditioned, or compounded, nature of all things.

Not in This Life

Don't assume that the Buddhist notion that the self is only a bundle of mental and physical impulses is entirely unheard of in Western philosophy. In fact, it closely resembles the view of self put forward by the Scottish philosopher David Hume, who characterized the self as "a bucket of ideas."

Filling in the Middle

Dependent origination and the Three Marks of Existence are central notions of Buddhist philosophy, and there's a lot of explaining that has been done in order to make sense of them. It should help to see how these ideas fit into the Buddhist Middle Way mentioned earlier in connection with the Buddhist recognition that neither asceticism nor luxurious living lead to enlightenment.

The ideas of conditioned arising and the Three Marks of Existence form the metaphysical basis for the Buddhist Middle Way. In practical terms, the Buddha's Middle Way strikes a compromise between harsh asceticism and a selfish desire for pleasure. In theoretical terms, the Middle Way strikes a compromise between the ancient Vedic ideals of Atman and Brahman—the essential absolutes of being and consciousness—and the reactionary view that there is no immortal soul, and existence is essentially a random and chaotic series of events.

Orient Expressions

Skandhas are groups or aggregates that constitute the various aspects of human existence and experience. They are **rupa** (body), **vedana** (feelings), **sanna** (perception), **samskara** (predisposition), and **vijnana** (consciousness). They are temporary conditions, therefore the self, which is based on them, has no essence. **Rupa** is the physical skandha. The others are **nama,** or mental.

The notion of conditioned arising says that all things—including everything with physical substance and the individual "self" or "soul"—are temporary forms. Nothing is permanent. The self, and all substantial things, are simply what happens when the right elements merge together for a time. Buddhists call these elements *skandhas*. The five skandhas can be thought of as fields of experience or as groupings of states of existence that make people what they are. Four of the skandhas are classified as *nama,* or mental. The fifth skandha, body, is *rupa,* or physical.

It's kind of creepy in a way, but according to Buddhists, what we think of as our self is really just an impermanent bundle of mental and physical impulses. In fact, the point is to realize that "you" are no more than the sum of your parts, and these parts will dissolve, leaving nothing there. The sooner you realize this, the closer you will be to achieving nirvana.

Of the mental skandhas, *samskara* (predisposition) deserves the most explanation, both because it is especially unfamiliar to Western thinking and because it poses a special obstacle to enlightenment. It stands for innate tendencies and impressions that build up as a result of past experience, including experience in previous lives. These tendencies are often subconscious, so they can be difficult to identify. Coming to terms with samskara can be a significant passage in the life of a Buddhist; it may be achieved after years of meditation.

Karma Dogma

The Boddhisattva Avalokita, while moving in the deep course of the Perfect Wisdom, shed light on the five skandas and found them equally empty. After this penetration, he overcame all pain.

"Listen, Sariputra, form is emptiness, emptiness is form, form does not differ from emptiness, emptiness does not differ from form. The same thing is true with feeling, perception, mental functioning, and consciousness."

—The Heart Sutra

Samskara is also one of the 12 links to existence depicted on the Wheel of Becoming, which you may remember from earlier in this chapter. Thus it is one of the factors of existence that bind people to the world. By the way, be careful not to confuse samskara with samsara. Samsara is the Hindu term for worldly reality and the cycle of death and rebirth. Buddhists recognize this concept, too. So you could say that your samskara keeps you trapped in samsara.

The Least You Need to Know

- The Buddha was born prince Siddhartha Gotama in the sixth century B.C.E. He renounced his comfortable existence to seek enlightenment as a wandering ascetic.
- The Buddha achieved enlightenment (nirvana) by following the Middle Way between the pursuit and the renunciation of pleasure. He taught this way to his followers.
- The Four Noble Truths of Buddhism hold that the world is full of suffering, suffering is caused by desire, suffering can be avoided through an extinguishing of desire, and the way to extinguish desire is by following the Eight-fold Path.
- The Eight-fold Path includes rules for moral living, mental and physical discipline, and intellectual knowledge.
- Dependent origination is the Buddhist theory of causality that says all things are changing, impermanent, and dependent on other things.
- Skandhas are fields of experience that make up what is commonly referred to as "the self."

Chapter 12

Flesh on the Bones

In This Chapter

- The development of early Buddhism
- Mahyahana and Theravada
- Arhats and Boddhisattvas
- Vaibeshika, Madhyamika, and Yogacara schools
- The decline of Buddhism in India

Statues of the Buddha exist depicting him before his enlightenment, when he was a half-starved ascetic. His bones and blood vessels show clearly through his skin, and his hollow face shows that he is absorbed in serious meditation. More familiar, however, are carved figurines of Buddha from China. He has a fat, protruding belly and an upturned, laughing face. If you didn't know, you would never guess that the two Buddhas are the same person.

Just as the Buddha himself was transformed, Buddhist philosophy underwent important changes as well as it grew and developed. The number of his disciples grew from a small handful to include monks, nuns, and lay believers throughout India and beyond. The bare bones of his teachings were fleshed out with commentaries, and Buddhist precepts were underscored and animated as they became incorporated into the lifestyles of various cultures.

The Buddha's message—or versions of it, at any rate—could be applied to just about any lifestyle, whether relaxed or rigorous, active or reflective. Buddhism became both more practical and more idealistic without losing its moral focus. As growing numbers of Buddhists found new and different paths to enlightenment, they came to believe that enlightenment was possible for everyone.

All Together Now

After 40 years of teaching and gathering disciples, the Buddha died, leaving behind a devoted community of believers. Many of these were committed to perpetuating Buddhism as a way of life. This community was, and still is, known as the *sangha*—the monks and nuns who embrace the teachings of Buddha. The sangha is one of the Three Jewels of Buddhism Buddhists take refuge in: the Buddha himself; the teachings of Buddhism, also known as the dharma; and the community.

Orient Expressions

The **sangha** is the Buddhist community, originally the order of nuns and monks that first embraced Buddhism. The sangha is considered one of the Three Jewels of Buddhism together with the Buddha himself and Buddhist teachings.

Baskets of Buddhism

Representatives of the Buddhist Sangha have held important councils six times since the death of the Buddha in order to discuss policy and doctrine. The first of these meetings is supposed to have taken place shortly after Buddha's death as leading Buddhists met with the intention of memorizing the major texts of Buddhism that had been written up to that point. These texts were written on palm leaves, which were stored in three baskets and thus are known as the Tripitaka, "three baskets": the Vinaya, containing rules for how monks and nuns were to behave (monks and nuns are expected to lead a more rigorous, disciplined life than other Buddhists); the Sutras, containing sayings and sermons of the Buddha; and the Abhidharma, containing explanations of Buddhist philosophy.

The Tripitaka may have been written originally in the Indian dialect known as Pali and translated into other languages as Buddhism spread, including Tibetan, Chinese, and Japanese. Some of the original Buddhist scriptures have been lost, but most exist in many languages, together with notes and commentaries that have been added through the generations.

Enlightened Empire

The spread of Buddhism increased tremendously around the middle of the third century B.C.E. when it was embraced as a religion by the Emperor of India, Ashoka (264–226). Ashoka was the grandson of Emperor Chandragupta, who founded the

Mauryan dynasty in the wake of the invasion of India by Alexander the Great. Legend has it that Asoka was an especially brutal Emperor who waged bloody battles to increase his empire. But Buddhists say all this changed when he converted to Buddhism. At that point, he became compassionate and civic minded and listened carefully to the requests of his people, building hospitals, roads, and water works.

In addition, he fostered Buddhism in his own realms and sent out teachers to spread it even farther. Asoka's daughter and son went in person to the island of Sri Lanka, and Buddhism subsequently took hold there. In the centuries that followed, monks spread Buddhism throughout East Asia and Southeast Asia. Buddhist monasteries and shrines were built all over India. As Buddhism spread and blended with other cultures, distinct Buddhist traditions developed.

Not in This Life

Don't be confused by subtle differences in the spelling of Pali and Sanskrit words for the same concept. Since Buddhism emerges out of Hindu philosophy, which was originally written in Sanskrit, Sanskrit is often used for Buddhist terms. But since some of the most important Buddhist texts were written in the Pali dialect, Pali words are often used. Compare the Sanskrit words, dharma, nirvana, and atman to their Pali counterparts, dhamma, nibbana, and atta.

Parallel Paths

The two main divisions of Buddhism are Theravada (or Hinayana) and Mahayana Buddhism. Theravada, meaning "way of the elders," is based on the Abhidharma teachings. (As mentioned at the beginning of this chapter, Abhidharma is one of the "three baskets" of Buddhist scripture.) Theravadins generally resist innovation, attempting to adhere to the Buddha's original teachings. You may say Theravada is "old-school" Buddhism. Mahayana, which means "greater vehicle," (in contrast to Hinayana, another name for Theravada meaning "lesser vehicle") is less rigid in following the Abhidharma. Partly because of its flexibility, it has gone over well with people of many different cultures. As a result, there are many different sects within Mahayana Buddhism, some of which you can read about in the following chapters.

Going Solo

The emphasis in Theravadin Buddhism is on personal enlightenment. Theravadins are chiefly concerned with themselves, or, actually, the conquering of selfhood. They hope to attain nirvana through meditation and by applying the insight that the world and the self are without essence. When this insight is grasped intellectually as well as realized through meditation as a higher state of consciousness, the Theravadin becomes released from the cycle of samasara that binds all creatures to an existence of suffering.

Theravadin monks recognize four stages in the process of enlightenment:

- First is the sotapanna, the "enterer of the stream." Those who have entered the stream—begun the process of Theravada discipline—will never again be born into life as anything less than a human being. In addition, they can expect no more than seven future reincarnations before achieving nirvana and release.
- Second is the sakadagamin, "one who will return once more." These monks will be reincarnated only once again before attaining nirvana.
- Next is the anagamin, "one who will not return." A nonreturner will be reborn into a heavenly existence before attaining nirvana.
- The fourth and highest stage of Theravadin Buddhism is the *arhat,* the "released one," who will attain nirvana at death. In the meantime, arhats remain alive, but have been purged of all worldly defilements.

Orient Expressions

An **arhat** is a Theravadin Buddhist who has achieved enlightenment and will be released from the cycle of samsara at death.

It's worth noting that the Theravadin path looks to the Buddha as a human example to follow, rather than as a divine figure to worship.

Dharma If You Do, Dharma If You Don't

An important philosophical school within Theravada Buddhism is known as Vaibeshika (not to be confused with Vaisheshika, the orthodox school of Hindu philosophy). The name refers to commentaries written on the Abhidharma, the portion of Buddhist scripture most closely concerned with philosophy. Vaibeshika stresses the doctrine of Dependent Arising that sees all things, including the self, as conditioned by skandhas, the groupings of things that make up the self described in the previous chapter.

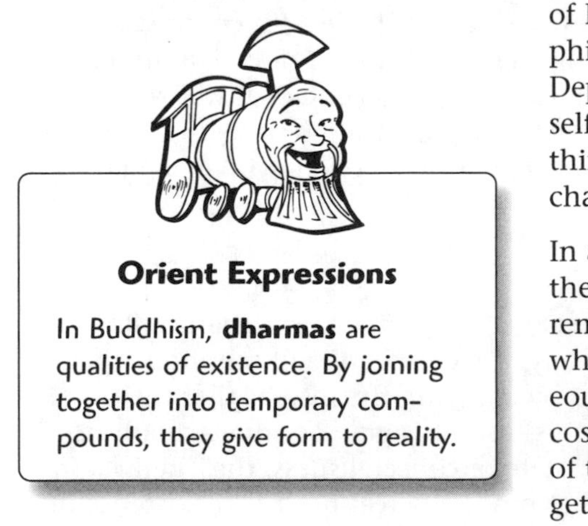

Orient Expressions

In Buddhism, **dharmas** are qualities of existence. By joining together into temporary compounds, they give form to reality.

In addition, Vaibeshika philosophy recognizes 82 further categories of existence called *dharmas*. You may remember the term dharma from Hindu philosophy, where it corresponds roughly to duty, law, or righteousness. To the Buddhists, dharma refers not only to cosmic law, but to the teachings of the Buddha (one of the Three Jewels) and to the qualities that work together to form reality.

The dharmas make the things of the world appear to exist. Yet the world as we perceive it isn't real; only the dharmas are real and permanent. Interestingly, Vaibeshika says they "arise" into being by moving backward through time from the future into the present. The present, then, is only a temporary appearance of the eternal dharmas as they pass from the future to the past.

Just as the skandhas that make up the self provide an explanation for how reincarnation can take place despite the Buddhist belief that there is no essential self, the dharmas explain how the world can exist and still be illusory and impermanent. Although the self and the world of things dissolve into their component parts, the skandhas and dharmas that constitute them will recombine into new forms.

Lotus Lore

Because it sees the dharmas as real things, Vaibeshika is considered a "realist" philosophy in Western terms. "Realism" can be applied to any philosophy that says things exist independently of the mind. An important realist philosophy in the West is empiricism, which forms the basis of modern science. The opposite of realism is idealism. Idealist philosophies hold that the mind is necessary for things to exist. Important Western idealist philosophers include Plato and Kant. The famous question, "If a tree fell in the forest and no one was there to hear it, would it make any sound?" is basically asking whether realism or idealism is true.

Divine Guides

Theravada has caught on mainly in South and Southeast Asia, including Sri Lanka, Burma, Thailand, Laos, and Cambodia. Mahayana Buddhism has spread even farther, to Tibet, Mongolia, Vietnam, Korea, China, and Japan. Like Theravadins, Mahayanas hope to attain nirvana, but unlike Theravadins, they believe that it is the job of the enlightened ones to help everyone else. Thus, in place of the Theravadin arhat, Mahayana Buddhists look to boddhisattvas, "seekers of enlightenment," analogous to Christian saints who assist ordinary people in a variety of spiritual ways.

Boddhisattvas include earthly human beings destined to become enlightened, as well as legendary, heavenly beings who have willingly postponed their release from samsara in order to help others. Mahayana Buddhists recognize numerous Buddhas and Boddhisattvas who appear on Earth in various reincarnations. In fact, the first

Boddhisattva is said to be Siddhartha Gotama (who became *the* Buddha) in a previous life. He accumulated the good karma necessary to become the Buddha by helping other Buddhas.

Thus, according to Mahayana belief, Buddhism predates the birth of the historical Buddha. Clearly, Mahayana Buddhism has a supernatural aspect that has helped it merge with the traditional beliefs of other cultures. Buddhas are not simply human beings who have attained release from suffering as they are in Theravada, but may be worshiped, prayed to, and offered sacrifices as divine beings. They are known for their compassion for all creatures.

The term "Boddhisattva" is sometimes used specifically to refer to one of the incarnations of the Buddha prior to his attainment of nirvana. Buddha is said to have gone through 550 lives, including both human and animal, on his way to Buddha-hood. Stories of his previous lives, known as Jatakas, were popular with monks in the early days of Buddhism, especially since the monks were not supposed to indulge in listening to earthly stories for mere entertainment. The Jatakas resemble the familiar beast fables of the ancient Greek writer, Aesop, in their recounting of the adventures of people and animals, from which moral lessons were derived. Supposedly, they were originally told to his disciples by the Buddha himself, who could remember all of his past lives upon attaining enlightenment.

Boddhisattvas are an appealing feature of Mahayana Buddhism since they offer guidance to monks and lay believers alike. Theravada, in contrast, tends to be more strictly monastic than Mahayana. Theravadin monks isolate themselves more fully from everyone else in seeking nirvana while, for Mahayanas, the search is more of a group enterprise. This is an additional factor that has helped Mahayana Buddhism catch on and merge with other cultures.

Orient Expressions

Tathata is the Mahayana concept of suchness. It refers to reality as it really is, apart from distinctions imposed by the ego-centered mind. One who sees reality in this way is a **tathagata,** "one who has gone thus." Tathagata is a term that is used to describe the Buddha.

Such a Suchness

Mahayana Buddhism has succeeded in assimilating a range of popular beliefs while still retaining an interest in scholarly philosophical questions concerned with the meaning of selflessness and impermanence. These questions are addressed in different ways by the two main philosophical schools of Mahayana. These are Madhyamika, "the middle teaching," and Yogacara, "the way of union."

Both of these schools draw on the Mahayana concept of *tathata,* or suchness. This refers to reality as it actually exists, apart from the way it appears to those who are deluded by their ego and worldly perceptions. One who understands tathata becomes a *tathagata,* "one who has gone thus," entering into a state of being in which conceptual distinctions disappear. All things become empty of self-oriented significance. They lose their "own-being," just as the tathagata loses his or her ego.

Filling in the Middle

Madhyamika is a philosophical school founded by Nagarjuna sometime around the second century C.E. Nagarjuna felt that the Theravada philosophers were getting carried away with their categories of dharmas used to explain reality. He advocated a return to the position of silence adopted by the Buddha when he refused to answer metaphysical questions. In place of the dharmas suggested by the Theravadins, Madhyamika philosophy asserts that nothing is real; all is void, or *shunyata*. Shunyata is the emptiness behind all appearances. It is the nothing that serves as the foundation for human experience.

Nagarjuna argued that there is nothing that can be said about existence. Words are not reliable and cannot be trusted to tell us the truth. Even the distinction between existence and nonexistence is invalid. This means philosophical speculation fails to supply adequate answers about the nature of reality. Recognizing the uselessness of philosophical speculation is a step forward in becoming liberated from worldly things.

Using the concept of shunyata, Madhyamika aims at going further than other Buddhists in dissolving the self. Not only the self and one's ideas are illusory, but the world itself is no more than an appearance. What's more, this appearance does not disguise emptiness, but *is* emptiness. When properly understood, reality is empty. The point is to reject the impulse to try to make something (or nothing!) out of anything. All attempts to conceptualize actually bind us to delusion. To fully understand this is to attain enlightenment.

Orient Expressions

Shunyata is void or emptiness, a term used by Nagarjuna to explain the underlying reality of all things and the failure of conceptualization to convey the truth.

The Logic of Nonlogic

Nagarjuna's critics objected that if we accept the idea of emptiness, the basic teachings of Buddhism, including the Four Noble Truths and the Eight-fold Path, have to go out the window, too. After all, these are conceptualizations; therefore, they must be invalid like all the others. Nagarjuna responded by saying that the truth of the Four Noble Truths and the Eight-fold Path are conventional and relative truths.

They are helpful in pointing the direction to the ultimate truth of shunyata, and therefore are valuable. But these teachings should not be mistaken for exact descriptions of the nature of reality—for tathata, or suchness. This is indescribable and beyond conceptualization.

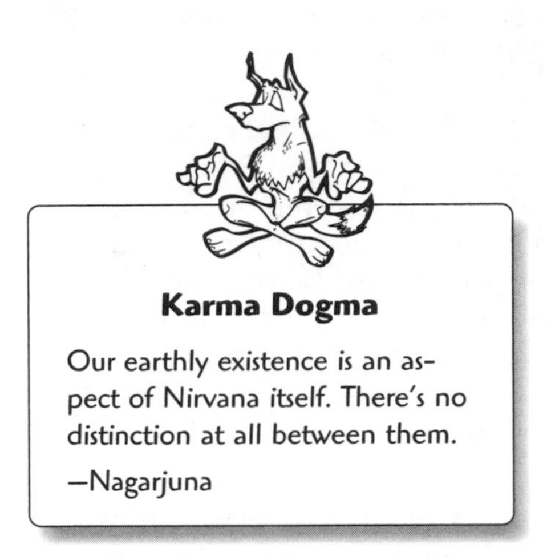

Karma Dogma

Our earthly existence is an aspect of Nirvana itself. There's no distinction at all between them.

—Nagarjuna

The concept of shunyata—the void—could be used to deny the distinctions between all concepts. In fact, Nagarjuna himself used it to challenge the distinction between nirvana and samsara. He suggested that attempts to free the self of desires could be understood as actually motivated by desire. On the other hand, the serene acceptance of desired things can indicate that desire has been transcended. As long as we're conceptualizing anyway, it's all relative.

Thus, even though Madhyamika philosophy sounds drastically nihilistic, it tended to instill a kind of "live and let live" attitude, in contrast with the more strict approaches to life practiced by Theravadins. As a result, Madhyamika emphasized the relaxed, accepting aspect of Buddhism, making it easier for more people to practice it in different ways.

Head Room

Yogacara, the "mind-only" school of Buddhist philosophy, developed during the fourth century. It was founded by two brothers, Asanga and Vasubandhu, who taught that consciousness alone is real. All things that appear to exist in the world exist only in consciousness. This teaching can be realized through yogic meditation in which pure consciousness is experienced.

Orient Expressions

Alaya-vijnana is "storehouse consciousness," the concept of Yogacara Buddhist philosophy that says mind is the only reality where distinctions disappear and existence may be understood in its "suchness."

Yogacarins believe that the distinction between consciousness and the objects, or contents, of consciousness is delusory. What we are aware of and the fact of our awareness are basically the same. In other words, things that appear to be objects of consciousness are actually attributes of consciousness. That they appear to have a separate, independent reality is a result of delusion.

When understood in their true nature, all things are attributes of a universal consciousness called *alaya-vijnana,* or "storehouse consciousness," that contains everything. Seen in this way, distinctions between various objects of consciousness and between consciousness and its objects disappear. This is the tathagata state, which can be reached through yogic meditation.

Not Fade Away

Buddhism is a highly paradoxical way of thinking. Much of the paradox has to do with the problem of separating the delusory appearances of conditioned reality from unconditioned nirvana. What seems most real is most delusory; what seems most empty is most complete. As with the truths of Hindu meditation, the only way to understand fully what Buddhism has to tell us is to become a Buddhist yourself and experience nirvana. But even this may involve ultimately having to decide for yourself just what nirvana is and just how you can achieve it.

And of course, the elusiveness and personal nature of Buddhist truths are a big part of their appeal, giving Buddhists the opportunity to explore existence in their own ways, taking guidance as needed from the teachings and the communities of Buddhism. Fortunately for non-Buddhists, these teachings are available to everyone. You don't have to be a full-fledged Buddhist stream-enterer to benefit from the wisdom of questioning conventional ideas, looking at reality with fresh eyes, and searching for a way to be at peace that works well in your own experience.

Many Buddhists insist Buddhism is not a religion, but simply a way. For others, it is clearly a form of worship with a priesthood and a community of believers. Buddhists can be found all over the world, all with varying ideas about what Buddhism is. And even in places where there aren't any Buddhists, you can still find the influence of Buddhism. This is especially true (paradoxically enough) in India itself, where organized Buddhism has all but died out completely.

Lotus Lore

Buddhism has been revived in parts of India in recent years as a result of the immigration to India of Buddhist monks in exile from Tibet. In fact, India is just one of several countries, including the United States, where exiled Tibetan Buddhists have relocated to escape political persecution from the Chinese government. Although Tibetan Buddhists have traditionally striven to maintain their seclusion from the rest of the world, political strife in Tibet has encouraged them to be more open about sharing their knowledge and beliefs with other countries.

There are a number of factors that led to the decline of Buddhism in India. Because Buddhism does not recognize the authority of the Hindu Vedas, Buddhists were considered heretical and suffered some persecution. They were also subject to persecution from the Muslims who invaded India and ruled there throughout much of the Middle Ages. Evidence for persecution can be found in the fact that many Buddhist texts originally written in Indian are known only from translations into other languages, such as Chinese. Many Buddhist writings in India were evidently destroyed.

Lotus Lore

Scholars debate the extent to which Buddhism influenced early Christianity. It has been suggested that rosary beads were introduced into Christianity by Buddhist monks, who carry similar beads. Another intriguing suggestion has to do with the legend of Saint Josephat, recognized by the Eastern Orthodox Church, which tells of the saint's renunciation of his comfortable life for a life of asceticism. Some say this legend stems from the story of Buddha's life, interpreting the name Josephat as an alteration of the Buddhist term, Boddhisattva, which means "seeker of enlightenment."

Yet even though Buddhism declined, it didn't disappear into thin air. Instead, it was partly reabsorbed into Hinduism. After all, the flexibility of Buddhism allowed it to merge with cultures outside India. The same flexibility helped it blend in with Hindu practices and beliefs as well, especially since Hinduism and Buddhism have so much in common to begin with. Meanwhile, Buddhism spread and flourished throughout Central and East Asia, adopting many different forms in the process. You can read about some of these varieties in the following chapters.

The Least You Need to Know

- Buddhism has an important monastic component. The Three Jewels of Buddhism include the sangha, or community of monks, as well as the Buddha himself and his teachings.
- The two main branches of Buddhism are the more conservative Theravada and the more progressive Mahayana Buddhism.
- Vaibeshika is a realist Theravada School that recognizes the existence of dharmas.
- Madhyamika is a relativist Mahayana school that emphasizes the concept of shunyata, the void.
- Yogacara is the mind-only school of Mahayana based on "storehouse consciousness."
- Organized Buddhism largely disappeared from India during the Middle Ages, but spread to many other countries.

Chapter 13

The Diamond Path

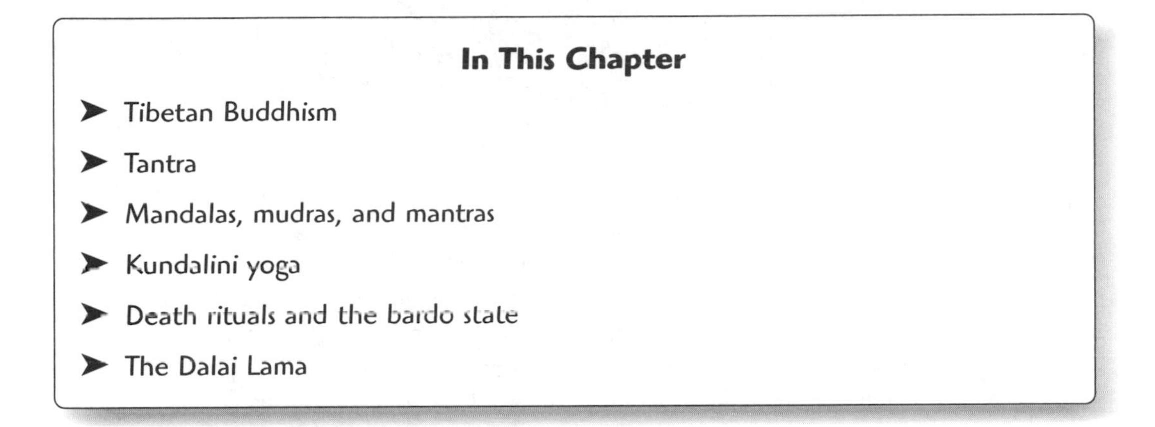

In This Chapter

- Tibetan Buddhism
- Tantra
- Mandalas, mudras, and mantras
- Kundalini yoga
- Death rituals and the bardo state
- The Dalai Lama

At least since the time when James Hilton wrote the fantasy-adventure novel, *Lost Horizon,* which tells the story of the Tibetan paradise of Shangri-La, Westerners have regarded Tibet as a magical and mysterious place. The magic and mystery is partly due to Tibet's seclusion but is greatly enhanced by the country's unique religious philosophy, which blends Buddhism with native Tibetan belief. This philosophy is a central feature of one of the most fascinating, beautiful, and civilized cultures on the planet—a culture which, sadly, is being engulfed by Communist China.

For centuries, Tibetan Buddhism has been the official state religion of Tibet. Yet while Tibetan Buddhism takes on a hallowed and solemn aspect, it is based in part on an exotic and esoteric Hindu cult known as tantrism. If you're like many Westerners, when you hear the word "tantrism," you immediately think of kinky sex rituals. Well don't get the wrong idea; Tibetan monks are celibate.

Even so, Tibetan Buddhism comprises a rich and paradoxical blend of unusual traditions, from its origins in secret tantric doctrine to its recent policy of openness to the West. Included in these traditions are a variety of cultural and artistic forms that express Tibet's unique philosophy. These traditions have only recently made their way beyond the Himalayas to encounter the West.

Up the Mountain

Scholars estimate that Buddhism first became introduced into Tibet during the sixth or seventh century C.E. At about the same time, Tibet developed its own writing, so the advent of Buddhism is closely associated with the first writings in Tibetan. As a result, Buddhism also became associated with progress, civilization, and the development of culture in general. By the end of the eighth century, Buddhism in Tibet won the support of the king. In fact, the earliest Buddhist writings in Tibet were translated by royal decree. Since that time, Buddhism has been the official religion in Tibet throughout most of the country's history.

Lotus Lore

Tibet has an aura of mystery in the West partly because of the popularity of the classic adventure-fantasy novel, *Lost Horizon,* by James Hilton, which depicts the utopian land of Shangri-La, a secluded paradise in the Himalayas where everyone is kind and no one grows old. Frank Capra directed the original movie version (1937), and the tale was remade as a musical in 1973. The story was so popular that Shangri-La became a familiar idea in America. President Franklin D. Roosevelt once joked at a 1942 press conference that a secret U.S. World War II airforce base was located in Shangri-La.

Tantra-lized

Tibetan Buddhism is known as Vajrayana, which means the "Diamond Vehicle." The name suggests that the teachings are enduring and precious, like diamonds. Alternatively, Vajrayana is sometimes translated as "the way of the thunderbolt." Still another name commonly applied to Tibetan Buddhism is Tantrayana, "the way of tantra," because it stems from a set of ancient Hindu and Indian Buddhist practices known as Tantrism.

Tantra has its roots in an Indian cult that worshiped the god Shiva together with his female manifestation, Shakti. Shakti is divine power or energy understood in Tantra to take female form. The union of Shiva, representing the male principle, with Shakti, the female, has special symbolic and ritual significance in Indian Tantra. As a result,

Tantra has acquired a reputation in the West for kinkiness—especially since the sexual symbolism of Tantra sometimes gets expressed as ritualistic sex!

In fact, there are two strains of Tantra, referred to as "right-handed" and "left-handed" Tantra. It's the left-handed variety that has become known for sex rituals. Right-handed Tantra makes use of sexual symbolism in ritual, yoga, and meditation, since male and female energy are important cosmic and internal forces. Actual sex, however, gets left out of right-handed tantric ritual. Instead, it's the symbolism that counts.

Not in This Life

Don't be put off by the attitudes of early Western scholars toward Tantra. When they first learned about it, some responded with prudish disgust to its sexual aspects, going so far as to suggest that the assimilation of Tantra by Indian Buddhists led to the corruption, decay, and eventual disappearance of Buddhism from India. Few serious students of Buddhism today accept this view.

Behind Closed Doors

Part of the idea behind left-handed tantric sex rituals is to gain control over the physical aspects of sex, much as, in ordinary yoga and meditation, the idea is to gain control of breathing and the activity of the mind. The height of this sort of tantric discipline for male yogis is to achieve sexual orgasm without ejaculating semen. (I don't know what this is like from experience, but I imagine it would be sort of like chewing on a piece of chocolate without salivating—not easy!) Anyway, kinky as it sounds, tantric sex ties in with the overall mind-body awareness and discipline that characterizes yoga in general. At the same time, it draws on ancient religious symbolism concerning the male and female aspects of the cosmos.

Tantra belief is ancient and no one knows for certain when it got started. It became especially popular in India during the Middle Ages thanks in part to the influence of Madhyamika Buddhism (which is described in the previous chapter). Madhyamika puts forward the idea that there is no real distinction between samsara and nirvana. The truly enlightened individual understands that the world of appearances is not a barrier to truth but an aspect of it.

Left-handed Tantra takes this idea a step further to say that experiencing forbidden pleasures—under ritualistic circumstances—can actually *lead* to enlightenment. By indulging in the very things that monks and ascetics have traditionally avoided, you can achieve heightened spirituality.

These forbidden things are known as *panca-makara,* "the five M's." They are …

- Madya (wine)
- Mamsa (meat)

- Matsya (fish)
- Mudra (fried grain)
- Maithuna (sex)

Orient Expressions

Panca-makara is "the five M's"—earthly pleasures forbidden to most monks and ascetics but used in left-handed tantric ritual to achieve a heightened spiritual condition.

Left-handed tantrists say that ritual indulgence in panca-makara is simultaneously an expression of devotion to the gods and a way of becoming god-like oneself. The idea is that the most worthy form of devotion to the gods comes from people who are most like the gods themselves. A way of becoming god-like is to enjoy pleasures ordinarily reserved for gods. In practicing maithuna—ritual sex—tantrists think of themselves as gods and goddesses.

Cosmic Flow

Some left-handed tantric writings suggest that asceticism is foolish and the mental and physical discipline of yoga is a waste of time. This anything goes, do-whatever-you-want attitude, however, is not the point of most Tantra, whether or not actual sex is involved. Instead—and certainly for the right-handed tantric Buddhism of Tibet—what is important is the interplay of energies that exist on various levels, including male/female, self/cosmos and nirvana/samsara.

In Tibetan Tantra, nirvana and samsara are not absolutely separate, as in Theravada Buddhism, nor are they ultimately indistinguishable, as in Madhyamika. Instead, the two can interact in a dynamic relationship that can lead to heightened states of being. The same can be said in Tantra of the distinction between male and female energies and between the self and the cosmos. Interaction between self and cosmos and between male and female are controlled through ritual, yoga, and meditation, and facilitated through symbolism expressed in sounds, gestures, and images.

Tantra is an especially symbolic form of Buddhism. It makes extensive use of mantras, mudras, and mandalas.

- Mantras are words and syllables imagined or spoken out loud during meditation.
- Mudras are physical gestures made with the hands during meditation.
- Mandalas are circular designs, often beautiful and elaborate, representing the self and the cosmos that are significant in ritual and meditation.

All three are used to bring about special symbolic, psychological, physical, and cosmic experiences.

Hand and Mouth

Mantras, as mentioned in previous chapters, are used in meditation to focus the mind. They include actual words and syllables with no self-evident meaning. Some may derive from ancient magic spells and are thought to produce psychic effects. Some are "seeds," syllables representing and encapsulating longer writings and ideas. The idea is that by condensing a sacred text into a single syllable or two and chanting the syllable many times, the power of the text becomes concentrated and can produce or enhance the energy flowing through the body, mind, and cosmos. The most famous tantric mantra is Om Mani Padme Hum, which literally means "Jewel in the Lotus." It has both sexual and spiritual connotations.

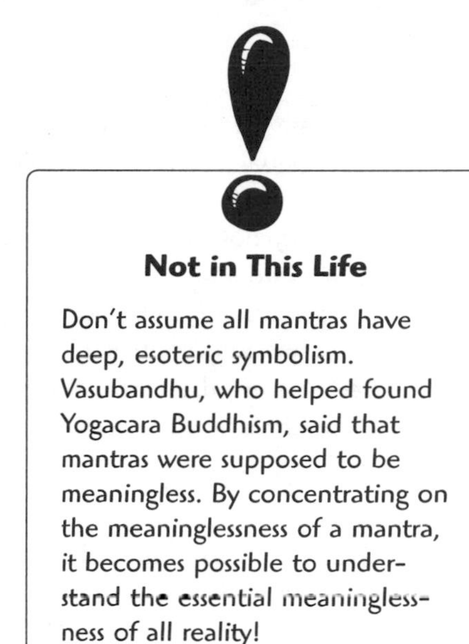

Not in This Life

Don't assume all mantras have deep, esoteric symbolism. Vasubandhu, who helped found Yogacara Buddhism, said that mantras were supposed to be meaningless. By concentrating on the meaninglessness of a mantra, it becomes possible to understand the essential meaninglessness of all reality!

Like mantras, mudras are thought to effect the flow of energy in meditation. One common mudra used in meditation places the hands in the lap with the palms upward and the fingers slightly overlapping. This symbolizes and facilitates inward concentration. Another familiar mudra is the mudra of blessing, in which the left hand is held up with the tips of the thumb and ring finger touching. Statues and paintings of the Buddha often show him with this mudra.

Wheels Inside of Wheels

While mudras and mantras can convey subtle and elaborate tantric symbolism, the most subtle and elaborate source of tantric symbolism is the mandala, a circular design representing the cosmos and the self that can be used in meditation and in ritual. These may be painted or drawn on the floor or made out of rice powder of various colors. Rice powder mandalas are something like sand paintings. They can easily be destroyed to show the impermanence of existence.

Mandalas are often divided into sections representing aspects of the self and the universe. In tantric initiation rituals, an initiate may be blindfolded and given a flower, which he then tosses on the mandala. The section in which the flower lands indicates a divine force that is particularly important to that person.

Features of the mandala may be imagined as areas within the self. This allows a person who meditates to explore his or her inner being symbolically, concentrating on various realms of the self in order to discover or experience existence in new ways. Mandalas may contain depictions of threatening gods and monsters representing forces that must be overcome through meditation. They also contain barriers to be passed through and realms such as palaces and paradises representing ecstatic and blissful states.

Lotus Lore

Some Westerners, most notably psychologist Carl Jung, have claimed that mandalas have a universal psychological significance that extends beyond Buddhist culture. Jung, who advanced the famous idea of the collective unconscious, says mandalas are universal symbols of psychological wholeness. Evidence for this theory includes magic circles and ritual designs from many cultures, including Christian church architecture. Even more striking, Jung found that mandala-like images appeared in dreams of patients who were in the process of successfully integrating aspects of their psyches that had been giving them trouble. These mandalas represented the spiritual wholeness of patients who successfully overcame psychological problems.

You might say mandalas symbolize the self, but the connection between the mandala and the self is more than symbolic in the minds of believing tantrists, for whom the body has a mystical aspect that can be realized through meditation and yoga. The mystical, or "subtle," body is filled with divine energy and connects the physical body to the universe. Mandalas then, function partly as maps of the mystic body, making it easier to explore.

Spiritual Snake-Charming

Concentrating on a mandala can help lend structure to tantric meditation. Another well-known tantric technique of structured meditation is *kundalini* yoga. This form of yoga is based on the view that the mystical body contains energy centers called *chakras*. Chakras are lotus-shaped nodes located along the spine and at the top of the head where energy currents intersect. The chakras can be stimulated by cosmic energy that lies dormant most of the time at the base of the spine. This energy is called kundalini, which means "serpent," because it is said to resemble a coiled up snake. When the snake is awakened, it can rise up through the chakras and produce self-realization and a revitalized mystical body.

Some forms of tantra recognize six main chakras, some seven. In Buddhist tantra, there are often only four. Each chakra corresponds to an aspect of consciousness, a material element, a mantra syllable, and a goddess. In between the main chakras are smaller ones.

To energize the chakras, the kundalini must first be awakened through yogic discipline. Then, through meditation, it must be guided up along the spine through each chakra in turn. Only the most skilled and dedicated kundalini yogis succeed in guiding the energy snake through all the chakras and into the highest one at the top of, or, as some say, above the head.

Orient Expressions

Kundalini yoga is a form of yoga that attempts to awaken the kundalini—cosmic energy in the form of a coiled snake—so that it rises through the **chakras,** or lotus-shaped energy centers of the mystic body.

Dying for Enlightenment

For Buddhism in general and, for that matter, Hinduism as well, one of the main purposes of yoga and meditation is to purify consciousness so that, at some point, either during life or after death, the self can be released into a state of nirvana or moksha. For Mahayana Buddhism, including tantric Buddhism of Tibet, meditation and yoga are not the only ways to attain nirvana. Mahayana Buddhists believe that the deeds of sages and holy people, especially Boddhisattvas, can confer enlightenment and release on ordinary Buddhists—even those who are not particularly skilled at yoga or meditation. This, as you may remember from the previous chapter, is one of the main factors that distinguish Mahayana Buddhism from the other main "vehicle" of Buddhism, Theravada.

Not in This Life

Many tantrists warn that you cannot hope to succeed in kundalini yoga without the help of a guru. In fact, gurus are so important in tantra that they are often considered an additional fourth jewel to the famous Three Jewels of Buddhism—the teachings of Buddha, the Buddha himself, and the sangha, or community of believers.

In Tibetan Buddhism, meditation, yoga, and spiritual guidance from others all work together in special ways to prepare people for enlightenment. Tibetan Buddhists believe spiritual masters can be especially helpful at the time of death. Death is seen as an important crossroad when the soul is faced with the possibility of attaining nirvana or, conversely, of rebirth into worldly existence. Gurus can be greatly helpful to the dying and the recently dead, giving the soul-in-transition its best chance of release from the painful cycle of samsara.

Out-of-Body Experience

The Tibetan tantric philosophy of dying has become well-known in the West through a work called the Bardo Thodol, or The Tibetan Book of the Dead. (A more literal translation of the title, Bardo Thodol, is "Liberation Through Hearing in the Bardo State.") The work describes what happens when the soul departs from the body and faces the possibilities of nirvana or rebirth. This transitional dying state is known as *bardo*.

During the process of death and when the body first dies, the soul enters a state of clarity or uncertainty. If the individual has attained purity of consciousness during life, the bardo state will be free of confusion. The soul enters the presence of a clear bright light and may pass through the light into nirvana. But if, like most people, the individual has led a confused, uncertain life, the confusion and uncertainty will be greatly increased in the bardo state. The soul will be terrified by the clear bright light and shrink from it, retreating instead to softer, dimmer lights that will lead it to rebirth in a new physical body.

Orient Expressions

Bardo, in Tibetan Buddhism, is a transitional state, especially the state of the dying and recently dead soul on its way to rebirth or nirvana. A **lama** is a high-ranking Tibetan Buddhist monk. The highest-ranking is the Dalai Lama, the spiritual leader of Tibet.

One way of understanding meditation, then, for Tibetan Buddhists anyway, is as practice and preparation for the bardo state. Someone who becomes calm, clear, and free of confusion through meditation while alive is more likely to remain clear in the bardo. All others are likely to lose their way in the bardo and get reincarnated as cockroaches. But fortunately, for those who have led a clueless existence, help is available at the time of death.

Getting Directions

The Bardo Thodol, in fact, includes detailed advice that can be read to the dying and recently dead—those in the bardo state. Ideally, this advice should be read by a great spiritual master who can best understand the situation, such as a *lama* or guru. A lama is a high-ranking Tibetan Buddhist monk, such as those in charge of monasteries. (The chief lama is the Dalai Lama, who is regarded as the wisest, holiest, and most compassionate of all Tibetan Buddhists.)

The Bardo Thodol forms the basis for death rituals practiced in Tibetan Buddhism. It was probably written in the eighth century, around the time when tantric Buddhism was introduced into Tibet, though its teachings may have been transmitted by word of mouth in India long before it was written down. The dead and dying who hear and obey the advice of the Bardo Thodol may be able to enter into the clear light of nirvana. If not, they may still be able to minimize their confusion and become reborn on a higher plane.

Hello, Dalai

Of course, in Tibetan Buddhism, as in all Mahayana Buddhism, not everyone who is able to obtain release from samsara and its suffering does so. Some choose to remain in the world to help others attain nirvana. In Tibetan Buddhism, the holiest monks are thought to be reborn in human state. Several years after an important monk dies, the other monks go out looking for him in his new incarnation. When found, the reincarnated monk is brought back to the monastery and trained to assume the position he held in the previous life. Talk about job security! Imagine getting to keep your job even after a prolonged leave of absence to die and be reborn!

Karma Dogma

Thy Guru hath set thee face to face before the clear light and now thou art to experience it in its reality in the bardo state where all things are like the void and cloudless sky, and the naked and spotless intellect is like a vacuum. At this moment, know thyself and abide in that state.

—Instructions from the Tibetan Book of the Dead to be read to a dying person

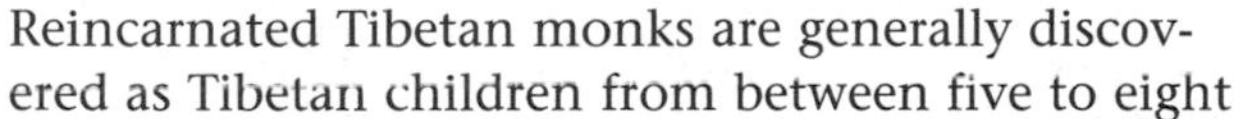

Reincarnated Tibetan monks are generally discovered as Tibetan children from between five to eight years old. These children are known as tulkus. When a prospective tulku is identified, he is tested to make sure he is still the monk he was before death. The test may include selecting some of the dead monk's possessions from a group of objects. When the right tulku is found, he is taken from his family to be raised in a monastery and trained in the way of vajrayana. Hundreds of tulku monks are thought to be alive today.

Among the monks who started out as tulkus are the present Dalai Lama, said to be the fourteenth in a continuing series of reincarnated Dalai Lamas. Unlike his predecessors, the current Dalai Lama has become something of a celebrity in the West. He has endorsed many books on Buddhism published for Western readers. He has also appeared in inspirational videos with Buddhist teachings. His life and the lives of other tulkus has even been the subject of several recent Hollywood films, including *Seven Years in Tibet, Kundun,* and *Little Buddha*.

The Dalai Lama's high public profile has to do with the fact that Tibet has been the subject of repeated invasions by China, which regards it as a part of the People's Republic and has selected its own "Dalai Lama" to rule there. The Tibetan Dalai Lama has had to flee Tibet and is living in exile in Dharmsala, India.

Traditionally, Tibet has been isolated, culturally and geographically, from the rest of the world. Its capital, the holy city of Llasa, has been walled off from outsiders, who are not ordinarily admitted inside. As a result, Tibetan Buddhism has been largely unknown to Westerners until recently.

Lotus Lore

In 1996, a group of Tibetan Buddhist monks from the Seraje monastery (originally in Tibet, now in South India) began fashioning a mandala at the Museum of Fine Arts in Houston. As the mandala was put together out of colored sand, footage of the event was posted on the Internet. Two weeks later, when the mandala was completed, the monks conducted a public ceremony during which they chanted requests to the Buddha for blessings for all living creatures. (The distinctively resonant sound of Tibetan chanting is increasingly heard in the West, now even in a car advertisement!) After the ceremony, the mandala was destroyed. Some of the sand was given away to onlookers.

Since the exile of so many Buddhist monks from Tibet, however, Tibetan Buddhists have become interested in sharing their knowledge and culture with the West. Tibetan monasteries have moved to other countries and have been opening their doors to interested Westerners. Spiritual teachers of Tibet, including the Dalai Lama, have been accommodating their teachings to Western audiences.

The Least You Need to Know

- Buddhism exerted a civilizing influence when it arrived in Tibet in the sixth and seventh centuries, helping to foster the first Tibetan writing.
- Tibetan Buddhism stems from Tantra, a cult that originated in India before Buddhism existed.
- Some tantric ritual involves sex. Tibetan Tantra does not; instead, it conveys symbolic meaning through mantras, mudras, and mandalas.
- The aim of kundalini yoga is to awaken cosmic energy that lies like a serpent at the base of your spine and to send it up through your chakras.
- The Bardo Thodol (the Tibetan Book of the Dead) contains instructions for what to do when you are dying and newly dead.
- The Dalai Lama has been living in India in exile from Chinese-ruled Tibet.

Chapter 14

Other Worlds

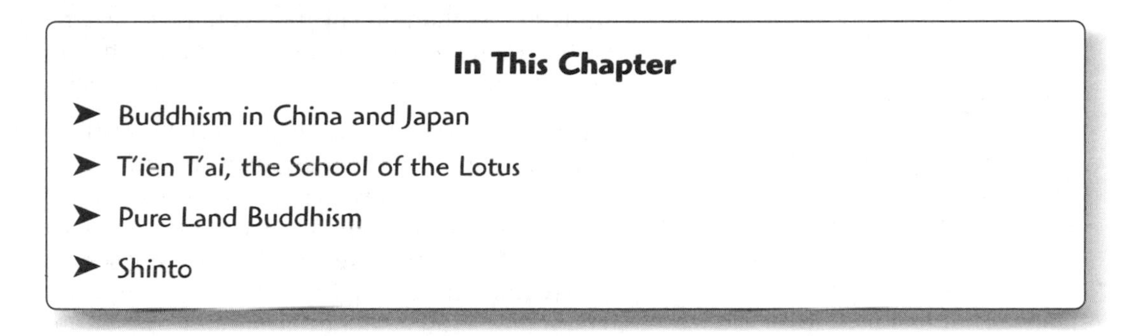

In This Chapter

- Buddhism in China and Japan
- T'ien T'ai, the School of the Lotus
- Pure Land Buddhism
- Shinto

The Mahayana Buddhists of China and Japan recognize many Buddhas in addition to Buddha Shakyamuni, the founder of Buddhism. Many Buddhas have their own legends, their own series of incarnations, their own specialties, qualities, and attributes, and they even live in their own worlds. In fact, the Buddhist universe is huge, with thousands of worlds beyond this one, inhabited by all manner of conscious beings.

The idea of many worlds isn't just Buddhist-style science fiction, but it illustrates the limitless variety of the universe in both cosmic and psychological terms. Just as the world we know isn't the only one, our limited knowledge doesn't begin to cover the range of consciousness it is possible to attain. You might say the other realms of the Buddhas represent higher states of consciousness. Ordinary human beings can have at least an indirect experience of these higher states by communicating with these worlds.

This cosmic idea figures into two strains of Buddhism that found wide acceptance, first in China and later in Japan. These are known as T'ien T'ai (Lotus School) and Pure Land Buddhism. Both of these forms of Buddhism emphasize the role of Buddhas and Boddhisattvas in helping ordinary people to attain enlightenment.

By the way, if you're looking to read about the most famous and influential form of Buddhism to take hold in China and Japan, skip to Chapter 15, "Now and Zen," on Ch'an (Japanese Zen) Buddhism.

A New Buddha on the Block

Buddhism was introduced into China during the first century C.E., but did not take root until centuries later. Unlike many other countries to which Buddhism spread, China already had its own highly organized civilization. Many predominant religious and philosophical beliefs centered around the state, so there wasn't much room for religious and philosophical innovations from outside.

Karma Dogma

The Confucians believed that it was unwise to spend time talking about such things as reincarnation. An early Chinese Buddhist named Mou Tzu replied by pointing out that Buddhists speak of reincarnation only because others want to know. He said, "Do Buddhists talk too much? We only answer the questions you ask us. Do bells and drums make noise by themselves? They make sound only when someone strikes them."

This was especially true since Chinese rulers have always been wary of outsiders, regarding their ways as less civilized than their own. What's more, most Chinese rulers and intellectuals focused more on worldly affairs than on spiritual concerns. As a result, Buddhism did not tend to get the kind of official government support it found, for example, in Tibet.

Another strike against Buddhism in the minds of many Chinese was its monasticism. Traditionally, the Chinese regarded family ties and responsibilities crucially important for both moral and practical reasons. Family relationships were the glue holding society together. Children had an obligation to honor their parents, even as adults, and an important way of doing this was to have children of their own. The monastic aspect of Buddhism, which required monks and nuns to remain celibate and leave their families, violated this basic Chinese belief.

Yet, despite the obstacles, Buddhism managed to take hold in China, especially among the common people. Many turned to Buddhism starting around the fourth century, in part as a source of solace and stability during times of political and economic turmoil. Sometimes, in opposition to the government, Buddhist monasteries began to serve valuable functions within society, sheltering the homeless, feeding the hungry, and providing refuge for those in need of asylum. Some monasteries even functioned as tax shelters and banks, giving people a place to keep their money to avoid taxes or borrow money in time of need.

Thus, while China gradually adapted to Buddhism, Buddhism adapted to China. It developed in ways that reflect the Chinese approach to life. Some of the more strict monastic rules governing the behavior of monks and nuns were relaxed. Some Buddhist monks, for example, could get married. At times, Buddhism was monitored and regulated by the government. Shrines and monasteries had to have official approval. Monks had to be certified. So, partly by conforming to the demands of the government and partly by filling needs the government couldn't supply, Buddhism became one of the three major beliefs of China, along with Taoism and Confucianism. (You can read about these other two in the following two sections.)

Like other Chinese ideas and practices, Chinese Buddhism spread to Japan, where it was changed even further. Buddhism was introduced in Japan during the sixth century, where it merged somewhat with native religious beliefs and, to an extent, provided a separate alternative. The Japanese did not have as highly organized a system of government as the Chinese, so Buddhism was able to merge more easily with the state religion, known as Shinto. At the same time, Buddhism was just one of the currents spreading to Japan from China, so it had to compete with Confucianism and Taoism for acceptance.

Not in This Life

When you look at the differences between Buddhism and native Chinese philosophy, don't lose sight of the similarities. The word *Tao,* meaning "the Way," was used to describe the way of the Buddha as well as Taoism. The Taoist term *wu-wei,* which means "effortless progress" or "growth," was used by early Chinese Buddhists as a word for nirvana.

The Lotus Serves Notice

One of the most influential of all Chinese Buddhists was Chih-k'ai (538–597), the founder of the school of Buddhism known as T'ien T'ai (or Tendai in Japan), which means "heavenly terrace." This is the name of the mountain where Chih-k'ai taught. Chih-k'ai combined the bookish, scholarly, and intellectual aspects of Buddhism with its broad, practical appeal, interpreting Buddhist scriptures in ways that had wide relevance for many people.

T'ien T'ai is based on a Mahayana scripture called *The Good Law of the Lotus Sutra,* or simply the *Lotus Sutra,* a work scholars believe was written in India during the second or third century, though many Buddhists say it was among the last teachings spoken by the Buddha himself. Chih-k'ai regarded the *Lotus Sutra* as the essence of true Buddhism, despite the fact that it is one of the later texts. It was not part of the original tripitaki, or "three baskets," of the Buddha's teachings.

Lotus Lore

The lotus, a kind of water lily from South Asia, is an important religious symbol in both Hinduism and Buddhism. The lotus features many petals and a sweet fragrance. According to a Hindu myth, the world was formed out of a lotus with 1,000 petals that emerged from the navel of the god Vishnu. In its center was seated the god Brahma. Much of the symbolic significance of the South Asian lotus has to do with the fact that the flower rises directly out of the water, blooming on its stem without touching the surface. Just as the lotus is untouched by the water, the enlightened Hindu or Buddhist is supposed to be untouched by the problems of existence. Thus the lotus represents purity.

All for One and One for All

One of Chih-k'ai's major accomplishments was to suggest a way of squaring the *Lotus Sutra* with the other Buddhist teachings that were written before it in a way that maximized the *Lotus Sutra*'s importance. Chih-k'ai said that the Buddha developed and improved his teachings as he went along, gearing them to different audiences. The earlier teachings aren't exactly wrong, but they are only partial approximations of the truth, intended for people who weren't quite ready to understand things as they are. The *Lotus Sutra,* in contrast, is the culmination of all Buddha's teachings and is thus the most important—at least according to Chih-k'ai.

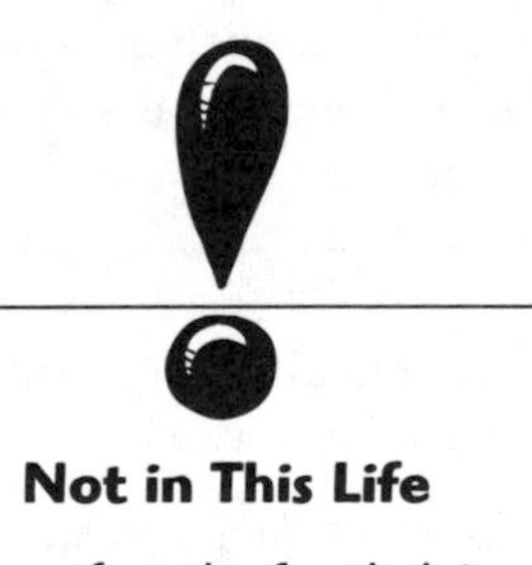

Not in This Life

Don't confuse the South Asian lotus with the kind of lotus mentioned in Homer's *Odyssey.* Homer's lotus is a shrub with edible fruit growing in North Africa. According to Homer, it has an addictive narcotic effect that makes travelers lose the desire to return to their homes.

According to Chih-k'ai's interpretation, the *Lotus Sutra* indicates that all things are intricately, cosmically connected. All beings are necessary parts of the cosmos. Without all the separate parts, the whole wouldn't be the same. The parts are as important to the whole as the whole is to the parts. Just as all beings depend on the cosmos in general for their existence, the cosmos depends on all beings.

This "all-in-one, one-in-all" theory of existence means that all things have Buddha nature. Everything is involved in a cosmic process of purification and improvement. This applies, of course, to people, too. As a result, T'ien T'ai emphasizes universal salvation. Everyone can achieve the goal of nirvana. They are aided in this by all the Buddhas who are filled with compassion for the suffering of living beings. The Buddhas want all creatures to attain Buddhahood. This means they are doing their best to help by listening to the prayers of ordinary people from their Buddha lands.

The *Lotus Sutra* says that those who pray and build shrines and make offerings to the Buddhas will find help in their efforts to attain nirvana. T'ien T'ai followers believed that those who do not offer praise to the Buddhas will be held accountable for their evil deeds and will go to hell to be judged. The idea that worship, rather than meditation, could lead to enlightenment became extremely popular among the common people.

Karma Dogma

Those who worship by folding two hands
Or by raising one hand
Or only by nodding their head
And those who give offerings to images of Buddha,
Even with only a flower,
Will eventually realize an infinity of Buddhas.
They will reach the highest realm.

—The *Lotus Sutra*

The Big Three

T'ien T'ai's all-in-one philosophy is rooted in the *Lotus Sutra*'s Harmonious Three-Fold Truth, which explains existence in terms of the cosmic qualities or attributes known as dharmas. (These are described in Chapter 12, "Flesh on the Bones.") Dharmas underlie all appearances, giving things their shape and nature.

- According to the first part of the Harmonious Three-Fold Truth, dharmas are empty. They have no self-being. This idea is in keeping with the concept of shunyata, the void, from Madhyamika Buddhism.
- The second part of the Three-Fold Truth says that dharmas are temporary. This contradicts Madhyamika Buddhism, which says dharmas are permanent. Because they are temporary, they depend on causation and therefore are empty in and of themselves.
- The third prong of the Three-Fold Truth says that the combination of emptiness and impermanence is in keeping with the Middle Way of the Buddha. (In China, the Middle Way dovetails with the Confucian concept of the Mean, or Medium, which means correct and balanced in a state of equilibrium.) The concept applies to natural and cosmic organization as well as to human thought and behavior.

The Big Ten

Chih-k'ai was interested in combining intellectual and philosophical teachings with meditative discipline. In fact, the *Lotus Sutra* provides some unique concepts for meditation. There are 10 realms, or states of consciousness, each associated with a kind of conscious being and an abode where these beings live. Although these realms are cosmic in nature, they are nonetheless temporary. Here they are

- **Buddhas.** There are many Buddhas in addition to "The Buddha." These are the highest beings in existence, having attained nirvana.
- **Boddhisattvas.** These are blessed beings who have postponed nirvana to help others attain enlightenment.
- **Private buddhas.** These are beings who have attained enlightenment but who do not help others do so as well. They are associated with the "lesser vehicle" of Hinayana Buddhism.
- **Direct disciples.** These are those who have attained enlightenment simply because they heard the Buddha speak in person.
- **Heavenly beings.** These include divine figures assimilated into Buddhism from other religions.
- **Fighting demons.** Legendary beings incorporated into Buddhism.
- **Human beings.** Perhaps you've heard of these creatures already. They're the hardest to pin down!
- **Hungry ghosts.** They lead a searching, dissatisfied, disembodied existence.
- **Beasts.** Dogs, cats, water buffalo, and other critters.
- **The damned.** Inhabitants of hell who are too evil and ignorant to live anywhere nicer.

Not in This Life

Don't assume that the early T'ien T'ai Buddhists imagined the various Buddha worlds existing somewhere in outer space on other planets. Actually, outer space is a fairly recent discovery. In fact, most of the planet Earth was unfamiliar to the early Chinese Buddhists. As a result, boundaries between "this world" and "other worlds" would have been unclear.

The top four of these realms are free from all desire. The lower six are the realms of desire. The lowest three realms are the realms of evil and unclean things.

Worlds Upon Worlds

Interestingly, each of these realms exists as an aspect of all the other realms, thereby subdividing each of them into 10 realms, making 100 realms of consciousness. Each realm of consciousness is further divided into 10 realms of "suchness." The realms of suchness are character, nature, substance, power, activity, causes, conditions, effects, retribution, and ultimate being. This makes 1,000 realms in all. Finally, each of these 1,000 realms is divided into three aspects. These are life, space, and dharma. All told, then, there are 3,000 realms of existence.

Each realm is presupposed and made necessary by all the other realms. Chih-k'ai and his followers believed they could intuit the interconnectedness of all the realms of existence by gaining insight into any single thought or impression. An isolated sound, sight, or event could contain an understanding of the whole universe. Seeing it could serve as a reminder that all things have Buddha-nature and can attain nirvana.

T'ien T'ai spread to Japan, where it became known as Tendai. It was introduced by a Japanese monk named Saicho (767–822) who isolated himself from the world by building a temple on Mount Hiei in Japan where he attracted followers. In time, this Japanese school merged with other strains, including Shinto, nationalism, and esoteric Buddhism.

Land Sakes

T'ien T'ai was not the only strain of Buddhism based on an ancient Indian sutra to take hold in China and spread to Japan. Another is Pure Land Buddhism, which remains today one of the most popular forms of Buddhism in the world. It is based on the *Pure Land Sutra,* written in India during the second century, and it emphasizes the effectiveness of prayer for attaining salvation. Interestingly, the Buddha to whom Pure Land Buddhists pray is not Buddha Shakyamuni, the founder of the religion, but another Buddha, known as Amitabha, or Amita, who vowed as a Boddhisattva to help all good-intentioned people who call on him.

In fact, Amitabha made 48 vows in all. It's vow number 18 that Pure Land Buddhists regard as especially important. This was the vow to lay his own enlightenment on the line for the sake of others. Pure Land Buddhists call this vow the Causal Vow because, in order to fulfill it, he created the Pure Land, where all those who believe in him will be reborn.

Karma Dogma

If, O Blessed One, when I have attained enlightenment, whatever being in other worlds, having a desire for right, and perfect enlightenment, and having heard my name and think on me with favorable intentions, if at the moment of their death, I do not stand before them to keep them from frustration, may I not attain to unexcelled, right, perfect enlightenment.

—Vow 18 of the Boddhisattva Dharmakara

Help from Above

Amitabha means "infinite light." He is also called Amatayus, which means "infinite life." The "light" symbolizes wisdom while the "life" symbolizes compassion. Thus he is thought to embody these qualities. Often, his devotees call him Amita, for short.

Amita wasn't always known as infinite light and infinite life. In fact, he first appears in Buddhist scripture as a Boddhisattva named Dharmakara. (Incidentally, according to scripture, it is Buddha Shakyamuni who tells the world about Amitabha.) While still a Boddhisattva, Dharmakara vowed to share his karmic merit with all other creatures to make it easier for them to attain enlightenment. In other words, he saved up all his good karma, which he stored up over centuries of lifetimes filled with good deeds. Then, instead of simply attaining enlightenment, he used his karma to create the Pure Land, a place for all well-meaning but struggling people who called on him for help.

Lotus Lore

The idea that Buddhas and Boddhisattvas assist ordinary people in attaining enlightenment is often considered a main distinguishing feature between Mahayana and Theravada Buddhism, but this isn't always the case. Sharing karmic merit is not unique to Mahayana Buddhism. In Burma, where Theravada Buddhism is practiced, pagodas are equipped with bells or gongs, which ordinary Buddhists may ring when they have done a good deed. The Burmese say that everyone who hears the gong will share in the good karma produced by the deed.

Buddhism did not start out as a salvation-oriented religion. The original idea was not for devotees to get divine help from a higher being. Gradually, however, salvation became popular in Mahayana Buddhism, especially with the lay Buddhists who didn't have the time or the training to meditate and study scripture as did the monks. Pure Land Buddhists are especially quick to admit that they would have little chance of attaining enlightenment without divine help. They see themselves—and all humanity—as evil and ignorant by nature. In adopting this attitude, Pure Land Buddhism resembles Christianity, which emphasizes the need of the sinner to accept grace.

Pure Land Buddhists believe it isn't necessary for them to meditate or to undergo ascetic discipline because Amitabha did all this for them when he was a Boddhisattva. In fact, Pure Land Buddhists are so dependent on grace that they believe nothing they do will make them enlightened without Amitabha's help. All they have to bring to the party, so to speak, is their faith in Amitabha. But even this faith doesn't come simply from them. It is a gift of grace from Amitabha Buddha.

The long-standing popularity of Pure Land Buddhism is evident from a wealth of art works representing the Pure Land Paradise or the hell to which sinful people go who do not believe in Amitabha Buddha. Pure Land continues to appeal to many Buddhists, especially in Japan, where it is known as *Shin,* in memory of a Japanese Buddhist named Shinran Shonin (1173–1263), who championed the faith. The Japanese also refer to the faith as *nembutsu,* which is short for *Namo Amida Butsu,* or "Praise be to Amida Buddha." This is the prayer that guarantees rebirth in the Pure Land to all who utter it.

Orient Expressions

Namo Amida Butsu, or **nembutsu,** which means "Praise be to Amida Buddha," is the prayer uttered in Japan by Pure Land (Shin) Buddhists who want to be reborn in the Pure Land.

Feeling Your Age

Of course, educated Buddhists knew that salvation as embodied by Pure Land Buddhism wasn't what Buddha Shakyamuni had in mind when he taught how to attain enlightenment. The earliest teachings of the Buddha stress individual effort in attaining enlightenment. Fortunately, however, Buddhists found an idea in the scriptures to explain and justify the new approach.

Mahayana Buddhists believe that the original teachings of the Buddha are the most beneficial, and they also believe that the Buddha's original disciples received the most benefit from them. After that, it's been downhill all the way. The ability of people to understand and obey the Buddha's teaching fades away the further removed in time they are from the Buddha's lifetime. To express this idea, Mahayana Buddhists identify three ages, or historical periods, during which the teachings were more or less understood.

The first age, which began when the Buddha died, is the Age of True Law. At this time, Buddha's followers could understand his teachings clearly. The second age (sources disagree as to the length of each age) is the Age of Reflected Law. This is when Buddhists kept up appearances, but had trouble realizing the Buddha's message. The third age is the Age of Impure Law. This is when no one knew what they were supposed to be doing to attain enlightenment.

The Pure Land Buddhists believed that the Age of Impure Law had come. The original significance of the Buddha's teachings had largely been lost. As a result, the best thing Buddhists could do was to pray for help. Fortunately for them, Amitabha Buddha pledged to help all who called on him. Pure Land Buddhists interpret the

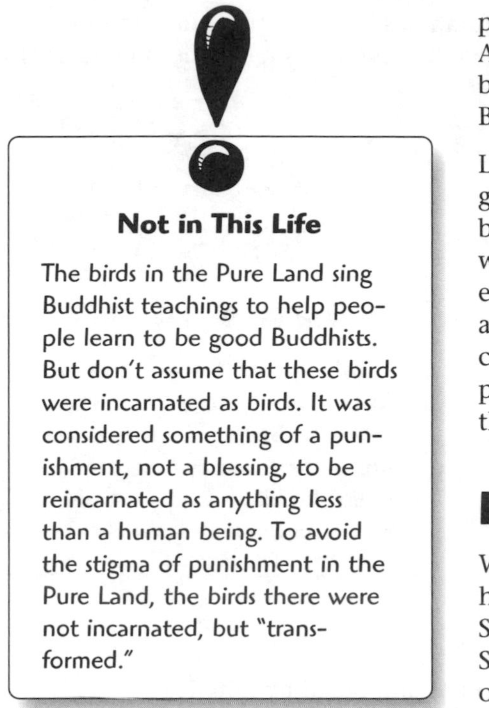

Not in This Life

The birds in the Pure Land sing Buddhist teachings to help people learn to be good Buddhists. But don't assume that these birds were incarnated as birds. It was considered something of a punishment, not a blessing, to be reincarnated as anything less than a human being. To avoid the stigma of punishment in the Pure Land, the birds there were not incarnated, but "transformed."

pledge to mean that all who call the name of Amitabha will not be reborn on Earth after they die, but will live as people in the realm of Amitabha Buddha.

Living in the Pure Land of the Amitabha Buddha is a good thing in itself, since it's a really nice place. The best thing about it though, is that it gives the people who live there a good opportunity to attain enlightenment. It doesn't have any of the evils, deceptions, and temptations that exist on Earth, so it's easier to concentrate on nirvana. Thus the Pure Land is not a permanent heaven, but a sort of halfway house for those on their way out of the cycle of samsara.

Into Shinto

When Buddhism entered Japan in the sixth century, it had to contend with the native religious philosophy, Shinto. The term Shinto means "way of the gods." Shinto gods are known as *kami*. There are thousands of kami, who live on Earth as well as in heaven. The imperial family, as well as the families of the more important Shinto priests, claimed to be descended from the kami. Thus, for centuries, the Japanese emperor was worshiped as divine. The Japanese adopted this belief until the aftermath of World War II. At that time, the emperor was declared officially mortal!

Orient Expressions

Kami are the gods of Shinto, the native religion of Japan.

In general, Shinto has coexisted alongside Buddhism (and Confucianism) throughout much of Japanese history. At times, the Buddhas and Boddhisattvas have been recognized as kami. Traditionally, however, the kami are worshiped as nature gods, and many myths tell of their doings on Earth and in heaven. They are said to dislike disorder, uncleanliness, and insincerity, so, as a result, many Japanese have avoided these shortcomings.

Shinto continues to exert a strong cultural influence in Japan. Shinto prayers to the kami are often said at the dedication of important buildings. Many Japanese families keep revered objects representing the kami in their homes. Shinto is also the name of a distinctive style of Japanese architecture.

The Least You Need to Know

- Despite the practical, worldly character of much Chinese thinking, Buddhism took hold in China and later spread to Japan.
- T'ien T'ai (Tendai in Japanese) Buddhism is based on the *Lotus Sutra* and emphasizes the cosmic interconnectedness of all things and the saving power of the Buddhas.
- Pure Land Buddhism teaches that those who pray to Amitabha Buddha will be reborn in the Pure Land where it will be easier to obtain enlightenment.
- Shinto is a native Japanese religion based on the worship of nature gods called kami.

Chapter 15

Now and Zen

In This Chapter

- Zen Buddhism
- The origins of Zen
- Satori and zazen
- Rinzai and Soto schools
- Zen koans

No other branch of Eastern philosophy has made such a big impact on the West or attained such popularity among Westerners as Zen Buddhism. And, perhaps not surprisingly, Zen is a big thing in the East, too, and has been for over a millennium. Zen has made its spiritual mark on just about every aspect of life from chopping wood to drinking tea to fixing a motorcycle to making war. To say nothing of just sitting still and not thinking!

In addition, Zen has given rise to a rich variety of stories, legends, poems, sermons, and riddles. And, as anyone who ever pays a visit to the local bookstore is well aware, it has also spawned a huge assortment of self-help, how-to, and inspirational books for Western readers. Yet despite all the hoopla, Zen somehow remains too profound for words. Words, formula, and dogma only stand in the way of the essence of Zen.

At the same time, though, words are useful in undoing the mistakes and confusion caused by words. The Zen masters express this idea by pointing out that you can remove a thorn from under your skin by using another thorn. So keep in mind, as you dig into this chapter, that the true meaning of Zen lies somewhere outside anyone's ability to say what it is.

Sitting Pretty

Zen, like other strains of Buddhism, developed in China in response to the teaching of Indian missionaries in the early Middle Ages before spreading to Japan. Zen is the Japanese equivalent of the Chinese "Ch'an," which is based in turn on the Sanskrit word *dhyana,* which is often translated as "meditation" in English. Many Zen types, however, prefer "sitting" as a more accurate translation, since the point of dhyana (or *zazen,* as it is called in Japanese) in Zen Buddhism is often not to *think* (as the term "meditation" implies) but *not* to think.

Orient Expressions

Dhyana is a Sanskrit word often translated as meditation. Early Chinese Buddhists called it Ch'an, and it became the name of an important school of Chinese Buddhism that spread to Japan where the school is called Zen and the dhyana meditation is called **zazen.**

Letting Go

Not thinking is, ironically, a key idea in Zen thought. According to Zen, self-conscious thinking gets in the way of being and doing. Thought—ideas, conceptions—aren't the same as actual existence. Thinking makes misleading distinctions within the flow of reality. It superimposes an extra, unnecessary layer on top of whatever is going on.

Perhaps you've noticed that some things become harder to do when you think about them. You become self-conscious or get wrapped up in your mind. As a result, you get anxious about how you appear to others or you start to second-guess yourself about the best way of proceeding. So, instead of just doing whatever it is in the simplest and most direct way possible, you end up adding unnecessary wrinkles in hopes of compensating for your doubts.

This is the problem that Zen tries to solve. The point is to free yourself of your own thoughts so you can have a more peaceful, harmonious, spontaneous existence. When your own mind doesn't get in the way, you can often act more simply, more naturally, and with greater effectiveness than you can when you are trying too hard, thinking too much, and psyching yourself out.

Karma Dogma

To make Buddha seek himself or to make the mind grasp itself, these are always impossible. We forget that as soon as our thoughts are at peace and all attempts at forming ideas subside, then the Buddha is revealed.

—Huang Po, a Chinese Zen Master

Zig-Zag Zen

The Zen approach of getting past thoughts has been applied to all sorts of activities. The original and most important purpose for Zen is to get past thinking in order to attain enlightenment, or *satori,* as it is called in Japanese (*tun-wu* in Chinese). At the same time, Zen practitioners realize that ideas are often necessary in pointing the direction. This is the value, for instance, of the Buddha's teachings. It's important, however, not to fix on the directions as if they were the goal. How to do something and doing it are very different things.

You might say that Zen is very self-conscious about becoming unself-conscious and very strict about not being too strict. This paradoxical attitude results in ways of thinking and acting that are often difficult to understand. In fact, Zen thinking frequently changes direction, turns on itself, and then appears out of nowhere in an entirely different place. But that's okay. After all, it's only thinking!

Orient Expressions

Satori is the Japanese Zen Buddhist term for enlightenment. This may come as the result of dedicated, disciplined effort, or in a sudden, spontaneous revelation.

Way Back Zen

Zen (or Ch'an) Buddhism is a distinctively Chinese and Japanese approach to Buddhism. In many ways it is similar in character to Taoism, which you can read about in Part 4, "'Way' Cool." Taoism existed in China long before Buddhism came along. Like Zen, much Taoism has to do with the rejection of conventional notions and ways of doing things. Taoists are interested in achieving harmony with nature, and this often involves doing away with human-made notions about what's important.

Zen can be understood as Buddhist Taoism. It reflects the attitude of the Chinese toward the Tao, or "the Way," applied to the Buddhist conception of enlightenment. Even so, Zen has become a distinct, parallel tradition. For one thing, since it is Buddhist, Zen emphasizes the importance of the sangha, or community of monks. It is thus more community-oriented than Taoism, which tends to encourage isolation and detachment. In addition, partly as a result of Zen's concern with individual awareness in a group setting, Zen ideas have been successfully applied to all kinds of activities Taoists don't generally participate in.

And, of course, as a strain of Buddhism, Zen has its own history that sets it apart from Taoism. This history is full of stories, legends, and events that express the teachings of Buddha Shakyamuni of India. In fact, Zen legend says that Zen teachings were not written down in Buddhist scripture but were passed by word of mouth from the Buddha to a special disciple named Kashyapa.

Say It with Flowers

The story goes that, when he first attained enlightenment, Buddha said nothing. He merely held up a flower. All the disciples looked quizzical except Kashyapa, who smiled. The smile indicated to Buddha that Kashyapa understood, and so it was supposedly through him that Zen was transmitted.

Zen teaching was passed along from teacher to disciple for generations until, as legend has it, the twenty-eighth patriarch, an Indian sage named Bodhidharma, brought it to China in 520 C.E. At the time, Buddhism had already reached China, where it gained support from Emperor Wu, himself a devout Buddhist. The legend goes on to tell of the origin of Zen in China in the meeting of Bodhidharma and the Emperor.

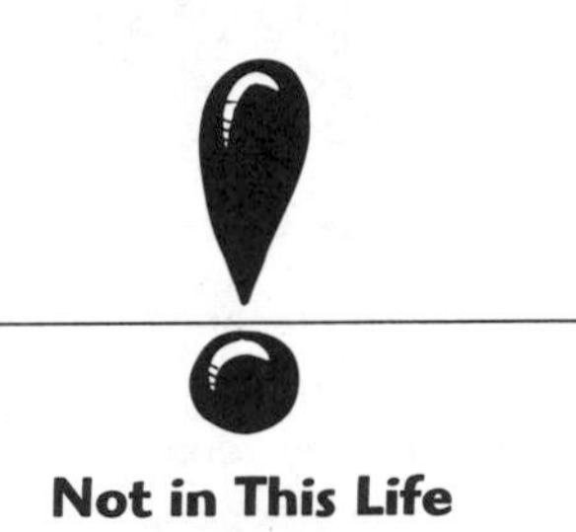

Not in This Life

Don't try to draw any rigid conclusions about the significance of Bodhidharma's mission to China. A famous Zen master, Ma Tsu, was once asked by a Zen monk, "For what purpose did Bodhidharma come to China?" Ma Tsu responded by reminding the monk that it would be appropriate to bow respectfully in the presence of a Zen master. As the monk proceeded to bow, Ma Tsu ran around behind him and kicked him!

Up Against the Wall

Emperor Wu requested an audience with the sage and, in the course of their discussion, told him about what great things he had done for Chinese Buddhism and for his people, such as build shrines and monasteries, roads and water works, and so forth. In keeping with the interest Mahayana Buddhism takes in good works, Emperor Wu asked Bodhidharma what sort of karmic merit he gained as a result of his actions. "No merit at all," was Bodhidharma's reply.

Taken aback, but still wanting to find common ground with the Indian wise man, Wu asked him what, in his opinion, was the essence of the Buddha's teachings. Bodhidharma answered abruptly, "There is no essence. The doctrine is empty." Feeling himself and his religion insulted, Wu asked, "Who are you to stand before me and tell me this?" Bodhidharma answered, "I don't know."

So Bodhidharma, in being true to his beliefs, failed to make a favorable impression on the Chinese Emperor. He traveled north and settled in a monastery where he sat in meditation facing a wall for nine years. (This wall is sometimes said to be a monastery wall, sometimes the wall of a cliff, and sometimes a psychological "wall" blocking out all outside impressions.) This superlative feat of doing nothing attracted followers, and Zen took hold and spread.

Lotus Lore

Zen Buddhists recognize Bodhidharma as the twenty-eighth patriarch of Buddhism and the first patriarch of Zen. His successor, the second Zen patriarch, was the Chinese monk Hui-k'o. According to legend, Hui-k'o remained with Bodhidharma for years and repeatedly asked to be taught. But each time, Bodhidharma refused. At last, in a desperate effort to show his earnestness and sincerity, Hui-k'o cut off his left hand and presented it to Bodhidharma. Swayed at last by this delightful token, Bodhidharma asked what it was Hui-k'o wanted to know. "My mind knows no peace," said Hui-k'o. "Okay," said Bodhidharma, "bring me your mind, and I will make it peaceful." "Well," said Hui-k'o, "the thing is, when I try to find my mind, I'm not sure where to look." "All right then," said Bodhidharma. "Consider it pacified." This brief exchange, sometimes considered the first mondo between a Zen master and his disciple, did the trick for Hui-k'o. He attained enlightenment at that moment.

The Long and Short of It

One way to think about the Zen approach to enlightenment is that, instead of worrying about how to obtain enlightenment and whether you are enlightened, you should simply free yourself of preconceptions and expectations. This freedom from expectations, in fact, *is* enlightenment—or is it?

Freedom may be enlightenment, but only until you say it is—until, in other words, you think you're enlightened. Then the preconceptions kick back in, and you need to free yourself again. In fact, there are various attitudes toward enlightenment within Zen. Some say enlightenment requires years of discipline, including concentrated periods of "sitting." Others say enlightenment can be triggered at any time and in any number of ways, especially by a sudden awareness of how the futility of ideas stands in the way of reality.

These two approaches represent the contrasting attitudes of two prominent schools of Japanese Zen known as the Rinzai and Soto schools. A basic idea common to both schools is that everyone already has a "Buddha nature"—the nature of an enlightened being. The trick is to *realize* it—to understand what this means and to avoid being fooled by all the things you might think it means but doesn't. Soto and Rinzai take different approaches to this process of realizing one's Buddha nature, known as the "short path" and the "long path."

Soto Voce

Rinzai is involved with the so-called short path tradition of attaining enlightenment. By following the short path, it is possible to experience satori, or enlightenment, at any time. In contrast, the Soto school is associated with the long path. Along this path, enlightenment may be attained only by years of self-discipline and meditation, or zazen.

Karma Dogma

Anyone at any time can achieve enlightenment by following the way of the Buddha .... Every person has the capacity to be influenced by Buddha's law. No one should feel he lacks the ability.

—Dogen, the founder of the Soto school of Zen Buddhism

The Soto school was founded in 1227 by Master Dogen (1200–1253). Dogen disagreed with the popular belief that people who lacked the spiritual capacity to study Buddhism and practice meditation could improve their karma by obtaining the blessing of a Boddhisattva or by making offerings or prayers. He believed that the way of the Buddha meant study and meditation for oneself, regardless of one's knowledge or capacity.

As a result, Dogen emphasized zazen as the best way for everyone to pursue enlightenment, especially provided that you meditate not for personal benefit, but to follow the path of the Buddha. He taught that even the sick and the dying should meditate since this would improve their chances of being reborn into Buddhism in a future life.

Dogen looked with disapproval on the methods of the Rinzai school, founded in 1191 by Master Eisei (1141–1215). This school emphasized a particular method of training involving tests and discussions between master and disciple. In Dogen's view, the focus on words missed the point of Buddha's teaching of the emptiness of all things. (Nevertheless, Dogen was himself an accomplished poet who wrote pithy and evocative expressions of the Zen state of mind.) Yet despite Dogen's objections, the Rinzai school flourished and became tremendously influential.

Koan Heads

In the Rinzai school, Zen monks attain enlightenment with help and guidance from their masters. This guidance sometimes takes the form of tests known as *koans* (or *kung-an* in Chinese). These are brief stories, verses, riddles, or question-and-answer sessions intended to train Zen monks to think and act spontaneously. Tied in with the practice of asking and answering koans are question-and-answer exchanges that take place between Zen masters and their disciples. These are called *wen-ta* in Chinese or, in Japanese, *mondo*.

Although koans are meant to be instructive, they do not simply contain a lesson. Instead, they are often paradoxical and even irrational, designed to sharpen the intuition and spontaneity of the person responding to them. The most successful koans trigger the experience of satori—the Zen Buddhist awakening into enlightenment. In addition, they illustrate how Zen thinking works and show how hard it is to pin down. Many koans and mondo anecdotes have been saved up over the years, illustrating how difficult it can be to distinguish between a satori experience, false enlightenment, and just plain confusion.

Orient Expressions

A **koan** is a story, verse, riddle, or question that is traditionally used in Zen to test and train monks. Ideally, a koan produces the experience of satori, or enlightenment, either after it has been contemplated over a period of time or else all of a sudden. The term comes from the Chinese word *kung-an,* which means case. **Mondo** are question-and-answer exchanges between a Zen master and a pupil. Mondo stories are often considered koans since they illustrate the nature of Zen.

You may already be familiar with the most well-known koan, "What is the sound of one hand clapping?" The answer, or response, depends on how you interpret the question. Sometimes the point is to meditate on the koan and attain greater awareness through reflection. Sometimes the point of a koan is to respond in a spontaneous and appropriate fashion, either by answering the question or performing some action that shows you are not confused by it.

Here are some other koans:

> Can you avoid stepping on your shadow?
>
> What is your true nature?
>
> Does a dog have Buddha nature?

The famous answer to this last one, offered by a Zen master of China, is "Wu," or no. The very fact that he gave so definite an answer has made everyone ever since wonder what he really meant—especially since a standard tenet of Mahayana Buddhism is that all things have Buddha nature.

Lotus Lore

The famous koan asking whether dogs have Buddha nature is taken up in the Summer 1999 issue of *Tricycle: The Buddhist Review,* an independent magazine on Buddhism. A variety of writers, from old times as well as the present day, offer their thoughts on this weighty topic. In addition, the cover features a photo of a dog sporting a Chinese Buddhist jacket, taken by world renowned dog photographer William Wegman. Are Buddhists totally hip or what?

Mondo Zen

Originally, koans were intended to trigger satori experience. Gradually, they became a standard feature in the training of Zen monks, with different types or levels intended for different stages of training. While they sometimes serve a specific purpose, they are also a major part of the lore surrounding Zen Buddhism. In fact, all kinds of Zen stories, anecdotes, and poems get referred to as koans, whether or not they are used to test disciples or trigger satori. For example, mondo (wen-ta) exchanges (and stories that get told about them) are often called koans.

Mondo question-and-answering isn't exactly your typical oral exam. Often, the point is not so much to learn Buddhist doctrine as to unlearn it—or, at any rate, to recognize that it's useless to cling to memorized rules and dogma. One famous mondo question asked of a Zen master by his disciple was, "Master, what is the first principle of Buddhism?" The answer was, "If I told you, it would be the second principle!"

In another mondo, a monk asked his master, "How can one become free?" The master responded with a question of his own, "Who has imprisoned you?" The monk then asked, "What is the Pure Land?" (See the previous chapter for a description of Pure Land Buddhism, which sometimes was combined with Zen beliefs.) The master responded, "Who has defiled you?" Then the monk asked, "What is nirvana?" The master came back with, "Who has subjected you to the cycle of birth and death?" (The opposite of nirvana.)

Missing the Pointer, Getting the Point

In addition to administering mondo questions-and-answers and koans, Rinzai masters have been known to practice all manner of unexpected methods to startle their disciples into enlightenment, even hitting or kicking them. One Zen story even tells of a master who cut off the finger of a novice. According to the story, the master was in the habit of raising his finger whenever he made a point in talking to his disciples. When the novice was asked what the master had taught that day, the novice simply raised his finger. Everyone at the monastery got such a big kick out of this that the novice kept it up. Whenever he was asked a question about anything, he would simply raise his finger.

One day, the master saw him do this, grabbed him, and cut off his finger. The novice ran off, but returned a short while later because the experience triggered enlightenment. His finger was a barrier in the way of his ability to understand. Without it, he could understand clearly.

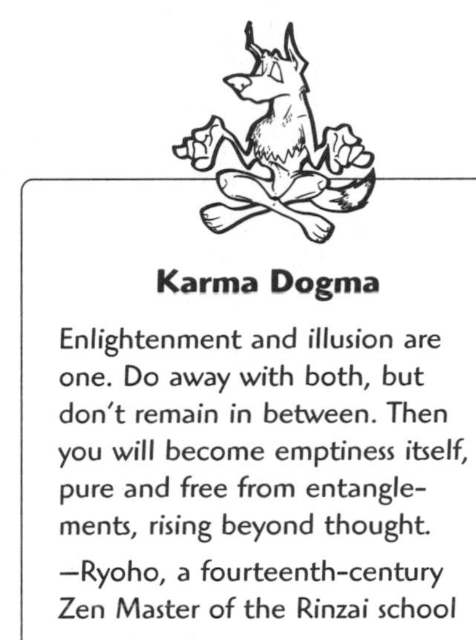

Karma Dogma

Enlightenment and illusion are one. Do away with both, but don't remain in between. Then you will become emptiness itself, pure and free from entanglements, rising beyond thought.

—Ryoho, a fourteenth-century Zen Master of the Rinzai school

Zen koans and mondo exchanges are often intended to help people see beyond their preconceptions about Buddhism. But the point is not simply that all ideas are misleading or pointless. In fact, many koans and mondo exchanges emphasize common sense. For example, a novice named Joshu entered a monastery and said to one of the masters, "I'm new here; please teach me." The master responded by asking, "Have you had breakfast?" Joshu replied that he had. So the master said, "Okay, now wash your bowl." It's not too hard to figure this one out. After eating, do your dishes.

Who, Me?

Knowledge is important, but it's also important to know when and how far to rely on it and to avoid becoming too fixed on any of it. Thoughts, ideas, and conceptions tend to stand in the way of enlightenment, but they can be used to clear the way to enlightenment as well. According to Zen, the existence of an idea also implies the existence of its opposite. If you say you are hot, it's because you're comparing the way you feel to something else, namely the feeling of cold. Heat and cold aren't absolute things, but are relative to one another. There is no hard and fast distinction between them. So it is with all concepts, even the concept of yourself.

Ordinary Miracles

The concept "yourself" implies the existence of its opposite—"not yourself." Where do you draw the distinction? However you define it, the distinction breaks down. The best way to see "yourself" is as a continuous part of a larger reality. Doing this can help you eliminate confusion in your life about how you should act and what you should be doing. Instead of thinking about what you should do and evaluating yourself and your actions, just do what comes naturally. According to the Zen attitude, spontaneous action, without prior expectations, goals, or agendas, often leads to the best results.

People who are into Zen say that, without expectations and preconceptions, life can be experienced as a magical or spiritual process. It becomes easier to appreciate just how miraculous life is when you stop thinking so much about yourself. A famous Zen poem points to this idea by speaking of the ordinary activities, chopping wood and carrying water, as miraculous feats. Obviously, these accomplishments don't exactly feed the ego. You don't say to yourself, "I sure am hot stuff on account of how well I chop wood and carry water!" Instead, the attitude is more like, "Isn't it amazing that these complex tasks can be done so easily without even thinking about them?" Almost automatically, with perfect spontaneity, you can do things like split logs with amazing precision, timing, accuracy, and power.

Zen-Fu

In the Far East, especially in Japan, this idea of spontaneous, intuitive action has carried over into many activities beyond just doing the chores around the monastery. Most notably and surprisingly, it has influenced the thinking of the Japanese warriors known as samurai. Samurai culture of the Middle Ages absorbed many aspects of Zen thinking, including the ideas of spontaneity and getting beyond concern for the self. These ideas are especially useful in fighting, where it is important to act without fear or hesitation and with maximum power and precision.

Lotus Lore

Books that apply Zen philosophy to life have been hugely popular with Western readers. The boom began in 1953 with Eugene Herrigal's *Zen and the Art of Archery,* which quickly became a bestseller and is still popular today. The same can be said for *Zen and the Art of Motorcycle Maintenance* (1974), by Robert Pirsig, an autobiographical novel in which the author's travels with his son trigger profound philosophical reflections. Ever since these two publications, there has been a torrent of "Zen and the Art of ..." books. Just a few of the many available are on golf, windsurfing, fatherhood, eastern cooking, the Internet, stand-up comedy, and casino gambling!

As a result of the influence of Zen on fighting strategy, many highly developed schools of martial arts took root in China and Japan. And from there, of course, "martial arts" has gone on to become a popular subgenre of low-budget action-adventure movies. In some of these movies, if you pay careful attention, you may be able to catch the heroes spouting Zen philosophy as they take out a small platoon of armed Ninjas with their bare hands and feet by doing a double backflip off the chandelier! In any case, you can read more about judo, jiu jitsu, and kung fu, as well as other Zen-influenced activities, in the final part of this book.

Fighting is not the only art form that has been heavily influenced by Zen. In fact, because of its emphasis on spontaneous, intuitive awareness, Zen thinking has inspired a range of artistic works, including poetry and painting. Often these art forms succeed in capturing and conveying the essence of a Zen feeling or insight better than a more thought-out, deliberate explanation could. You can read about Zen in the arts, both in the Far East and in North America, in Part 6, "Living Wisdom."

The Least You Need to Know

- Zen legend says that Zen Buddhism was brought to China by the Indian monk Bodhidharma during the sixth century.
- Zen emphasizes spontaneity and intuition while cautioning against a reliance on conventional ideas and rules.
- Two major Zen schools in Japan are the Soto school, which follows the long path of lifelong meditation, and the Rinzai school, which follows the short path of sudden enlightenment.
- Koans are stories and riddles used in Zen training to test and illuminate monks.
- Zen has influenced many activities in Japan, including martial arts, poetry, and painting.

Part 4
"Way" Cool

Chinese philosophy is cultured, worldly, and elegant, yet at the same time, simple and profound. Of its many branches, perhaps the most simple and most profound is known in China as "the Way"—the Tao. Taoism has helped many generations of Chinese in their efforts to attain a harmonious way of life.

Perhaps to a greater extent than any other philosophy in the world, Taoism succeeds in combining and reconciling practical action and spiritual awareness. It is almost scientific in its observation of the things of the world and almost mystic in its respect for the unseen. Never controlling, yet always powerful, the Tao is the simplest concept in the world and the most difficult to define.

Because Taoism is both practical and inspiring, it has become familiar in the West as the underlying philosophy of a barrage of inspirational "how-to" books on everything from quantum physics to Winnie-the-Pooh. These books show that Taoist thought can be applied in just about any situation, yet they tend to gloss over—or completely ignore—the circumstances of Taoist thought and practice in China.

So here's an account, not only of the ideas, but also of the origin and history of Taoism in China, including explanations of esoteric strands of Taoism that may surprise you. In addition, you can read about how Taoism relates to other important philosophies in China, particularly Confucianism and the Yin-yang School.

Old Masters

In This Chapter

- The first Chinese philosophers
- Chinese versus Indian and Western thought
- Social turmoil and the wane of feudalism
- The Hundred Schools and the Six Schools
- Taoism versus Confucianism

Much Chinese philosophy has caught on in the West because of its focus on harmony (which is something many Westerners feel they could use more of in their hectic, frazzled lives). But this emphasis on harmony did not develop in China under harmonious circumstances. Instead, it originated, together with the first philosophies in ancient China, during difficult times beset with wars and corruption in government.

The golden age of Chinese philosophy was marked by social strife and political upheaval. Early Chinese philosophy responded to these problems with the kind of hardheaded, clear-eyed recommendations for dealing with disaster that set the philosophical tone in China for centuries to come. As a result, Chinese thought has a direct and ongoing relevance to life. And this thought has been a major force in influencing the course of Chinese civilization.

You could say that the ancient Chinese philosophers stepped up to the task of figuring out how human life should be conducted within a great civilization, and Chinese people ever since have listened to them and adopted their ideas. Out of many proliferating philosophical schools, the two major streams of Chinese thought emerged—Confucianism and Taoism—which have combined to shape the lives and attitudes of many generations of Chinese.

Living in the Real World

China is one of the oldest civilizations in the world, and philosophy has long held a prominent place in Chinese culture. From the beginnings of Chinese philosophy around 600 B.C.E. (which is, incidentally, about the time Western philosophy got started in ancient Greece), the Chinese have cultivated wisdom, not simply in order to escape from, or reflect on, life and its challenges, but as a way of dealing with the business of life. Hence philosophy's special importance and practical character in China. These qualities help set it apart from the philosophies of other parts of the world.

Lotus Lore

Organized religion has played a major role in shaping government and politics throughout much of the history of Europe and in India. In both regions, widely held religious doctrines, devout rulers, and powerful priesthoods made religion a crucial aspect of the state through the sixteenth century and beyond. In fact, the separation of church and state did not become a widely accepted ideal in the West until the eighteenth century. In contrast, organized religion has not exerted nearly as strong an influence in the history of China. Instead, the doctrines influencing government and justifying the state have been largely philosophical, with Confucianism supplying the moral direction for leadership.

Ideas with a Difference

Broadly speaking, Chinese philosophy differs from the philosophy of India in focusing more directly on practical worldly matters. Chinese thinking tends to be less concerned about transcendence, timelessness, and absolute existence than Indian thought. Instead, it is more concerned with helping things go smoothly—in minimizing strife, hardship, and worry—by acting in harmony with society and with nature.

At the same time (and again, speaking in general), Chinese philosophy differs from Western thinking in emphasizing society as a whole rather than the individual. Although there is a pronounced practical aspect at work in both Chinese and Western philosophy, Chinese philosophy looks more at group dynamics than at individual power and virtue. Westerners, in contrast, are more individualistic.

As a result, Westerners tend to think about whether they are good or bad, important or insignificant, strong or weak, without considering how they relate to, or fit into their society. They generally see themselves as individuals who are defined from within. They think of themselves—and of all people—as responsible for themselves and their own character and development. In contrast, the Chinese have tended to define themselves in terms of their social roles and their relationships with others. They think more about the importance of the collective than about the individual.

Same Difference

Of course, not all Chinese philosophy is collective and not all Western philosophy is individualistic. Chinese Taoism, for example, even while focusing on collective harmony, recognizes the value of individual expression and the uniqueness of each person's particular nature. And Marxism, to take a Western example, focuses on the importance of collective action and well-being.

Yet, in some ways, these exceptions prove the rule of the difference between Western and Chinese thinking. Taoism has become extremely popular in the West, perhaps because it provides Westerners with a new way to think about and express their individuality. Meanwhile, Marxism was adopted in China, no doubt in part, because it provides a modern approach to collective thinking.

Karma Dogma

Classes, state power, and political parties will die out naturally and humanity will enter the era of the Great Harmony.

—Mao Tse-tung, the first Chairman of China's Communist Party, adapting Marxist philosophy to traditional Chinese thinking

Getting Wise to the Times

Chinese culture had already developed to an advanced stage before philosophy got started. There was writing, religion, codes of honor, metal works, highly developed agricultural techniques, and domesticated animals, including the horse. There was an elaborate feudal system of government and economics in which the peasants grew crops and made things, and the rulers kept the peasants in line. But still no philosophy. At least not until times of acute social upheaval when the old feudal order was challenged.

At that time—again, around 600 B.C.E.—the leaders and officials of the many Chinese city states began to wonder what to do. Some hearkened back to the "good old days" of legend when wise benevolent emperors brought the gifts of civilization to the grateful masses. Others abandoned the old ways and instituted drastic new measures to secure power at any price. Still others adopted policies based on caution, flexibility and gentleness in hopes of restoring peace. Lots of people had ideas about what should be done. Many were former officials who had lost their places in government. Others were educated as ministers and were seeking positions from wise rulers who were ready to listen to them.

Lotus Lore

An anecdote about the Duke of Sung illustrates the impracticality of the outmoded code of honor of the Chinese nobility during feudal times. In 650 B.C.E. the Duke's soldiers were poised to attack an invading army. The Duke's subordinates urged him to take action while the enemy was crossing a river and would be hampered in defending itself. But the Duke refused, saying it was dishonorable to attack a foe who was not prepared. So the Duke's forces waited until the enemy was safely across the river and was fully mustered and ready for battle on the other side. The enemy promptly crushed the Duke and his army.

Troubled Waters

This era of political instability and the proliferation of philosophical ideas began during what was known as the "Spring and Autumn" period, named for a historical document on events of the time called the *Spring and Autumn Annals*. This was the time of Confucius, the most influential Chinese philosopher of all time. It was a difficult, tumultuous period that followed in the wake of an era of stability and was followed by even more turbulent times.

Chinese history is full of ups and downs, yet Chinese civilization has been remarkably resilient. Prior to the series of revolutions in the twentieth century, culminating in the rise of Communism, Chinese government consisted of a succession of imperial dynasties stretching back into legendary times.

Dynasty: The Series

Here's a list of dynasties and other important periods and events in the history of ancient China leading up to the rise and spread of Chinese philosophy:

- **The Hsia Dynasty** (pre–1500 B.C.E.). This dynasty is legendary. Only scant archeological evidence for its existence has been found.
- **The Shang Dynasty** (1550–1027 B.C.E.). An advanced material culture that introduced the spoked wheel and the domesticated horse.
- **The Chou Dynasty** (1027–256 B.C.E.). A culture with highly developed ritual and moral codes admired by Confucius. This was the height of the feudal system in China.
- **Period of the Spring and Summer Annals** (722–487 B.C.E.). Time late in the Chou Dynasty when the feudal system was deteriorating, and new, larger states came to power through military force. This is the time of Confucius and the dawn of Chinese philosophy.
- **The Warring States Period** (480–221 B.C.E.). A time of widespread warfare among Chinese states and the downfall of the Chou Dynasty. Many new rulers and would-be rulers arose. Often these new rulers were interested in hearing philosophical advice.
- **The Ch'in Dynasty** (221–207 B.C.E.). This dynasty's founder, the Duke of Ch'in, augmented his power by instituting totalitarian measures on his subjects, forcing them to contribute heavily to his war effort. In this way, he unified China (which takes its name from Ch'in). The Duke of Ch'in called himself Ch'in Shih-huang, the first Emperor of China. He replaced feudal government with a provincial system in which ministers in the provinces were responsible to the central authorities. To consolidate his power, he ordered the construction of the Great Wall, as well as the infamous burning of the books.
- **The Burning of the Books** (213 B.C.E.). By decree of Ch'in Shih-huang, all books except those on agriculture, medicine, and divination were burned. This was an attempt to eradicate the vestiges of Chou culture that dominated China prior to the Ch'in. As a result, many books on philosophy from the height of China's philosophical period were destroyed. Fortunately, a number of books were preserved in secret by scholars willing to risk severe punishment. Even so, records of the philosophy of ancient China are sketchy, thanks to Emperor Ch'in.

Actually, the Dynastic Chinese didn't refer to their country as "China," but as *Chung-kuo,* which means Middle Kingdom. This name indicates that the Chinese saw themselves in the middle, surrounded by "barbarian" peoples on all sides. Since ancient times, the Chinese regarded their own culture as the only civilization on the planet. The eventual arrival of traders and missionaries from Europe didn't make them rush to change their minds!

Boys Named Tzu

Thus China's golden age of philosophy was actually something of a mess, politically speaking. Philosophers proliferated, as men who lost careers in public office attempted to sort out the growing problems of statecraft. A few of these became well known for their wisdom and came to be called by the informal but honorary title, *Tzu,* which means master. Some of the best known Tzu's are Kung Fu Tzu (known in the West by the Latinized name, Confucius), Lao Tzu, Chuang Tzu, Meng Tzu (better known in the West as Mencius), Mo Tzu, and Hsun Tzu.

Orient Expressions

Tzu is an honorary title applied to many famous Chinese philosophers, including Kung Fu Tzu, the philosopher whose name has been Latinized as Confucius.

Advisors for Hire

Burning questions addressed by these philosophers included whether the ancient rituals were still important, when and how to use force in governing, whether it was better to be loved or feared as a ruler, and even whether it was possible for an individual to exert a positive influence on society. Most of these ideas respond in some way to the social upheavals that were taking place, and were aimed at making the troubled political situation more stable.

Lotus Lore

The noted scholar and historian Liu Hsin (46 B.C.E.–23 C.E.) advanced a theory about the origin of the many schools of philosophy in ancient China: He said that it was once part of an official's job to pass his knowledge along to his successor. Thus, there was no difference between teachers and officials, hence there was no need for philosophers. When the Chou Dynasty fell, many officials were thrown out of their posts. These ex-government officials became private teachers in order to spread their knowledge. Liu Hsin goes so far as to link various philosophical schools with the governmental departments that supposedly gave rise to them. Liu Hsin's idea is intriguing but probably inaccurate.

Many philosophical teachers and scholars began traveling around in search of government posts or of followers who would help spread their teachings. That time is sometimes referred to as "the period of the hundred schools." If there ever were this many philosophies in ancient China, any record of most of them has disappeared. Who knows how much ancient Chinese philosophy was lost in the burning of the books!

The historian Ssu-ma Ch'ien (145–86 B.C.E.) lumps the hundred schools into six larger schools. Some of these, as you'll see, are more important than others. Not all six have much relevance today, but Ssu-ma's classification shows the range of ancient Chinese thought, including philosophies that continue to shape the way people live.

Karma Dogma

In the world, there is one purpose, but there are a hundred ideas about it. There is a single goal, but the paths toward it are various.

—The "Great Appendix" of the *I Ching*

Ancient Curriculum

Here are the six schools as Ssu-ma describes them. All of them emerged before 200 B.C.E. and the rise of the Ch'in Dynasty.

- **The Yin-yang School.** This school gets its name from the universal principles, yin and yang, which are said to be aspects of all things. The school emphasizes cosmology, the form and workings of the cosmos. Yin-yang philosophers studied the motions of the stars and the changing of the seasons, among other natural phenomena.
- **The School of Literati, or Scholars.** This is another term for Confucianism, the philosophy founded by Confucius, who believed in the value of studying the classic literature written during the Chou Dynasty. Confucianism, of course, evolved far beyond its focus on scholarship to become the most important and influential philosophy in China's long history.
- **The Mohist School.** This school was founded by the sage Mo Tzu, who advocated universal love and happiness, and prosperity for the lower classes. He was an influential rival of Confucius in his day, but many of his ideas later became absorbed into Confucianism.
- **The School of Names.** A group of logicians who liked paradoxical ideas and debating about abstract concerns. They focused on "names" as opposed to actual things.
- **The Legalists.** These philosophers believed that the best way to govern was by imposing and enforcing strict laws. They held that human nature is inherently

bad, so that people will only do right when they are forced to. This view opposes the ideas of the other Chinese political philosophies, including Confucianism, Mohism, and Taoism.

- **The Taoists.** These philosophers advocated avoiding conflict and controversy by acting in harmony with nature and the circumstances at hand. Taoism went on to become one of China's most important philosophies.

Lotus Lore

Ssu-ma Ch'ien is remembered in China not only for writing historical records of great importance to Chinese historians, but for courageously defending a devoted Imperial Cavalry Commander named Li Ling who, after battling the Huns for days on end, ran out of food and supplies and finally surrendered to save his men. Emperor Han Wu-ti regarded surrender unacceptable and, as punishment, had Li Ling's wife and children put to death. Ssu-ma Ch'ien reacted in a public appeal to the Emperor praising Li Ling for his honor, devotion, and prudence. Han Wu-ti was displeased and had Ssu-ma arrested and tried for insubordination. The famous historian was found guilty and punished with castration!

To these six schools mentioned we can add the school of strategy, epitomized by General Sun Tzu, the author of the *Art of War*. This work provides advice on how to fight, how to lead soldiers, and how to deal with the enemy. In addition to being an influence on the development of martial arts in China and Japan, it was also studied by many of China's leaders, including Mao Tse-tung.

Two Left Standing

Of all these schools, the two most important are the Scholars (Confucianism) and Taoism. To the extent that the other schools didn't disappear entirely, they became largely absorbed by one of these two main philosophies. Thus, although the early Confucians abhorred the attitude of the Legalists, Confucianism became so entrenched that many Legalist-type Confucians emerged—wily and selfish, in contrast to the kinder, more benevolent Confucians.

In fact, Confucianism came to dominate all Chinese political philosophy up until the twentieth century. Throughout the history of dynastic China, Confucian ideals were incorporated into the official imperial system for selecting ministers, who were expected to be well-versed in the ancient classics and prepared to implement policy in the spirit of Confucian leadership.

The major alternative to Confucian philosophy throughout most of China's history is Taoism, which emphasizes solitude and private contemplation, as opposed to the Confucian ideals of study and active leadership. It has been said that, in dynastic China, everyone was a Confucian during times of public success and a Taoist in times of failure and during retirement. Yet, despite its emphasis on quiet living, the Taoist philosophy has a lot to say about how to act effectively. In fact, it has much in common with the philosophy of Sun Tzu, whose *Art of War* applies the concept of the Tao to military situations.

Lotus Lore

The Tao, like Zen, has inspired a flood of inspirational, educational, and practical guidebooks for Western readers. Among the most well-known are the best-selling *The Tao of Physics* (1976) by Fritjof Capra and *The Tao of Pooh* (1983) by Benjamin Hoff. Scores of other books apply Taoist thinking to such subjects as cooking, sex, parenting, pet care, business management, financial investment, sports, law, physical and mental health, art, religion, and everyday life.

Taoism in China is so flexible, in fact, that it has thrived and spread under the name of an imported religious sect, namely Buddhism. As you may remember from the chapter on Zen, this school (called Ch'an Buddhism in China, Zen in Japan) developed when Buddhism arrived in China and merged with Taoism. Thus Zen and Taoism have much in common. You could see Zen as an aspect of Taoism, or Tao as an aspect of Zen.

Sorting the Systems

In a way, the "hundred schools" of ancient China can be boiled down into just six or seven and then further reduced to only two—the official philosophy of Confucianism and the private philosophy of Taoism. Yet within these two main strands are many divergent and coalescing threads. What's more, as you may have guessed, Confucianism and Taoism aren't totally separate. Although, traditionally, Confucians and

Taoists have often been critical of one another, the two philosophies were largely reconciled in the life and thinking of Dynastic China. They represented alternative aims, values, and lifestyles. Confusians and Taoists often aired disagreements that reflected opposing attitudes toward society and nature. To the Confucians, society was of paramount importance, while to the Taoists, nature was more significant.

Yet both philosophies emphasize harmony as a major aim of thought and action. Confucians sought to cultivate harmony within the social order while the Taoists attempted to live in harmony with natural processes. This focus on harmony isn't surprising when you consider what a mess things were when these two philosophies got their start. As rulers of the various Chinese states became embroiled in conflict during the Spring and Autumn and Warring States periods, the old codes of honor in governing and in warfare were abandoned. Martial law and totalitarianism became increasingly common. Confucians and Taoists alike complained of widespread corruption in government.

Karma Dogma

The whole world is a rising torrent. Who can change it? As for you, rather than follow a gentleman who runs from one prince to another, shouldn't you instead follow a man who flees the world entirely?

—Words of a hermit to a disciple of Confucius, from the Confucian *Analects,* 18:6

Hide or Seek

Disagreements between the two philosophies arose over the best way to respond to the crisis. The Confucians felt it was the duty of members of the educated class to seek office as ministers of state and try to exert a positive influence on the troubled situation. The Taoists, in contrast, felt that getting involved in state affairs would only make matters worse. They believed there was nothing to be done to improve the situation but wait until the trouble subsided on its own. So, while Confucians traveled around China looking for government jobs that would enable them to apply their principles, Taoists retreated to the countryside to become hermits.

In fact, Confucius himself spent many years in search of a government position under a virtuous ruler. As he traveled around, he came into contact with Taoist hermits who made fun of him for trying to change things. He responded by saying that any other course besides seeking office would involve ignoring his duty.

Enter the Dragon

Legend tells of an encounter between Confucius as a young man and the Taoist sage, Lao Tzu, who is credited with writing the founding work of Taoism, the *Tao Te Ching* (the *Book of the Way and Its Power*). Confucius approached the elderly sage and started a discussion about the Confucian ideals of benevolence and righteousness. Lao Tzu responded by asking, "Why expend so much energy carrying a big drum in search of the son you have lost?"

Lao Tzu's words are cryptic and mysterious, in keeping with his reputation for thinking on a different level from most ordinary people. The point of his question could be to suggest that, in making a big deal about benevolence and righteousness, Confucius was actually looking for something that was lost. Lao Tzu was saying, in other words, that if Confucius actually were righteous and benevolent, he wouldn't need to go around talking about these qualities.

Lao Tzu went on to criticize Confucius for attempting to change people from their natural ways by speaking of praiseworthy ideals. He suggested that it was all just a lot of grand talk vainly attempting to compensate for the fact that natural human goodness had disappeared. He compared the position of Confucius and his followers to that of fish in a dried-up pond, trying to keep each other wet by gasping. Human beings in organized society, in other words, are like fish out of water. The wise thing to do under the circumstances, Lao Tzu concluded, would be to leave off the talk and avoid society altogether.

The meeting with Lao Tzu is said to have left Confucius speechless for three days afterward. Finally, he compared Lao Tzu to a dragon—mysterious and powerful. And he admitted that he had nothing to say in his own defense.

Karma Dogma

It is wrong to refuse to take office. If the relationship that binds a father and son together may not be set aside, who can set aside the relationship between a ruler and his ministers? ... The reason the gentleman tries to get a place in office is that he believes this is right, even though he may be aware that his principles will not succeed.

—Words of a disciple of Confucius to a hermit

Meeting of the Ways

Lao Tzu's criticism of Confucius was not the last word in the disagreement between Confucianism and Taoism. Years later, the Confucian Hsun Tzu accused the Taoists of being "blinded by nature and without knowledge of humanity." Mencius, another important Confucian, criticized the Taoist sage Yang Chu by saying that Yang wouldn't pluck out a single hair from his head to save the world. In other words, he was selfish and irresponsible and wouldn't lift a finger to help others.

Despite periodic sniping on both sides, Confucianism and Taoism have coexisted in China for centuries, with many Chinese accepting the basic tenets of both. Throughout the Dynastic period, many Taoists regarded Confucius as a great sage, while many Confucians adopted Taoist principles. Elements of both philosophies continue to influence Chinese thought today.

The Least You Need to Know

- In general, Chinese philosophy is more worldly and practical than Indian philosophy and more collectively oriented than Western philosophy.
- Chinese philosophy originated during a turbulent period in Chinese history as feudalism gave way to a large, centrally controlled empire between around 600 and 200 B.C.E.
- Many of China's first philosophers may have been former public officials forced out of work by political turmoil.
- Taoism and Confucianism emerged as the two major strains of Chinese philosophy.
- Early Taoists tended to avoid society, while the Confucians sought employment as ministers of state.

Tao or Never

Taoism has long-ago, faraway origins that are shrouded in mystery. The Tao itself is a mysterious principle, often said to be indefinable and incomprehensible. Yet despite its legendary beginnings and mystic suppositions, Taoism manages to convey down-to-earth common sense and an ability to grasp the big picture. The Tao runs through everything, including nature, the human psyche, and politics.

Taoism is an all-encompassing philosophy, providing a point of view on just about everything. There are many strains of Taoism. Among its most important thrusts is its philosophy of nature. Many see nature as the heart of Taoism since it provides the best model for how the Tao, or "the Way" works. By looking at how the Tao works in nature, the Taoist sage brings his own actions into harmony with the Tao.

The Taoist philosophy of nature has features in common with Western science and, at the same time, with religion. Like science, it is based on the observation of impersonal principles. Yet unlike science, Taoist principles are not primarily concerned with the material things nature is made of. Like religion, Taoism recognizes an unseen power that directs the course of natural things. Yet this power does not care how people behave. This power, the Tao, is to be observed and imitated, but need not be worshiped.

Tapping the Source

Taoism has been a major strand of Chinese philosophy for as long (or almost as long) as Chinese philosophy has been around. Actually, it may be more accurate to say that Taoism consists of several strands. It is a philosophy of nature, of human behavior, and of physical and psychological health. It is also a mystic religion whose lore includes mythic beings and imaginary places. Different kinds of Taoist ideas have been embraced by philosophers, priests, magicians, rulers, artists, hermits, and practically everyone else in China. This chapter focuses on the natural Tao observed and described by ancient Chinese philosophers, together with background on how this concept got started.

Orient Expressions

The **Tao** is a Chinese term usually translated as "the way." It includes the way of heaven, of nature, and of humanity.

Since the Tao is all-encompassing, it includes natural process, reason, truth, goodness, or even, in some views, God. Incidentally, Taoism isn't the only Chinese philosophy that recognizes the concept of the Tao. Confucianism refers to it as well, putting a slightly different spin on the idea.

A Way Out

Scholars disagree about how Taoism got started. According to legend, it was founded by the sage Lao Tzu around 600 B.C.E. The story goes that Lao Tzu's mother became pregnant with him just by watching a falling star. (You'd think they'd invent special glasses to prevent this sort of thing from happening!) As if this weren't unusual enough, she carried the future philosopher in her womb for over sixty years before giving birth. By the time he was born, Lao Tzu knew how to talk and had white hair. In fact, the word Lao means "the old boy."

The ancient Chinese historian Ssu-ma Ch'ien says that Lao Tzu was also known as Lao Tan, who served under the emperor as a court record keeper. Times were hard in those days—the years leading up to the infamous "warring states period" from 403–221 B.C.E. China was divided into many city states, which maintained power by making war on one another. This, of course, made everyone's life miserable. Even those who were not directly involved in the fighting suffered. Farmers and merchants were heavily taxed to support the army while rulers and governing officials lived in constant fear of conspiracy, intrigue, and revolt.

Everywhere he looked, Lao Tzu saw people making things worse through foolish and selfish behavior. In a vain attempt to make things better for themselves, it seemed that everyone was fanning the flames of conflict. Eventually he became so disgusted with society that he simply took off by himself and was never heard from again. By this time, as legend has it, he was about 160 years old.

Fortunately for the future of Taoism, Lao Tzu's route out of the emperor's realms and on to his new life as a hermit took him through the Han-Ku pass. The keeper of the pass was a man named Yin Hsi, who happened to be skilled in predicting the future by reading natural events. Thus he knew that a great sage would be passing through and recognized Lao Tzu as the man he expected. Yin Hsi asked Lao Tzu to write a book telling everything he knew before leaving society. And Lao Tzu complied by writing one of the most famous books of philosophy ever written, the *Tao Te Ching*.

Tao in Print

The title, *Tao Te Ching* (usually pronounced *dow duh jing*) literally means "Way Power Book" or, as we would say in English, "The Book of the Way and Its Power." This classic has been well-known in China for many centuries and has been widely read in the West as well. In fact, it has been translated into English dozens of times—more times than any other Chinese book. Its popularity stems in part from its probing philosophical insights.

It is sometimes referred to as "the book of 5,000 characters" since this is the number of characters (pictographs used in Chinese writing) used to write it.

Lotus Lore

There are two widely used systems for "Romanizing" Chinese writing today—the Wade-Giles and the Pinyin systems. This book uses the Wade-Giles system, which is older and has been repeatedly revised along the way. This system makes use of apostrophes (') to indicate hard consonants. Thus "ch'in" is pronounced like the place below your lips while "chin" is pronounced like the stuff they put in martinis. The Pinyin system is based on the method used for Romanizing the Russian Cyrillic alphabet. It uses "zh," for a sound somewhere between the North American *r* and *j*, and "x" for a sound that is close to *sh*.

So Lao Tzu went off by himself, leaving his wisdom behind him. Some Taoists say that he never died, but achieved immortality. He has been worshiped as a God by certain religious Taoists, even though this kind of piety is inconsistent with the Taoist philosophy of nature. But then again, there are several different—and conflicting—interpretations of Lao Tzu's ideas, since different groups in China have adopted and emphasized different aspects of the teachings of the *Tao Te Ching*.

In recent years, scholars have expressed doubts about whether Lao Tzu wrote the *Tao Te Ching*—and even whether he actually existed. They also disagree about when the book was written. Many believe the *Tao Te Ching* is a compilation of wise sayings by several different people. And there's a growing consensus that it was written for the first time around 250 B.C.E., some three and a half centuries later than Lao Tzu is supposed to have lived.

In any case, all the various opinions about the origin of Taoism are little more than educated guesses. There are few historical facts about the subject, so no one can say for certain what its origin was. Yet, despite the controversy over who wrote the *Tao Te Ching* and when it was written, no one disagrees about its importance as the foundational book of one of the most widely cherished of the world's philosophies.

A Fork in the Way

The *Tao Te Ching* is an important book within two very different strains of Taoism known in China as *Tao Chia* (contemplative, or philosophical Taoism) and *Tao Chiao* (magic, or religious, Taoism). It appears that Tao Chia was the original form of Taoism, and that Taoism acquired occult ideas from other sources later on.

Orient Expressions

Tao Chia is contemplative, or philosophical, Taoism, studied and practiced as a down-to-earth yet mystic way of life. **Tao Chiao** is magic, or religious, Taoism, practiced in hopes of attaining immortality and divine blessing.

Sages Versus Priests

The philosophical strain, Tao Chia, talks about the Tao in terms of nature and the human condition. Although the Tao is a mystery, it reveals itself in understandable ways. By observing these ways, we can figure out how to act and think about life. In this philosophical sense, the Tao isn't divine or magical, so there's no particular reason to worship it.

Tao Chiao sees the Tao as a divine force. Religious Taoists have believed that by tapping into this force it is possible to obtain special powers, most notably immortality. You can read about religious Taoism in more detail in Chapter 19, "Tao and Forever," but for now, the point is that religious Taoists have looked to Lao Tzu and other philosophical Taoist writings in formulating their beliefs. Philosophical Taoists, however, do not look for divine or magic significance in the Tao Te Ching.

Sage List

The *Tao Te Ching* is often looked at as the heart and soul of philosophical Taoism, but it is just one of several important Taoist writings produced during the early years. And Lao Tzu is just one of several famous Taoist sages. Here's a list of the biggest names in early philosophical Taoism, together with the writings associated with them:

- **Lao Tzu.** The legendary founder of Taoism supposed to have written the *Tao Te Ching* around 600 B.C.E. Scholars say, however, that the book may have been written by several authors as late as 250 B.C.E. (Incidentally, the *Tao Te Ching* is also known as the *Lao-tzu*. Similarly, other Taoist books are named for the sages who supposedly wrote them.)
- **Yang Chu.** A Taoist recluse who probably lived around 350 or 400 B.C.E. He is thought to have been pessimistic and fatalistic, with an "every man for himself" attitude. He shunned society and ridiculed attempts to improve things through active involvement. His views became associated with hedonism, the philosophy of doing whatever the heck you feel like. He is not known to have written anything, but his philosophy is described in the Taoist writings of Lieh Tzu.
- **Chuang Tzu.** A sage who lived from 369 to 286 B.C.E., he wrote *Chuang-tzu,* which is a favorite Taoist text among intellectuals who enjoy its rich imaginative qualities. The *Chuang-tzu* is generally more concerned with spiritual matters and less concerned with political affairs than the *Tao Te Ching*.
- **Lieh Tzu.** Still another sagely author of a Taoist text called the *Lieh-tzu,* written around 300 B.C.E. This work is more accepting of Confucian philosophy than other Taoist works.

Lotus Lore

Chuang Tzu (369–286 B.C.E.), the Taoist sage who wrote an important book on Taoism, is perhaps best known outside of China for his famous "butterfly" brain teaser. He says that he once dreamed he was a butterfly. While he was dreaming, he thought he actually was a butterfly and had no idea that he, Chuang Tzu, existed at all. Then he woke up and realized who he was. But then he had to wonder: Maybe he is really, after all, a butterfly dreaming he is Chuang Tzu!

Book of Mysteries

The *Tao Te Ching* is well worth reading and thinking about, but it isn't exactly easy to understand. This is partly because ancient Chinese is a tricky language that often presents ideas in an ambiguous way. In addition, Lao Tzu's style (assuming Lao Tzu is the one who wrote it) is often vague. He tends not to go into a lot of detail to explain what he means. He'll say something and abruptly go on to something else, leaving you to figure out for yourself what, if anything, the two have to do with each other.

Karma Dogma

The Tao is bottomless
Like the source of all things.
It blunts edges that are sharp.
It unties tangled things.
It softens all lights.
It unites the world into a whole.
It is like dark, deep water that
exists forever.

—The *Tao Te Ching*, section 4

Naming the Unnamable

It isn't simply that Lao Tzu's style lacks clarity; it makes the *Tao Te Ching* poetic as well as philosophical, expressing meaning on many levels at once. Parts of the book that seem to be about physical health can also be interpreted as statements about good moral behavior. When it seems to be talking about nature, it could also be interpreted to be about human interaction. In fact, the multilayered significance of the *Tao Te Ching* is in keeping with the concept of the Tao.

The *Tao Te Ching* says right off the bat that "the Tao that can be spoken of is not the true Tao." The true Tao is an unknowable mystery. And even if you're sagely enough, like Lao Tzu, to have a sense of what it is, you still can't pin it down with words. Lao Tzu goes on to describe it as a principle of nonbeing that gives rise to all things. It is empty in itself, but it nurtures the universe—not because it cares for things in a personal way; it doesn't. The Tao, according to Lao Tzu, is not filled with love like God, but is neutral toward created things. Yet the Tao enables things to exist and regulates them in a harmonious way.

The Way, in a Way

Because the Tao can't be defined literally, Lao Tzu uses a number of metaphors to convey a rough idea of it.

- It is like the hollow space inside the hub of a wheel. This hollow space allows the wheel to turn on its axle and can thus be seen as the source of its power. Yet it is empty in itself.
- It is like the hollow shape of a bowl or cup, which, because it is empty, can contain things.

- It is like a bellows (a sort of collapsible box used by blacksmiths that blows air for heating fire). It is empty yet inexhaustible. In fact, because it is empty, it can never be depleted.
- It is like water which makes no resistance. If you throw something at it, the object passes right through. If you put something in its path, it simply passes around it. Yet it is capable of wearing away even the hardest rock. And it is unstoppable.
- It is also a "mysterious female force." The *Tao Te Ching* associates the female with giving birth and with passivity. Thus the Tao is fertile and nurturing yet it is not directly controlling.

To Be or Not to Be

Lao Tzu associates the Tao with "nonbeing." Chuang Tzu, however, implies that it is a substance that exists inside all things. Both agree that it produces things and enables them to exist. The Tao is thus a philosophy that developed from observing nature. This is what gives it its down-to-earth, practical quality. Yet it is obviously very different from Western science, which is also based on observations of nature. The difference is that while Western science is interested in learning about nature in order to control it, Taoism is interested in learning about nature in order to adapt to it.

Taoism sees nature as a harmonious balance. This balance in nature makes life possible, but, of course, the balance involves death. Just as without death there could be no life, so without weakness, there could be no strength; without sickness, there could be no health. The Tao is responsible for both sides of the balance. Recognizing this balance helps you adapt to it, so you waste less effort working against natural processes.

Tao Fu

The Tao never changes, but manifests itself through the natural world as constant change. Things can only change so far before they balance themselves out. Taoists understand natural balance in terms of the concept of *fu,* or return. Fu is the return of all things from a state of extremes to a state of balance. As a famous maxim from the *Tao Te Ching* puts it, "reversal is the movement of the Tao."

Orient Expressions

Fu, a Chinese word for return, is the Taoist principle of balance or equilibrium. All extremes return to a state of balance with their opposites.

Fu is a natural process, but it can also be applied to human fortunes. Fu means that no one's life is simply good or simply bad, but involves many combinations of the two. You can't have one without the other. If things are going badly for you, the good news is that they are bound to improve because things are constantly changing. If you suffer misfortune, the next logical change that will take place is that something fortunate will happen. If something lucky happens to you, it only makes sense that something unlucky will happen. It all balances out.

The Good with the Bad

Taoists tell a story illustrating the concept of fu in human affairs. There was a Taoist farmer whose horse ran away. This was bad news since the horse was valuable and also necessary for running the farm. The farmer's neighbor heard about his bad luck and said, "Gee, that's too bad." The farmer merely shrugged and took it in stride.

The next day the horse came back, bringing with it a wild horse it had befriended in its absence. The farmer's neighbor couldn't believe the farmer's good luck and said, "Wow, two horses! How about that!" The farmer merely shrugged again and acted like it was no big deal.

The next day, the farmer's son tried to put a saddle on the new horse. The horse wheeled around and kicked him in the leg, breaking a bone. A doctor came to set the broken leg and said it would take months to heal. Again the neighbor came to offer his sympathies. Again the farmer was unconcerned.

The next day, army officials came to the farmer's house looking for young men to draft into the emperor's army to fight a war that was a big bloody mistake. Most thought it was not only unjust, but futile. Tens of thousands of soldiers were being killed or wounded. The army officers were about to collar the farmer's son and drag him off to the war until they noticed his broken leg. "Can't fight like that," they said and went on their way. The neighbor, who happened to be there at the time, said, "Wow, your son sure picked a good time to break his leg." The farmer, of course, shrugged.

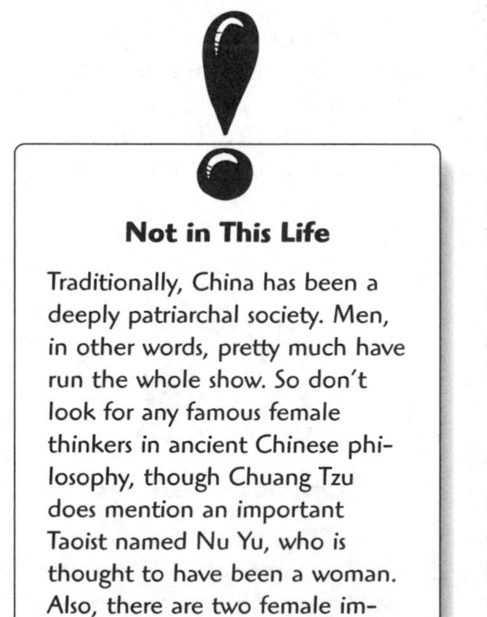

Not in This Life

Traditionally, China has been a deeply patriarchal society. Men, in other words, pretty much have run the whole show. So don't look for any famous female thinkers in ancient Chinese philosophy, though Chuang Tzu does mention an important Taoist named Nu Yu, who is thought to have been a woman. Also, there are two female immortals among the eight immortal sages of religious Taoism.

In the Balance

Fu applies to all things, including natural and human events. It is the return of all things to their source. Since the source of being is nonbeing, all things that exist return to a state of nonexistence. Things that live die; things that are formed decay. This is not simply a bad thing, but involves a balance between good and bad.

Philosophical Taoists accept this situation as natural and in keeping with the Tao. They are unconcerned about death because, to their way of thinking, the Tao never changes. Chuang Tzu and Lieh Tzu even suggest that death is meaningless. Philosophically speaking, the point is that death is not only unavoidable, but makes it possible for life to go on. Life is a cycle, and to participate fully in the cycle, you have to accept the fact that it's going to come to an end.

Not all Taoists look at things this way, however. The religious Taoists, who you can read more about later, interpret the statements of Chuang Tzu and Lieh Tzu as saying that death can be conquered by learning to harness the magical power of the Tao. Thus they believe that by living in harmony with nature, a Taoist sage can transform himself (or herself) and attain immortality.

Better Halves

Fu is only one aspect of the Taoist conception of balance. Another is the famous symbolic pair of opposed principles, *yin* and *yang*. Yin and yang are opposed, complementary concepts representing dark and light, female and male, negative and positive, passive and active, etc. Everything in existence works through a combination of yin and yang characteristics. Thus, although yin is considered female and yang male, all men and women have both yin and yang characteristics.

Orient Expressions

Yin and **yang** are the passive and active principles of the universe, recognized by most schools of Chinese philosophy. The interplay of yin and yang are perpetually in flux, giving shape to the changing world.

The concepts of yin and yang didn't originate with Taoism, but Taoism incorporated them so that both religious and philosophical Taoists recognize them. The interplay of yin and yang is perpetually at work in natural and human events, so that things continually change and balance out, in keeping with the Tao.

Although yin and yang can be considered elements of Taoist philosophy, there is a so-called Yin-yang School of ancient China that is more or less distinct from Taoism. This school uses yin and yang to explain everything from the physical workings of nature to the course of human history. Unlike Taoism, the Yin-yang School doesn't focus heavily on how to live and act in accordance with the Tao, which is the subject of Chapter 20, "Opposites in Flux."

The Least You Need to Know

- Legend says Lao Tzu lived around 600 B.C.E. and wrote the *Tao Te Ching*. Some scholars say the book was written some 250 years later, possibly by many writers.
- The Tao, or the Way, refers to nature and human nature simultaneously.
- Two strains of Taoism are the contemplative and religious schools. The contemplative school is based on living and acting according to principles found in nature. The religious school is preoccupied with immortality.
- In philosophical Taoism, the balance, harmony, and effortlessness of natural processes provides a model for human action.
- Fu and yin and yang are two concepts that help explain the Taoist conception of natural balance and harmony.

Chapter 18

Tao and Later

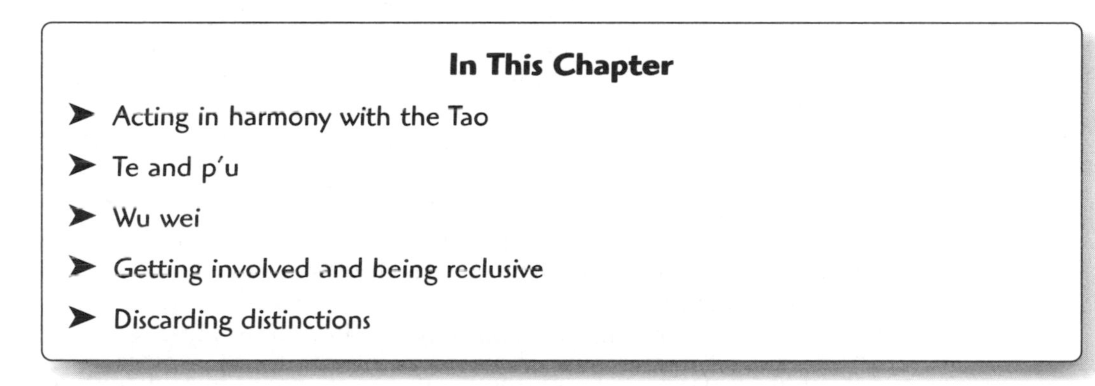
In This Chapter

- Acting in harmony with the Tao
- Te and p'u
- Wu wei
- Getting involved and being reclusive
- Discarding distinctions

This chapter talks about how to act, given the Taoist view. So-called "contemplative" (as opposed to "religious") Taoism isn't just about sitting and thinking, but about finding the best way of dealing with life's problems. Tao, after all, means "the Way," not "the idea" or "the point of view." This includes the way to act and to live, as well as the way to think.

Taoist behavior is simple, natural, and unassuming. Taoist leaders aren't bossy; Taoist workers aren't ambitious; Taoist sages don't make a big deal about their wisdom or their accomplishments. This is because the harder you try to succeed or look good or gain power, the more conflicts you'll generate and the more resistance you'll run into. So, instead of exerting yourself for no good purpose, the thing to do is make use of the natural tendencies of the situation in order to get what you want, and to realize that what most people want isn't worth the trouble.

This effortless, harmonious approach to life has set the tone for millions of people in China for centuries. It has also caught on with many in the West who see Taoism as a sensible response to the hype, high pressure, greed, and complexity of existence in the late twentieth century.

Inner Freedom

The Tao is the universal way of nature that allows all things to exist in all their variety. Each living thing has its own nature, qualities, and power. This power is called *te,* the principle that allows things to be what they are. Ideally, the actions of all living things are expressions of their te, their power or virtue. As far as people are concerned, te is the power of the Tao applied in human life. If you don't act according to your te, it's because you lack free will for some reason, generally because your actions are limited by laws, conventions, or responsibilities.

Orient Expressions

Te is the power of the Tao. It is the principle that enables things to be what they are and is expressed differently by each living thing.

Express Yourself

Te is a natural thing, so it doesn't require any study or sophistication to acquire or control it. The best way to tap into your own te is by not trying to change or develop in any particular way. Be as simple as possible—even childlike. The more you try to be smart or smooth or stylish, the more you end up crowding out your te. If you work at becoming sophisticated, all you are doing is trying to conform to external ideas about how to act. The more you conform, the less chance your te has to express itself. If, on the other hand, you can be simple and unassuming, your te will come through without resistance.

As an illustration of the dangers of conformity and the nature of te, Chuang Tzu discusses the difference between a duck and a crane. A duck has short legs that enable it to paddle around in the water where it eats while floating on the surface or diving underneath. A crane, in contrast, has long legs that enable it to wade in the shallows as it searches for food. Each creature has a different te. The duck would be unhappy with a crane's legs and vice versa.

The example goes to show that we shouldn't expect people to behave like one another any more than birds do. What works for one person may not work for someone else, so it's wrong to impose standards and rules. If your society imposes rules (as all societies do), the best thing is to avoid society. And, while you're at it, you might want to avoid picking up on social cues about how to act. Instead, keep to yourself and keep things simple.

The Tao of P'u

The Chinese term for this plain-and-simple attitude is *p'u*. P'u is usually translated as "uncarved block," but the original meaning seems to have been more like "unfinished (roughly sawn) lumber." The idea is that there's nothing wrong with rough edges. Your rough edges are actually a part of you, and it would be too bad to lose them, especially since they can be an advantage in many situations.

Orient Expressions

P'u is the Taoist term for a simple, unassuming attitude. It is often translated literally as "uncarved block," meaning lumber that has not had its rough edges smoothed off.

P'u refers not only to your external appearance. It's not only about dropping facades. It also has to do with your inner state. To be simple inside is to have few desires. The more you want, the more complicated your life gets as you struggle to satisfy your cravings. If, on the other hand, all you want is to eat when you're hungry and sleep when you're tired, it's easier to live simply.

The Way of the West

If you're like many Westerners, you probably have mixed feelings about the idea of p'u and the value of simplicity. Modern living often seems like one headache after another. Just dealing with the car, for example, means parking, maintenance, license, insurance, registration, safety and environmental inspections, and remembering where you left the keys. Then there's the other car, the TV, the computer, the stereo, the air conditioner, the food processor, the washing machine, and whatever else you have that can seem like it's more trouble than it's worth.

And there's the endless stream of advertising trying to make you think you want even more stuff. By the time you've finished doing the work to pay for it all and after you've written checks for the credit card bills and figured out your taxes, there's hardly any time left over to use any of it, much less do things you feel like doing. After spending a full five-day week on the job followed by a weekend spent running errands, Taoist simplicity can start to make a lot of sense. Why not just say "to heck with it all" and go off and live in a cave somewhere?

But then, on the other hand, who wants to live in a cave? Even if you find a way to feed yourself and stay reasonably warm and dry without worrying about rent or mortgage payments, what about friends and family? Do they go out the window along with the microwave? To a point, complexity is an unavoidable part of modern life.

Lotus Lore

Ancient Taoist recluses were not all morally opposed to society for its own sake, but often had practical reasons for avoiding public life. The political climate of China during the early years of Taoism meant that many people had to go into hiding for their own safety. Others abandoned society in order to make a statement about corruption in government.

Different Flows

Actually, not all philosophical Taoists are recluses living in caves. In fact, there's a whole range of attitudes toward society at work in the ancient Taoist writings. Sometimes, Taoism is about getting away from it all. At other times, the idea is to deal with the complexities of social life in the simplest possible way.

Contemplative Taoism, in other words, points in two directions. On one hand, it's a practical philosophy aimed at helping people get what they want out of life. By acting in harmony with the Tao, you can harness its power, its te, and be more effective in the things you do. If you want to govern, you can be a better leader. If you want to fight, you can be a better fighter. Te can even help you get people to do what you want them to without their even realizing it. You can accomplish anything you want because you have the power of the Tao backing you up.

On the other hand, Taoism is a mystic philosophy that shows that worldly things are unimportant. Desire, ambition, hope, and fear are vain. From this perspective, acting in harmony with the Tao means renouncing worldly goals and going off by yourself to be a sagely hermit like the early Taoist recluses. There's really no point in trying to influence other people. In fact, trying to make a difference only ends up making things worse.

Thus Taoism describes two approaches for practicing p'u and acting in accord with te. One is for those who are engaged in public affairs. This approach focuses not only on obeying the dictates of your own te, but on dealing with other people in ways that won't restrict theirs. The point is to work with others while obeying your own nature while allowing others to obey theirs.

The other approach recognizes the difficulty of preserving your own freedom and acting in accord with te when you're involved in a complex human society. Getting involved with others often means that someone ends up sacrificing their free will and losing the ability to express te. This second approach, then, is for those who are ready to go off by themselves in order to enjoy and cultivate their freedom in peace and quiet.

Hanging Loose

But there's no reason why you can't adopt both of these two somewhat contradictory attitudes at different times, depending on the situation. In fact, there's a key Taoist principle that talks about doing just this, called *wu wei,* which means inaction, or nondoing. Paradoxically, the wise way to act is through inaction. The point of wu wei isn't to do nothing, but to do things the easy way, without engaging in conflict. Whatever you do, be modest and flexible. Don't assert your own ego or tell others what to do.

Orient Expressions

Wu wei is the Taoist principle of effortlessness or inaction. By adopting wu wei, the Taoist sage accomplishes things without encountering resistance.

Although the Tao is powerful, its power is effortless. The wise person who sees that effortlessness is the most effective way of doing things can adopt this principle in his or her own life. Doing things the easy way makes them go more smoothly. Don't look for trouble or try too hard; just go with the flow. Sometimes this involves taking action and other times it involves stepping aside.

Leading Lightly

Both of these approaches—taking action and standing aside—are evident in the life and teachings of Lao Tzu. He is supposed to have renounced the world to go off by himself. Yet his book, the *Tao Te Ching,* includes advice to rulers and government officials on how to lead more effectively. Before leaving society, he evidently worked as a keeper of court records. In other words, he was something of an official historian, so he must have understood the ups and downs of the state and its rulers. He knew about rulers who rose to power only to be quickly overthrown again, and he also knew about those who ruled in peace and security. He saw these ups and downs, like the changes that take place in nature, as responding to the Tao.

All in the Timing

Lao Tzu suggests that to act in harmony with the Tao requires a good sense of timing. It's possible to exert a profound and helpful influence on the course of events if you tackle problems early, before they get a chance to develop into full-blown disasters. "Nipping problems in the bud" is the best way to deal with them.

Karma Dogma

Difficult things in the world can be handled when they are easy.
Big things in the world can be accomplished
By seeing to their small beginnings.
Thus the Sage never wrestles with big things.
Yet he alone is able to achieve them.

—*Tao Te Ching*, chapter 63

On the other hand, when situations have already developed, it's usually best to try to live with them, even if they aren't ideal. In fact, the worse things are, the sooner the problems will blow over. Just waiting is often the best course of action. Stepping in to try to change a bad situation is likely to make it worse.

Although it may seem counter-intuitive, the idea of wu wei is to act when things are going well in order to preserve the favorable situation. "Ride the wave," in other words. Take advantage of the times. That way, you can work with things as they are and prevent undesirable changes. When things are bad—and they will always become bad sooner or later—the thing to do is wait it out and let things cool down on their own. Thus, by following the principle of wu wei, you can accomplish more by doing less.

Kid Gloves

Lao Tzu applies wu wei as a way of influencing people. The best way to govern people is to leave them alone as much as possible. Don't stand in the way of anything they want. Instead, simply make sure they want as little as possible. Allow them to be happy with what they have by being discreet about your own possessions. Don't display luxuries or make yourself look superior; that way, no one will envy you. Don't teach people things they don't know or get them to desire things they don't have. This will only make them feel dissatisfied and cause trouble.

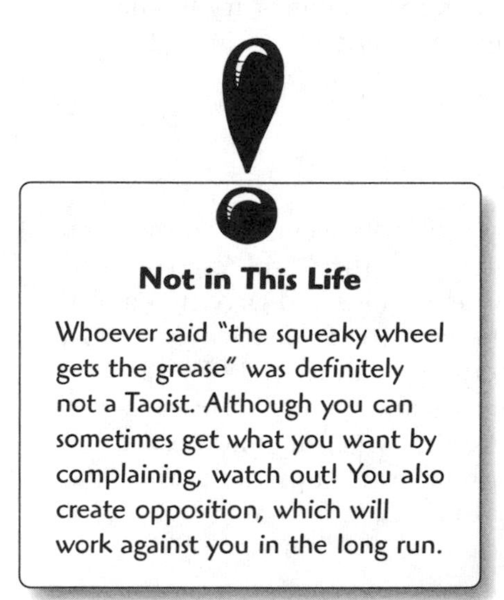

Not in This Life

Whoever said "the squeaky wheel gets the grease" was definitely not a Taoist. Although you can sometimes get what you want by complaining, watch out! You also create opposition, which will work against you in the long run.

If people are causing trouble, don't stand in their way. Merely stand aside or continue on your own course. Ignore them as much as possible. When they run out of steam and look around them and see you standing right where you were to begin with, they will feel foolish and realize you know exactly what you're doing. And, since you haven't opposed them, they won't regard you as their enemy. This will make it easy for them to change and do things your way. If they don't regard the situation as a conflict, they won't worry about whether they come out ahead of you. If you don't compete against them, they will see that their actions aren't having any effect, and they'll fall into line.

Lao Tzu believed his approach to government was good not only for the ruler, but for his subjects. The people will be happier if you don't boss them around too much. Rather than telling them what to do, simply lead by example, and they will learn. What's more, they'll think they figured everything out for themselves! Of course, this means you may not get the credit you deserve for your tactful leadership, but that's not a bad thing. If you get lots of credit, others will envy you and start causing problems, so it's actually better to stay out of the limelight.

Practical Tao

Wu wei can be applied by anyone who understands the Tao, whether or not he or she happens to be in charge of an ancient Chinese kingdom. It can work with kids if you're a parent or a teacher. It can work when you're dealing with any kind of bureaucracy. Red tape can be much easier to cut through if you don't argue with the people you're dealing with, whether they're secretaries, receptionists, agents, clerks, or whoever. In fact, it's been said that the Chinese invented bureaucracy, so it's good to know they also invented a way to deal with it in Taoism!

Lotus Lore

For close to two millennia, the Chinese Empire has been run by what was both the largest (in terms of territory) and the oldest bureaucracy on the planet. It started during the third century B.C.E. and quickly extended farther than the Roman Empire would reach at its height. Some scholars believe Chinese bureaucratic techniques influenced the rise of bureaucracy in the West. Chief in importance among these techniques is the Chinese examination system for selecting and evaluating officials, instituted during the Ch'in Dynasty. The ancient Chinese examination system appears to have influenced the Civil Service Examination system in Britain, which started in the nineteenth century to serve the British Empire.

Let's say you need to get something—information, documents, an official stamp, or whatever—from a big agency. You suspect someone screwed up somewhere, and your file has been lost in the shuffle. All you want is to get what you need as quickly as possible so you can leave and get on with your life. But there's this huge, impersonal system with lots of working people in it who would rather be somewhere else. They have to deal with millions of annoying little problems every day, so no one is going to be particularly concerned with yours. So what do you do?

Red Tape Tips

Here's a list of pointers for using wu wei to cut through red tape.

- ➤ Don't be in a hurry. Being impatient is unlikely to get anyone to speed up what they're doing. They're more likely to think that the quickest way to get rid of you is to ignore you until you leave in a huff. On the other hand, if you make yourself comfortable, someone will come up and ask if they can help you.
- ➤ Don't be bossy or argue with anyone. When you disagree with what someone tells you, don't insist you are right, but explain your problem and ask for advice. If they tell you you're out of luck, say "thank you" and try getting help from someone else.
- ➤ Don't act like you know everything. If something went wrong, let whoever's dealing with you discover it for him- or herself. If this happens, the person will feel they've accomplished something and will be more likely to want to get involved in finding a solution.
- ➤ Don't make it seem as though you think your problem is particularly important. Act like you're just curious about how things work. If you seem interested in what people are supposed to be doing, you may get them to think more carefully about how they deal with you.

Karma Dogma

How does the ocean come to rule the rivers?
Because it lies lower than they do.
Thus the ocean rules the rivers.
Thus the sage reigns over the people by humbling himself
And leads people by putting himself behind them.

—*Tao Te Ching*, chapter 66

Quitting Time

And finally, in addition to knowing when to wait and when to act, there's still another aspect of wu wei—knowing when to leave. The Taoist sage never boasts about his or her accomplishments or knowledge. When the job is done and there's nothing more to do, there's no point in hanging around and getting in the way, no matter how important you used to be or how smoothly you did your job.

The Taoist knowledge of when to quit is exemplified by Lao Tzu's famous retirement. He left and was never heard from again. Although it is sometimes said that he was so disgusted with society that he wanted nothing more to do with it, he may simply have felt that, after finishing his work, it was time to quit.

Low Profile

The tendency of Taoists to avoid society and go off by themselves started even before the *Tao Te Ching* was written (which, as you may remember from the previous chapter, may or may not have been written by Lao Tzu). This tendency was later emphasized in the work of the second-most-famous Taoist sage after Lao Tzu, Chuang Tzu. Chuang Tzu says we're better off renouncing worldly ambition and seeking out peace and quiet away from public affairs.

Lotus Lore

The Confucian *Analects,* which record the sayings and actions of Confucius, tell of encounters Confucius and his disciples had with recluses who exhibited something of a Taoist attitude toward social problems by teasing Confucius for attempting to improve the world. These recluses regard the strife in China during Confucius's time as hopeless and suggest that the wisest course of action is to stay out of public affairs altogether. Confucius responds by saying that it is not in his nature to "herd together with birds and beasts," but to associate with human beings.

The Tao of Slacking Off

According to Chuang Tzu, the more ambitious you are, the more responsibilities you have to take on. The more responsibilities you have, the less free you are. The less free you are, the more you have to restrict your te. Thus public success results in a life of doing things you don't want to do. It makes more sense to avoid success. Instead of moving up the ladder, you can be happier staying where you are. You'll have fewer responsibilities, fewer headaches, and more free time.

In fact, in Chuang Tzu's view, the further away from organized society you can be, the better. Customs, conventions, rules, and laws all pose restrictions to free will. Chuang Tzu compares these things to the harness on a horse and the tether through the nose of an ox. They get people to act according to external guidelines without their own free choice.

Included in customary restrictions on free choice are ideas about good and evil. Chuang Tzu suggests that concern with good and evil is actually a waste of time. This notion is one of the most challenging aspects of Chuang Tzu's philosophy. Right and wrong are not absolute, but come into being in opposition to one another. From the point of view of wrong, right is wrong and wrong is right. They are only two opposing sides. The only way to be right is not to assert any notion of good or rightness at all.

All Judgments Aside

To exemplify this idea, Chuang Tzu points out that there are virtuous thieves. As a class, they have their own unwritten moral code, and recognize that some thieves follow this code more closely than others. They take their work as seriously as government officials. The only difference is that they work for different people and follow a different set of rules.

Chuang Tzu picks up on a point made previously by Lao Tzu in saying that ideals of good behavior came into existence only when that behavior ceased to be the natural, obvious way to behave. People, according to Taoism, are naturally good. But when, as a result of social corruption, they lapse out of their natural goodness, they invent standards of goodness to keep each other in line. According to Chuang Tzu, these standards do more harm than good. By getting stuck on the standards of goodness, we lose touch with our inherent way of being.

Karma Dogma

To love the people is the first step to injure them. To practice righteousness in order to make an end to war is the root from which war is caused. Any attempt to bring about what we think is good while we have an ulterior motive is a bad plan .... Benevolence and righteousness are no better than hypocrisy.

—*Chuang-tzu,* 24–2

The Taoist answer to the problem of good and evil is to do away with the distinction. Either things are natural and in harmony with the Tao or they aren't. There's no point in arguing about right and wrong. The argument is a mistake to begin with.

Good and evil and right and wrong are not the only distinctions that belong in the trash can of conventional thinking. All distinctions cause opposition and trouble and distract people from acting in harmony with the Tao. In fact, any idea or behavior that requires a lot of thought, reasoning, and sorting is inconsistent with the Tao because the Tao is both perfectly simple and impossible to explain.

The Least You Need to Know

- Te is the Taoist term for the power of the Tao that allows individual creatures to act according to their own nature.
- P'u is the Taoist principle of simplicity. It includes simplicity of action as well as simplicity of motive (having few desires).
- Wu wei is the Taoist concept of nondoing or inaction, which means doing things in such a way and at such a time as to encounter the least resistance.
- Contemplative Taoism includes advice for avoiding society as well as advice for dealing with society, including advice to rulers of state.
- Taoism recommends discarding conceptual distinctions, including the distinction between good and evil.

Chapter 19

Tao and Forever

In This Chapter

- Religious Taoism and Taoist hygiene
- Alchemy and the Five Elements
- The Immortals and the Blessed Islands
- Ch'i Kung (Qigong)
- The Yellow Turban Rebellion and the Falun Gong movement

Taoism is best known in the West as a philosophy of nature and of human action taken in harmony with nature. Among the many benefits of acting in harmony with nature are psychological tranquility and good physical health. These factors, of course, can lead to a long life. So one of the big drawing points of Taoism is the promise of living a long time. Many Taoists have taken this idea of longevity and run with it, taking Taoism to all sorts of fascinating places.

Longevity, according to many Taoists throughout Chinese history, can be attained through a variety of methods, including alchemy, fitness exercises, meditation and controlled breathing, and spiritual beliefs. Longevity is just the beginning—a beginning without an end, in fact, in that some strains of Taoism offer the hope of immortality. In fact, many Taoist legends tell of sages who have become immortal through a variety of esoteric and occult techniques. This Taoist pursuit of immortality has blended with other traditional Chinese religious beliefs, resulting in a vast array of gods and other divine beings, including the 36,000 gods who live inside your body!

While many Taoist beliefs about health and longevity can seem bizarre, many have had a big impact in the fields of health and "alternative medicine." In fact, much of Chinese medicine has its roots in Taoism. And, as you probably realize, Chinese medical techniques have been making a progressively larger impact on the mainstream. So this chapter goes to show that some of the strangest ideas can have common origins with some of the most useful ones.

The Tao of Pre-Chem

Taoism has performed many functions within China's history—cultural, political, religious, and practical. Taoist mysticism, for example, ties in with traditional folk beliefs in China. Taoist religious movements have had significant political impact, providing an organized voice for the common people. And Taoist alchemy and hygiene have given rise to important ideas in Chinese medicine and fitness. In fact, just as alchemy in the West is one of the roots of Western science, Taoist alchemy has evolved into the Chinese way of understanding the mind, the body, and the environment.

Eye of Newt...

The development of science in the West helped establish a clear distinction between magic and technology. Before the rise of science, people interested in the nature and workings of things practiced alchemy. Alchemists performed experiments on chemical substances to learn about their natural, as well as magical, qualities. They believed that the substances they worked with were somehow connected with their own spiritual states. They believed, in other words, that their ability to produce chemical reactions demonstrated not only their knowledge of chemical substances, but also their spiritual power as alchemists.

Orient Expressions

Fang hsien tao, "the way of recipes and immortality," is Chinese alchemy, the art of discovering the secrets of immortality by means of chemical experiments.

Since ancient times, different traditions of alchemy have been practiced in the West and in China. Chinese alchemy is an aspect of Taoism, tied to Taoist ideas about harmony and balance in the natural world and in the human body and spirit. Traditional Chinese alchemy is known as *fang hsien tao,* "the way of recipes and immortality." Like the Western alchemists, many Taoists hoped to discover the elixir of immortality through a combination of chemistry, or "recipes"; spiritual discipline; and magic.

All That Glitters

Many of the recipes used by Chinese alchemists involved a substance known as cinnabar, a reddish ore containing mercury. It was thought that eating cinnabar or eating out of a dish that was made of cinnabar could help make you immortal. Some Chinese alchemists attempted to transmute cinnabar to gold, both to get rich and to develop spiritual power. Others believed that eating cinnabar would convert the bones to gold and the flesh to jade, thereby rendering them impervious to decay. (This may sound good to you, put don't try this at home! Because cinnabar is mostly mercury, it is actually poisonous.)

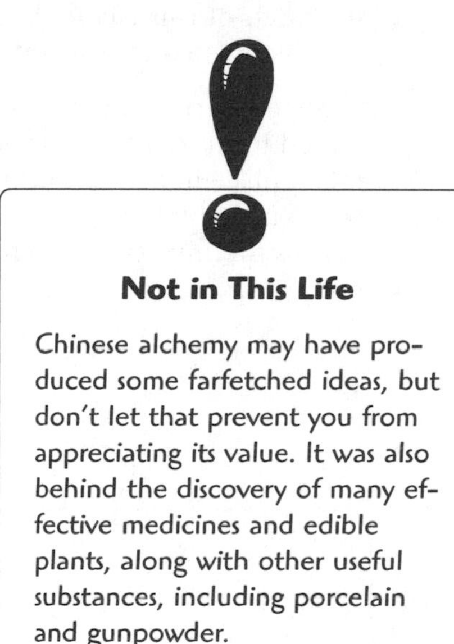

Not in This Life

Chinese alchemy may have produced some farfetched ideas, but don't let that prevent you from appreciating its value. It was also behind the discovery of many effective medicines and edible plants, along with other useful substances, including porcelain and gunpowder.

Cinnabar was such a fascinating substance to many Taoists that it became a symbolic component of the human body. Three "fields of cinnabar"—in the head, the chest, and the abdomen—supposedly constitute energy centers. These energy centers are thought to radiate good health. The bad news is that a worm lives in each one, responsible for producing diseases. These worms were thought to eat grain. So Taoists tried to vanquish their inner worms by eliminating grain from their diets.

Magic in High Places

Some Taoist wise men managed to get imperial support for their ideas. During the Ch'in Dynasty, a Taoist magician named Lu enjoyed the patronage of Emperor Ch'in Shih. It seems the two men had a falling out, however, that resulted in Master Lu fleeing the emperor's court. The emperor reacted by having 460 scholars and magicians executed!

Another famous Taoist wise man was Li Shao-chun, who enjoyed favor at the court of Emperor Wu Ti during the Han Dynasty. Wu Ti desired immortality, and Li Shao-chun instructed the Emperor in his alchemical wisdom, including experiments with cinnabar. Another approach Li Shao-chun recommended was sacrifice to Tsao Chun, the God of the Stove—the first important Taoist deity.

Tsao Chun, worshiped in China long before the rise of Taoism, was the first important Taoist god and remains in important Chinese religious traditions. This god is not only the kitchen god, he also has the title of Director of Destinies. In this capacity, he has the job of deciding how long people have to live. Therefore, he became significant in the Taoist pursuit of immortality.

Emperor Ch'in Shih and Emperor Wu Ti are both said to have believed that there were islands off the coast of China where immortals lived. Both emperors sponsored expeditions in search of these islands. Li Shao-chun told Emperor Wu Ti that he would become immortal by viewing the mythical island of P'eng Lai, which was supposed to be floating around in the China seas. So Wu Ti not only funded expeditions in search of this island, but spent time wandering around on the coast in case the island happened to drift into view of shore.

Li Shao-chun claimed to have seen P'eng Lai himself and claimed as well to have attained immortality. He even gave "eye-witness" accounts of famous events that had taken place in China during the previous century! Wu Ti was evidently persuaded completely by Li Shao-chun's claims. Even when the wise man died during the emperor's lifetime, the emperor chose to believe that he had merely moved out of his body.

Lotus Lore

Taoist alchemy managed to secure imperial patronage throughout much of Chinese history, with mixed results. In 820 C.E., the emperor Hsien Tsung took a longevity pill administered by his Taoist alchemist, Liu Pi. Soon afterward, he dropped dead! Despite such occasional failures, Chinese legends tell of many lucky, skillful, and virtuous people who succeeded in obtaining immortality. These immortals, or hsien, are popular figures in folklore and are thought to offer assistance from time to time to worthy human followers.

High Fives

Although Taoist alchemy focuses on the idea of immortality, it has other features. For one thing, it has developed an elaborate system of corresponding categories based on the idea of Five Elements. This system can be used to explain just about everything from unexpected weather and tummyaches to the course of human history.

Braving the Elements

According to Taoist alchemy, the world is made up of five elements: air, earth, water, fire, and metal. These elements are a key feature in a whole system of cosmic correspondences, including five directions (North, East, South, West, and Center), five internal yin organs (liver, heart, spleen, lungs, kidneys), yang organs (gall, stomach, large intestine, small intestine, bladder), and many other categories pertaining to physical and natural conditions, including five tastes, five colors, five emotions, five seasons (with late summer as a separate season), five climates, and numerous others.

The elements interrelate in different ways, both nourishing and destroying one another. Wood is said to produce fire, fire produces earth, earth produces metal, metal produces water, and water produces wood. Conversely, water subdues fire, fire subdues metal, metal subdues wood, wood subdues earth, and earth subdues water. It was thought that these rules could be applied to explain and predict all kinds of situations.

For example, the legendary Hsia dynasty was associated with wood. It was supplanted by the Shang dynasty, which was associated with metal. The notion that metal can subdue wood was thus used to explain why the Hsia Dynasty fell to the Shang. Similarly, the Chou Dynasty, associated with fire, supplanted the Shang. The idea was that this progression would repeat itself in an endless cycle.

The Lay of the Land

Another interesting application of the Five Elements is in the ancient art of Chinese geomancy (divination from signs found in the earth) known as *feng shui,* which means "wind and water." Traditionally, feng shui practitioners are employed to determine the most auspicious sites and designs for public buildings, temples, and graves, as well as the best time for constructing them. In plotting the features of a building, including the locations of doors, windows, and even furniture and decor, they take into account the presence of beneficial energy and evil spirits, as well as harmony with the environment, based on an interpretation of the setting in terms of the five elements.

Orient Expressions

Feng shui (literally "wind and water") is the ancient art of Chinese geomancy, or earth divination, used to identify the best sites for buildings and graves.

Feng shui has recently become a trendy design concept. Feng shui consultants will tell you how to maximize the positive energy flow in your home or business environment by identifying the "dragon lines" running through the room and balancing and harmonizing the space with the environment. Feng shui fans claim that a harmoniously situated environment reduces stress and makes everyone in it happier.

The Five Elements are still used by some practitioners of alternative medicine and Chinese fitness as a way of understanding the interplay of various aspects of the body. They can also be used in conjunction with the concepts of yin and yang to indicate the balance and interdependency of natural forces.

Mystical Fitness

Alchemy is only one aspect of a long and rich Chinese tradition for achieving physical and mental harmony through concentration and exercise. This tradition is sometimes called the Hygiene School of Taoism. The Hygiene School has led to some pretty far-out beliefs, yet it has also resulted in approaches to health and medicine that have been increasingly recognized in the West as effective and beneficial.

Living on Air

Some "hygiene" Taoists believed that they could learn to survive by nourishing themselves on their own breath and saliva. In doing so, they hoped to purify their bodies and become immortal. They also attempted to improve the circulation of their breath throughout their bodies, directing it in a controlled way by force of concentration. This was thought to ward off diseases.

These approaches to attaining immortality are known as "embryonic respiration," since it was thought that embryos inside the womb ate and breathed this way. The idea is to hold your breath while guiding it throughout the body. Meanwhile, you accumulate saliva which is supposed to provide a pure form of nourishment. As you may imagine, it takes great skill and spiritual wisdom to succeed in gaining immortality this way! Nevertheless, a number of Chinese legends tell of people who managed to pull it off.

Karma Dogma

Even if you do not believe wholeheartedly that life can be lengthened and immortality attained, what have you got to lose by trying it?

—Ko Hung, a Chinese alchemist of the fourth century

Some Taoist adepts added a new wrinkle to the practice of embryonic breathing in the form of 36,000 gods which were supposed to live inside the body. These interior gods were said to serve different purposes in regulating bodily processes. (The interior gods were thought to have a kind of bureaucratic function modeled after the Chinese system of government. Thus they were not exactly regarded as bodily engineers and custodians, as Westerners might imagine.)

The presence of gods inside the body means that death occurs only when the gods leave. Fortunately, they could be enticed to stay through concentrated devotion to them—that is, by visualizing them and meditating on them. They could also be placated by the avoidance of meat and wine, which offends them. In addition, they could be pleased by good deeds.

Bang the Gong

Slightly less far-out approaches to Taoist hygiene and fitness are still practiced today, not only in China but all over the world. The Chinese term for mind/body fitness is familiar to most Westerners as a branch of Eastern martial arts: *kung fu* (pronounced *gong fu* in China). Actually, kung fu does not refer simply to a way of hitting people with all parts of your body as you fly through the air in slow motion (as you might think from watching the famous TV series of the '70s and '80s starring David Carradine). Kung fu is the general Chinese idea of physical and mental discipline. It includes the physical training and exercise system of *t'ai chi*. But perhaps the best known approach to kung fu in China is *ch'i kung* (often written in the Pinyin romanization system as *qigong*).

The "ch'i" in "ch'i kung" is a Chinese word whose original meaning is breath. Thanks in part to the spiritual breathing exercises of the old hygiene school Taoists, the word ch'i took on the additional meaning of "life force," or energy. Ch'i is thought to travel through the body along certain channels known to practitioners of acupuncture. Ch'i is also the energy that flows through the environment known to practitioners of feng shui (wind and water geomancy). Thus ch'i kung (qigong) is a mind/body discipline intended to improve the flow of ch'i through the body.

Orient Expressions

Kung fu (gong fu in Pinyin) is the general term used in China for mind/body discipline. **T'ai chi** is a well-known form of kung fu, and so is **ch'i kung** (qigong in Pinyin). **Ch'i** is the Chinese word for breath that also means life force or energy.

State Versus Spirit

In addition to ch'i kung, another form of kung fu, falun kung (Falun Gong), has been spreading around the world in recent years. Falun gong combines mind/body discipline with spiritual beliefs derived from Buddhism as well as Taoism. This movement is quickly growing and is becoming a major spiritual force in China, much to the dismay of the Chinese Communist government. More on falun gong later in this chapter in the "Gut Feelings" section.

It might help to put the Falun Gong movement in perspective by comparing it to a powerful religious movement that swept through China during the second century. This was the Taoist sect known as T'ai P'ing Tao, the Way of Great Peace (not to be confused with the T'ai P'ing Rebellion of the nineteenth century in China). As the ancient imperial government tried to suppress this movement, it sparked the famous event known as the Yellow Turban Rebellion.

Tie a Yellow Turban

During the Han Dynasty, a Taoist religious organization became organized with a hierarchy of priests who taught salvation. The religion snowballed into a popular movement. It had begun as a faith-healing cult, when a Taoist healer, Chang Ling, began attracting attention and gathering followers. He was succeeded by his descendants, who became religious leaders after him. (One of these successors became a warlord and the ruler of the runaway state of Han-chung, which successfully maintained its independence from the empire for thirty years before surrendering.)

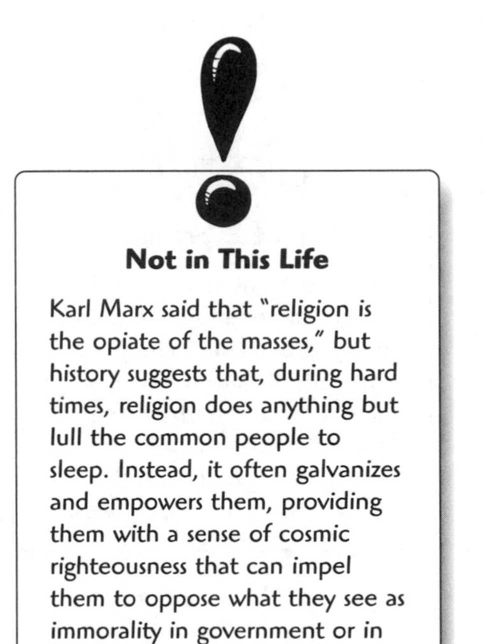

Not in This Life

Karl Marx said that "religion is the opiate of the masses," but history suggests that, during hard times, religion does anything but lull the common people to sleep. Instead, it often galvanizes and empowers them, providing them with a sense of cosmic righteousness that can impel them to oppose what they see as immorality in government or in enemy groups.

The Chang sect was only one of several Taoist religious organizations. During the waning years of the Han Dynasty, organized religious Taoism was spreading throughout China, largely because of hard times made worse by corrupt government. High taxes were imposed in order to pay for a luxurious lifestyle for the emperor and to help ward off the constant intrigues that beset the imperial court. Meanwhile, the people had to cope with intermittent famines and outbreaks of disease. In poverty, sickness, and despair, people flocked to religion for the hope it had to offer.

Part of the hope involved spiritual sanctity and health for the believer, but there was also an apocalyptic tone to the religion. Many believers thought that the divine powers in heaven would soon intervene to put a stop to the wicked leadership on Earth. Needless to say, the imperial government was not happy with this idea.

The most popular of these Taoist movements at the time was the T'ai P'ing Tao, the Way of Great Peace. This was probably an ecstatic sect, in which believers were healed through public confession of their sins. The faithful were also expected to be truthful, avoid stealing, and abstain from alcohol. In return, they could hope to obtain recognition in the afterlife and be awarded administrative positions there; then, they could hope to work their way up to become full-fledged immortals! And, while many hoped to make a difference in the government in heaven, they also hoped, no doubt, for changes on Earth.

Most of China fell under the influence of the religion. The Imperial Government became exasperated with the astonishing popularity of the Way of Great Peace. In 184 C.E., it issued warnings to religious leaders that the religion's activities would be suppressed. Enraged by the threat of suppression, members wore yellow headcloths in a display of defiance. This was the beginning of a conflict between church and state that lasted about 20 years; it was known as the Yellow Turban Rebellion.

Although religious fervor waned in the following centuries, Taoist religion remained a vital cultural force in Chinese life. During intermittent periods in Chinese history. It also exerted political force. For example, despite the fact that Taoism and Buddhism have merged to produce important philosophical currents, organized Taoism and Buddhism have during certain periods been antagonistic. Most notably, in 446 and 485, influential Taoists in government organized large-scale persecutions of Buddhists.

Lotus Lore

Like Zen Buddhism, Falun Gong combines Buddhist and Taoist ideas, but does it in a very different way, emphasizing personal spiritual and physical health through mind/body exercise. Falun Gong methods are much easier to learn and practice than a Zen—you don't have to spend your life in a monastery to master them. As a result, it is popular with working people who want to tap in to cosmic energy.

Gut Feelings

The Yellow Turban Rebellion was not the last time Taoist sectarians came into conflict with the Chinese state. These days, Taoist spirituality is on the upswing again, with thousands of Chinese in search of more out of life than Communism has to offer. The new movement, Falun Gong, like the ancient Way of Great Peace, combines salvational thinking, faith healing, physical exercise, and moral teachings. And, like the Yellow Turban leaders, Falun Gong leaders have recently run into trouble with the Chinese government. Members of the Communist Party who practice Falun Gong have been detained and "reeducated" in the basics of communism.

The founder of Falun Gong, Li Hongzhi, is currently living in America, but the Communist party wants the U.S. to extradite him back to China. The Chinese government condemns the movement as superstitious, counterproductive, and subversive. Spokespeople for the movement deny that it has any sort of political agenda, suggesting it is simply intended to promote health and well-being.

Falun Gong refers to the Taoist mind/body "gong" aspect of the movement, which is also known as falun dafa. "Dafa" refers to Buddhist Law, which the movement reinterprets in its own way to square with the idea of mind/body power and wholeness.

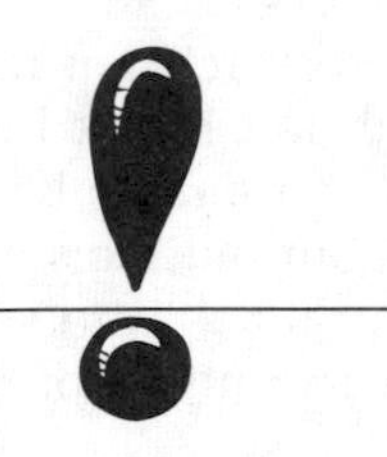

Not in This Life

The swastika did not originate in twentieth-century Germany but in ancient India. The word swastika derives from a Sanskrit term meaning well-being. The symbol was adopted by some Buddhists who thought it to be the seal of Buddha's heart, and its use was spread to China by Buddhists in the second century, long before it became an emblem of Falun Gong.

At the center of the Falun Gong doctrine is the falun, which combines the Buddhist idea of the wheel of dharma with the Taoist idea of the cycle of yin and yang, both of which can be understood to represent revolving cosmic energy.

The falun is an intelligent sphere of spinning energy located in the abdomen. It absorbs cosmic energy from the universe, especially if you cultivate its power through Falun Gong. The falun is symbolized by a rotating swastika, an ancient emblem that originated in India (and was later appropriated by the German Third Reich. Followers of falun dafa hasten to point out that they are not Nazis!).

In addition to physical and spiritual empowerment through mind/body exercises (Falun Gong), falun dafa teaches the basic principles of truth, compassion, and forbearance. Since its origins in 1992, it has mushroomed all over the world, with centers throughout North America, Europe, Australia, and China.

The Least You Need to Know

- Taoist alchemy aimed at discovering the secrets of immortality through elixirs, hygiene, and the search for the legendary Islands of the Immortals.
- The theory of the Five Elements has been used to explain the natural world, human health, and historical change. It is a traditional idea in Chinese medicine and geomancy (feng shui).
- Taoist religion has come into conflict with the Chinese state at different times in history, notably during the Yellow Turban Rebellion and recently in the attempts of the Communist government to suppress Falun Gong.
- Falun Gong blends ch'i kung (qigong) exercises with traditional Taoist hygiene and Buddhist spirituality.

Chapter 20

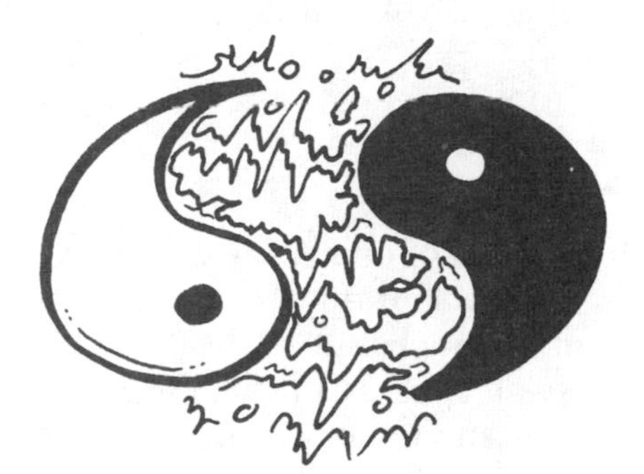

Opposites in Flux

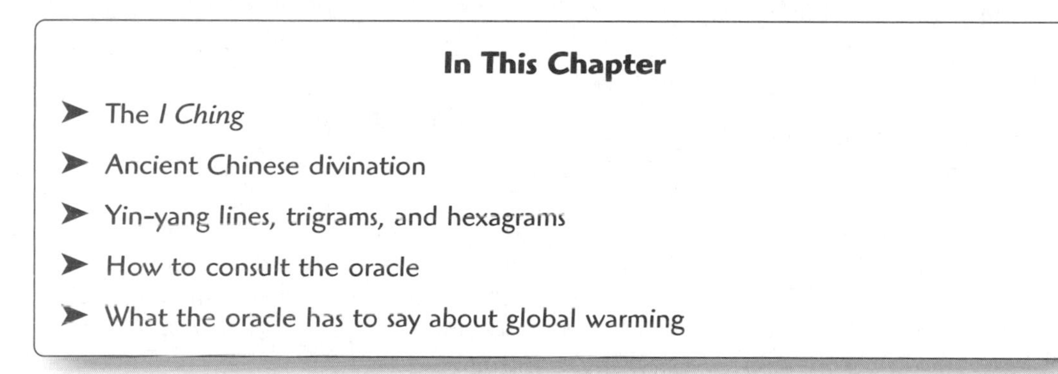

In This Chapter

- The *I Ching*
- Ancient Chinese divination
- Yin-yang lines, trigrams, and hexagrams
- How to consult the oracle
- What the oracle has to say about global warming

The *I Ching* (pronounced *ee jing*), or *Book of Changes,* is a work like no other. It combines a Confucian view of political and moral philosophy and a Taoist view of natural processes within a system of divination. Its origins are extremely ancient, predating the times of Confucius and Lao Tzu, yet it continues to be popular today as a source of moral guidance, spiritual insight, and occult knowledge.

One of the things that makes the *I Ching* unique is its interactive nature. You ask it questions, and it responds—often in surprisingly specific fashion—to the particular questions you ask. Of course, making sense of the answers can require a certain amount of interpretive flexibility, but what do you expect from an ancient Chinese oracle?

Because it is interactive, the *I Ching* enables those who use it to apply its philosophy to their lives in their own ways. Here you can get a sense of how this can be done. But keep in mind, interpreting the *I Ching* is not an exact science. Those who consult the oracle must rely on guesswork and intuition as well as philosophical knowledge in order to understand its meanings.

Here, after describing the book and its philosophy and explaining how it can be used, this chapter tells the story of a close encounter of the oracular kind in which the *I Ching* reveals its answer to a problem that is currently plaguing all of humanity. Although I've done my best to figure out what it all means, others may see things differently!

Karma Dogma

Because it is a book of divination, you might think the *I Ching* consists of occult philosophy aimed at teaching secrets that ordinary people can't understand. In fact, its teachings include the practical advice to leaders: "He who is easy to understand is easy to follow." The point is not deep dark mystery, but common principles of practical action and social morality that everyone can appreciate.

Either Oracle

The *I Ching* is both a system of divination and a collection of advice used in ancient times by men of affairs, such as government officials, ministers, and rulers. Thus, despite its mysterious, oracular aspect, much of its wisdom is essentially practical, reflecting the value of getting along with others, leading and following wisely, managing things effectively, understanding the motivations of others, and seeing how one fits in with the larger society.

The Tao of Chou

Much of the advice contained in the *Book of Changes* is directed to the *chun tzu*, or "the superior man." The term appears in many works on Confucian philosophy as well. The intended audience for these works was originally someone in a responsible position, someone socially superior to others (remember that China during the Chou Dynasty was a feudal society). But of course, the superiority implies moral superiority as well, and the advice in the *Book of Changes* is intended to foster not only effective leadership skills but the kind of personal integrity that can benefit society as a whole. This does not mean guys with big heads, but people with a good sense of how their actions affect others.

Some women who use the *I Ching* are understandably unhappy about the sexist implications of much of its language. Since the book seems to be by, for, and about men, you might think that the oracle is antifeminist. To find out for myself, I asked it what it thinks about feminism. The response was "Gathering Together" changing to "Shock, the Arousing." This seems to me like a pretty clear way of saying "Sisterhood is powerful," despite the fact that the commentary mentions "the superior man"! So I'd say it's safe to disregard the guy-talk if you don't like it and focus on the philosophical and oracular significance of the book. Or, if you prefer, you can get yourself a copy of the *Women's I Ching* by Diane Stein.

The general philosophy of the *I Ching* is public-minded, reflecting the orientation of its first commentators, the early Confucian scholars. In fact, the book includes a set of 10 appendixes known as the Ten Wings, which were traditionally supposed to have been written by Confucius himself, but were probably written during the centuries following his lifetime. The bare bones of the book, however, came into existence long before Confucius lived. Its oracular system is said to have been developed by the legendary King Wen, founder of the Chou Dynasty. The words that serve as oracular pronouncements were supposedly written by Wen's son, the Duke of Chou. Many of the earliest historical references to the book call it "the Changes of Chou."

Orient Expressions

Chun tzu means "superior man" and indicates moral as well as social superiority. The term appears frequently in the *I Ching* and in works on Confucian philosophy, including the *Analects of Confucius.*

Whether or not the Duke of Chou actually wrote the interpretations of the oracle lines, many of them reflect the keen interest in politics he would have had. At the same time, they also draw on agriculture, astronomy, family relationships, and other aspects of daily life in ancient China.

All of these areas of life get woven into the *I Ching*'s ancient symbolism, expressed in poetic sayings, that supply the basis of the book and form a bridge between the oracular "changes" and the philosophical commentary of the Ten Wings.

Order of the Day

The changes themselves are based on an elegantly patterned system of broken and unbroken lines representing yin and yang, respectively. As you may remember from Chapter 17, "Tao or Never," the Yin-yang School is an ancient philosophy that accounts for cosmic order and change—natural, social, and historical—in terms of the interplay of the opposed and complementary principles of yin and yang. Yin is female, dark, cold, passive, and receptive while yang is male, light, hot, active, and creative. Yin characterizes the earth while yang characterizes heaven, yet they are not separate areas of existence, but are aspects shared by all things.

Karma Dogma

The *I Ching* was made on the principle of accordance with heaven and earth. It therefore shows, without gaps or confusion, the course of heaven and earth.

—The Great Treatise appendix to the *I Ching*

Yin and yang, earth and heaven, are extremes that balance each other. The opposite poles are necessary to one another and neither is more important than the other. When yin and yang fail to unite properly, the result is disharmony of some kind. This can take the form of flooding, drought, or infestation in the natural world; strife or political corruption in society; or mental or physical decay at the personal level.

Drawing the Lines

Thus the interplay of yin and yang governs all aspects of existence. Yin and yang can be used to explain pretty much everything that matters in human life. In the *I Ching,* yin and yang are conceived of in various combinations to represent ideas, relationships, and situations. The book consists of a system of yin and yang groupings together with explanations for what they mean.

Yang is represented by an unbroken line (_______) while a broken line (___ ___) represents yin. These lines are organized into eight groups of three lines each, called trigrams. Each trigram has its own set of characteristics. Each one also represents a member of the family. (Family relationships are extremely significant in ancient Chinese culture and play an important role in Confucian philosophy as well as the I Ching.)

It Takes Three to Yin-Yang-O

Here are the eight trigrams of the *I Ching,* together with their names, their place in the family, and their characteristics:

The Eight Trigrams of the *I Ching*

——— ——— ———	Ch'ien, the creative, heaven, strong, active, the father
— — — — — —	K'un, the receptive, earth, yielding, passive, the mother
— — — — ———	Ch'en, the arousing, thunder, impulse, oldest son

continues

continued

The Eight Trigrams of the *I Ching*	
– – —— – –	K'an, the abysmal, water, danger, second son
—— – – – –	K'en, keeping still, mountain, third son
—— —— – –	Sun, the gentle, wind or wood, penetration, oldest daughter
—— – – ——	Li, the clinging, fire, clarity, second daughter
– – —— ——	T'ui, the joyous, lake, happiness, third daughter

Lotus Lore

The *I Ching* is often compared to the well-known Western divination tool, the Tarot, since both provide fortuitous symbolic responses to questions. Tarot cards were invented during the Renaissance for use in European courts. The *I Ching* was invented approximately 2,000 years earlier for use by rulers and officials of state. Using the Tarot involves interpreting pictures and symbols drawn from Medieval society and hermetic (alchemical) philosophy. Using the *I Ching* involves interpreting hexagrams made up of yin and yang lines together with the traditional poetic and philosophical commentary on them.

The Big Picture

Each trigram, built up of yin and yang lines, has attributes and a place in the family but does not represent a situation. Situations are constructed by combining two trigrams into hexagrams containing six yin and/or yang lines. In all, there are 64 hexagrams constituting all possible combinations of the trigrams. Taken as a totality, the 64 situations represented by the hexagrams function as a kind of map of human existence, indicating—in poetic and philosophical terms—the various circumstances that make up human life.

In other words, the 64 hexagrams represent the changes the *Book of Changes* is named for. The idea is that the world is constantly in flux, so that situations continually arise, change, and give way to new situations. There are times of prosperity and deprivation, power and weakness, opportunity and obstacles, and many other circumstances configured by the hexagrams.

Out of the Limelight

To take one example, here's the hexagram called *Ming I,* "Darkening of the Light":

Ming I, "Darkening of the Light"

— —

— —

— —

——

— —

——

Notice that this hexagram is made up of the Li trigram, representing fire, on the bottom; and the K'un trigram on top, representing Earth. The light, in other words, is covered up, so the situation represented by the hexagram has to do with keeping oneself or one's qualities hidden. Like most of the hexagrams, this one represents a situation that can be seen either as a problem or an opportunity. Seen as a problem, the hexagram suggests that your abilities are going unrecognized. Seen as an opportunity, it suggests that you have a chance to make a positive impact on others by working behind the scenes.

In addition to the general situation represented by the hexagram, each of the lines within it stands for a specific aspect of it. Thus, although some hexagrams are more favorable than others (Darkening of the Light is among the more unfavorable ones) the individual lines represent various positive and negative aspects of it. These lines may change, depending on the results of the divination. This change illustrates the Taoist principle that things tend to convert into their opposites.

There are many ways to use the *Book of Changes*. You can just read around in it for its poetry and philosophy or you can consult the oracle. Some believe that the oracle can predict the future and actually tell you how to deal with events that are about to take place. Others find the oracular sayings a useful stimulus to reflection, providing helpful perspectives on whatever it is they have on their minds. Using the *I Ching* oracle involves thinking about problems in creative ways, which can trigger insights that you might not otherwise have. In addition, the *I Ching* philosophy tends to take a wide view of things, which can help you look past your own personal assumptions and presuppositions.

Karma Dogma

Tao gave birth to one, one begat two, two begat three, and three gave birth to all the myriad things.

—*Tao Te Ching*, chapter 42, a passage often used to account for the organization of the *I Ching*

Shell Game

Although the *I Ching* hexagrams were developed in ancient times during the Chou Dynasty, they may have evolved out of a divination system that is even more ancient. This older system involved the use of tortoise shells and the shoulder bones of oxen. Small holes were drilled into the shells and bones, which were then heated until they cracked. The cracks were interpreted in such a way as to yield answers to whatever was being asked.

Not in This Life

When charged with being illogical, some who rely on the *I Ching* oracle defend themselves by pointing out that logical deduction cannot account for the infinite number of factors that might affect a situation. Thus, even when making important decisions, it is wise to accept the fact that we cannot know everything, and to let ourselves be guided in part by faith, or chance, or intuition.

In time, the tortoise shell and ox bone system was replaced by a system using lines, representing yin and yang, that could be drawn by hand. The yin-yang lines evolved into the full-fledged *I Ching*. As an oracle, the *I Ching* was traditionally consulted by a group of priests or magicians who identified hexagrams by sorting handfuls of yarrow stalks. Adding and subtracting the stalks according to a particular formula results in an odd or even number of remaining stalks, which indicates a yin or a yang line. Going through this routine six times produces a six-line hexagram.

This may seem like a complicated rigamarole to go through just to determine the difference between yin and yang six times at random. But each line is actually more than simply yin or yang. The lines can also be either changing or unchanging. Changing lines in a hexagram are accompanied by additional commentary and advice that is often more specific than the overall remarks that accompany each hexagram. What's more, a hexagram that has changing lines changes to a new hexagram. Thus, in asking the oracle a question, the answer may come as a single hexagram and the commentary about it, or it may include that hexagram and commentary plus the commentary on one or more changing lines plus a new hexagram and its commentary. In this way, a whole story can unfold in answer to a single question.

So the yarrow stalks determine whether each line is yin or yang and changing or unchanging. After each run-through, the priests were left with from six to nine yarrow stalks. Six means changing yin, seven means unchanging yang, eight means unchanging yin, and nine means changing yang. Why am I telling you all this stuff, you ask? In case you want to try it for yourself. And don't worry if you don't happen to have a sheaf of yarrow stalks; you can generate changing and unchanging lines by flipping coins.

Flip three coins at a time for each line. Assign heads a value of three and tails two. The total value of all three coins will be from six to nine. Three heads gives you a changing yang line; three tails a changing yin; one tail and two heads is an unchanging yin; one head and two tails is an unchanging yang. Changing yin lines are drawn with an x in the gap (-x-); changing yang lines are drawn through an O (-O-). By the way, if you do try this yourself, you'll need a copy of the book so you can see what the lines mean.

Lotus Lore

Different translations and editions of the *I Ching* vary widely in how they organize the commentary and how much commentary is provided. Some include only the bare bones statements attributed to the Duke of Chou. Others include the Ten Wings commentary and even commentary on the commentary. You may have to shop around to find a translation that you find enjoyable. Among the most reputable are those by the crusty pioneer Sinologist, James Legge (who has deep respect for Confucian philosophy, but none whatsoever for occult beliefs) and the Baynes-Wilhelm translation, which comes with an introduction by world-renowned psychologist Carl Jung. The Baynes-Wilhelm translation is the one quoted in this chapter.

Worldly Wisdom

For now, here's a sample of the *I Ching's* wisdom. I've asked the oracle a question about global warming. This weighty environmental issue clearly concerns everyone. For a little over a decade now, scientists have been saying that pollutants released into the air are responsible for an enhanced greenhouse effect as they prevent many of the sun's rays from reflecting back out of the earth's atmosphere. As a result, global temperatures are rising, prompting changing weather patterns that threaten to upset the balance of life on the planet. Environmentalists argue that drastic measures should be taken to curtail the greenhouse effect, but representatives of industry have denied the severity of the problem.

So, in order to set the world straight, I consulted the *I Ching*, asking, "What should be done about global warming?" I must say, the answer surprised me, both because it was unexpected and because it makes perfect sense as a specific, intelligent answer to the question. I have to admit, though, it took me a while to see what the oracle's pronouncement meant.

Lotus Lore

A number of Western thinkers of note have taken the *I Ching* seriously. Among them are seventeenth-century Dutch-born philosopher Baruch Spinoza, who was fascinated by the mathematical beauty of the whole sequence of hexagrams. More recently, Swiss psychologist Carl Jung has used his theory of "synchronicity" to account for the uncanny ability of the oracle to provide apt responses to questions. And more recently still, New Age philosopher Fritjof Capra (author of the *Tao of Physics*) sees the structure of the *I Ching* as analogous to the S-matrix theory of particle physics in its understanding of the dynamics of change.

Moving Heaven and Earth

After flipping coins, I generated *T'ai*, "Peace," the eleventh hexagram. This is one of the most auspicious hexagrams of all, indicating a harmonious interrelationship between earth and heaven. It further signifies the happy and productive cooperation between high and low, the powerful and the needy. Here's what it looks like:

T'ai, "Peace"

— —

—x—

— —

———

———

—o—

Notice the changing lines in the first and fifth position, which I'll talk about later. As you can see, the Ch'ien trigram, representing heaven, is on the bottom. The K'un trigram, representing earth, is on top. To most Westerners, this may seem like an unnatural and topsy-turvy state of affairs. According to the *I Ching,* however, this is an optimal situation that takes place when powerful leaders place themselves at the service of devoted followers who lack power. The result is fruitful activity that benefits everyone.

In keeping with this idea, the commentary on the hexagram says:

> *Peace. The small departs,*
> *The great approaches.*
> *Good Fortune. Success.*

And

> *Heaven and earth unite. The image of Peace.*
> *Thus the ruler divides and completes the course of heaven and earth.*
> *He increases and regulates the gifts of heaven and earth, and so aids the people.*

After I took a moment to think about it, I saw that the hexagram addressed the necessity of balancing heaven and earth. The "ruler" here, I suppose, could be taken to represent God, but I'm inclined to interpret it as standing for human government, which passes environmental laws and sets industrial standards. In fact, an important purpose of government is stewardship of our natural resources or, as the oracle says, "to regulate the gifts of earth and heaven and so aid the people."

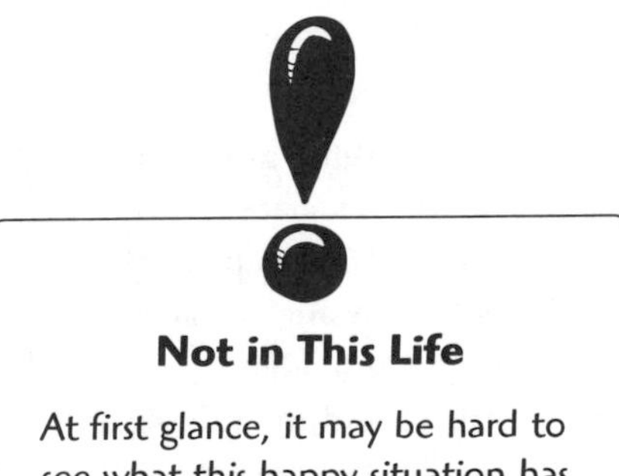

Not in This Life

At first glance, it may be hard to see what this happy situation has to do with global warming, but if you think about it, it's pretty clear that the balance of heaven and earth is the issue at hand and that this balance, if managed properly, can have beneficial effects on humanity.

Global warming, of course, is an issue related to stewardship of the planet and the gifts of heaven and earth. So it looks like we're on the same page with the oracle, right? But hold on, things are about to get pretty murky. As I mentioned, there are two changing lines in this hexagram, and each one comes with its own commentary. The first line says:

> *When ribbon grass is pulled up, the sod comes with it.*
> *Each according to his kind.*
> *Undertakings bring good fortune.*

And the fifth line says:

> *The Sovereign I gives his daughter in marriage.*
> *This brings blessing and supreme good fortune.*

Talk about optimism! It's hard to imagine a more favorable situation. What happened to the imminent disaster to be caused by global warming? And what do marriage and ribbon grass have to do with anything?

Lotus Lore

The line descriptions attributed to the Duke of Chou are often said to be derived from the relationship of each line with all the others. For example, in the Peace hexagram, the first of three yang lines would be "pulling up" more of its kind with it. Thus the ribbon grass metaphor. The fifth line is said to be the place of the ruler in all the hexagrams. In the Peace hexagram, the ruler's place is occupied by a yin line, considered weak, but in this case, a good thing, because it complements the corresponding stronger line below in the second position. This suggests the idea of a powerful woman marrying a worthy underling.

Grass Roots

Well, as I mentioned, the *I Ching* was originally developed with men of affairs such as government officials in mind. So, as commentators explain it, ribbon grass getting pulled up represents worthy ministers being appointed to office and bringing helpful supporters with them. This is a good situation showing that everyone wants to get involved in their own way. It's clear, however, that this interpretation doesn't apply very specifically as a response to our question about global warming.

But ribbon grass getting pulled up does provide a powerful image of deforestation, which, as you may know, is one of the causes of global warming! As the forested area of the planet—particularly the rain forest—diminishes, more carbon dioxide remains in the atmosphere, which augments the greenhouse effect. It's easy to picture ribbon grass getting pulled up as a God's-eye view of intensive activity on the part of the lumber industry.

So why is this a good thing? Why do "undertakings bring good fortune"? Let's think about this in connection with the commentary on the fifth changing line about the Sovereign I giving his daughter in marriage. The situation is usually taken to mean that the sovereign's daughter was the most powerful woman around, but that, despite her position, she would be a dutiful and submissive wife to whoever she married. This ties in with the unity of heaven and earth connected with the whole Peace hexagram. Those in high places willingly serve those beneath them, resulting in prosperity and good fortune all around.

But again, we have to reinterpret the commentary to see how it applies to global warming. Obviously, the daughter given in marriage by the sovereign represents the planet Earth itself, given to humanity by its creator, God. This gift—the earth and the natural resources it contains—is the source of all human well-being. Seen in this light, it makes perfectly good sense that the ribbon grass being pulled represents one of the uses being made of this gift.

In other words, the oracle is reminding us that even though global warming may result in natural imbalance, it does so as a result of the fact that human beings are making use of natural resources. And it is good that we do this. In using these resources, we are maintaining and developing human civilization.

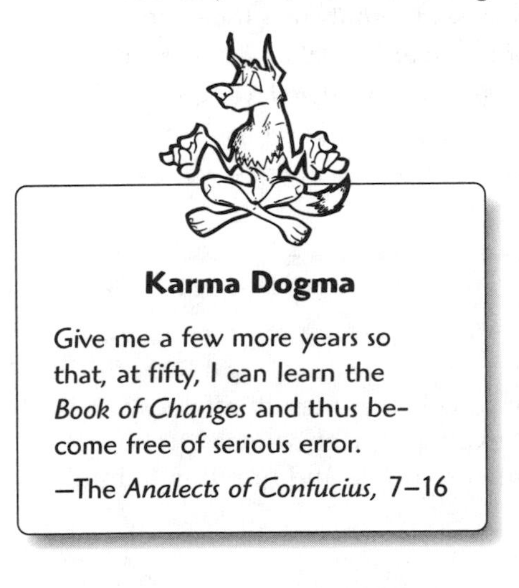

Karma Dogma

Give me a few more years so that, at fifty, I can learn the *Book of Changes* and thus become free of serious error.

—The *Analects of Confucius,* 7–16

I have to admit that this isn't what I expected to hear from the oracle. Even after reflecting on this cheery prognosis, I continue to worry about the fate of the planet and regret the gradual but accelerating disappearance of the wildlife and human cultures that depend on the rainforest and other natural areas for survival. But I also realize that my own ability to participate in civilization depends to a great extent on industrial products such as paper (you know, the stuff this book is printed on), which is made from trees with the help of the whole industrial process. Industry, after all, sustains the lifestyles of pretty much everyone who doesn't live in a grass hut and collect their food out of the forest.

Going to the Well

But of course, the oracle has more to say about our situation. The changing lines result in a new hexagram, number 48, which is Ching, "The Well." It looks like this:

Ching, "The Well"

— —

——

— —

——

——

— —

This hexagram is made of the Sun trigram on the bottom, which represents wood, and the K'an trigram on top, which represents water. This suggests the idea of wood dipping into water, or a wooden bucket being lowered into a well. In the *I Ching*, the Well hexagram means pretty much what Westerners mean when they talk about "going to the well." The well is there. You go there hoping to get what you want. Sometimes you get it. Sometimes you don't.

Here's what the commentary says:

The town may be changed but the well cannot be changed.
It neither decreases nor increases.
They come and go and draw from the well.
If one gets down almost to the water
And the rope does not reach or the bucket leaks
It brings misfortune.

And

Thus the superior person encourages the people at their work
And urges the people to help each other.

The well is significant in connection with global warming or, at any rate, in connection with the use and conservation of natural resources, because it represents the most vital resource of all—water—as well as the most ancient civilized means of providing this resource for the people who make use of it. Civilization is also referred to symbolically as "the town." Finally, it is civilization that determines whether or not we will be able to continue making use of natural resources. Civilization is made up of everyone who is a part of it. To be a part of civilization, you have to do whatever it is you do to help make it work—your job, in other words.

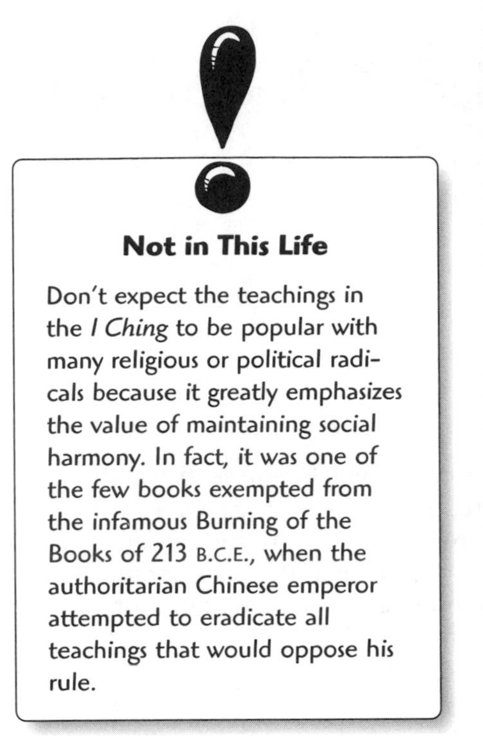

Not in This Life

Don't expect the teachings in the *I Ching* to be popular with many religious or political radicals because it greatly emphasizes the value of maintaining social harmony. In fact, it was one of the few books exempted from the infamous Burning of the Books of 213 B.C.E., when the authoritarian Chinese emperor attempted to eradicate all teachings that would oppose his rule.

Having jobs is our civilization's way of enabling people to develop, access, use, and share the things we need. Thus civilized work is a good thing and results in a much better situation than, say, social chaos! Hopefully, our civilization will be able to continue functioning. Hopefully, its rope won't break and its bucket won't leak. Obviously, no one wants to waste or destroy natural resources, but concern for the environment shouldn't stop us from continuing to make use of them. We have to make use of them in order to do our work and help others do theirs.

Although the *I Ching* includes elements of both Taoist and Confucian philosophy, the oracular message here is pretty thoroughly Confucian. Whereas Taoists tend to identify with nature rather than civilization, the Confucians regard civilization as their top priority. The Taoist point of view would undoubtedly be that we should save the rainforest and restore the natural balance at any cost. Confucians would respond that the most important kind of balance is social balance and this balance should not be disturbed by preventing people from doing their jobs. You can read more about Confucian philosophy in Part 5, "Sages in Service."

The Least You Need to Know

- The *I Ching,* or *Book of Changes,* was developed during the ancient Chou Dynasty for use by rulers, ministers, and others in positions of social responsibility.
- The *I Ching* combines a Confucian view of society and a Taoist view of nature within an elaborate system of divination based on yin and yang lines.
- The *I Ching* oracle probably developed out of an older method of divination that involved reading cracks made in tortoise shells and ox scapula bones.
- Use of the *I Ching* today requires creative interpretation of its poetic images in order to apply them to contemporary concerns.

Part 5

Sages in Service

China is unique among the great civilizations of the world in having, for most of its long and rich history, an official philosophy—as opposed to a state religion. This official philosophy is Confucianism, based on the teachings of China's most venerable sage, Kung Fu Tzu, known in the West as Confucius. Confucius's teachings were directly instrumental in maintaining the bureaucracy that ran the Chinese Empire.

Yet Confucianism is much more than a set of guidelines for Chinese bureaucrats. It is an idealistic, yet down-to-earth vision of society that aims at fostering peace and prosperity through harmonious relationships between leaders and their subordinates. In cultivating such relationships, Confucianism stresses the importance of civilized and gentlemanly behavior, appreciation for culture, and unflagging personal integrity.

It is by building a bridge between personal integrity and the ideal of a harmonious society that Confucian teachings have had such a tremendous impact on China. Of course, in being put into practice as an official bureaucratic program, this ideal has often fallen short of its goal as a result of corruption and stagnation. Yet for the most part, Confucianism has served its purpose for many centuries and continues to provide wise guidance for squaring personal conduct with the needs of society.

Chapter 21

Confucius Says

In This Chapter

- The life and teachings of Confucius
- Social harmony and personal integrity
- Yi and jen
- The rectification of names
- Li and the constant mean

If you're like many Westerners, you first heard of Confucius as a kid listening to other kids tell "Confucius says" jokes. You probably realized that there really was a man named Confucius who wasn't actually a comedian. In fact, Confucian philosophy has been tremendously important in China, where it was the official state philosophy up until the twentieth century.

Confucius is widely considered the greatest teacher and philosopher of China and, by some, the greatest that ever lived anywhere. Although he did not present his ideas in a schematized, highly organized way, all of his thinking tends toward one major goal: How to act in such a way as to maximize the harmonious functioning of the state. Many oppose his ideas as being too caught up with conformity and obedience. For Confucius, acting to serve the state doesn't limit individual freedom; it lends significance to one's actions and character.

Personal character, for Confucius, is the key to a harmonious society. When members of society—especially rulers and public ministers—cultivate wisdom, integrity, and compassion, the entire society will be peaceful and prosperous. Confucius was so committed to this vision of society that he devoted his entire life to attempting to bring it about—both as a teacher and as a minister of state.

The Man from Lu

Confucius, or Kung Fu Tzu, as he is known in China, is thought to have lived from 551 to 479 B.C.E. during a turbulent period in Chinese history when the great Chou Dynasty was on the wane and many small states vied with one another for power. He was born and spent most of his life in the principality of Lu, where Chou culture had made a big impact. Confucius himself was a devotee of Chou ideals and sought to preserve them in his teaching. In the process, he explained and justified them in new ways, stressing their practical and moral significance.

Lotus Lore

Legend attributes the cultural accomplishments of the ancient Chou Dynasty to the first Chou rulers, King Wen and his son, the Duke of Chou. But by Confucius's time, the dynasty and its culture were in decline. Nevertheless, Confucius's home state of Lu was ruled by descendants of the Chou, and Lu was widely considered to be a holdout of Chou culture. Confucius deplored the fading of Chou tradition and saw it as his mission to preserve and spread the ancient Chou teachings both as a teacher and as a minister of state.

Old Ways, New Thinking

Though he claimed to be merely a transmitter of traditional Chou wisdom, his original perspective on the importance of tradition lent coherence and purpose to his teachings. He recognized that social harmony depends on many factors, especially wise and benevolent leadership—in other words, on the competence and integrity of those in power. He believed integrity in leadership could be strengthened through respectful observance of the many traditional rituals of state. These rituals, he felt, preserved the earnestness and sincerity of those involved.

You might say Confucius was the first sociologist. He saw that traditional rites had a positive influence on society and that breakdowns in the social order were accompanied by a general disregard for tradition. But beyond this insightful observation, he had a deep sense of the practical need for personal integrity among rulers and public officials, so he taught aspiring public servants how to practice virtuous behavior for the sake of society as a whole. Yet, while Confucian virtue is rooted in ceremony and tradition and has a practical emphasis, Confucius advocated taking an almost spiritual interest in practical affairs.

Open Enrollment

Although little is known for certain about Confucius's background, he is thought to have descended from a noble family that had fallen on hard times by the time he was born. If so, this helps account for his tendency to stress personal integrity rather than wealth and power. Yet he saw that personal integrity was entirely dependent on one's ability to influence society for the good. In keeping with this view, he was committed to public service.

In his youth, Confucius was appointed to minor positions in the local government, such as superintendent of granaries, and later, supervisor of the care and feeding of sacrificial animals. These posts were not prestigious or especially demanding, yet Confucius filled them conscientiously. Though he took his work seriously, he was evidently capable of doing far more than keeping track of grain and livestock.

The details of his life are sketchy, but we know that at some point, around the age of 22, Confucius opened his own school. He may have seen teaching only as a sideline, but it became his most important work. In fact, Confucius is sometimes said to have been China's first private teacher.

Prior to Confucius's school, education was restricted to the nobility. As a result, only the nobility could serve in government since public service required education. Confucius believed that the lowly of birth could be trained as well as the highborn to become good ministers of state. He offered instruction to whoever could pay the modest sum of 10 strips of dried meat. Confucius's innovation of offering everyone, including the poor and lowborn, the opportunity of getting an education and serving in government eventually became adopted as official policy throughout the Chinese empire.

Confucius's teaching emphasized traditional rites, music, literature, and history, but despite this liberal arts curriculum, the school had the specific purpose of training people to serve in government. Confucius adopted the theory that a broad education focusing on culture and personal virtue was the best preparation for ministers of state. The idea was that a good understanding of culture and tradition would enable the future public servants to appreciate what it was they were working for—what society was, how it worked, why it was important, and how it could best be maintained and strengthened.

The Rite Stuff

Confucius himself came to be considered something of a specialist in the ancient rites; he traveled to other cities to study how they were practiced. The Chinese word for ritual, *li,* is an important concept in Confucian philosophy. It refers not only to ritual activities, but to the traditional rules of conduct and, even more generally, to good manners. In fact, the performance of rituals was thought to foster proper behavior.

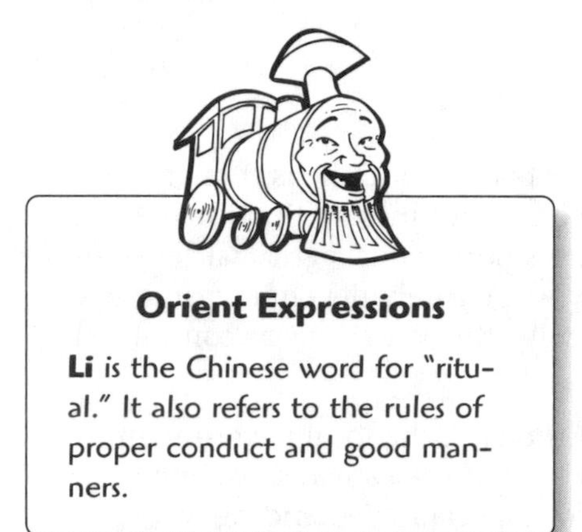

Orient Expressions

Li is the Chinese word for "ritual." It also refers to the rules of proper conduct and good manners.

Confucius's knowledge of the rites bolstered his reputation as a teacher and as a government official. Properly performed rituals lent credibility to government proceedings since they were thought to establish good relationships between heaven and the ruler and between the ruler and his subjects. This was especially useful in Confucius's time, which was fraught with social turmoil. Leaders and officials often seized power through violence and intrigue, resulting in hardship and instability for everyone. The traditional rites enabled some rulers to demonstrate sincerity and concern for the greater good. This, in turn, helped bolster their claims to legitimacy. Because Confucius was highly respected and knew the proper way to perform the rites, several leaders wanted him to work for them. So Confucius's knowledge of the right way of doing things helped him advance in government in his home province of Lu.

Take This Job and Shove It

In fact, Confucius came to hold a position as a minister of law and a diplomat in Lu. He had considerable influence with the governor and succeeded in improving Lu's political and economic standing with rival neighboring states. But at some point, around 497 B.C.E., after serving at his post for about four years, he resigned and left Lu, evidently because he was dissatisfied with the actions of his ruler. Although Confucius believed it was his duty to serve in government, he also believed it was morally wrong to serve a bad ruler who refused to take good advice.

Some say that Confucius left his post after taking part in a sacrificial rite and not receiving his due share of the meat that was distributed afterward. The point is not simply that Confucius was miffed about not getting what he had coming to him, but that the breach of propriety, a sign of more serious problems with the leadership, was an excuse to leave tactfully. Another story says that the governor of Lu was bribed by the head of a neighboring state with the gift of a bevy of singing and dancing girls! He became so engrossed with these women that he neglected state affairs.

In either case, Confucius felt his only recourse was to walk away. As a minister, he could not have improved the situation by arguing with his ruler. In fact, for a minister to criticize his ruler was not only useless, but foolish and dangerous since he could be suspected of disloyalty and severely punished. Simply leaving was the most effective way of offering criticism, but, of course, it meant that Confucius was out of a job. He set off in search of a new post somewhere else, taking many of his disciples with him and continuing to teach as they journeyed on.

Karma Dogma

The Master said, "When the way prevails in government, speak and act in an upright manner. When the way does not prevail, act in an upright manner but speak with humility."

—The *Analects of Confucius*, 14–3

Road Scholars

So Confucius and his followers traveled through the provinces in search of an enlightened ruler who would be willing to put Confucius's principles into practice. Some people they met on their way even laughed at them, regarding the mission as hopeless. Times were so volatile and corruption so deep-seated that no one in power was interested in giving Confucius a chance.

During his travels, he occasionally acknowledged the hopelessness of his cause, yet he continued to search for a position, regarding it as his duty. In fact, he never succeeded in getting a suitable post in government, and, after 13 years on the road, he returned to Lu. The 13-year job search wasn't a complete failure, however, since it must have provided his students with a unique opportunity to see the world while learning about it from an experienced and disciplined master. In fact, many of them succeeded in getting posts where their teacher had failed.

Although Confucius did not succeed in his long-held ambition to become a minister of state, he did not consider his efforts a waste of time. In fact, when he was asked why he did not serve the state, he responded that simply keeping up friendly relations with others as a private citizen constitutes honorable service.

Confucius was 68 when he returned to Lu and reconciled himself to teaching. He died five years later. His disciples recorded and collected his teachings into a book known in China as the *Lun Yu,* which means "collected sayings," or "collected discussions." In the West, the book is known as the *Analects of Confucius*. This is the main source of the philosophy that became the most influential way of thinking in Chinese history.

Lotus Lore

The sayings of Confucius are known as **Lun Yu** in Chinese, which means "collected sayings," or "collected discussions." James Legge, the pioneering student of Chinese literature in the West, first gave the *Lun Yu* the English title of *Analects* (which is a scholarly word meaning discussions). Most of the passages in the *Lun Yu* begin with the phrase "The Master said ..." giving rise to many Western parodies in the form of "Confucius says" jokes. In case you're wondering, the real Confucius actually did not say "He who lives inside a glass house dresses behind a brick window!"

Do-Gooders

A list of all the important principles of Confucian philosophy would read a lot like the boy scout motto: "Trusty, brave, true," etc. And, on the surface, the Confucian *Analects* can seem like nothing more than a bunch of guys sitting around reminding each other always to be good. The whole Confucius thing is easy to dismiss as a lot of pious, sanctimonious, self-satisfied hot air. What can really remind Westerners of long hours spent painfully in Sunday school learning to be good, is that Confucius expected his followers to take joy in learning to act like Dudley Do-Right clones.

If you pick up the *Analects* expecting the witty banter of urbane intellectuals, you'll be disappointed. And there's little of the humor, irony, and imagination that you can find in the old Taoist works like the *Chuang Tzu* and the *Tao Te Ching*. But after all, Confucius was running a school for future professionals. The point is to learn public service, not private feelings. As a result, there isn't much to joke about—just a clear, consistent sense of what's right and what's wrong and why, together with how to put what's right into practice and get what's wrong out of the picture.

But even though Confucius's teachings are geared toward public service, they focus heavily on personal cultivation. He taught his students that their practical ability depended on their knowledge, virtue, and integrity as individuals. "Being good" for Confucius is not simply a way to feel good about yourself, but a way to help make society function more smoothly. This goodness involved a whole range of things, including being able to appreciate poetry, fulfilling your responsibilities to others, and knowing when to keep your mouth shut.

Respecting Others, Being Respectable

There are two basic, interrelated ideas underlying all of Confucius's teaching. One is called *yi,* or righteousness. This means acting according to how you ought to act based on the situation. To act in keeping with yi is to act blamelessly and with sincerity to uphold your responsibilities to others. Tied in with this notion of righteousness is *jen,* or humanity, goodness, and benevolence. This includes love and compassion for others based on an appreciation of human nature and human society.

Jen supplies an important reason for behaving in accord with yi. Doing the right thing fosters humanity. This doesn't mean being totally self-sacrificing and being nice to everyone regardless of who they are. How you treat people and how you conduct yourself depends on the social effects your actions will have. Thus, according to Confucius, you don't treat a person who behaves badly with the same respect with which you treat a good person. In fact, a good person resents bad behavior because of the harmful effects it has on others.

Similarly, you have a right to enjoy the good things in life as long as you get them through appropriate means. After all, you're a part of society just like everyone else, so when things go well for everyone, you should join with others in reaping the rewards. In fact, helping others get good things is the best way to get them for yourself.

Orient Expressions

Yi is the Confucian concept of righteousness, involving just and appropriate behavior. **Jen** is the Confucian concept of humanity, goodness, and benevolence involving compassion for others. The word also means human being and, more particularly, a gentleman.

Two-Way Streets

Confucian philosophy is largely about teamwork, but it's also about obedience, loyalty, and leadership. In fact, Confucius paid close attention to all the different kinds of relationships that exist between people. Some occupy positions of leadership, others are followers. Confucius believed everyone's position in society should be clearly defined.

As he saw it, society was held together by social relationships of five types: husband and wife; parent and child; ruler and subject; sibling and sibling; friend and friend. Each type has its own structure and its own responsibilities. Confucius believed

Karma Dogma

A man of humanity is one who, wishing to establish himself, establishes others, and wishing to gain wisdom, helps others gain wisdom.

—The *Analects of Confucius,* 6–30

that, for society to run smoothly, everyone must understand and carry out their responsibilities to others.

What he saw around him was far from the ideal he envisioned: The five traditional relationships holding society together were degenerating and, as a result, society itself was falling apart at the seams. To counteract the problem, he recommended a stricter observance of the duties involved in the five social relationships.

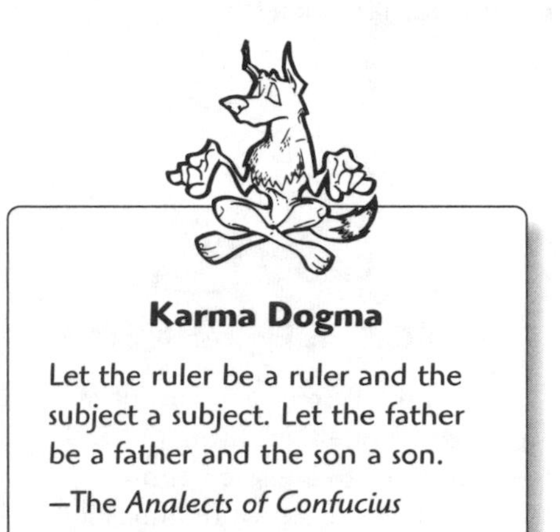

Karma Dogma

Let the ruler be a ruler and the subject a subject. Let the father be a father and the son a son.

—The *Analects of Confucius*

Parents, for example, have the responsibility of caring for their children until they are old enough to take care of themselves. Children, in return, owe a debt of gratitude to their parents throughout their entire lives and even beyond. This includes obeying them in youth, caring for them in their old age, and observing burial, mourning, and sacrificial rituals when they are dead. And, of course, the child who is obedient to his or her parents has a right to expect the same kind of consideration from his or her own children. Thus the parent-child relationship not only works both ways, but perpetuates itself.

What's more, the father-son relationship establishes the proper values and attitudes to be followed in the ruler-subject relationship. Confucius believed that a good son was unlikely to be a rebellious subject, while a good father was unlikely to be a tyrannical ruler. Thus the ability to uphold the responsibilities of close relationships reinforces the ability to uphold other social responsibilities as well, contributing to the harmony and stability of society as a whole.

Hanging in the Balance

One reason Confucian ministers of state required so much knowledge of culture and propriety is that they had to understand, cultivate, and balance all the social positions involved in the relationships holding society together. They had to be able to act as rulers, subjects, parents, children, friends, and siblings as the various occasions required. Thus, they had to be able to balance out wisdom and humility; benevolence and loyalty; simplicity and refinement; respect and courage; generosity and prudence.

An Official and a Gentleman

A potential minister should be a special kind of person whose understanding and respect for society enables him to follow the right course and adopt an appropriate attitude with complete sincerity, regardless of the situation. Thus, a sense of balance is crucial. Confucius called this balance *chung yung,* the "constant mean." *Chung Yung* later became the title of an important work on Confucian philosophy known in

English as *The Doctrine of the Mean*. The idea behind the constant mean and its doctrine is "do everything thoroughly, but don't overdo anything. As a subordinate, be respectful but not obsequious. As a leader, be authoritative but not arrogant."

Confucius saw that without the proper sense of balance, even virtues become faults. He believed this balance was best attained by learning and practicing the rituals. For example, he pointed out that even yi, the important virtue of compassion, could lead to foolishness. But tempered by the awareness of society that is fostered through ritual, yi cannot become merely sentimental or weak minded.

On the other side of the coin, and to take another example, Confucius said that courage without the respect fostered by ritual can lead to rebelliousness. Ritual, after all, involves a balancing of forces through a meeting of high and low. In ritual, various levels of society work together with a common purpose and in a clearly defined manner. So, by studying ritual, Confucius believed his students could see how to harmonize all the elements of society in order to put courage, compassion, and the other virtues to good use.

Looking Out for Number One

The emphasis on ritual in Confucius's teaching reinforces another point he repeatedly makes, namely that sincerity is crucial in whatever you do. Unless you're sincere, all your personal abilities and attributes are just a lot of window dressing. You may be smooth, polished, and refined, but you won't be any use to the common people, who don't have the time or inclination to worry about polish. When combined with sincerity, however, your cultivation is an honor for you, to the ruler who employs you, and to the people you lead.

Lotus Lore

A disciple once asked Confucius what he would have to say about a person who was liked by everyone in town. The sage responded that such a person was not on the right track. The disciple proceeded to ask what Confucius would say about a person who was disliked by the whole town. He responded by saying that this person wasn't headed in the right direction either. The best sort of person, said Confucius, is one who is liked by all the good people in town and disliked by all the bad ones.

This kind of sincerity can be fostered through an understanding of the rites, since they teach you to subordinate your own abilities and accomplishments to a higher good. At the same time, however, Confucian sincerity is more than self-sacrifice. Your own will and judgement are important as well. In fact, Confucius says it's a mistake to do things simply in order to please or impress other people. Instead, you should do things because they are right. This includes doing things that are right for you as well as for society.

Public Spirit

So Confucius taught that self-cultivation involves finding an appropriate compromise between your own desires and the good of society. These things don't necessarily have to be opposed to each other, but can work together. A society that doesn't enable its members to prosper is not a good society and should be changed. On the other hand, an individual who does not support society is not a good person and should change his or her attitude. According to Confucius, the best guidelines for achieving this harmony between personal needs and desires and the good of the public are provided by the rites.

Ritual reminds everyone that there are things that are more important than any single individual. It draws everyone's attention to the higher purpose behind what they do. It requires everyone involved to submit themselves together to this higher purpose. Confucius believed that when everyone in society recognizes and respects this higher purpose, society will become harmonious. In this way, ordinary life and daily work takes on a religious significance and everyone involved becomes inclined to devote themselves to the common cause.

Just what Confucius's religious beliefs were has been subject to debate. He once said to "respect the spirits but keep them at a distance." On another occasion, one of his disciples asked him how to serve God and the spirits, and he answered by asking, "How can you serve God or the spirits when you don't even know how to serve humanity?" No doubt the answer shut that disciple up in a hurry! The fact is, Confucius doesn't have much to say about divine and supernatural forces.

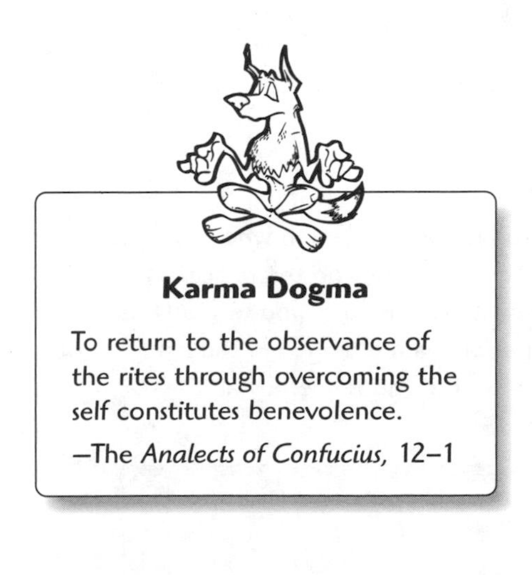

Karma Dogma

To return to the observance of the rites through overcoming the self constitutes benevolence.

—The *Analects of Confucius*, 12–1

Even so, he was clearly interested in drawing on religious feeling and putting it to use in upholding social harmony. You might say he treated the idea of social harmony itself as a spiritual thing—revering it and devoting himself to it. If so, he evidently believed there were many ways to practice the "religion" of social harmony, depending on your position in life. For himself and his students it meant studying the ancient classics of literature and history, which you can read about in the following chapter.

The Least You Need to Know

- Confucius was China's first teacher to accept commoners as pupils.
- Confucius's school was intended to prepare his students to fill government positions. The teaching stressed social harmony and personal integrity.
- Confucius left an important position in public service because he was dissatisfied with the leadership of the ruler.
- Although Confucius traveled throughout China for 13 years in search of a ruler who would give him a chance to practice his principles as a government minister, he was unable to get acceptable work in public service.
- Confucius stressed the importance of the five social relationships: husband and wife; parent and child; ruler and subject; sibling and sibling; and friend and friend.
- Confucius believed that studying traditional ritual practices was important for balancing one's desires, cultivating sincerity, and appreciating the higher purpose of society.

Chapter 22

It Is Written

In This Chapter

- The Six Classics
- The Li Chi
- Law versus ritual
- Sincerity and filial piety
- The Confucian Tao

Confucian philosophy has a lot to do with books, not simply because it is written down in books, but because, according to the Confucian way of thinking, books provide an important link between civilization and the individual. By reading books and learning how to interpret them, one cultivates oneself, gaining knowledge of culture and humanity and increasing one's powers of understanding and refinement. This in turn enables civilization to flourish. As the leaders of society become cultured and educated, the whole society becomes peaceful and prosperous.

One of the most important books in Confucian philosophy is the *Li Chi,* the *Book of Rites*. This book not only describes the traditional rites of ancient China, but explains their purpose in social and personal terms, showing how tradition, individual character, and society are interrelated. Through ritual, Confucians believed all Chinese could cultivate the right attitude for improving society.

This attitude is based on sincerity and filial piety, which were seen as natural human feelings capable of being directed in positive ways to maximize both public and personal well-being.

Although the rites and the qualities they encourage are seen as natural, they also require continuous effort to maintain. The person who can maintain these qualities through practice, study, and performance of the rites is thought to be a worthy leader and a loyal follower.

By the Book

Among all the ancient Chinese books that existed around the time of Confucius, six are often mentioned as the ones he used in his teaching. These are the Six Classics, consisting of the *Book of History,* the *Book of Odes,* the *Book of Rites,* the *Book of Music,* the *Spring and Autumn Annals,* and the *Book of Changes* (the *I Ching,* which was described in detail in Chapter 20, "Opposites in Flux"). Together, these works made up the curriculum of the earliest Confucian scholars.

Lotus Lore

Even into the early part of the twentieth century, Chinese Confucians continued to see the Six Classics as the foundation not only for civilized learning, but for civilization itself. Some looked to the Classics as a way to help China preserve her autonomy from the West. Others hoped their model of civilization, based on the Classics, would spread to the West, and even looked for prophetic signs that the early Confucians intended their philosophy to become the basis for a unified world government and civilization.

Study Guide

These books are so closely associated with Confucius that scholars associated with the Chinese interpretive tradition known as the New Text School regard him as their author. An alternative tradition, the Old Text School, regards Confucius as the editor and commentator of these Six Classics. In fact, few scholars today think Confucius either wrote or edited the books, some of which even appear to have been written after his lifetime.

But Confucius did teach the subjects they cover—known as the Six Disciplines. He stressed the importance of these subjects to personal cultivation and to civilization in general.

Confucius's ideas about how to use the Six Disciplines became fleshed out by later writers who describe the specific benefits to be gained by studying each of the Six Classics. These benefits are understood to include personal qualities cultivated by individual scholars, but also qualities exhibited by society as a whole.

Confucian Reading List

Here's a list of the Six Classics together with the Chinese name for each book and the personal and public attributes that can presumably be gained from studying each one:

- ***Shih Ching,* the *Book of Odes.*** This book consists of 305 poems that may have been sung to the lute at court during the Chou Dynasty. It is said to teach human motives and the qualities of gentleness, beneficence, and sincerity.
- ***Shu Ching,* the *Book of History.*** This is a collection of ancient speeches and prayers uttered on historical occasions stretching back to the beginning of the early Chou Dynasty. It teaches human events and breadth of understanding.
- ***Li Chi,* the *Book of Rites.*** This is a compilation describing and justifying ceremonial procedures, probably put together by Confucian scholars after Confucius's lifetime early in the Han Dynasty. It teaches respect, modesty, and earnestness.
- ***Ch'un Ch'iu,* the *Spring and Autumn Annals.*** A brief yearly chronicle of events in Confucius's home state of Lu covering the period from 722 to 481 B.C.E. It teaches duties and the powers of discrimination and judgement. (The *Spring and Autumn Annals* are actually so brief that they don't say much about the history of the period. Fortunately for historians, a commentary on the annals, known as the *Tso Chuan,* probably written during the third century B.C.E., provides more detailed information.)
- ***Yueh,* the *Book of Music.*** A classic text on music which may have existed, but is not known to exist today. The Yueh was said to teach harmony, generosity, and ease.
- ***I Ching,* the *Book of Changes.*** A book of divination and philosophical commentary stemming from the early Chou Dynasty. It teaches the movements of yin and yang, as well as subtlety, refinement, and calmness.

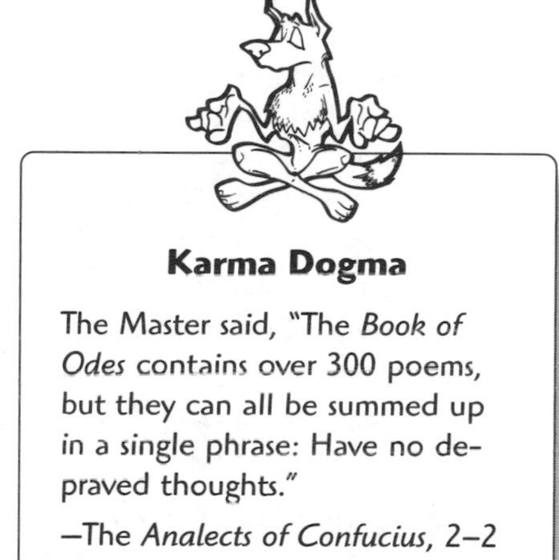

Karma Dogma

The Master said, "The *Book of Odes* contains over 300 poems, but they can all be summed up in a single phrase: Have no depraved thoughts."

—The *Analects of Confucius*, 2–2

On the Rite Track

Of all these books, perhaps the one that does the most to tie all of Confucian philosophy together is the *Li Chi*. This is partly because of the important place of ritual in ancient Chinese society and in Confucian philosophy. If you think of the essence of Confucianism as putting old traditions to new uses, you'll find reinforcement in the *Li Chi,* the book that stresses this idea most fully.

Lotus Lore

Although the Six Classics were important books to Confucius and his scholars, they are not the most important sources of Confucian philosophy. For that, we need to turn to the Four Books, written after Confucian ideas had had a chance to sink in. They include the *Analects, The Great Learning, The Doctrine of the Mean,* and *Mencius*. Together, they show the directions Confucian philosophy took following Confucius's lifetime. Two of the Four Books, however, *The Great Learning* and *The Doctrine of the Mean,* were later incorporated into one of the Six Classics, namely the *Li Chi, Book of Rites*. Thus the Confucian philosophy of ritual became one of its defining and most highly developed features.

Against the Law

The *Li Chi* explains *li*, or ritual, by contrasting it with laws. Both rites and laws were designed by the ancient Chou leaders to govern and regulate human conduct, but while the laws control bad actions after they have already been committed, rituals prevent bad actions by regulating the desires and feelings of people. In this way, Confucian philosophy emphasized the practical aspect of ritual. What law does through threats, restrictions, and punishments, ritual does through positive reinforcement of good and appropriate feelings and behavior.

The positive aspect of ritual makes it much preferable to law in the eyes of the Confucians. Ideally, there shouldn't have to be any laws. The state could, in theory, be well-ordered just through the power of ritual alone. The idea is that people who practice the rituals with sincerity are incapable of acting in such a way as to harm society.

Whether people act in a harmful or a beneficial way depends on how they deal with their desires. The Confucian scholars recognized that all people have desires, and felt that, on the one hand, these desires are natural and should be expressed and satisfied. On the other hand, they saw that unless desires are regulated, they can upset the balance of society. They looked at ritual as the best way of regulating desires, setting appropriate limits on how feelings should be expressed, as well as on how honors and gifts should be bestowed.

Not in This Life

Of course, not everyone in ancient China felt the same way about ritual as the Confucians. The *Lao-tzu* refers to the rites as "the mere husk of loyalty," emptily standing for things no one sensible really believed in. Another philosopher, Mo Tzu, who lived shortly after Confucius's lifetime, saw the rites as a waste of money that should be used for more practical things.

To Give and to Receive

The *Li Chi* separates the rites into five categories:

- Marriage rites
- Mourning rites
- Military rites
- Entertainment rites
- Sacrificial rites

The most important of these were the sacrificial rites, which were thought to be the profoundest expressions of feeling. During these rites, offerings were made to the ancestors and to leaders and other important figures of the past.

Karma Dogma

When there is devotion in making offerings to the dead, how much more will there be so to the living! Therefore, it is said that when the sacrificial rites are understood, the people are filial.

—The *Li Chi*

The *Li Chi* explains the emotional significance of the sacrificial rites in terms of the comfort they bring the living. Rationally, everyone knows that the dead who are offered sacrifices cannot enjoy them, but it is reassuring for those who offer them to imagine that they could. The idea is that the ritual involves a compromise between the foolishness of acting as though the dead were alive and the cold-heartedness of writing them off as no longer important. As an expression of this idea, ritual objects that had a place in the rites often went unused; for example, musical instruments were left out of tune. The fact that these instruments cannot be played symbolizes death.

While the ritual supplies comfort without delusion to those left behind, all the preparations for it, as well as the ritual itself, serve to refine and discipline the spirit of those who perform them. This refined discipline fosters the qualities necessary for good leadership and loyal service in political and administrative affairs. What's more, the ritual fosters personal integrity without encouraging excessive pride. By performing a ritual, you humble yourself in submission to the dead and, in doing so, you become ennobled and purified inwardly.

Owing It All to Mom and Dad

The ancient rituals of sacrifice were performed twice a year—in spring and autumn—by adults expressing devotion to their dead parents. The *Li Chi* stresses the importance of the inseparable connection between parents and their children, even after death. The sacrifice ritual serves to maintain this connection. In fact, filial piety—devotion to one's parents—is considered one of the most important qualities nurtured by ritual. The *Li Chi* does not expect the sacrifice to serve any beneficial purpose to the souls of the dead. Rather, ritual devotion to one's dead parents benefits the individual and, therefore, the state.

According to the *Li Chi* (as well as other Confucian sources), each individual has a lifelong responsibility to his or her parents and to the family name. This responsibility is fulfilled not just by taking care of your parents when they are old, but also by striving to bring honor to them through your actions and achievements. This also involves taking care of yourself and your reputation.

For example, many ancient Chinese regarded their bodies as the property of their parents, given to them for use and safekeeping. As a result, they were especially careful to avoid foolish and reckless behavior that could lead to permanent injury. One Confucian sage is even said to have called his disciples together shortly before his death so they could witness the fact that he had kept his body whole and functioning all his life.

This kind of scrupulous attention to oneself was thought to carry over into one's public actions. In this way, filial piety becomes a model for honorable action in general, especially the kind of activity that serves the state. It is said that the ancient sage kings of China brought harmony to the state by starting with their own families. They brought harmony to their families by regulating their own actions, and they regulated their actions by cultivating and purifying their minds. In this way, by going to work on themselves, they laid the foundations of civilization.

Lotus Lore

Confucians regarded it as a duty to one's parents to preserve one's body whole and in good working order. In Dynastic China, this duty had significance that extended beyond mere care in avoiding physical accidents. For one thing, it lent added disgrace to the brutal punishments for wrong-doing inflicted by the state, which often involved the chopping off of body parts. The duty to the body was also used as an argument against monastic Buddhism in China. Buddhist monks typically got their heads shaved. Some Confucians interpreted this (unreasonably enough) as an act of disrespect toward one's body.

Starting Small

Confucian philosophy emphasizes the value of paying attention to little things—of sweating the details—as a way to accomplish big things later on. Big things can't be done all at once, but result from the accumulation of many smaller things. This is true of society, which is a big thing made up of many individuals. In turn, the character of each individual in society develops gradually out of small things. This means it's a mistake to let little things slide even though they may seem unimportant. These little things all add up.

Sincerely Yours

The best way to approach any undertaking, whether it's big or small, is with sincerity. Sincerity, or *ch'eng,* is considered a divine quality exhibited by heaven as it interacts with the earth in producing and maintaining all things. It is also a human quality that can be developed through continued effort.

Orient Expressions

Ch'eng is the Chinese word for sincerity, which is an important Confucian virtue that can be developed by imitating the natural and beneficial nature of heaven.

Knowledge and learning are important in perfecting one's mind, but sincerity matters even more. Thus, even if you don't know how to do something but are sincere in your attempts, you're better off than someone who knows how but is not sincerely concerned about the outcome. The *Li Chi* expresses this idea by referring to the situation of a young woman bringing up her first child. Even if she never studied how to raise children, her attitude is naturally sincere.

Maintaining one's sincerity is vitally important in taking successful and appropriate actions, but it isn't always easy to do. It can require constant self-scrutiny and application. This may sound funny if you're from the West, where we usually think of sincerity as a quality that cannot be cultivated and just happens naturally. Either you're sincere or you aren't.

In China, however, because sincerity is considered natural, it can be fostered by imitating nature. Nature is tireless and constant in its workings and seeks nothing in doing what it does. These are also the qualities of a sincere individual. In addition, sincerity can be achieved by eliminating all discrepancies between inner feeling and external action. This means not fooling others or being deceived by yourself.

All the Rest

The *Li Chi* says that the way to maintain sincerity is by coming to rest before taking action. In other words, in conducting one's affairs, one should not run around like a chicken with its head cut off. Don't go from one thing to another without stopping for breath. Don't get drawn into doing a lot of multitasking! Obviously, the old Confucian sages weren't thinking about the Western work week when they came up with the idea of coming to rest!

Karma Dogma

Only he who has most ch'eng [sincerity] can develop himself to the utmost. Able to develop himself, he can develop other people. Able to develop other people, he can develop other things. Able to develop things, he can further the beneficial operations of heaven and earth.

—The *Li Chi,* chapter on the *Doctrine of the Mean*

Nevertheless, the idea is that mental clarity and sincerity depend on focus and preparation that can only come during times of inactivity. While resting, you can think about how to do what you're doing, as well as why it's important. Then you'll be able to do what you have to do thoroughly and with the proper frame of mind. To illustrate the value of coming to rest, the *Li Chi* compares the mind to a pool of water that is tranquil and clear only if it has had a chance to settle after being stirred up. Another metaphor is the bow (as in bow and arrows) that is ruined if it is never unstrung.

A familiar equivalent to the Confucian idea of resting is "finding your center." If you are centered you aren't exerting any unnecessary energy. You're not out of kilter, so you're not confused, disturbed, or dissatisfied. This helps if you want to be clear about what you're doing before you start doing it. This clarity and centeredness are good prerequisites to sincerity. Sincerity, in turn, is an infectious attitude that can influence others for the better, increasing your chances for success.

Setting the Standard

Confucian leaders believed in using themselves as a standard for measuring the behavior of their followers. In this way, leaders who wanted to hold their followers to high standards had to maintain their own best behavior. The idea is that if the leaders are good, the followers will be good also. Because of the importance of having good leaders, the Chinese have traditionally seen ambition as an honorable trait. If you are a good person, it is your duty to become as influential as possible so that more people will become good like you.

This ties in with the Confucian version of the Biblical teaching known in the West as "the Golden Rule." The Bible says, "Do unto others as you would have others do unto you." Confucius said, "Don't do to others what you don't want them to do to you." For Confucius, this meant treating superiors with loyalty and respect and treating subordinates with benevolence.

Obviously, the stress on fitting in with society is balanced in Confucian philosophy by the stress on self-cultivation and sincerity. In other words, Confucianism isn't just about conforming to the group, as many Westerners have assumed. Within Confucian thinking, it may even be appropriate to work to change society if you're dissatisfied and believe it is unjust. But before you go lobbying congress or stirring up public sentiment for your cause, you need to get your own act together and make sure you aren't simply lashing out in anger or frustration with your own life.

How to Tao

Self-cultivation in order to have a positive influence on society is the Confucian version of the Tao. If you looked at this book's previous section on Taoism, you may remember that the Tao means "the Way," which the Taoists saw as the way of nature. For Confucians, the Tao is the way of humanity. Unlike the Taoist Tao, which is effortless, the Confucian Tao can require tremendous exertion and energy to practice.

Be Smart, Be Nice, Be Strong

According to the *Li Chi,* the three requirements for practicing the Confucian Tao are *chih, jen,* and *yung.*

- **Chih** (wisdom) is practiced by studying the traditions and appreciating their beneficial effects on yourself and on the rest of society. In addition, it means being continually honest about your own needs, abilities, and motives and paying attention to how your actions influence other people, and you have to apply your knowledge and sincerity in doing whatever you can for yourself and for society in general.
- **Jen** (compassion) is fellow-feeling for other people. Jen is sometimes translated to mean human-heartedness. This involves realizing that your own feelings and

desires are shared by other people. This doesn't mean having equally strong feelings for everyone, however, since not all people hold the same relationship to you and not all people are equally worthy of respect.

➤ **Yung** (fortitude) involves working hard to carry out your actions thoroughly and maintain your good attitude constantly throughout your life. If necessary, it can mean standing up to adversaries or meeting other kinds of challenges. Then again, it may simply mean doing what you're supposed to be doing day in and day out, whether or not you get the appreciation you deserve!

The Long Haul

For some, the Confucian way comes naturally. Because of the Confucians' sincerity and devotion, they enjoy their work and have no difficulty teaching others, following their superiors, and generally maintaining harmonious relations. In fact, Confucius said that it is right to take pleasure in these things, since enjoyment makes it easier to do the work well.

Karma Dogma

The Master Said, "At fifteen, I set my heart on learning. At thirty I was established. At forty I became free from doubts. At fifty I understood the decree of heaven. At sixty I was obedient. At seventy I could follow my heart's desire without overstepping propriety.

—The *Analects of Confucius,* 2–4

For others, the Tao of Confucius poses more difficulties. They may lose interest in things, feel unappreciated, have trouble disciplining themselves, or tend to discipline themselves too harshly. Or they may succumb to greed or other temptations or weaknesses. Such difficulties, however, are no reason to give up.

In fact, Confucius himself admitted to having lapses from time to time. You can't really blame him since his whole life was basically a long series of disappointments! But the goal he set for himself was not so much to accomplish anything in particular in public life, but to get to the point where doing the right thing was second nature and enjoyable. In other words, he wanted the "way" of his desires to conform to the "way" of acting in harmony with others. According to the *Analects,* he succeeded in doing this at the age of 70!

The Least You Need to Know

- Confucian teachings are based on the Six Disciplines, which became the basis for the Six Classics, including the *Book of History,* the *Book of Odes,* the *Book of Music,* the *Spring and Summer Annals,* the *Book of Changes,* and the *Book of Rites.*
- Confucian philosophy contrasts ritual and law, seeing ritual as positive reinforcement and law as negative.
- By practicing the rites, Confucians hoped to cultivate personal virtue and thereby improve society in general.
- Among the most important qualities fostered by the rites are filial piety, sincerity, wisdom, compassion, and fortitude.
- Confucius claimed to have succeeded in squaring his desires with the decree of heaven by the age of 70.

Chapter 23

The Three Sages

In This Chapter

- Mo Tzu, Mencius, and Hsun Tzu
- Human nature and behavior
- Universal love and the three tests
- The Four Beginnings and the Four Complete Virtues
- Sagehood and its rewards

During the Warring States Period (480–221 B.C.E.), when governments vied with one another for a tenuous hold on power, philosophers hearkened back to an idealized past in which China was ruled by sage kings who epitomized wisdom, benevolence, and virtue. They believed that these kings came to rule China not through force or intrigue or hereditary succession, but through merit. Because they were the most capable rulers, they were selected by the will of heaven to govern the realm.

This ideal was behind the efforts of the most important philosophers of the time as they tried to understand human nature and direct natural human tendencies toward a peaceful, prosperous state. They reasoned on the human potential for wisdom and virtue and suggested ways to develop and tap this potential. In theory, all individuals could become sages, and, hopefully, one of them would step forward and take the reins of government.

These philosophers were, next to Confucius, the best-known non-Taoist philosophers of the classical period of Chinese philosophy: Mo Tzu, Meng Tzu (known in the West as Mencius), and Hsun Tzu. Mencius and Hsun Tzu were Confucian philosophers who applied themselves to explaining and developing Confucian principles. Mo Tzu set himself against Confucianism, although, like Confucius, he stressed the importance of social harmony in practical terms.

A Guy Named Mo

Little is known about the life of Mo Tzu (ca. 480–380 B.C.E.), China's leading non-Taoist philosopher next to Confucius. He may have come from Lu, the state where Confucius was born, or from Sung, which bordered Lu to the south. Although he is now considered much less important than Confucius, he was widely respected during his life and led a group of about 180 devoted followers. This group grew and stayed together even after his death, adopting a new leader they called the Chu Tzu, or Great Master. The Chu Tzu held command over the Mohists, so together the group constituted a powerfully organized political force.

Lotus Lore

Mo Tzu's followers were said to have made it a point of honor to die for a worthy cause. Meng Sheng, a leader of a Mohist group, sided with a ruler who was defeated by a more powerful rival. In order to show the world where he stood and how deeply he held his convictions, he killed himself. In a show of solidarity with their leader, close to 85 disciples also committed suicide. Even more Mohists would have killed themselves, but they were commanded not to by the man Meng Sheng appointed as his replacement.

Lovers and Fighters

Mo Tzu may have come from China's class of warriors or knights—known as *hsieh*—who often traveled around China during the Warring States Period, offering their services to rulers in need of fighting men. These warriors had a firm code of honor requiring them to stick together and support one another. Mo Tzu's philosophy can be understood as an elaboration and extension of this knightly code. Ironically, although Mohism seems to have developed out of the traditions of China's warrior class, it is best known for the view that all people should practice universal love.

The knightly code of the hsieh required them to love and care for one another. Mo Tzu said that this principle should be applied to all people. He reasoned that society's problems all stemmed from strife and oppression and that these hardships could be eliminated if people practiced universal love, treating strangers with the same devotion one has for one's own family. In practice, Mo Tzu's philosophy of universal love was not completely against violent action where necessary. In fact, Mo Tzu's followers were prepared to fight in defense of small states and weaker families oppressed by larger and more powerful ones.

Thus, universal love for Mo Tzu is primarily a practical value intended to improve society. He also taught that loving feelings and actions benefit the individual as well since, in the long run at least, they will be returned by others. At the same time, independently of practical reasons, Mo Tzu believed in a loving God who wants human beings to love one another. So Mo Tzu's teachings were both practical and religious. Even so, his chief standard for thought and action was benefit to the people. He believed that measures to improve the lot of commoners were the most helpful and necessary.

Not in This Life

Mo Tzu's philosophy of universal love was far from universally accepted. It gave rise to many philosophical arguments between the Mohists and other philosophers as to the relationship between loving behavior and righteousness. The Mohists advocated capital punishment for murderers and were willing to fight for a worthy cause. As a result, they were accused of logical inconsistency by rival schools.

Answer Me These Questions Three

Mo Tzu defined the most important human virtues in terms of their beneficial influence. Loyalty, for example, is behavior that benefits the ruler. Filial piety is behavior that benefits one's parents. According to Mo Tzu, the best people are those whose actions provide the most benefit for the most people.

Benefit to the people is the standard for the third and most important of Mo Tzu's "three tests" used for judging the correctness of moral principles. To determine whether a principle is good or bad, Mo Tzu said it should be subjected to the three tests of judgement. These measure the principle according to its foundation, its truth, and its applicability.

The foundation of a principle, according to Mo Tzu, is the will of heaven and the spirits and precedents set by the great sage kings of China's past.

In other words, valid principles come from spiritual and traditional sources. This does not rule out new ideas, however, especially since Mo Tzu himself was an original thinker. The truth of a principle should be tested by the witness of the common people. If the people accept a principle as true by adopting it or acquiescing to it, then it should be accepted as such in fact.

And finally, the applicability of a principle determines whether it's beneficial when put into practice, especially in government. This last test is the most significant. Thus, while Mo Tzu's philosophy leaves room for tradition and spirituality, its main thrust is its practical benefit for the commoners.

Crossed Paths

Mo Tzu's emphasis on benefit for the people, in and of itself, does not directly contradict the teachings of Confucius. After all, Confucius stressed the importance of social harmony, which can easily be interpreted as being concerned with public benefit. Yet in setting forth specific recommendations about how to benefit others, Mo Tzu expresses many disagreements with his predecessor. In other words, Confucius and Mo Tzu advocate taking different paths to reach a similar goal.

Lotus Lore

Mo Tzu, like the Confucian philosophers, idealized the ancient founders and rulers of the Chou, Shang, and the legendary Hsia Dynasties. According to legend, civilization was founded and developed by the Five Emperors—Fu Hsi, Shen Nung, Huang Ti (the Yellow Emperor), Shao Hao, and Shun Hsu. These were semi-divine rulers who supposedly invented the necessary elements of civilization, including agriculture, writing, domestic animals, pottery, etc. The Five Emperors were succeeded by the sage kings, who were not considered divine, but were said to have ruled with complete wisdom, benevolence, and virtue. These included the famous Three Kings—Yu, the founder of the Hsia Dynasty, T'ang, who founded the Shang, and Wen, who founded the Chou. The sage kings were considered to have attained rule of China not by military force or hereditary succession, but by the will of heaven. Thus they represent the Chinese ideal of meritocracy—government by those most fit to rule.

Bones of Contention

The Mohist ideal of universal love, for example, contradicts the Confucian teaching of the importance of the five human relationships and, more generally, the Confucian belief that different people should be treated differently depending on their moral worthiness. Confucius believed that people should be accorded varying degrees of respect and consideration depending on how closely related they are and depending on how virtuous they are. Mo Tzu argued that none of these things matter. We should love others equally and universally, regardless of whether we are bound by any social ties.

Another important point of disagreement between Mo Tzu and Confucian teachings concerns the value of ritual. Confucius taught that observance of the rites improves individual character and social harmony. Mo Tzu, in contrast, complained that the rituals involved an unnecessary expense. Lavish ceremonials wasted money and didn't produce any tangible benefits. Therefore, they should not be practiced.

Karma Dogma

To believe that spirits don't exist while studying sacrificial ceremonies is like learning the rules of hospitality without entertaining guests or like casting nets where there are no fish.

—Mo Tzu in criticism of Confucian ritual

Mo Tzu criticized Confucius's ambiguous attitude toward the belief in the ancestral spirits that the rites were intended to honor. Confucius said the rites should be practiced not for the sake of the spirits, but for the sake of the living. Mo Tzu argued that it was absurd to hold sacrifices for spirits you don't believe in. This is especially true considering the time, energy, and expense the rituals involved.

Thrifty Thinking

In a related, broader complaint against Confucian teaching, Mo Tzu argued that Confucius's ideas about self-cultivation and moral improvement were impractical and time-consuming. He pointed out that the traditional period of mourning to be observed by a son for his dead father was three years. (Actually, the length of the mourning period was two years and one month, but it was called "three years" anyway.) Mo Tzu said this was an excessive length of time and involved great personal inconvenience. Someone in mourning wasted time and energy that could be better spent doing more productive things.

Mo Tzu believed that Confucian scholarship was also too much trouble for most people and the benefits too intangible to make the effort worthwhile. He complained that Confucian self-cultivation was not materially productive and therefore was an inefficient use of time and energy. Instead, Mo Tzu advocated thrift and hard work for everyone as a way of improving the well-being of society in general and the common people in particular.

In general, Mo Tzu adopted and defended the point of view of the lower classes in China in a way that contrasted to that of Confucius, whose point of view was an extension and reworking of aristocratic beliefs. While they were both concerned with the well-being of the commoners, Mo Tzu believed in the importance of obedience and loyalty to superiors. He wanted to improve conditions for the poor and oppressed but did not see revolution as a good way to achieve this.

Lotus Lore

Some say Mo was not originally Mo Tzu's name, but a nickname indicating an interesting fact about his background. "Mo" is a Chinese term for the harsh punishment of branding criminals. Mo Tzu may have been such a criminal himself and have come to be called Branded Master by his disciples, who wanted to acknowledge his humble background and the hardships he had undergone. The brand may actually have been considered a kind of badge of honor by those who sympathized with his cause of improving the lot of the poor.

A Meng Among Men

Mo Tzu was not the only philosopher of the Warring States Period to find fault with the teachings of Confucius. In addition, the Taoist Chuang Tzu had criticisms to offer (as well as parodies) of Confucius and his wisdom. And, if the legends are true, Chuang Tzu's Taoist predecessor Lao Tzu also had stern and pointed reproaches for Confucius, which he offered in person. But despite the anti-Confucian backlash, Confucian ideas grew and spread, thanks to the work of his disciples and their disciples after them.

The best known Confucian philosopher next to Confucius himself was Meng Tzu, or Mencius, who lived around 370–290 B.C.E. Mencius studied under a disciple of Confucius's grandson, Tzu-ssu, who is supposed to have written the *Doctrine of the Mean,* a famous classic and one of the Four Books of Confucian scholarship. Mencius's own writings, called, believe it or not, *Mencius,* make up another of the Four Books. In order to explain and extend the teachings of Confucius, Mencius developed new ideas, many of them based on the concept that human beings are innately good.

Good at Heart

Mencius believed that people naturally want to help and protect one another as a result of innate feelings. When we see others suffering, we naturally want to help them. When we do wrong, we naturally feel ashamed. Yet, although these positive tendencies are natural, strife, poverty, and other social problems can lead us to abandon them.

The good news is that they can be developed into virtuous behavior with the proper training. Thus he called these natural tendencies the Four Beginnings, because they are the starting point of human goodness. According to Mencius, these innate traits distinguish human beings from other animals.

The Four Beginnings, with the right training, can be developed into the Four Constant Virtues. It should come as no surprise that these virtues include some of the more important Confucian values, since Mencius's ideas are designed to support Confucianism.

Karma Dogma

That in which humanity differs from the lower animals is not much. The mass of people throw it away, but the superior men preserve it.

—*Mencius,* 4:2–19

Starting Off Right

Here are Mencius's Four Beginnings, together with the Four Constant Virtues that grow out of them:

- **Sympathy.** This is what we feel when we see another person suffering. With the right training, this feeling can be developed into the virtue of jen, which is human-heartedness, or compassion.
- **Shame and dislike.** This is what we feel when we see evil in ourselves or in other people. This feeling can be cultivated into the virtue of yi, righteousness.
- **Modesty and deference.** This is what we feel when we see virtue that is superior to our own. This feeling can develop into a sense of propriety. Propriety is the virtue that is exercised in observing the traditional rites, or li. As a result, the word li is used to refer to the rules of proper conduct.
- **Right and wrong.** Last but not least, everyone has an innate sense of right and wrong. This sense provides a natural guide for all our actions. This sense can be developed into the virtue of chih, wisdom.

Making It All Worthwhile

When the Four Beginnings are all cultivated to the extent that they become fully established within an individual's character, that person, according to Mencius, becomes a sage, or *sheng*. Establishing them, of course, means putting them into practice in dealing with others. The best way to do this is to go into government service since, in keeping with Confucian philosophy, it is desirable for the most virtuous people to become leaders.

Orient Expressions

A **sheng,** or sage, is among the most highly venerated figures of China's Classical Period. Not simply a wise man, the sage was also virtuous and capable of taking the reins of government.

Whether or not you become a leading minister of state, the lofty goal of sagehood is within the reach of all who apply themselves through study and reflection. What's more, the experience of being a sage is portrayed in somewhat more positive terms by Mencius than by Confucius. Confucius wasn't unhappy about being a sage, of course, but part of his amazing achievement was to be content despite the fact that his lifelong efforts went largely unrewarded and even unrecognized.

Confucius associates sagely fulfillment with enjoyment of what is right and with satisfaction with what he calls "the decree of heaven." Despite this link between wisdom and the decree of heaven, Confucius often suggests that wisdom and the other virtues are their own reward—that a sage does not seek any reward or compensation for his efforts. Thus, a sage who has been able to have a positive influence on society can enjoy being a part of a better world. In contrast, a sage who has not been able to exert much of an influence can take satisfaction in having done his best.

Beyond these things, there's not a lot of pleasure to be derived from being a sage that isn't available to everyone else. Arguably, there's even less to enjoy since a sage has to be disciplined about how, when, how much, and with whom to take pleasure! So the rewards of being a sage as Confucius depicts them aren't likely to entice everyone in the neighborhood to rush out and apply for the job.

Mencius makes sagehood seem a little more appealing by suggesting that it confers mystic benefits. The sage is capable of achieving unity with the universe by becoming selfless and attaining perfect sincerity. In addition, he comes into possession of a mystic force through the prolonged practice of righteousness.

An anecdote from the book of *Mencius* illustrates the sage in action. It seems that there was a powerful king who became upset as he watched a bull struggle in terror as it was about to be slaughtered in sacrifice. The animal seemed almost human in its awareness of what was going on, and its effect on the king was heightened by the king's knowledge that the animal was innocent of any wrongdoing. Filled with sympathy for the beast, he ordered that a sheep be substituted as the sacrificial offering. Learning of this, Mencius approached the king and suggested that he apply his feeling of sympathy in managing his kingdom by showing more kindness and compassion to his subjects. The king replied by admitting that the reason he was unsympathetic toward his subjects was because of his desire for luxury and power, which drove him to subject his people to hardships on his behalf. Mencius responded by pointing out that all people shared the king's love of power and luxury, so that the king had even more reason to sympathize with his subjects, hence even more reason to treat them with compassion.

Down on the Farm

Although there is a mystical streak in the teaching of Mencius, he also pays attention to practical economic matters. He devised a method of distributing land and labor so that farming families could have equal plots to farm, and so they could be taxed fairly. This is known as the "well field system." The idea is that a large square area of land could be divided into nine equal smaller squares and farmed by eight families. Each family would farm one square for itself and help to farm the ninth square in common with the other families. Each family would keep what it produced on its own square. The goods produced on the ninth common square would go to the government.

Thus Mencius hoped to set guidelines that would enable peasant families to become prosperous and not unduly burdened by taxes. Like Confucius, he emphasized the importance of wisdom and benevolence in high places. In fact, Mencius distinguished between the ideal ruler, the sage king, who governed with human-heartedness toward all his subjects, and the typical tyrannical warlord who tried to exploit the people for personal gain.

Contrasting Confucian

Among venerable Confucians, at the opposite extreme from Mencius is Hsun Tzu (ca. 300–240 B.C.E.), who offered an entirely different account of why people should cultivate themselves. In fact, he opposed Mencius's ideas in many respects, yet he became the preeminent Confucian scholar of his day.

Lotus Lore

Although Hsun Tzu was the greatest exponent of learning in his day, his disciple, Li ssu, was hugely instrumental in curtailing private teaching and study in China. Li ssu became the chief minister to the Emperor Ch'in Shih Huang-ti and, in an effort to consolidate the emperor's power, recommended the infamous decree that resulted in the burning of most of the books in China.

The most striking difference between Mencius and Hsun Tzu is that, whereas Mencius said human nature is basically good, Hsun Tzu said it is basically evil. He believed that intellect and culture were necessary to counteract the bad innate tendencies of

Karma Dogma

Although the way of heaven is deep, the sage does not try to understand it. Although it is great, he does not devote any effort to it. And although it is refined, he does not scrutinize it. This is what is meant by not competing with heaven.

—Hsun Tzu

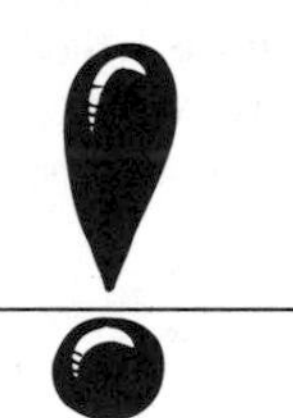

Not in This Life

Hsun Tzu's tendency to regard nature as devoid of divine influence did not mean he did not respect it. He argued that people should allow natural resources set periods of time to replenish themselves. For example, he recommended closing off streams while fish were spawning, restricting the cutting down of saplings, and imposing legal hunting seasons to protect game.

individuals. By using and developing the intellect, people come to realize the practical need for society and for social order, so they develop rules of conduct, enforced through laws and fostered through ritual, in order to guide behavior in a positive way.

Thus, while Mencius saw self-cultivation as a way of developing positive innate tendencies in human nature, Hsun Tzu saw it as a way of controlling negative ones. And while Mencius suggested that virtue conferred mystical benefits on the person who developed himself, Hsun Tzu saw self-cultivation in strictly practical, human terms. In addition, while Mencius saw nature and heaven as forces that the sage can identify with, Hsun Tzu said that the sage should not attempt to understand heaven except as a way to make appropriate use of nature.

According to Hsun Tzu, self-development has nothing to do with heaven. Heaven, for Hsun Tzu, is not divine, but natural, and nature doesn't show people how to behave; culture does. For this reason, human beings should leave the workings of heaven alone and concentrate on practical matters only. This means not getting involved in matters beyond human knowledge and human control.

In keeping with this attitude, Hsun Tzu placed less emphasis on virtue and personal goodness than on learning. His philosophy relies on intelligence and scholarship as a way of avoiding the pitfalls of human nature. Hsun Tzu himself was extremely learned and promoted study of the Confucian classics while providing critical analysis of other philosophies. These criticisms were generally based on logic rather than morality.

You might think from all this that Hsun Tzu was completely devoid of idealistic beliefs. In fact, however, Hsun Tzu was like other Confucians in idealizing the sage kings of the past. He provided elaborate explanations to justify the view that they attained rule of China through merit and experience rather than heredity, politics, or military force.

The Least You Need to Know

- Mo Tzu taught universal love and frugality in order to benefit the common people.
- Mo Tzu criticized Confucians for spending money and effort in learning the rites when it could have been better spent in productive work.
- Mencius taught that human nature is innately good and should be cultivated into the Four Constant Virtues.
- Mencius proposed a system for equitable land use and taxation in which nine equal plots would be cultivated by eight families.
- Hsun Tzu stressed learning as a way of controlling evil tendencies and drew a sharp distinction between human concerns and the workings of heaven.

Chapter 24

Official Business

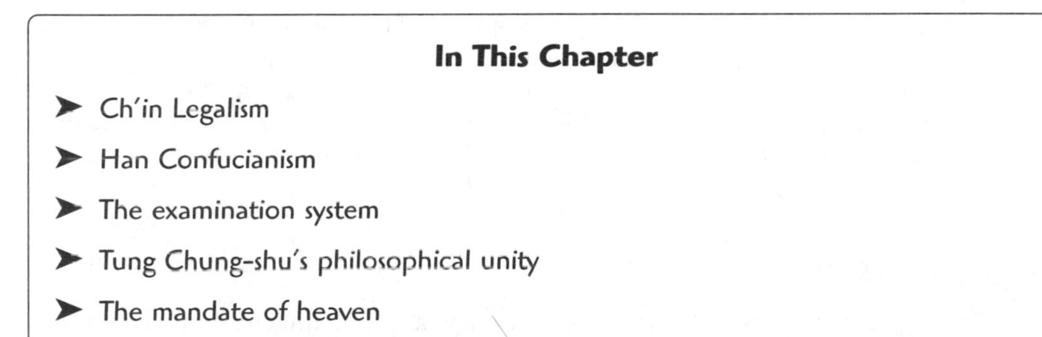

In This Chapter

- Ch'in Legalism
- Han Confucianism
- The examination system
- Tung Chung-shu's philosophical unity
- The mandate of heaven

Not quite 350 years after his death, the moral teachings of an out-of-work public servant were adopted as the official philosophy of the Han Dynasty, one of the greatest regimes in Chinese history. The move reflected the belief that those who were most cultivated and learned were also the most virtuous and best fit to rule. It drew on widespread public veneration of Confucius, the Sage of Lu, as well as on resentment toward atrocities committed by the emperors of the preceding Han Dynasty. In addition, the move was intended to establish a meritocracy—a rule of the best—in China in place of the authoritarian rule of the Ch'in.

Of course, in putting Confucius's teachings to this unprecedented use, the Han emperors changed Confucian philosophy. It became more systematized, mixing with theories about the laws of nature, the direction of history, and the workings of heaven. As a complete system, it laid the basis for a new unification of political, bureaucratic, and philosophical ideas.

Thus Confucian philosophy attained tremendous prominence and remained the state philosophy throughout the history of imperial China. The scholar-administrators who served in the Chinese government had more status than members of all other professions. They based their policies on Confucianism more than on any other philosophy.

Ch'in Up

At the conclusion of the Warring States Period, the State of Ch'in emerged as China's dominant power, and the Ch'in Dynasty began. The first Ch'in emperor consolidated his rule by instituting harsh laws with severe punishments for lawbreakers. He tried to extend his power over the thinking, as well as the behavior of his people. So he decreed the infamous Burning of the Books in 213 B.C.E. in which hundreds of philosophical texts were destroyed.

But the Ch'in government wasn't completely opposed to philosophy. In fact, the severe methods it put in practice were largely the outgrowth of the teachings of the philosophical school known as Legalism. Legalism helped supply a rationale for harsh methods of government and, by extension, for the rise of the Ch'in Dynasty itself.

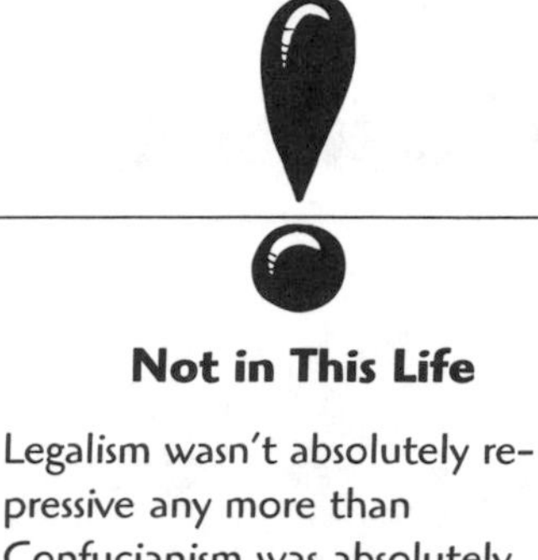

Not in This Life

Legalism wasn't absolutely repressive any more than Confucianism was absolutely benevolent. In fact, both philosophies have important features in common, including an emphasis on social and political stability. An early Legalist named Kuan Chung was admired by Confucius for his political skill.

Legal Matters

The Legalists did not revere the legendary sage kings of ancient times as the Confucians did. Instead, they believed that it didn't require any unusual degree of wisdom or virtue to rule an empire, but only the ability to make firm, clear laws and to appoint ministers to enforce them and abide by them. According to the Legalist school, the ministers do all the hard work of running the state while the ruler merely keeps the ministers in line through rewards and punishments.

Ch'in Legalism broke down the business of ruling into three components. These are *shih,* or power; *fa,* the law; and *shu,* which is method of government. All three were considered necessary for a well-run state. Power depends on the military and economic force of the ruler; laws depend on his will; and shu is provided by the Legalist philosophy.

Whereas the Confucians believed that the ruler should rely on laws as little as possible and rule instead by setting a good example, the Legalists saw laws as crucial for maintaining order. And, to enforce the laws, strict punishments were necessary. The importance of laws for controlling the masses extends to the method of delegating official responsibility for their enforcement. An official must have a clearly defined role so that he can be held responsible for the results he produces. If he does what he is supposed to do, he should be rewarded. If he fails, he should be punished. There is no need to take extenuating circumstances into consideration since this might give other officials the wrong idea about their own responsibility. This way, the ministers' focus is strictly on results.

Orient Expressions

Shih is power, **fa** is law, and **shu** is method. Together they make up the three basic principles of government according to Legalism.

Stick and Carrot

Rewards and punishments were said to be "two handles" for controlling the people. Unfortunately for just about everyone but the ruler, these were not always as clearly defined as the laws. They were based on the arbitrary whim of the emperor, who was free to dole out favor and retribution however he saw fit.

As you might imagine, this made life under the Ch'in Dynasty unpleasant for most people. The commoners were hard pressed to make a living, pay taxes, and keep out of trouble. Government officials were in danger of falling out of favor either by making a mistake or as a result of the political intrigues of those who wanted to rise quickly into the emperor's good graces. In fact, one of the leading Legalist philosophers of the time, Han Fei Tzu, was forced to drink poison as a result of a plot by a former pupil.

Han Fei Tzu says rulers should take direct, authoritative measures in dealing with the common people, but when government ministers deal with their rulers, they need to be extremely cagey in order to stay in their good graces.

He gives advice for coddling and manipulating rulers so as to be liked and trusted. The idea is to influence the ruler by subtly playing on his vanity, which has a deeper effect. For example, if the ruler thinks highly of his own intelligence, the minister should pretend to be not quite as smart as he is on any given matter. One way to do this is by *not* making the best possible recommendations when asked. Instead, the minister should come up with mediocre ideas for what to do and acknowledge how weak the ideas are. Eventually, the ruler will hit on the intelligent course of action. Then the minister should approve heartily of "the ruler's" idea.

Karma Dogma

If your ruler has an ignoble purpose that he cannot put aside, praise its merits and make light of the harm it can do. If he has lofty ambition but is too weak to realize it, point out its flaws and reveal its disadvantages.

—Han Fei Tzu

The minister should avoid obvious flattery since no one likes a yes man. So, in order to make the ruler happy and put him in a trusting mood, the minister should look for other people who have virtues in common with the ruler and praise them. If the ruler likes to think of himself as bold and decisive, the minister should praise the bold and decisive actions of others. Similarly, the minister should avoid criticizing others who have the same faults as the ruler.

The crafty approach to politics recommended by Han Fei Tzu contrasts sharply with that of Confucius, which emphasizes the values of sincerity and righteousness on the part of public ministers. Eventually, Confucianism won out as the official governing philosophy of China. But, of course, Legalism didn't entirely disappear; with the fall of the Ch'in Dynasty, it went underground. After that, the writings of Han Fei Tzu and other Legalists failed to gain the cultural importance in China that Confucian writings attained.

Upper Han

In fact, the Ch'in Dynasty didn't last long and soon fell apart amid revolutionary agitation. In its wake, the Han Dynasty (206 B.C.E.–220 C.E.) came to power. Like the Ch'in before it, the Han relied on newly developed philosophical ideas to maintain itself, but it turned to ideas that contrasted sharply with Legalism (not that Legalist methods disappeared entirely). But the official philosophy was a much kinder, gentler way of thinking. This was a form of updated Confucianism that incorporated much of the thinking of the Yin-yang School. The new hybrid was adopted as the official state philosophy. Though the adherents of the new thinking called themselves Confucians, they espoused many ideas that were not originally part of Confucius's teachings.

Looking Good

Han Confucianism was, in some ways, a reaction against the ruthlessness of Ch'in Legalism. Confucianism, after all, advocates fostering harmony through ritual rather than compelling obedience through the threat of punishment. In addition, by adopting Confucian thought as an official state philosophy, the Han government found ways to legitimize itself. The official philosophy suggested that Han rule was not only virtuous and enlightened, but historically inevitable and even a manifestation of the will of heaven. Thus Confucianism was used as political propaganda.

The official move to make Confucianism the state philosophy was intended to serve many purposes at once. Chief among these was to unify philosophical thinking in China in order to minimize political strife. The emperor hoped that, with just one state philosophy, there would be no dissent. Not only did the emperor hope to introduce a single, common way of doing things, he wanted general agreement on its purpose. Perhaps even more important from his perspective was his desire for a way of thinking that would regard the newly established Han Dynasty as just and legitimate. The teachings of Confucius, together with the sage's reputation for wisdom and integrity, served the needs of the new regime perfectly.

Lotus Lore

During the Han period, Confucianism gradually received greater and greater imperial support. The empire sponsored Confucianism in many ways. A university was founded where Confucianism was taught and officials were trained; conferences on Confucian teachings were organized; texts of the Confucian classics were carved in stone slabs, which were put on public display; and a civil service examination system qualifying applicants for official positions was instituted based on Confucian teachings. The empire even ordered that sacrifices to Confucius be held.

Han Hindsight

During the years following his death, Confucius's reputation gradually grew, and he came to be regarded as a truly great sage. Some even regarded him as divine. Many believed that he wrote the Six Classics that were used as the basis of Confucian education. An important Han official named Tung Chung-shu even suggested that Confucius had a master plan, expressed in the Six Classics, for bringing about an ideal government. So scholars combed through the old books looking for evidence to support this theory.

Many Han Confucians believed Confucius was actually the man appointed by heaven to rule China in the wake of the Chou Dynasty but that his rightful position was usurped by the Ch'in. They believed he wrote the *Spring and Autumn Annals* to express his views of proper government. This idea of Confucius as king paved the way for the view adopted in later generations that he was a god.

Confucius came to be seen as a kind of prophet of the Han Dynasty. The Confucian writings were interpreted not just as explanations of the ancient Chou traditions, but as anticipations of the Han. In interpreting the classics in this way, Tung Chung-shu and his followers suggested that heaven itself intended to install the Han as rulers of China.

Karma Dogma

When one serves one's parents with love and reverence while they are alive and serves them with grief and sorrow when they are dead, the fundamental duty of humanity is fulfilled, the meaning of life and death is completely understood, and the duty of the child to the parents is completed.

—The *Hsiao Ching,* Classic of Filial Piety

Office Work

The element of propaganda was not the only reason the Han adopted Confucianism as the official state philosophy; there were more basic practical and philosophical considerations. For one thing, the bureaucratic elements of Confucianism suited the Han administration. The Confucian ideals of loyalty and order fit in well with the big, centrally controlled imperial society inherited by the Han rulers from their Ch'in predecessors. At the same time, the importance of family relationships in Confucianism reinforced the traditional social structure based on large family groups.

Gravy Train

While the Han rulers used Confucianism both to make themselves look good and to help keep family and administrative relationships in place, they tried to organize the government through Confucian principles. Confucius taught that the most virtuous people make the best ministers and that one of the best ways to become virtuous is to study and cultivate oneself. It only stands to reason, then, that if a ruler wants good ministers, he should employ the best scholars. This is exactly what the Han leaders tried to do.

In 136 B.C.E., the Han emperor Wu Ti passed an edict declaring that, of all the teachings current in China, only the Six Classics of Confucian scholarship would receive official sanction. Philosophers would be permitted to study and teach whatever they wanted, but only Confucian philosophy would get imperial support. As a result, Confucianism flourished, and other approaches shriveled in comparison.

Confucian learning actually became an important meal ticket for China's best scholars. Henceforward, all candidates for government employment would be selected largely on the basis of their knowledge of the Six Confucian Classics. This meant not only that Confucianism was officially recognized as the imperial philosophy of government, but that Confucian scholars would be trained as government leaders.

Lotus Lore

Two competing approaches to scholarship developed during the Han period: the New and Old Text Schools. "Old Text" refers to the style of writing used before the Ch'in burning of the books. The Old Text School began when some books written with this ancient script were discovered. The New Text School claimed that these books were forgeries, and they based their interpretation of Confucian philosophy on reconstructions of the burned books. In turn, the Old Text School accused the New Text School of adding new, non-Confucian ideas to the ancient teachings. Scholars today tend to think that both criticisms were justified. The Old Text School did use forged documents, and the New Text School did add new ideas to the old teachings!

Passing the Test

In order to locate the most talented Confucian scholars, a system of examinations was put into practice. The examinations were administered regularly throughout China to all those who wanted positions in government. The examinees wrote essays in response to questions that centered around the Confucian Classics. Those writing the best essays qualified for government posts. The idea was to put in place a system of government and administration based on merit.

The idea took hold and stuck. The examination system and the scholar-administrator became features of Chinese bureaucracy for centuries to come. Scholars and government officials were paid well and enjoyed tremendous prestige.

Not in This Life

The examination system in imperial China was intended to identify potential government officials based on merit. In practice, however, the system didn't always work. For one thing, cheating on the tests was not uncommon. Test takers with connections in high places were sometimes able to find out the questions ahead of time.

It seems likely that the practice of employing scholars in government had a beneficial effect on the stability of Han rule in more ways than one. According to Confucian theory, scholars are most fit to rule. History also suggests that during times of trouble, it is often the educated classes who produce rebel leaders and ignite insurrection. The Chinese approach of employing scholars in government effectively prevented this source of conflict!

All Together Now

The examination system of imperial China was first proposed by Tung Chung-shu (ca. 180–100 B.C.E.), the same influential minister and scholar who interpreted the Six Classics of Confucianism as a prophecy of the Han Dynasty. Tung Chung-shu, in fact, was chiefly responsible for making Confucianism the official Han Dynasty philosophy. He did this in part by applying Confucian teachings in new ways—most notably by proposing the examination system. He also added new ideas to the old teachings, such as the notion that Confucius's writing anticipated Han rule. In addition, he combined Confucian philosophy with other traditional philosophical beliefs.

For Heaven's Sake

For example, according to Han Confucianism, the ruler reigns according to the mandate of heaven. This means that cosmic, natural, and social forces all work together to fulfill the will of heaven, which controls all things. In fact, "the mandate of heaven" is an ancient idea in Chinese thinking. Throughout the history of imperial China, the emperor is known as "the son of heaven."

The Han Confucians believed that the power of the emperor over his subjects corresponds to the power of heaven over the earth. Heaven influences the earth by making it fruitful and productive in spring, summer, and fall, and by making it barren in winter. Similarly, the emperor enables the people to flourish and be productive by rewarding them for good work and obedience and by punishing them for unruliness. The rewards of the emperor correspond to spring, summer, and fall while the punishments correspond to winter.

Seen in a negative light, this view of imperial power as god-like makes the welfare of the people completely dependent on the whim of the emperor. With no system of checks and balances, the ruler could do whatever he wanted. Nothing could stop him from oppressing his subjects. (Nothing, that is, except the courage of his ministers who, according to Confucian tradition, were expected to risk their lives, if necessary, by offering advice and criticism even when the emperor didn't want to hear it!)

There is a plus side, however: The idea that the emperor corresponds with heaven clearly shows that it's the emperor's job to help the people flourish, just as it was considered heaven's job to make Earth a fruitful place. In fact, if the emperor wanted to convince people that he had the mandate of heaven, he had to rule in such a way as to provide for his subjects. Otherwise, he risked triggering a revolution.

"Heaven" to the Chinese is quite different from the God of Western religion, who has absolute power, is said to be "jealous" and unknowable, and is completely separate from Earth. The Chinese concept of heaven exists in close relation to the earth and interacts with it. It is a natural, as well as spiritual, force. Therefore, the mandate of heaven gave the emperor absolute power, but also implied moral responsibilities and at least a certain amount of benevolence.

Lotus Lore

The "mandate of heaven" is the Chinese concept of rule by divine right and may first have been claimed by the ancient Chou kings in order to justify their overthrow of the Shang rulers who preceded them. Mencius reinterpreted the concept by saying that the best sign of the mandate of heaven is the approval of the people. Many Chinese emperors, however, were more superstitious than Mencius and listened to the prognostications of magicians and soothsayers who interpreted the will of heaven through natural events, such as floods and storms. This superstition was intensified by the fact that the mandate was generally understood to be temporary. The traditional Chinese view of history is cyclical, and it was widely believed that each dynasty would be succeeded by another in time.

State of Union

Tung Chung-shu's brand of Confucianism was a blend of Confucian thought and his own ideas. He also incorporated ideas derived from the Yin-yang School, many of which were popular at the time with the common people. Thus, by making Yin-yang ideas a component of Confucianism, Tung Chung-shu helped to unify separate philosophies under one way of thinking.

The Han rulers were happy with this philosophical unification because they hoped it would promote political unification. They believed that the more the people and public officials believed the same things, the more stable the government would be. In fact, the Han rulers inherited this idea from the Ch'in emperors before them. But while the Ch'in relied mostly on the coercive measures of the Legalists to control the thinking and behavior of the people, the Han tended to use the benign precepts of Confucianism, together with new interpretations of what they meant and how to apply them.

The Yin-yang School focused on principles for explaining the working of nature, including yin and yang and the five elements. (You can read about the five elements in Chapter 16, "Old Masters.") In mixing the Yin-yang teachings with Confucianism, Tung Chung-shu tried to give the social and moral principles of Confucius a natural and cosmic justification. Thus, where Confucius said that something was morally right, Tung Chung-shu would say it was not only right, but natural and cosmic.

Lotus Lore

In 79 C.E., a major conference was held in China's capital city that was attended by important Confucian scholars. The purpose of the conference, sponsored by the emperor, was to discuss the Confucian classics and iron out disagreements as to their interpretation. The record of this conference is known as the *Comprehensive Discussions at the White Tiger Hall.* (The White Tiger Hall was the name of the building where the conference was held.) The book served as an official interpretation of Confucian teachings on every topic and is largely consistent with the ideas of Tung Chung-shu and the New Text School.

Cosmic Morality

Tung Chung-shu took the Confucian concept of the five relationships (parent/child, ruler/subject, husband/wife, friend/friend, and sibling/sibling) and explained them in terms of yin and yang. In the parent/child relationship, the parent occupied the yang polarity while the child occupied the yin position. In the ruler/subject relationship, the ruler is yang while the subject is yin.

Orient Expressions

Hsing is the human potential for good as described by Tung Chung-shu, who associated it with the yang principle. **Ch'ing** is the propensity of feelings and desires, which Tung associated with the yin principle.

Tung Chung-shu identified three of these relationships as more important: parent/child, ruler/subject, and husband/wife. These relationships, according to Tung Chung-shu, form the basis of social morality. He calls them the three *kang*. A kang is a cord used in the mesh of a net to which other cords are tied in making the net. Thus the three kang, or relationships are the basis of society.

Tung explained personal qualities as well as human relationships in terms of yin and yang. He said all people have a natural potential to be good. He called this potential *hsing* and associated it with the basic constitution of the self. In addition, people have feelings and desires that can either complement or crowd out the good potential. These desires are known as *ch'ing*. Hsing represents the yang aspect of the human character while ch'ing represents the yin. Through training, study, and personal cultivation, hsing can be developed and put to good use, and ch'ing can be controlled.

The best way to develop one's hsing is by concentrating on the five chief Confucian virtues, known as *ch'ang*. Tung identified these as compassion, righteousness, conduct, wisdom, and good faith. He associated these five virtues with the five elements of the Yin-yang School. Human morality should be based on these ch'ang virtues as well as on the three kang relationships. Ch'ang represents personal good behavior while kang represents good social relationships. Together, they represent the virtuous life, known as *kang-ch'ang*.

Tung Chung-shu said that everyone is capable of leading a virtuous life but most people need help from the government. He saw it as the job of the scholar-administrator to help people cultivate their virtues and keep their desires in check. Ironically, despite his tremendous influence on Chinese bureaucracy, he never rose very high in public office. Yet he was said to be a devoted scholar, and his writings were studied by followers for centuries after his death.

Orient Expressions

Kang is a term for the cords in the mesh of a net, used by Tung Chung-shu to refer to the three most important human relationships: parent/child, husband/wife, and ruler/subject. **Ch'ang** refers to the five chief Confucian virtues, according to Tung Chung-shu. **Kang-ch'ang** is the virtuous life involving both personal goodness and social ethics.

The Least You Need to Know

- Legalism is the philosophy of ruling through strict laws and harsh punishments. It was adopted by the leaders of the short-lived Ch'in Dynasty.
- Many Han scholars reinterpreted the Confucian classics as a blueprint for the Han Dynasty's rule.
- Confucianism became the official state philosophy during the Han period, when public officials were selected by examinations based on Confucian learning.
- Tung Chung-shu was largely responsible for developing the rationale for the examination system and the employment of Confucian scholars in government.
- Tung Chung-shu elaborated the ancient concept of the "mandate of heaven," which gave heaven's approval to the ruler.

Chapter 25

The Way Revisited

In This Chapter

- Neo-Confucianism
- Chu Hsi and the principle of nature
- Wang Yang-ming and the principle of mind
- Neo-Confucianism and Buddhism
- The fall of imperial China and the rise of Communism

A renaissance in Confucian thought and culture took place in China beginning around the tenth century C.E., which, in the minds of many historians, marked the high point of Chinese civilization. This rebirth came with prosperity, growth, peace, and stability throughout the empire and involved a new approach to Confucianism as the old classics were reinterpreted in light of Buddhist and Taoist influence. The result was that Confucianism became more cosmically oriented on the one hand and more focused on the mind and consciousness on the other.

The philosophy known in the West as Neo-Confucianism is known in China as *Tao Hsueh Chia,* the School of the Study of the Tao. The Tao referred to here is both the cosmic Tao of the Taoists and the social Tao of the Confucians, brought together into a synthesis that set the tone for philosophy in China throughout the remainder of the imperial era. In many ways, the ancient Confucian ideal of a harmonious and cultivated civilization was realized.

Thanks largely to this cultural and philosophical legacy, Chinese civilization peaked early (during the Dark Ages in Europe) and remained on a high plateau for centuries. In fact, China's culture was so much more sophisticated than its neighbors' that the Chinese acquired a habit of isolation and self-reliance. But China's efforts to remain aloof from the rest of the world failed in the nineteenth and twentieth centuries when the empire was overrun by Westerners bent on free trade.

In with the New

The rise of Neo-Confucianism represents the third major stage of Confucian thought in the history of China. First, there was the age of Confucius himself around 600 B.C.E. Next, centuries later, starting around 200 B.C.E., came Han Confucianism with its implementation of Confucian principles in government and bureaucracy. Confucianism lent stability to Han rule, but the order didn't last. Incursions of hostile foreign powers and internal schisms divided the realm. Surprisingly, however, the Chinese empire and Confucianism bounced back.

Lotus Lore

Because foreign conquerors did not have a written language of their own, they were forced to learn Chinese writing to administer their states. In this way, China's cultural cohesion was preserved amid repeated political upheavals. Europe, in contrast, remained fragmented after the fall of the Roman Empire, possibly because European kings could use the Roman alphabet to write in their native languages, thereby enabling the countries of Europe to develop cultural autonomy.

The Han Dynasty fell in 222 C.E., and the Chinese empire would not be united again for almost four hundred years, when the S'ui Dynasty established control in 589. Yet the fact that the empire managed to regroup after being divided and conquered by foreign powers is remarkable. One possible factor accounting for the resiliency of imperial China is Confucian philosophy. It may be that the Confucian principles of wise and benevolent leadership had such a strong appeal that they never completely disappeared. Another factor may be China's unique written language. Because Chinese writing does not represent vocal sounds like the Roman system, Chinese characters cannot be used to write non-Chinese languages.

New and Improved

Confucianism and the Han Dynasty flourished together for 400 years before Han rule weakened and gave way. Under the Han, the Chinese population grew too fast for the government bureaucracy to keep order. Although, to an extent, Confucianism supported the bureaucratic order, it also placed great importance on family ties. As a result, large and powerful families emerged whose interests competed with the good of China as a whole.

In the wake of the Han, the Chinese Empire fell apart into a number of kingdoms whose sway was neither extensive nor prolonged. This is known as the Six Dynasties period, from 222 to 589. During this time, Confucianism preserved much of its official status among administrators but lost the respect of many educated Chinese who became disgusted with society and politics.

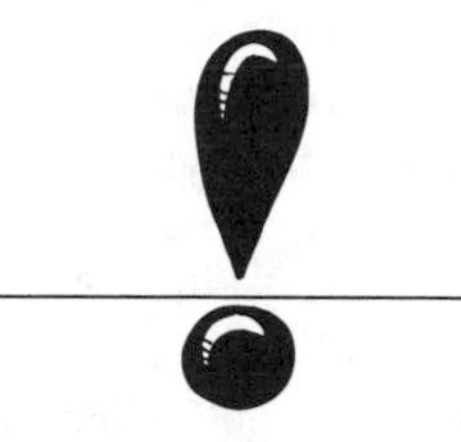

Not in This Life

Not all the dynasties of imperial China were actually Chinese dynasties. The Yuan Dynasty (1279–1368) was a period of Mongol rule. The last dynasty, the Ch'ing (1662–1912), was a long succession of Manchu emperors. Despite foreign rule, however, Chinese cultural and administrative institutions were preserved. It proved more efficient and effective for foreign rulers to use them than to introduce new systems.

In the skeptical climate of the Six Dynasties period, Taoism and Buddhism rose in prominence. Retirement from public life came to seem wiser than Confucian public service. Yet the decline of Confucianism wasn't permanent. Confucian ideals came roaring back with the reunification of China under the Sui (589–618) and T'ang (618–907) Dynasties. From this point until the fall of the Chinese Empire and the start of the Chinese Republic in the twentieth century, Confucianism remained a major basis of cultural prestige and political stability.

Neo-Confucianism succeeded largely because it helped the empire succeed, providing a reliable system of managing its economic and political affairs. It also succeeded because it incorporated elements from competing philosophies—Buddhism and Taoism. As Confucian scholar-administrators began to think about Buddhist and Taoist teachings, they applied them to their understanding of the Confucian classics. In effect, this provided a kind of official sanction for new and popular ideas, keeping Confucianism abreast of the thinking of the times. This was the timely blend of Confucianism, Taoism, and Buddhism that took hold during the T'ang Dynasty.

Reading Between the Lines

Neo-Confucianism involves, simultaneously, an incorporation of Taoism and Buddhism and a reaction against them. Although the Neo-Confucians borrowed from

Karma Dogma

A man may become a sage through his nature (hsing). A man may betray his nature through his feelings (ch'ing). Happiness, wrath, pity, fear, love, hate, and desire are the seven courses of the feelings. When the feelings are stirred up, they drown out man's nature.

—Li Ao, Neo-Confucian scholar of the ninth century

Buddhist and Taoist thinking, they pretended to have come up with the new ideas on their own and they continued to criticize Buddhists and Taoists!

Of the two, Neo-Confucianism regarded Buddhism with special antagonism. This is partly a matter of national pride since Buddhism came from outside China. Yet Buddhism provided a valuable stimulus to Confucian thinking.

Some Neo-Confucians regarded the ideal of Confucian sagehood in terms similar to Buddhist enlightenment. Just as Buddhists believed that the original teachings of the Buddha were transmitted through a chain of leading disciples down from the Buddha's time to the present day, Neo-Confucians believed that the Confucian Tao originated with the ancient sage king, Yao, who passed it along to his successors until it reached Confucius, and later Mencius.

The idea of succession suggests there is a hidden element to the ancient teachings that could not be written down, but had to be communicated in person from teacher to disciple. Without this personal communication, which was thought to involve special training as well, the writings expressing the Confucian Tao could not be properly interpreted. It was widely thought that the line of succession was broken after Mencius, so that no one after him understood the true teachings. Nevertheless, the Neo-Confucians set themselves the task of recovering the lost, unwritten teachings.

Amazingly enough, some of these lost teachings bear a striking resemblance to Buddhist teachings! Of course, what was really happening was that the Neo-Confucians were going back and interpreting the Confucian classics along Buddhist lines and pretending that the new, Buddhist elements were Confucian in origin and were there all along.

Buddha Within, Confucius Without

You may remember from the previous chapter that the Han Confucians made a distinction between selfish feelings (ch'ing) and the natural human potential for good (hsing). Under the influence of Buddhism, the Neo-Confucians began to think about ch'ing in terms of the Buddhist attitude toward desire. Desire, for the Buddhists, is a cause of suffering and delusion and stands in the way of enlightenment, which can only be attained through inner tranquility.

Taking their cue from the Buddhists, the Neo-Confucians considered inner tranquility a way of overcoming desire. What's more, they identified this idea, not as a Buddhist teaching, but a Confucian one, which they located in the Confucian classic, *The Doctrine of the Mean*. This work, as you may remember from Chapter 19, "Tao and Forever," is part of the *Li Chi,* or *Book of Rites,* and talks about the importance of coming to rest as a way of maintaining sincerity (ch'eng) in one's actions.

The Neo-Confucians interpreted "coming to rest" as being equivalent to the inner tranquility of the Buddhists. By coming to rest, you can overcome your own selfish desires and attain sincerity. This sincerity is an important Confucian virtue that leads to wisdom. For the Neo-Confucians, sincerity leads to the enlightenment of the sage, just as tranquility through meditation leads to Buddhahood for the Buddhists.

A Man of Reason

The most important Neo-Confucian was Chu Hsi (1130–1200). More than any other philosopher, he brought together the separate currents of Buddhism, Taoism, and Confucianism into a way of thinking that generations of Chinese after him continued to accept. Chu Hsi was schooled in the Confucian classics at an early age and passed the imperial examination at the age of nineteen. Despite his ability, his rise in the ranks was hampered by his frank disagreement with his superiors on political matters and by what were at the time his unorthodox interpretations of the classics. In fact, one of his superiors was so irritated by Chu Hsi that he put in a request to the emperor to have him beheaded!

But Chu Hsi was able to keep his head on his shoulders and put it to good use as the leading Neo-Confucian philosopher. He did not get far with his career as a government official, however, but he did make the most of his free time by writing books and commentaries. His work did not receive official recognition until after his death when he was made an honorary duke.

Lofty Ideas

Like other Neo-Confucians before him, Chu Hsi incorporated Buddhist and Taoist elements into his thinking. In doing so, he added a Confucian account of natural and cosmic principles not found in original Confucianism. Chief among these principles is the concept, stemming from Taoism, of the *t'ai chi,* or Supreme Ultimate.

Orient Expressions

Li is a Neo-Confucianist term meaning "ultimate principle," which was thought to determine the nature of all things. **Ch'i** is the matter or substance of all things that takes shape through the influence of li.

Many Taoists believed that t'ai chi consisted of yin and yang and accounted for natural processes of the universe, as well as the nature of humanity. Chu Hsi explained t'ai chi as a principle beyond physical things which makes these things what they are. This principle applies to human behavior as well as to natural processes. He called this principle *li* (not to be confused with the Confucian concept of li, meaning conduct or ritual).

Corresponding to li, or principle, is *ch'i,* which means matter, the material substance things are made of. According to Chu Hsi, there are two ch'i: yin and yang. Thus, yin and yang are actually physical substances that make up the material world and take their shape in different things according to li. All things have li, according to Chu Hsi. Their li gives them their nature.

Clearing Things Up

While Chu Hsi's philosophy provides a way of thinking about the natural world, it has moral implications as well. Li exists in human beings and accounts for the human capacity for goodness. But not all people are able to act on this capacity because our ch'i gets in the way. Although ch'i gives us our physical form, it poses an obstacle to our li, or human nature. This causes us to act badly and prevents us from understanding why our actions are bad. Fortunately, it's possible, through study and self-examination, to understand our own li and avoid bad behavior.

Chu Hsi compares li (human nature) to a pearl, and ch'i (matter) to a pool of water. He imagines the pearl sitting in the pool and says that the water may be more or less clear or muddy depending on our virtue and understanding. Ignorant and evil people have the same nature as wise virtuous folks, but their ch'i is different. In the wise and virtuous, ch'i is like calm, clear water that enables the pearl of li to be seen in all its luster. In the evil and ignorant, ch'i is like muddy water. Animals, says Chu Hsi, also have a virtuous nature, but their ch'i is like thick mud, so it's nearly impossible to see.

Lotus Lore

Chu Hsi's philosophy is described in Chinese as *Li Hsueh,* which is often translated into English as Rationalism. In Western philosophy, Rationalism is the theory that human beings are capable of knowing things through reason alone, independently of experience. The preeminent Western Rationalist is Rene Descartes, who believed the human mind included a physical aspect that was subject to delusion, as well as an immaterial soul that was incapable of error. Descartes's distinction between the material mind and the immaterial soul resembles Chu Hsi's distinction between ch'i and li. An analogous rationalist view can be found in the Hindu and Buddhist understanding of *citta,* or consciousness, which may be more or less pure and spiritual and more or less polluted by physical concerns, including desires.

Nature Meets Society

The central idea of Chu Hsi's philosophy—that li is at work in all things—accounts both for the natural world and for human nature. And it suggests continuity between humanity and the world, based on human understanding. To know things as they are, to see clearly and accurately, goes along with having a virtuous nature. Knowledge and goodness go together. This means that studying is an especially virtuous activity.

In keeping with this attitude, Chu Hsi emphasized a passage from *The Great Learning*, one of the Four Books of Confucian scholarship, which says "the extension of knowledge lies in the investigation of things." By investigating things, Chu Hsi doesn't mean going out and conducting scientific experiments; rather, he means we should continually notice that the nature of all things accords with li. By observing the li in external things, we can cultivate the li in ourselves. The sage, according to Chu Hsi, is someone who recognizes li in the things of the world and in himself and acts in accordance with it.

Chu Hsi's emphasis on the nature of things and the understanding of the individual are not in and of themselves important thrusts of Confucian philosophy—at least not before Chu Hsi came along. Confucius himself didn't have a lot to say about how the understanding works or about the nature of the physical world, or whether these things were controlled by some sort of overarching principle. Confucius pretty much limited his focus to personal conduct, interpersonal relationships, and society as a whole.

In Chu Hsi's philosophy, however, Confucius's teachings on conduct, relationships, and society are explained in terms of li—human nature and the nature of things. In fact, Chu Hsi says that society has its own li, which a leader needs to understand in order to govern effectively. This is why the task of leadership should be reserved for the sage. Those who come to power by means of force may exert control over people, but they will not be able to govern properly without an accurate knowledge of the nature of things, including knowledge of society and of themselves.

Buddha Bashing

The rational aspect of Chu Hsi's philosophy—the focus on the innate ability of the mind to understand the truth—reflects Buddhist influence on Confucianism. Buddhism is deeply concerned with the nature of consciousness and the interrelationship between consciousness and observable reality. Chu Hsi drew on Buddhist influence in other ways as well. For example, he advocated a form of meditation—not in order to transcend the self as in Buddhism, but as a means of self-evaluation. By sitting quietly and reflecting on one's actions and character, it is possible to gain the necessary insight for self-improvement.

Yet despite the affinities between Neo-Confucians and Buddhists, Chu Hsi was strongly opposed to Buddhism. He criticized Buddhists on both practical and theoretical grounds. Like other Confucians, he objected to monastic living since it broke up the traditional family and isolated monks from the rest of the society. Chu complained not only that monastic Buddhism was bad, but also suggested that it was hypocritical in its attitude toward family relationships. The Buddhists claimed that family relationships were not important. Chu Hsi said the Buddhists actually demonstrated their importance by forming monastic societies based on artificial versions of natural family relationships. In other words, he accused the Buddhists of inventing a substitute for the kind of relationships they claimed to do without.

The head monk served as ruler, with the other monks as subjects. Teachers served as fathers, and disciples occupied the role of sons. More experienced monks were like older brothers to novices. This, according to Chu Hsi, shows the natural inevitability of the Confucian relationships and indicates that Buddhism is missing the point.

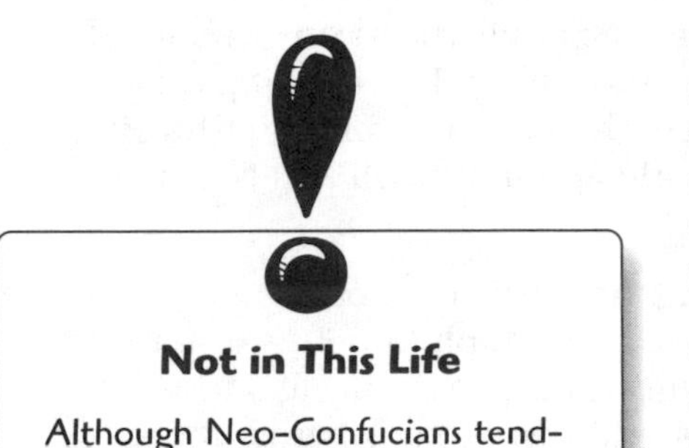

Not in This Life

Although Neo-Confucians tended to criticize Buddhism, Buddhist influence incited some Neo-Confucians to change their attitude toward Confucius and the Six Classics of Confucianism. They maintained that a sage who attained enlightenment had no need to thoroughly study the classics since the knowledge would be superfluous.

Chu Hsi also complained of the Buddhist tendency to confuse consciousness with ultimate reality. In his view, consciousness, or the mind, is separate and different from the overarching principle of li. To mistake one's own mind for the overarching principle itself is to fail to see how one fits in with the rest of reality and to fail to appreciate the importance of other things, including human society.

In addition, Chu Hsi objected to the Buddhist concept of shunyata, or void. Buddhism teaches that existence, including the self, is impermanent and therefore empty. Chu Hsi compares this concept of shunyata with his concept of li, saying that li is not empty, but real and lasting. To take emptiness as an ultimate principle is to do away with reality.

High Ideals

Chu Hsi represents one of two main branches of Neo-Confucianism—the Rationalist School (Li Hsueh, study of principle). In contrast to this school is the Idealist School (Hsin Hsueh, study of mind). The leading idealist Neo-Confucian philosopher is Wang Yang-ming (1472–1529), who lived during the Ming Dynasty. He emphasized the concept of Universal Mind.

Can't See the Forest for the Bamboo

Like other Neo-Confucians, Wang Yang-ming talks about the principle of li, which transcends and organizes reality. For Wang, however, li is not synonymous with nature, as it is for Chu Hsi, but with mind. Mind, for Wang, is universal, embracing heaven, earth, and humankind. The mind works through an intuitive awareness of this unity. At the level of the individual, this mental connection is experienced as the Confucian virtue of compassion, or jen, that enables us to identify with and understand the things of the world.

Not in This Life

The power of the mind does not have an equal effect on good and bad alike according to Wang Yang-ming. He says that a good thought is not truly good unless it is put into practice. On the other hand, an evil thought is evil even merely as a thought.

Wang Yang-ming arrived at this understanding of li as mind after years of wrestling with a statement found in *The Great Learning,* "The extension of knowledge lies in the investigation of things." This statement was famous at the time thanks to the teachings of Chu Hsi who wrote commentary on it. Wang wanted to put this idea to the test for himself. Here's how, according to his biography, he went about it:

> He began "investigating things" with a grove of bamboo plants and went out to observe and study them to see what he could learn. He remained in the grove for days on end until he finally got sick and had to go inside. After all this effort, he learned nothing in particular about bamboo. Dissatisfied with his efforts to understand things, he turned to Taoist teachings, which he found more to his liking. But when he tried to square these teachings with those of Confucius, he couldn't make them fit.

Mind Meld

His problem with investigating things remained unresolved years later when he got in trouble at court over an argument with a powerful eunuch. (You can read more about eunuchs in Chapter 27, "Bedroom Wise." For now, it's enough to say that whenever eunuchs attained political power in imperial China, it was generally taken as a sign of corruption in government. Confucians, in particular, regarded them as impure.) As a consequence of this argument, Wang was banished to a remote and isolated province, thus putting his political career on hold.

It was in exile that Wang Yang-ming came to his important discovery. It was late at night, and he lay awake in bed, when suddenly it hit him. He got up and started shouting and dancing around the room. From that moment on, he regarded li, the ultimate principle, as Universal Mind. Without Mind, neither the principle nor the things of the world could exist.

Lotus Lore

Idealism is a Western philosophical term that can be applied to Wang Yang-ming's philosophy since it refers to the idea that nothing exists independently of the mind. Famous Western idealists include Plato, Immanuel Kant, and Bishop George "If-a-tree-falls-in-the-forest" Berkeley. The Buddhist Yogacara (Mind-only) school is another important brand of idealism that may have had an indirect influence on Wang Yang-ming.

As a result of this discovery, he proposed an interpretation of "extending knowledge" by "investigating things" that differs sharply from Chu Hsi's view. Knowledge of things can be gained not through detached observation and study, but intuitively. Because things owe their very existence to the Mind, it is in terms of Mind that they must be understood. And the most important lesson is that there is no significant difference among things. The whole universe is an expression of Mind.

Alien Nations

Neo-Confucianism shows how flexible Confucian philosophy can be in its ability to appropriate influences from other philosophies and still maintain its own identity and function as imperial China's official doctrine. By incorporating elements of Buddhism and Taoism, Neo-Confucianism became capable of appealing to many Chinese who might otherwise have become Buddhist or Taoist. This no doubt helped the empire maintain stability in the face of divergent ways of thinking. But when China was confronted with Western influences, it turned out to be a different story.

Stemming the Tide

Toward the final years of the Chinese empire, Neo-Confucianism faced the task of responding to new political, religious, and philosophical ideas from the West. To an extent, Neo-Confucianism went on to absorb elements of Western thinking as China became increasingly exposed to Westerners. Confucian assimilation of Western ideas, however, posed an increasingly greater challenge, and it was ultimately less successful than it had been with Buddhism and Taoism. Nevertheless, for a while at least, Confucians absorbed a limited degree of Western influence while preserving their Chinese identity.

Starting in the sixteenth century during the Ming Dynasty, Christian missionaries arrived in China to spread the gospel of Christ. They succeeded in winning some converts but, on the whole, the Chinese were resistant to the new faith—especially since those who embraced Christianity were expected to renounce all other religious practices, including ancestor worship. Nevertheless, the Christians made enough of an impact to inspire many Confucians to take a more religious attitude toward their beliefs. They began hailing Confucius as a divine, as an uncrowned king, and as a prophet of world peace.

Later still, near the collapse of the empire, a group of Confucian reformers attempted to introduce Western social and political ideas in Confucian guise. They tried to make Confucianism more liberal in hopes of peacefully changing the system of government to a modern constitutional monarchy. The attempt failed, however, and many of the reformers were assassinated.

Lotus Lore

After the fall of the last Chinese Empire in 1912, a congress met in 1915 to draft a constitution for the new Republic of China. One of the proposals put forth generated heated debate. This was a measure to adopt Confucianism as the official state religion of the republic. In a compromise, the congress agreed to accept Confucianism not as a religion, but as the basis of ethical procedure. Although the provision was duly written into the constitution, it was never carried out.

All the Tea in China

During the final years of the empire, the Chinese administration did its best to keep Western influence out of China. One reason for this policy was to maintain control over trade. China produced many luxury goods, including silk and porcelain, that were in demand in Western countries, but there was little from the West (other than gold and silver) that the Chinese wanted in return, despite the many technological innovations the West had to offer. In fact, the Chinese tended to regard Westerners as uncultured barbarians and, as a result, underestimated Western achievements in science and technology.

Eager to exploit Chinese markets and frustrated with the trade imbalance caused by Chinese protectionism, Western countries resorted to smuggling opium into China from Turkey and India. Though outlawed by the Chinese government, opium trade was so highly profitable that opium smuggling was condoned by many Western governments. As the Chinese cracked down on the smugglers who had the official support of the West, tensions escalated into war.

The Opium Wars of the nineteenth century proved disastrous for China. The Chinese lost and were forced to yield to Western demands that included special privileges for Western traders. Hong Kong was ceded to British control. China was further weakened by the Sino-Japanese War of 1894 to 1895. Antiforeign resentment reached a fever pitch at the turn of the century as the Boxer Rebellion broke out. The Boxers, as they were known in the West, were a militant nationalist group called the *I Ho Chuan*—the Society of Righteous Fists—bent on eradicating foreigners and foreign influence in China.

The Boxers brutally massacred foreign businessmen, officials, and missionaries but vented most of their anger on Chinese who had converted to Christianity, killing them in large numbers. The uprising was officially denounced by the imperial government in statements to the West, but in reality, the Boxers met no official resistance, and the group marched to Beijing and besieged the section of the city controlled by foreigners. The rebellion was eventually put down by Western troops, and the Chinese government was assessed a stiff fine it was unable to pay.

Orient Expressions

I Ho Chuan was the Society of Righteous Fists, better known to the West as the Boxers, a group of militant nationalists who terrorized Westerners and Western sympathizers in China at the turn of the twentieth century.

Unable to curb the conflicting forces vying for power in China, in 1911, the last emperor abdicated. For a time, China became a nominal republic under the military leadership of General Sun Yat Sen, but the struggling new regime failed to secure necessary support from the West. With assistance from Soviet Russia, Communism in China gathered steam under Mao Tse-tung, who led a successful revolution and became Chairman of the People's Republic of China in 1949.

The Least You Need to Know

- The Chinese Empire fell apart in 222 but reformed again almost 400 years later. After this, Confucianism was revived and was sustained until the empire fell again in 1912.
- Neo-Confucianism, which blends Confucian, Buddhist, and Taoist teachings, reached its peak around the tenth century.
- Chu Hsi was an influential Neo-Confucian of the Rationalist School. He believed the mind is innately capable of understanding itself and all other things, thanks to a transcendent natural principle called li.
- Wang Yang-ming was an important Neo-Confucian of the Idealist School. He believed that a Universal Mind contains all that exists.
- Efforts to square Confucianism with Western ideas failed amid antiforeign resentment as the empire fell apart.

Part 6

Living Wisdom

Eastern philosophy, as you may have noticed by now, is not an activity restricted to old men with long white beards who live on mountaintops or in ivory towers. It goes on in the minds and actions of ordinary people in the process of leading their lives. It has a profound influence on just about everything people do.

In this part, you can read about the applied, practical aspect of Eastern ideas—how these ideas have influenced the way people eat, have sex, fight, stay healthy, create artwork, do business, and practice politics. You may learn how to incorporate Eastern wisdom into your own way of doing things. In fact, you may be surprised at the extent to which Eastern thinking is already a part of your life.

Chapter 26

Food for Thought

In This Chapter

- Food and philosophy in the East
- Food in Hindu religious sacrifice
- Sacred cows and vegetarianism
- Legalist and Confucian ideas about food
- Taoism, eating, and health

Of all the subjects of philosophical speculation, food is among the most thought-provoking. Different eating styles invariably come with their own mindsets since the way people eat influences the way they think and vice versa. Because food is so important to life, it is important to philosophy.

It's no surprise that Eastern philosophy should have a lot to say on the subject. In fact, it may not be mere coincidence that India and China have not only produced some of the world's most influential philosophies, but also some of the most widely eaten cuisines. After all, knowing how to eat is an important aspect of knowing how to live. It only makes sense that the two should develop side by side in both of these Asian civilizations.

If you've ever received good advice from a fortune cookie, you already know that food and philosophy go together in Chinese culture. The same can be said of India, although the reasons are vastly different. In China, food acts as the center of social life and forms the basis of personal health. In India, food is often considered holy and is to be shared with the gods who helped to provide it. Food for thought, anyway—worth keeping in mind the next time you order takeout!

Different Tastes

Various philosophical traditions in India and China recommend a range of attitudes toward eating—from near complete abstinence to downright gluttony. In China, some Taoists have attempted to survive without eating so as to purify their bodies. In India, Hindus, Buddhists, and Jain ascetics have imposed strict limitations on eating—in some cases, even to the point of self-starvation.

Lotus Lore

In a Taoist legend, a man fleeing for his life from his enemies had to abandon his infant daughter in a grave with only a few days' supply of food and water. Years passed before he could return to the grave where he expected to grieve over her remains. To his joy and surprise, he found her still alive where he had left her! Astonished, he asked her how she'd lived without food or water. She answered that there was an invisible man in the grave with her who'd taught her how to survive on her own breath and saliva. He was a Taoist immortal who had purified himself beyond having need of his body, which had died and been buried in the grave.

On the other hand, there is a pronounced sensual side to the cultures of both civilizations that looks favorably on food as a means of self-indulgence. In China, the Taoist philosopher Yang Chu was said to be a hedonist. And the Taoist Pure Conversation School had members who devoted their lives largely to eating and drinking. There were also hedonists and Epicureans among Indian philosophers. Food, as well as sex, is an element of certain Tantric rituals aimed at achieving maximum sensual gratification. Members of the materialist Carvaka School advocated self-indulgence on all fronts simply because they believed in no higher power than the self.

Yet, despite their many similarities in other ways, in their philosophical attitudes toward food, India and China are generally different from one another. The difference can be summed up in the Chinese emphasis on social and economic stability and personal physical health and the Indian emphasis on spirituality.

Food for the Gods

The people of India have always taken a deeply spiritual approach to food. Many Hindus regard food as a link between the gods and humans; the thinking is that food is produced through their joint efforts. People till the soil, plant and tend crops, harvest them, and prepare the food, and gods make the food grow and control the weather and climate. In appreciation of this, many Hindu religious rituals enact the sharing of food between Hindu gods and those who worship them. You might say that Thanksgiving in India comes much more often than once a year—but that doesn't mean they sit and stuff themselves while watching football on television!

Much Hindu spirituality is also expressed by not eating. Virtually all of the many different religious groups in India observe dietary restrictions particular to them. Some foods are eaten only in limited amounts or at certain times, under certain circumstances, with certain people. Other foods are never eaten. These restrictions vary, not only from group to group, but within historical periods. History shows that religious food restrictions in India have changed dramatically over time, suggesting links between religious observance and food availability.

India's many food restrictions and food rituals serve other purposes in addition to expressing religious spirituality. Anthropologists have found that they provide a means of feeding the poor and needy and of maintaining boundaries between social groups, such as tribes and castes. (Some castes won't eat certain foods eaten by other castes or eat in the presence of other caste members.) Yet despite the particular relevance of food-spirituality to Indian society and culture, certain of its key features have been adopted by outsiders. The popularity of vegetarianism in the West, for example, owes a lot to India.

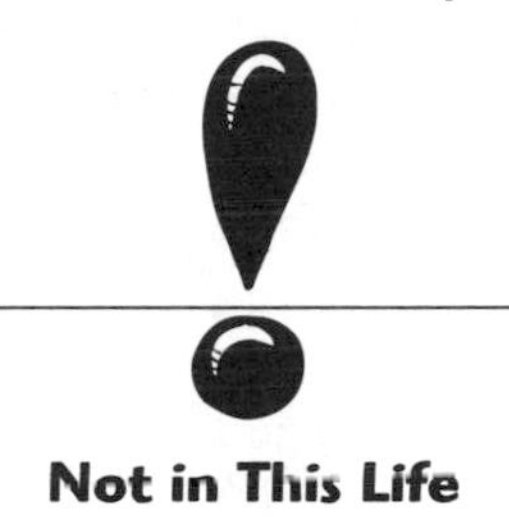

Not in This Life

Though the caste system traditionally imposes restrictions on who can eat with whom, these restrictions can be overridden by sacred food rituals that allow the sharing of food across caste boundaries. In contrast, some food rituals serve to reinforce caste distinctions.

Holy Pleasure

For millions of Hindus, feeding the gods is the basis of many important religious rituals. Often, food is placed in front of statues of the gods as a sacrificial offering. After the appropriate amount of time, the "leftovers"—called *prasad*—are eaten by the faithful. But not all the food is necessarily eaten. In traditions practiced by certain worshipers of Krishna, small likenesses of the god are sculpted out of cow dung. A small bit of food is placed in the navel of the cow-paddy statues. These statues, or the idols of other gods, may be bathed in milk, or ornamented with flowers, jewels, perfume, or other luxury items.

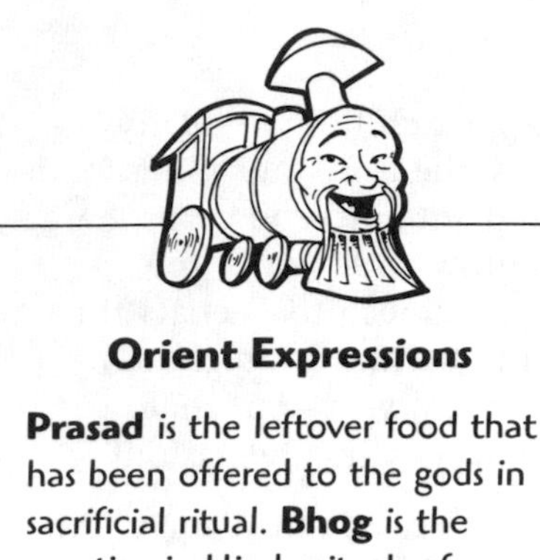

Orient Expressions

Prasad is the leftover food that has been offered to the gods in sacrificial ritual. **Bhog** is the practice in Hindu rituals of providing the gods with pleasurable things, including food, music, and adornment. It is a way of sharing the fruits of human labor and divine providence.

This practice of providing the gods with pleasurable things is known as *bhog*. Bhog includes the food, ornamentation, and music offered for the god's enjoyment. Ceremonies involving bhog may be performed in temples by locals or by visitors on pilgrimage, in the home, or in ashrams by monks and nuns.

At this point, you may be surprised to learn that many Hindus regale their gods with things, such as food and music, that are enjoyable to the senses. After all, Hindu philosophy says that everything that appeals to the senses is an aspect of maya—worldly delusion—and, as such, forms an obstacle to the experience of moksha—release from the bonds of karma. In other words, if Hindu philosophy is as anti-worldly as it sounds, why does Hindu religious ritual focus so much on worldly things?

For one thing, not everyone plans on becoming enlightened and liberated right away. Enlightenment generally takes many lifetimes, so there's plenty of time to stop and smell the flowers along the way. And the practice of religious ritual is part of dharma—the duties of life all people must observe. In fact, the gods, too, have their own dharma, so they are not above the enjoyment of worldly things either.

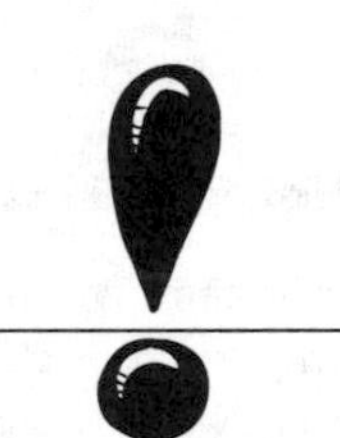

Not in This Life

Believe it or not, you don't necessarily have to use actual food to perform sacrificial food offerings to Hindu gods. In some cases, where food is not available, it is considered acceptable to make the offering mentally, imagining the food that should be offered while chanting one's mantra.

Staying Hungry

Of course, typical Hinduism (if there is such a thing) is far from a hedonistic religious philosophy. Many Hindu sects place strict limitations on eating. One reason for staying away from the dinner table (at least for spiritual adepts) is that worldly pleasures such as eating are vain and should be renounced. Of all Indian religions, Jainism is the most ascetic. Jain monks and nuns are expected to think nothing at all of the pleasures of eating. It is said that Mahavira, the founder of Jainism, cared for food so little that he starved himself to death.

Self-starvation is pretty extreme, of course, but limitations on food is a common element of much Indian religious and philosophical practice. The idea is that if you're hung up on food, you can't experience consciousness to its full, heightened extent.

Mastering the desire to eat is thus considered an important achievement in the life of a religious ascetic. Of course, everyone has to eat at least a certain amount, but some ascetics regard eating as no more than a necessary bodily function, much like going to the bathroom. As a result, they eat in private.

Some food restrictions apply to many Hindus who are not religious ascetics. Even among those who indulge their appetite, many are careful about what they eat—especially when it comes to meat. This restriction is in keeping with the principle of ahimsa, which is respect for all living things. Animals are thought to be so closely connected with people that individual souls may inhabit the bodies of animals or humans in the course of successive lifetimes. This helps account for widespread vegetarianism in India.

Don't Have a Cow

Of all India's taboos on meat, the most important is the prohibition against eating beef, since the cow is sacred. Cow worship has baffled many Westerners, especially the British colonialists in India, who couldn't understand why cows and bulls were revered rather than eaten in a country were malnourishment was so widespread. In fact, the *sacred cow* seemed so irrational that the phrase came to stand for anything false that is blindly accepted as dogma. As a result, politicians today still speak of bad ideas as sacred cows.

It turns out, however, that in practical terms, the sacred cow of India makes a lot of sense. American anthropologist Marvin Harris made the famous argument that cows and bulls were actually worth more to India alive than as food. They are necessary to India's agriculture as plow animals. Their milk and clarified butter, or ghee, are staples in the diet of most Indians. What's more, cow dung is an important source of fuel that burns relatively cleanly and without a bad smell.

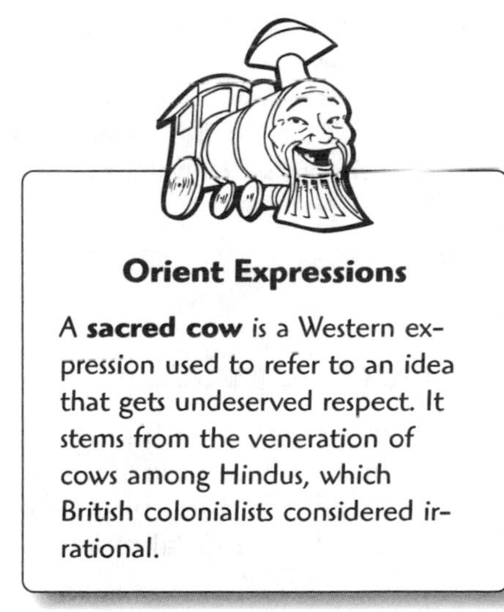

Orient Expressions

A **sacred cow** is a Western expression used to refer to an idea that gets undeserved respect. It stems from the veneration of cows among Hindus, which British colonialists considered irrational.

The species in question is the zebu ox, which is so hardy that it can survive on husks and stalks and things people can't eat. This means that sacred cows don't put any strain on the human food supply, while they contribute to it a great deal as plow animals, milk givers, and fuel providers. Using them as meat would curtail the food supply by making the unplowed fields less productive. Hindus revere the cows as a way of acknowledging their value to the economy and as a reminder that eating them could endanger that value.

Where's the Beef?

Hinduism, however, hasn't always revered and protected the cow. In fact, the ancient Vedas specify cows as important sacrificial animals. In many cultures, animal sacrifice is a significant means of sharing meat with all the members of the community. At one time, this was true in India, as the Brahmins offered up sacrificial cows to the gods and shared the meat with the group. But as the population increased and cow sacrifice became less practical, the taboo on beef kicked in.

This taboo did not originate in Hinduism, but got started by the two main alternative religious philosophies of India—Jainism and Buddhism. Only after these other religions introduced it did Hinduism adopt the idea of the sacred cow, perhaps as a way of keeping up in the spiritual competition among these religions. Ironically, because the cow was already important in Hinduism as a sacrificial animal, the religion was able to draw on tradition in instituting rituals for worshiping it. The act of sacrificing cows and distributing beef became a ritual that served the purpose of revering and protecting the cow.

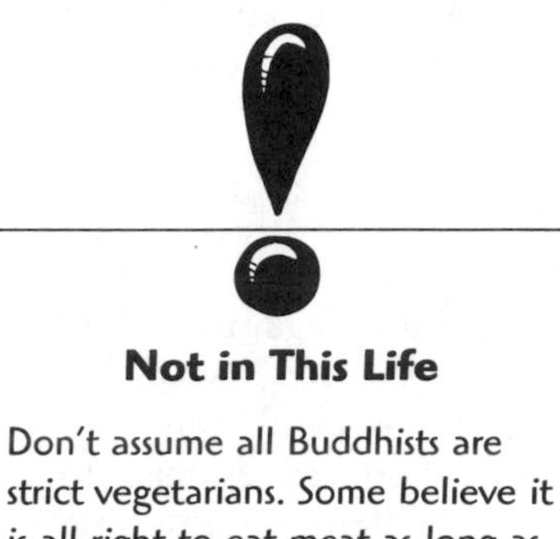

Not in This Life

Don't assume all Buddhists are strict vegetarians. Some believe it is all right to eat meat as long as it has been killed by non-Buddhists. In some countries, Buddhists sanction the eating of fish they have caught in nets, saying that the fishermen didn't actually kill the fish, but merely took them out of the water before they died!

This feature of Hinduism is tremendously important to many Hindus who regard cow protection as central to their religion. Some students of Indian culture have even suggested that the reason Buddhism died off in India after spreading to other countries is that it had no ritual means of protecting cows, but relied exclusively on the teaching of ahimsa. This may have made it less popular than Hinduism, which reveres cows through ritual as well as teaching.

Food Service

In general, the Chinese have been as practical in their attitudes toward food as the Indians have been spiritual. As a result, Chinese philosophy talks about food, not so much in relation to the gods, but largely in terms of political economy, human health, and social morality.

Growing Concerns

The ancient Legalist philosophers recognized agricultural production as one of the keys to a successful empire. Only with food surplus resulting from flourishing agriculture is it possible to secure the other resources, such as an army and a legal system, necessary for governing an empire. In fact, its thriving agriculture enabled the state of

Ch'in to gain the power to rise above its rivals and unify China for the first time under Ch'in rule.

Centuries later the Confucian philosopher Mencius drew on the idea of the importance of agriculture in laying out plans for helping the common people prosper. This was a system for allotting land and distributing labor in equal shares. Perhaps more important to Mencius's ideas were his suggestions for conserving natural resources. He proposed off-seasons for hunting, fishing, and lumbering so as to give trees, fish, and game animals time to replenish themselves. For more about Mencius, see Chapter 23, "The Three Sages."

Table Manners

Confucius himself often spoke to his disciples about food and eating. While he appreciated the importance of food to the political economy, he regarded diet as a matter of conduct and personal discipline. He saw proper eating habits as a way of showing respect and consideration for others, as a sign of personal integrity, and as an expression of the higher values of society. He was especially concerned with distinguishing between sacrificial food offerings as a way of showing respect for tradition and sacrificial offerings as a way of showing off one's wealth.

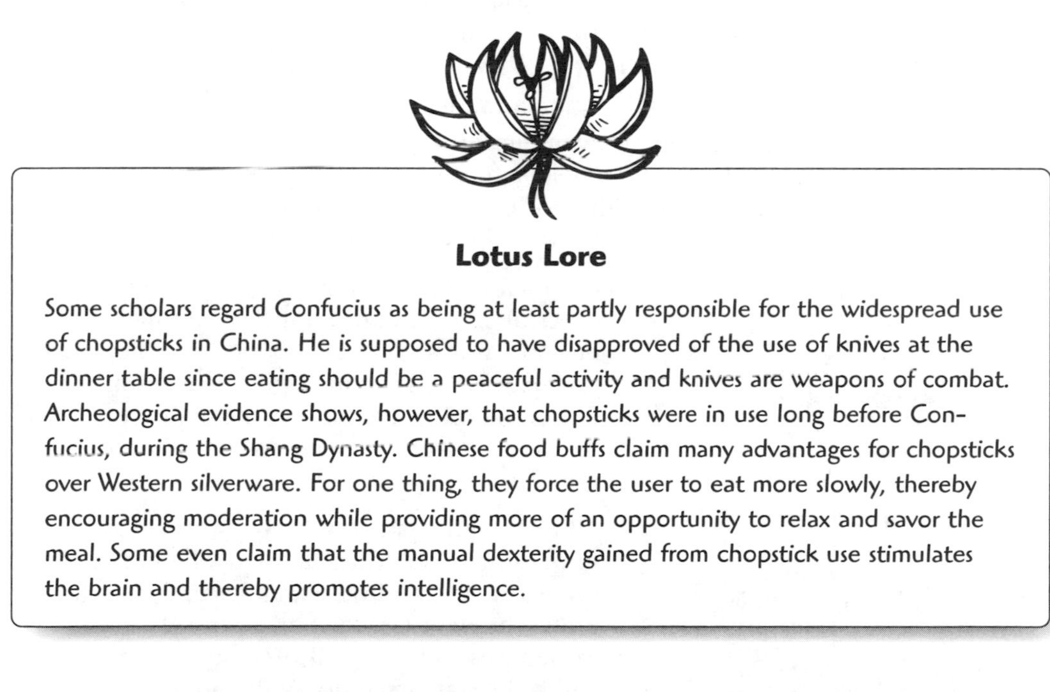

Lotus Lore

Some scholars regard Confucius as being at least partly responsible for the widespread use of chopsticks in China. He is supposed to have disapproved of the use of knives at the dinner table since eating should be a peaceful activity and knives are weapons of combat. Archeological evidence shows, however, that chopsticks were in use long before Confucius, during the Shang Dynasty. Chinese food buffs claim many advantages for chopsticks over Western silverware. For one thing, they force the user to eat more slowly, thereby encouraging moderation while providing more of an opportunity to relax and savor the meal. Some even claim that the manual dexterity gained from chopstick use stimulates the brain and thereby promotes intelligence.

Snobbery in the form of showing off expensive possessions is certainly as familiar in the West today as it was in Confucius's time. If you spend your money on expensive things, people tend to be impressed, whether you spend it on clothes and cars in the

U.S. or on fancy sacrificial rites in ancient China. Confucius felt that this kind of showing off is bad for society since it leads to disharmony between rich and poor.

A story in the *Confucian Analects* illustrates the problem and shows something of Confucius's subtle teaching style. It seems that one of his disciples was called away on official business. The disciple's mother was a poor woman with no one to look after her in her son's absence. Fortunately for her, another disciple took notice of her and asked Confucius for some grain out of the school supplies to give to the woman. Confucius said to give her only a very small, insignificant amount.

The disciple asked for more, and Confucius said to give her only an insignificant amount more. Knowing that the amount Confucius specified would be of little help to the woman, the disciple decided to increase the amount by a great deal and made her a generous gift of the school's grain. When Confucius heard about this, he responded in few words, saying only two things. First, he pointed out that the son away on business left with well-fed horses and was elegantly dressed. Then he said that it was right to give help to the needy, but not right to give to maintain the stylish appearance of rich people.

The son, in other words, spent his money to look good for his trip instead of to take care of his mother. In helping the mother out, the other disciple was, in effect, enabling the son to get away with his misdeed. The son's vanity led him to neglect his mother, and by giving grain to the mother, the other disciple was going along with the son's reprehensible action.

The point is that if you spend money to hide your poverty, rather than to take care of your needs and responsibilities, you make things worse for everybody. For this reason, Confucius said that it's impossible to get good advice from an official who is ashamed of poor food and clothing. He also recommended being modest and sincere whenever offering sacrifices rather than making a big show of it.

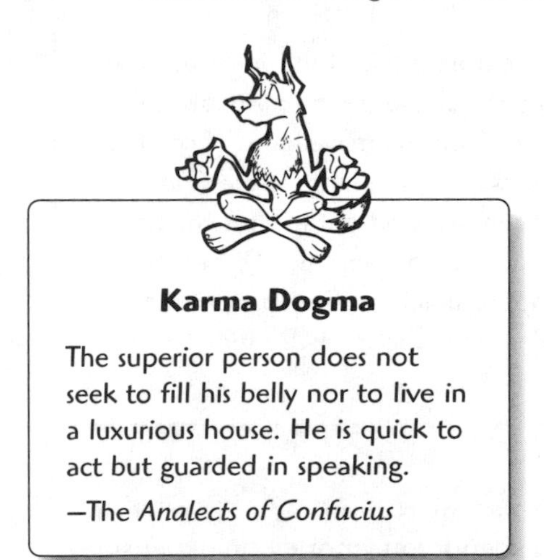

Karma Dogma

The superior person does not seek to fill his belly nor to live in a luxurious house. He is quick to act but guarded in speaking.

—The *Analects of Confucius*

Confucius admired those who were able to remain cheerful and content despite their impoverishment, but not, as in Indian philosophy, for the sake of spiritual benefits to be gained from mastering the desire for sensual pleasure. Rather, the ability to cope cheerfully with poverty shows you have the right personal priorities.

All this might lead you to believe that Confucius was something of a Puritan. Actually, he had nothing against wealth and pleasurable things if obtained under the right circumstances. In fact, if you have earned wealth as a result of good service to the state, and if the state itself does not subsist by oppressing the poor, then it's your duty to spend money on your appearance in keeping with the dignity of your position. Speaking of public ministers, Confucius says, "It is a disgrace to be poor and humble when the Tao prevails in government, just as it is a disgrace to be rich and proud when the Tao does not prevail."

The Tao of Dining

Confucian philosophy's basic concern with food is with its social and economic significance. In contrast, Taoism and the Yin-yang school have merged in looking at the effects of food on health and longevity. Much of the food-wisdom derived from these Chinese sources has spread around the world and has had an especially strong impact on the business of alternative medicine and herbal remedies.

Not in This Life

Rice is not nearly as popular a crop in Europe as it has always been in China, in part because Europeans have shunned the marshy environments where rice thrives in order to avoid malaria-carrying mosquitoes that breed there.

Spice of Life

Yin-yang Taoism sorts the world into analogous sets of five categories or characteristics based on the five elements: wood, water, earth, metal, and fire. Corresponding to these are the five tastes and five smells. The tastes are sweet, bitter, sour, salty, and piquant (hot). The smells are fragrant, scorched, rancid, putrid, and rotten. (Most of these smells may not seem very appetizing, but if skillfully blended, they can yield good results.)

The tastes and smells are traditionally used in correspondences with the five elements' relationships as guides in determining the effects of foods on the body. The body is thought to contain an ideal balance of the five elements. If these elements become unbalanced, sickness can result. The balance can be restored by eating foods that have a preponderance of the needed characteristic.

Another closely related approach to using foods as medicine involves categorizing foods as "hot" or "cold," depending on their supposed effect on the body. Classifications of hot and cold differ, depending on the source and on whose body, but, in general, cold foods are blander, and hot foods are more intensely flavored. The right balance of hot and cold foods in the diet was thought to result in optimum health.

Another aspect of many foods is *pu,* which means strengthening. Strengthening foods are said to restore or enhance depleted energy, or ch'i. They are thought to increase virility, strength, stamina, and intellect. The meat of predatory animals, such as the snake, and the fin of the shark are generally considered rich in pu, as are foods that are exotic and hard to get, including birds' nests. (As you know if you're a big Chinese food fan, certain kinds of birds' nests are actually used in making soup.)

Orient Expressions

In traditional Chinese lore, **pu** is a category of food thought to strengthen the body or provide a special source of energy.

The pervasive interest in foods as health remedies has helped make Chinese cuisine incredibly rich and various. This diversity has also been widened by food scarcities in China, encouraging people to go out and try eating just about everything. Animals such as the eagle, dog, monkey, sea cucumber, and jellyfish all have a place on the Chinese menu.

Well-Blended Stew

Variety in food, according to the Taoists, mirrors the variety that goes into natural and social harmony. In answer to a ruler who complained that few people agreed with his policies, the philosopher Yen Tzu responded that society is like a soup with many flavors that harmonize to yield a complex and delicious dish. Thus, although few people agreed with what the ruler said, their views actually harmonized to produce a balanced state policy.

The connection between food and harmony was more than just a metaphor in the minds of many imperial Chinese. During the T'ang Dynasty, it was believed that the emperor's diet had both cosmic and political significance. To make sure the imperial gastro-intestinal system was in harmony with the larger movements of the state and the natural world, the emperor employed a retinue of dietitians who made sure that each meal consisted of the proper food items in accordance with the changing seasons and ceremonial occasions. The emperor never ate with foreign visitors since it might upset the regularity of the realm!

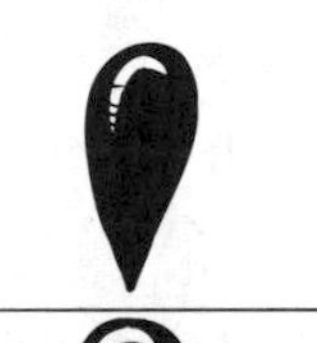

Not in This Life

It is widely believed that noodles were invented in China and introduced into Italy for the first time by Marco Polo, who traveled to China toward the end of the twelfth century. Actually, this isn't true. Noodles were probably invented in Western Asia and spread east to China and west to Italy well before Marco Polo's famous journey.

Despite the interest in variety in the diet, much Tao-oriented cooking emphasizes naturalness and simplicity. The idea is to make predominant use of foods that are easy to get, and to prepare them in a way that requires minimal effort and sophistication. This approach is considered healthy, convenient, and harmonious with the environment. At the same time, however, there is a more hedonistic approach to eating that values unusual delicacies and elaborate preparation. Both these approaches have left their legacy in Chinese cuisine.

The Taoist preoccupation with food as a source of health dovetails with the efforts of religious Taoism to discover the secret of immortality. One approach in this quest was to make a commitment to avoid eating. Taoists hoped that if they could learn to subsist on nothing but their own breath and saliva, they would become purified and freed from physical sickness and decay. The other approach was to try to transmute the bones and flesh of the body to durable materials by eating cinnabar and other minerals that could be dissolved or ground up. It seems clear to most people today that either of these practices is much more likely to shorten than to prolong life! (For more on religious Taoism, see Chapter 19, "Tao and Forever.")

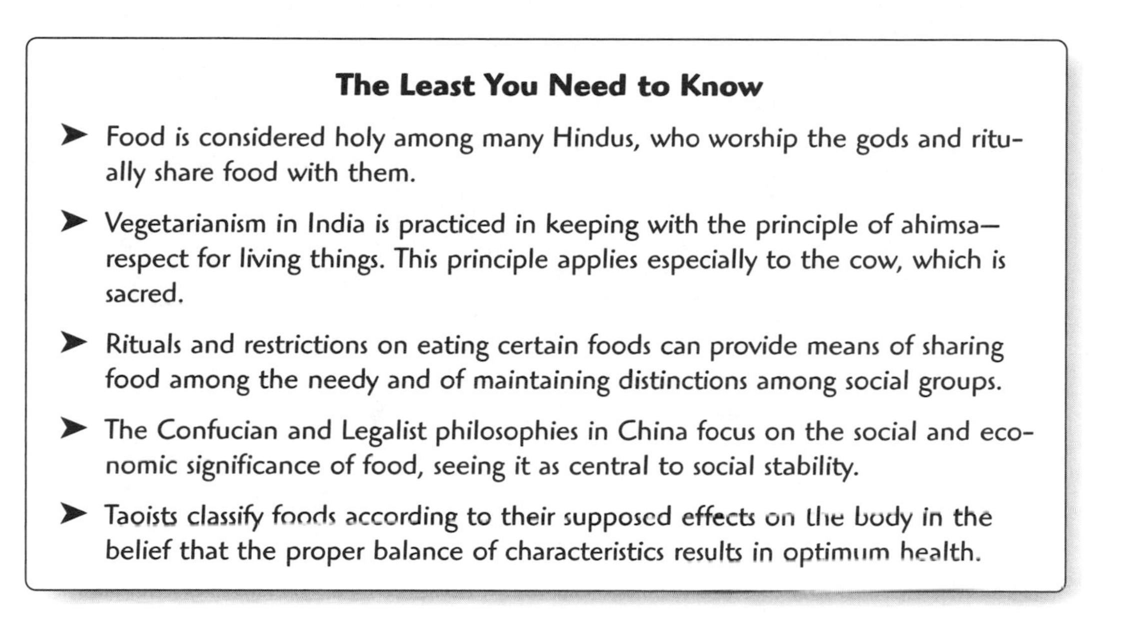

The Least You Need to Know

- Food is considered holy among many Hindus, who worship the gods and ritually share food with them.
- Vegetarianism in India is practiced in keeping with the principle of ahimsa—respect for living things. This principle applies especially to the cow, which is sacred.
- Rituals and restrictions on eating certain foods can provide means of sharing food among the needy and of maintaining distinctions among social groups.
- The Confucian and Legalist philosophies in China focus on the social and economic significance of food, seeing it as central to social stability.
- Taoists classify foods according to their supposed effects on the body in the belief that the proper balance of characteristics results in optimum health.

Chapter 27

Bedroom Wise

In This Chapter

- Philosophies of love and sex
- The *Kama Sutra*
- Tantric sex ritual
- Sex and marriage in imperial China
- Castration and foot binding

Many consider sex one of life's biggest mysteries and deepest joys. It connects us to life like no other activity. It leads to new life, and it calls to us in a way few can resist. On the other hand, under the wrong circumstances, it can get you into a lot of trouble. It can entangle you with obligations or stigmatize you with a bad reputation. Because of its tremendous potential for harm and for good, it is alternately celebrated and condemned all over the world.

As a spiritual matter, sex provides, simultaneously, a release from the conventional experiences of living and a profound union with another person. As a practical matter, sex can require tremendous thought, care, and sacrifice so as to manage it in a way that doesn't jeopardize other priorities in life. For some, sex is a mystic pleasure. For others, it's a pleasurable mistake.

Regardless of your attitude toward the subject, you may be interested to know something about sex ideas and sex practices from India and China. I can't promise that this chapter will help you improve your sex life, but you should get a wider sense of what sex is all about after reading up on the traditions of sex and marriage described here. If you aren't aware of how much fun it can be, you have a chance to find out. If you didn't realize how difficult sexuality can make life, you can find out about that, too.

Hindu How-To

Of all the many and various writings of India, perhaps the best known among Westerners is the *Kama Sutra*. This is a fairly short but comprehensive guidebook to sex, written sometime around the third or fourth century by a worldly pundit named Vatsyayana. The *Kama Sutra* is indeed an eye-opening book, impressive in both scope and detail.

Lotus Lore

Kama, the Sanskrit word for "pleasure," is also the Hindu god of Love. Kama, like Cupid, shoots people and gods alike with his bow and arrow, causing them to fall in love. According to legend, Kama was commanded by Indra to shoot Shiva, so that he would fall in love with Parvati and marry her. Kama's love arrow did its job, but Shiva became enraged with him and incinerated him on the spot. Kama's wife entreated Shiva to bring Kama back to life, which he did, but in spirit only; his body was burned away for good. So Kama became an invisible god, present wherever two lovers meet. Along with his bow and arrows, he carries a lasso and a hook for ensnaring people into love.

Book of Love

In India, the erotic arts were developed and perfected by courtesans trained in the craft from an early age. Accounts of their knowledge and skill were recorded in sutras—advice literature—where they could be studied, not only by other courtesans and their patrons, but by ordinary married folks. This, as you can imagine, put a sexy new wrinkle in the marriage sutras already familiar to many Indians. The *Kama Sutra* combines the somewhat stodgy rules of etiquette found in the traditional marriage literature with the wisdom gleaned from experienced courtesans.

It includes useful subjects such as how to satisfy the varying tastes of women from different parts of India. It also provides a detailed account of virtually every aspect of sex play, including a description of the different kinds of noises most commonly made during sex. There are even recipes for making aphrodisiacs.

In fact, it tells the educated young man and woman of medieval India just about everything they could want to know about conducting a satisfying sex life. Topics include what sort of partners are appropriate for each other, how to attract the opposite sex, role playing, sexual etiquette, foreplay, and, of course, sexual positions. The *Kama Sutra* takes broader social factors into consideration, describing the use of go-betweens, the life of courtesans, and customs governing marriage. There's even a list of 64 arts—hobbies, pastimes, and accomplishments—recommended for the sophisticated fourth-century swinger!

Best of all, the work draws on the rich philosophical background of the Vedas and Upanishads, as well as on older sutras on the subject of sex that have since been lost. Completely absent from the book is any suggestion that having sex might stand in the way of spiritual enlightenment. Note that the sutra was written two or three centuries before the rise of India's most ascetic religion, Jainism, and before Buddha had refined the art of abstinence. Celibate monks were not common in India when the *Kama Sutra* appeared.

Married or Not

Kama, or pleasure, is an important philosophical concept in India since it is one of the four purusarthas, or main goals of life. (All four of these are described in Chapter 3, "East Meets West.") The other three purusarthas are dharma (duty), artha (wealth), and moksha (spiritual liberation). Although many Indians combined these four goals over the course of their lifetimes, it was considered appropriate for different people to devote themselves to a greater or lesser extent to each of them. A wandering ascetic would not be concerned with kama or artha. Similarly, a young girl would not focus much attention on moksha.

Throughout most of Indian history, there has been a certain amount of tension between the merits of leading an ascetic existence and the claims of householding and family life. One interesting legend tells of an ascetic named Jaratkaru who, ironically, experienced enlightenment into the higher moral purpose of raising a family. One day, while he had been deeply absorbed in tranquil meditation, he'd had a frightening vision of his ancestors. They were hanging over the side of a pit on the end of some vines, calling out in desperation for help. At the bottom of the pit were all kinds of people-eating beasts, such as snakes and tigers. As if this wasn't bad enough, a little rat scurried around on the wall of the pit, gnawing away at the vines from which the ancestors dangled.

Jaratkaru looked over the edge and was overcome with concern for their plight. "Can I help you?" he asked. "No," they answered, not realizing who he was. "Only our descendent, Jaratkaru, can help us, for this pit is the Hell of Oblivion and Forgetfulness, the vines from which we cling are our Hope for the Future, and the rat which gnaws the vines is Time itself. If only Jaratkaru would marry and have children to continue the family line, we would be saved from the pit. But alas, he is a wandering ascetic who takes no thought of us!" At this, Jaratkaru snapped out of his meditation and went off in search of a wife. (And perhaps he got a copy of the *Kama Sutra* beforehand so he'd know what to expect!)

Kama is considered an especially appropriate preoccupation for a young man who has recently completed his study of the Vedas. In fact, traditional Indian advice books recommend that men put off marriage until after they have finished their Vedic education. Marriages are often arranged in traditional Indian society, and girls were typically married off before reaching puberty. The *Kama Sutra* indicates, however, that both men and women were able to exercise a certain amount of freedom in choosing their own spouses and lovers. This was especially true of urban and court society where widows or courtesans and single or married men could seek out the companionship of the opposite sex without family interference.

Karma Dogma

When a man makes up to a woman, and she reproaches him with harsh words, she should be abandoned at once. When a woman reproaches a man, but at the same time acts affectionately towards him, she should be made love to in every way.

—Kama Sutra

The *Kama Sutra* provides advice for conducting both marital and extramarital relationships. (After all, fun is fun, no matter who you're having it with!) Some of the techniques it describes would be considered kinky by most of us; in addition to a variety of sexual positions, there's a description of eight different kinds of bites! (Evidently, hickies go way back!) There's even a section devoted to different kinds of scratching.

The *Kama Sutra* manages to be frank and explicit about sex without losing sight of the fact that it is an extremely playful activity. For example, the book provides suggestions for how to assume the role of the opposite sex, and for pretending that kissing is a contest in which the "loser" is expected to act bitterly disappointed while the "winner" swaggers around triumphantly—at least until the tables are turned in the next round!

Kissing and Telling

Without going too (ahem) deeply into the subject, you may find it worthwhile to sample the sorts of things the *Kama Sutra* covers—strictly for educational purposes, you understand. Here's a list of some of the many kissing techniques the book describes. Maybe you'll find some you've never tried.

- **The straight kiss.** This is the standard, unvarnished, lip-to-lip smooch. All other kisses are variations on this theme.
- **The kiss in name only.** This is when partners touch lips without moving them at all, as if they were statues. It's a good place to start since it can only get better from here!
- **The throbbing kiss.** This is done with the upper lip held completely still and the lower lip pushed back and forth in a throbbing motion.

- **The touching kiss.** Touching tongues, that is; hand holding is also recommended.
- **The bent kiss.** This is when one or both partners bends their neck way up or down. If you and your partner are extra limber, you can try this with one of you behind the other bending forward and the other bending back.
- **The turned kiss.** This is a good one for those with a flair for the dramatic. While standing or reclining slightly to one side, grab your partner's head gently but firmly with both hands and guide it to your face.
- **The pressed kiss.** This is just like the straight kiss, only you push harder.
- **The greatly pressed kiss.** A straight kiss taken to the third degree. Don't forget to come up for air!

Sex Rites

Strangely, the erotic tradition of the *Kama Sutra* mostly disappeared from India during the rise of Buddhism and Jainism. Fortunately for India, sex didn't disappear entirely, but people started looking at it in a completely different way—less as an end in itself than as a symbol for other things. Ritual sex and sex symbolism became an important feature of Tantrism, including both Hindu and Buddhist Tantric practices.

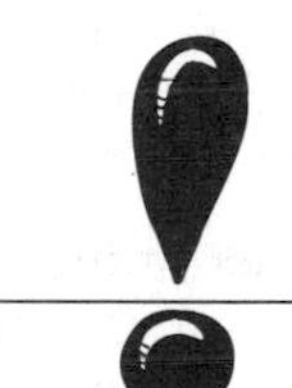

Not in This Life

Don't write off the Buddhist view of sexuality as useless or outdated. According to Buddhist psychotherapist Mark Epstein, M.D., Buddhist philosophy and meditation can be valuable tools in understanding and dealing with emotional problems caused by unfulfilled sexual desires. In his book, *Thoughts Without a Thinker: Psychotherapy from a Buddhist Perspective* (1995), Epstein describes Buddhist teachings as largely consistent with much of Western psychology.

Tantrism adopts a paradoxical view of sex. It recognizes sex as one of the main sources of desire standing in the way of transcendence and enlightenment, but it also recognizes that, to the enlightened and transcendent adept, desire has no harmful effect. Sex, after all, is not considered bad in itself, but is a problem only to the extent that it binds us with desire. The god-like state of enlightenment is immune from the negative influence of sexual desire.

Tantrists believe that a good way of attaining enlightenment is to behave as if you have attained it already. So, in order to exercise an enlightened attitude, they practice rituals in which the usual taboos are systematically violated in ritual fashion. And the "climax" of the ritual is—you guessed it—flying to the moon! Not all Tantrists practice ritual sex. For many, sexual union is important chiefly as a form of spiritual symbolism rather than spiritual practice.

Orient Expressions

Yab-Yum is the union of the divine male and female principles in Tibetan Tantric Buddhism. It represents the nonduality of nirvana and samsara.

In Hindu Tantrism, the sexual union is represented by the mating of Shiva and Shakti. In the Buddhist Tantrism of Tibet, archetypal copulating figures are called *Yab-Yum,* the divine male and female. Yab-Yum figures locked in embrace are common subjects of Tibetan religious art. For Tantric Buddhists, the union of the divine male and female symbolizes the nonduality of nirvana and samsara, the transcendent actual and its delusory physical manifestation.

Slippery Business

The Chinese have not traditionally regarded sex as primarily pleasurable for its own sake, but chiefly as a means to an end. For the religious Taoists, sexual practices were a feature of the range of techniques employed in the attempt to gain immortality. For the male adept, for example, controlling the release of sperm during sex sometimes went along with controlling the circulation of the breath through the body.

For the Confucians, sex was one of the seven desires every cultivated person needed to control, indulging in them only in moderation so they wouldn't interfere with the important business—running the empire. In addition, for the leading families in the empire, sex was strictly a means of perpetuating the line. As a result, sexuality was strictly controlled by law, custom, and ritual in such a way as to maximize the chances of producing male descendants.

Karma Dogma

Man and woman need one another. They hold in the mouth or spit, each nourishing the other. Male and female are mixed together, each seeking according to nature.

—Ancient Taoist teaching

Double Standard

In theory, women, as human representatives of the Yin principle, were the equal complements of their Yang counterparts, the men. In keeping with this idea, Confucian teaching called for husbands and wives to be mutually respectful of one another. Mothers and fathers alike were mourned in the rites that were so crucial to imperial Chinese culture. In practice, however, the lot of women in imperial China was far inferior to that of their husbands. Although some had a say in household affairs, most had to do what they were told or were sent packing.

Most Chinese philosophy is by, for, and about men, so it doesn't say much about the hard lot of women, which reflects the importance placed on maintaining the ancestral male line. Women in well-off families were tightly controlled to prevent unwanted pregnancies. Women in poorer families were often less rigidly controlled, but were just as often married off against their will or obliged to make a living through prostitution. For many women, the only available form of protest against intolerable treatment was suicide.

Pulling Strings to Tie the Knot

In imperial China, marriages for the young were typically arranged by the parents. When it was time for a son to be married, a likely bride would be selected, and a go-between would be sent to learn her birthday and other vital statistics. These would be turned over to a Feng Shui expert (a geomancer) who would study her horoscope to determine whether she would make a suitable match for the son. If the stars were in line, the leaders of the families involved (the fathers or grandfathers) would settle on a bride price.

Marriages were often arranged long before either of the parties was old enough to wed, sometimes in infancy or even before birth. Marriage contracts could be so important that, even if one or both of the intended spouses died in the interim, the marriage ceremony would still be held! These "spirit marriages," performed in honor of the dead, were celebrated with the same pomp and circumstance surrounding ordinary marriages and were considered just as binding.

In these ceremonies, a slip of paper holding the deceased's name filled in for the actual living spouse to be. Women who married these slips of paper were considered legally married and could expect to be provided for by the family of what was considered her late husband. In turn, she was expected not to remarry. All widows, in fact, were discouraged from marrying again after the death of their husbands.

After a costly wedding ceremony, the bride would go to live with her husband's family, returning to her family only as a guest or in the disastrous case of divorce. Women who were divorced for disobedience to their husbands were sent back to their parents.

Adultery on the part of a woman was punishable by death. Men, in contrast, were answerable only to whoever was responsible for the women they slept with. A man could be killed for committing adultery with the wife of an important man or forced to marry the unwed daughter of a respectable father.

A Man's World

You've probably noticed by now that social relations in imperial China were not exactly based on the ideal of equality. People were not thought to have civil rights, but sets of different responsibilities and privileges based on their position in society.

Women could rise to occupy important positions within the household. In rare cases, this enabled them to wield power outside the home. Famous examples are Empress Wu of the T'ang Dynasty and Empress Dowager Tzu Hsi of the Ch'ing Dynasty. In general, however, women were said to be *san ts'ung,* or "three times obedient." In childhood, they were expected to obey their fathers; as married women, they were to obey their husbands; and as older women, they were to obey their grown sons. Women had no higher calling than to bear sons to their husbands so as to maintain the husband's family name.

Orient Expressions

San ts'ung is an expression used in imperial China that literally means "three times obedient." It described the social predicament of women who were expected to obey their fathers, husbands, and grown sons.

For men, it was a different story. They could have as many partners as they could arrange to get. Prostitutes, known as flower girls, worked legally. In addition, men commonly took concubines. Thus, unless a woman happened to be the number one wife, she had to obey her superiors in a whole pecking order of ladies of the house. If they could afford large families, husbands often took concubines in addition to their wives—especially if the wives had failed to bear male children.

The concubines had rank and household power according to their seniority. As you might imagine, this could make for a complicated family life. Children had to learn to recognize any number of different "mothers" and learn to treat each one in keeping with her status while maintaining a special relationship with their biological mother.

The largest households were those of the emperors, some of whom kept hundreds of concubines. Assembling such enormous harems was an official procedure closely resembling the examination system for potential government officials. Candidates were brought in from all over the empire and carefully inspected for health and appearance. Finalists underwent a try-out period as ladies in waiting at the palace. Finally, the lucky winners were signed on as imperial concubines. When one of these concubines happened to give birth to the emperor's oldest surviving son, she became the most important woman in China, no matter how humble her own parents may have been.

Chop Chop

Because the imperial concubines were a large group of the most beautiful young women in China, plighted solely to the Son of Heaven (the emperor or crown prince), they required special protection. On the one hand, the protectors had to be strong and manly enough to fight off attackers. On the other, they had to be gentle with the ladies; and they could never, under any circumstances, become sexually involved with them.

Lotus Lore

One of the best-known women of Chinese history is Wu Tse T'ien, who came out of nowhere, became an imperial concubine at age 12, and usurped the throne of the T'ang empire, which she held for 25 years until her death in the year 705. She came to power by persuading the emperor to divorce his wife and install her as imperial consort. When the emperor died, she held on to the throne through a policy of intimidation and intrigue, arranging the assassinations of her political opponents. Ruthless as she was in the palace, she turned out to be a benevolent ruler, lowering taxes, reducing the army, and weeding out corruption in government.

The job, in short, required men who were willing to make the supreme sacrifice. These were the imperial eunuchs, specially castrated (actually, this was not a surgical procedure, but involved a single, decisive chop with a hatchet!) to prevent any unwanted hanky-panky with the concubines. You might think that there wouldn't exactly have been a whole stream of applicants for the position, but times were so hard for some Chinese men that even the loss of their best and closest friends was not too great a price to pay for a life of luxury at the palace.

In addition to the obvious drawbacks to becoming a eunuch, they had to endure widespread contempt. They were generally regarded as unclean and unnatural. One reason eunuchs were despised is that they occasionally exerted pressure on the emperor and thus came to wield influence in government through intrigue. This did not go down well with imperial advisors and others who saw the eunuchs as a corrupting influence.

Foot Fetish

Before moving along to more pleasant topics in the next chapter, and as long as we're on the subject of physical mutilation, you may want to read about the practice of foot binding, especially since this tradition ties in with sexuality. Back in imperial days, small feet on women were considered incredibly sexy. The good news is, almost all Chinese women are born with small feet. The bad news is, the small feet invariably grow into larger feet unless drastic measures are taken.

And drastic measures were indeed taken among upper-class Chinese families, beginning in the Sung Dynasty and on into the twentieth century. Starting around age five, girls' feet were tightly and continually wrapped in heavy cloth. As a result, the bones of the feet became mangled as they were forced to grow in under the heel. Needless to say, this effectively crippled the women who underwent the practice; they had to be helped around wherever they went—which usually wasn't far.

Lotus Lore

The customs of foot binding and concubinage reached their peak during the Sung Dynasty, apparently as a response to the growth in size of Chinese cities. More wealthy families living in cities meant that there was less and less for the women in those families to do, since women were never employed in official jobs. Without the chance to work on the farm or in household production of goods as country women often did, they became almost useless except as wives, mothers, and mistresses. This drastically limited their social significance to the roles of sexuality and motherhood.

The mangled feet resulting from foot binding were known affectionately as golden lilies and were highly prized as especially beautiful. It seems that bound feet were a way of showing the world that the woman who had them was good for nothing but sitting around and looking pretty—and that the man who could afford to support such a woman was rich and powerful. Thus foot binding was a status symbol as well as a sexual turn-on. As a result, women participated more-or-less willingly in the practice. At any rate, it was the women of the household who supervised the foot-binding procedure.

Of course, European traders and missionaries were appalled to find so many women hobbling around on feet that had been mutilated on purpose. They wondered how anyone could think that deliberate mutilation was sexy. But, of course, it would be a long time before tattoos, body piercing, liposuction, and breast augmentation surgery would become fashionable in the West!

The Least You Need to Know

- The *Kama Sutra* is a how-to sex guide compiled around the third or fourth century in India by a pundit named Vatsyayana.
- The *Kama Sutra* combines accounts of the lives and skills of Indian courtesans with advice about marriage and marriage customs.
- Hindu and Buddhist Tantrism employ sex rituals and sex symbolism representing the nonduality of nirvana and samsara.
- The strict marriage customs of imperial China were intended to perpetuate the family name and bloodlines.
- Among the most graphic signs of class and gender inequality in imperial China are the custom of foot binding and the practice of employing eunuchs in the imperial palace.

Chapter 28

Kung Fu Fighting

In This Chapter

- Eastern fighting and philosophy
- Sun Tzu's *Art of War*
- Samurai culture and bushido
- Eastern martial arts

Imagine being perfectly calm, at peace, and aware of everything around you, despite the fact that you are surrounded by turmoil and confusion and your life is in danger. Thanks to years of training, you have attained perfect clarity of mind and control of your body. You understand the desires and motivations, strengths and limitations of your enemies. You know you are on the side of right, so you are unconcerned about yourself and care only that justice is done. You may be called upon to spring into action at any moment, and you will act with timing, power, and precision made possible only through generations of accumulated wisdom and experience, stretching back into the mysterious past of the Far East. Yes, Grasshopper, you are a martial arts master!

And you're not alone! The merging of Eastern philosophy and Eastern fighting has become tremendously popular all over the world during this last century, especially during the past few decades. Martial arts centers can be found in the United States in just about every city block and suburban neighborhood. Books and movies recounting imaginary Eastern adventures are everywhere. American kids are at least as likely to make believe they are ninjas as cowboys. Corporate executives study Eastern military strategy to get an edge on the competition.

To many Westerners, the Eastern notions of harmony and enlightenment can seem a little vague and airy on their own. When these notions are applied to individual performance and combat situations, however, they can suddenly become important and exciting. It's no wonder that martial arts buffs look back into the history of Eastern thought and find applications to combat and self defense everywhere.

Rising Sun

Eastern philosophy tends to oppose war and violence. Nonviolence is the basis of the principle of ahimsa, or respect for all living things, which has been observed for centuries by Hindus and Buddhists. The early Taoist sages opposed conflict for other reasons, namely that it fails to solve problems and, indeed, tends to make them worse. Confucius had little to say about war or fighting, since the traditional gentleman-scholar of China was more concerned with the arts of peace.

Yet despite the pervasive pacifism of the East, the first and perhaps the most famous military treatise ever written is Chinese. This is *The Art of War* by Sun Tzu, who lived around 500 B.C.E. Some Chinese scholars have ranked this work alongside the Confucian classics for its depth of wisdom. Sun Tzu himself is said to have defeated an army of 300,000 soldiers with only 20,000 of his own men.

The great Chinese historian Ssu-ma Ch'ien tells a story that suggests something of the intense seriousness with which Sun Tzu approached the study and practice of warfare. According to this story, the king of Sun Tzu's home state of Wu read Sun Tzu's book and asked him if its principles of discipline could be applied to women. Sun Tzu said they could and agreed to prove it by conducting drills for women for the king's inspection. So Sun Tzu mustered the imperial concubines, assigned the chief concubines as officers, and instructed them in military drills. But when he gave commands, instead of performing the drills, they simply burst out laughing. Undismayed, he announced his rule: When orders are not obeyed because they are unclear, it is the fault of the general, but when orders are clear and are still not obeyed, it's the fault of the officers.

Karma Dogma

To conquer the enemy without fighting is the highest excellence.
—Sun Tzu, *The Art of War*

He again explained the instructions and gave commands to drill. Again the women burst out laughing. This time, said Sun Tzu, the orders were clear, yet they were not obeyed. This is the fault of the officers, and they shall be executed. True to his word, he had the chief concubines beheaded on the spot. After appointing new officers from the ranks of the concubines, he again gave the order to drill, and this time the order was promptly carried out. When the king learned of the loss of his chief concubines, he grieved, but was convinced nevertheless that Sun Tzu knew what he was doing, so he appointed him commander in chief of the army.

No Illusions

Sun Tzu takes a cold, rational, and practical approach to war. He looks at it not in terms of morality or politics, but purely as a tactical matter. He talks about the many variables in waging war, its effect on the state, its risks, its gains, and the factors leading to success or failure—all in dispassionate, practical terms.

He says a ruler should not engage in conflict unless he has ample reason to think he can win. Winning depends on an accurate knowledge of one's own forces and preparedness, as well as a knowledge of the enemy. This knowledge includes everything from a grasp of the politics behind the conflict to an understanding of the terrain of the battlefield and the weather. And, of course, the army has to be organized with a clear, efficient command structure.

So far, this may seem to resemble the typical Western approach to the problem: Figure out everything you can about the situation and design a strategy to control it. Beyond this rationalist attitude, however, is an Eastern awareness of the ebb and flow of momentum, and concern with the psychology of those involved. Taking these factors into account, the military strategist determines the right moment to attack and retreat so as to capitalize on the enemy's weaknesses and avoid playing into his strengths. This is generally consistent with the Taoist attitude of letting things happen and exerting the minimal effort necessary to accomplish one's goals. Sun Tzu is not generally considered a Taoist, but he may have been influenced by Taoist thinking.

Many Ways to Win

In keeping with this idea of minimal effort, it is significant that Sun Tzu isn't interested in military conquest for its own sake; in fact, he advocates political and economic pressure as preferable to combat. If you can win without having to go into battle, so much the better. You not only conserve your own power, you assimilate the resources of your opponent without having to destroy things.

Sun Tzu's work has been studied eagerly by many, including political leaders and corporate executives. Sun Tzu himself suggests, however, that warfare does not make for a desirable way of life, though he doesn't elaborate on the life of the warrior. In fact, part of what makes his thinking noteworthy is that it disregards so much of the philosophical and ceremonial baggage traditionally associated with war. In Sun Tzu's eyes, warfare is not about honor and chivalry, as it was to many others of his day. It is a practical matter of power, politics, and strategy.

Living by the Sword

Not until many centuries after Sun Tzu's death did warfare become a widely recognized, philosophically based way of life. This happened in Japan under the feudal

Orient Expressions

Shoguns are Japanese warlords who ruled in Japan from the twelfth to the nineteenth centuries. **Samurais** were Japanese knights or warrior-administrators who formed the top layer of the **bushi,** or warrior class in Japan. The bushi followed a strict code of honor known as **bushido,** or way of the warrior.

leadership of the *shoguns,* warlords who established hereditary military dictatorships with the help of warrior-administrators called *samurai.* The samurai were at the top of a large warrior class known as *bushi.* This class adopted a strict code of honor based on the traditional Japanese family, Chinese Confucianism, and Zen. This code is known as *bushido,* the way of the warrior.

Bushi League

The bushi were expected to be fiercely loyal and undergo any hardships required of them by their leaders. They were even expected to commit suicide (hari-kari) if necessary. At the same time, they were cultivated in the arts. Many were poets and painters. Many also developed fighting techniques as gentlemanly arts. Much as Chinese Confucians enriched themselves by studying books, the bushido of Japan cultivated themselves through arts such as swordsmanship, archery, and hand-to-hand combat. The bushido was a leading influence on Japanese culture for many years, and the samurai remains something of a romantic figure in Japan, not unlike the cowboy in the United States.

Bushido was deeply influenced by Zen. This may seem incongruous, since Buddha abhorred killing, but aside from this little detail, Zen and the warrior's lifestyle worked together very well. Zen teachers have pointed out that warriors are often especially quick to cut through the conventional ways of seeing things and can appreciate reality in their own ways. This is because they take little in life for granted. Because they can expect to die at any moment, they often live fully in the present and react spontaneously to whatever happens. This attitude is very much in keeping with Zen.

Thus the bushi took their own approach to Zen thinking, adapting it as their own. They developed their own version of the sangha, or Buddhist brotherhood, and came up with their own warrior koans to train and test their understanding. They applied their knowledge of Zen principles to warfare and the warrior's life in general.

Fighting Form

Japan was actually not in a constant state of warfare during the seven hundred years of shogun rule. In fact, for much of the time, things were downright peaceful. Thus it was probably a good thing that the bushi had a philosophy that gave them something to think about besides fighting each other. Nevertheless, even in times of peace, many bushi wanted to maintain their fighting form and display their courage and prowess, so they developed techniques for use in hand-to-hand combat and staged competitions to show them off.

These formalized techniques were known as jujitsu, which means "gentleness technique," so-called because it is a means of fighting without weapons. Many different styles of jujitsu developed. Jujitsu contests were serious business. It is said that the most highly skilled in the art sometimes fought to the death in order to prove their superiority. Yet it's hard to say whether jujitsu was actually used in combat. Some say it served as a kind of formal substitute for battle. Others say it developed in response to edicts issued during the nineteenth century, preventing most samurai from carrying weapons.

Lotus Lore

Several martial arts, most notably karate, developed on the island of Okinawa where a local version of bushido was cultivated by the warrior class. In the seventeenth century, Japan annexed Okinawa and passed laws forbidding the possession of weapons. This apparently led to the development of weaponless fighting techniques, as well as techniques involving the use of household tools and farm implements. Some of these implements are still recognized as part of the arsenal of certain martial arts styles. These include the kama (a sickle), the bo (a cudgel), the sai (a short club), and the nunchuk (a rice flail).

Samurai traditions faded with Japan's increasing involvement in trade with the West, but unless you've been asleep for the past 100 years, you know that martial arts didn't disappear. Instead, they've become possibly the most widespread, influential, and glamorized aspects of traditional Eastern thought and culture.

The phenomenal popularity of Eastern martial arts began in 1882 when a jujitsu master named Jigoro Kano (1860–1938) opened a school where he taught his own style of jujitsu, which he called judo, or "gentleness way." The school was a big success, and judo was taken up by men, women, and children throughout the East in the early years of the twentieth century. In 1911, judo was widely taught as an important part of the physical education program in Japan. Later, it was the first martial arts form introduced in the West in the wake of World War II. Meanwhile, other martial arts forms developed in China and Korea have spread throughout the world.

In Style

Martial arts have many uses. They are practiced as competitive sports, as self-defense, as physical fitness, as spiritual and intellectual discipline, and for show. Martial arts stem from colorful cultural traditions that add to their appeal. In fact, various styles of martial arts have mushroomed to such an extent that it can be hard even for experts to tell them apart. These different styles tend to branch off and recombine with one another, so they can be difficult to keep track of. But because they are closely related philosophically, it's possible to describe them all at once in general terms.

Inside Outside

Much of the mystique—and hence, the popularity—of martial arts has to do with the fact that they have roots in Eastern philosophy—especially Zen and the Tao. For example, a common teaching among many martial arts systems is to do things with minimal effort. From a practical standpoint, this means using your body as efficiently as possible. This can involve the ability to time one's movements in order to achieve the best results; the ability to make use of the movements or force of one's adversary to use them to one's own advantage; and the ability to achieve harmony between mind and body so as to sharpen the decision-making process.

Lotus Lore

Many, but not all, martial arts instructors say that, outside of practice and competition, martial arts should be used in self-defense only, never to attack. This idea hearkens back to the Chinese philosopher Mo Tzu, who was a member of China's warrior class and founded a school of philosophy based on the warrior code observed at the time. Despite this warrior's background, he emphasized the concept of universal love among all people.

Thus, despite the fact that martial arts can require lots of practice, discipline, and physical exertion, they are typically in keeping with the Zen and Taoist principle of wu wei, or effortlessness. Unnecessary effort stems from a cluttered mind, resulting in indecision and haphazard movement. The mind should be clear so the body is capable of spontaneous and purposeful action. The mind/body connection works both ways. Practicing physical movements is a good way to clear the mind, and clearing the mind is a good way to sharpen physical movements.

This helps explain why many see martial arts and philosophical understanding as two aspects of the same path. Just what this path is, however, varies with different styles and different practitioners. In general, the relation between martial arts and philosophy falls into two headings, internal and external. External styles are those that use philosophical wisdom as a tool for improving prowess in fighting. Practitioners of external styles regard the development of martial skill as a worthwhile goal in itself and see philosophical knowledge as one way of achieving this goal. Internal styles, in contrast, regard physical prowess as a tool for developing philosophical knowledge. They regard enlightenment, spirituality, and mind/body harmony as ultimate goals and see physical practice as a way to attain it.

Forms of Expression

The external-internal distinction is only one way of characterizing the martial arts. After all, since Eastern fighting is an art form, it's capable of exhibiting many different qualities.

Two more important distinctions are hard and soft. Hard styles are those that take a direct, aggressive approach to combat; this means hitting and kicking to incapacitate your opponent and avoiding being kicked and hit by blocking, rather than stepping aside. Soft styles, in contrast, are lower-impact and more evasive than confrontational.

Still other distinguishing characteristics are linear and circular. Linear styles are those involving direct, head-on attack and defense. They tend to be hard styles. Circular styles involve sidestepping and sweeping attack motions in the attempt to put an opponent off balance. They tend to be softer styles.

These distinctions are not categories of different forms, but are characteristics that may be more or less present in any particular style or even in an individual's approach to the style. This is especially the case since many practitioners blend ideas and techniques from different styles. This blending is often a source of debate among martial arts buffs, some of whom are sticklers for tradition, whereas others are interested in trying new things.

Karma Dogma

Absorb what is useful.

—Bruce Lee, martial artist

Hit List

Here's a list describing just a few of the better-known styles of Eastern martial arts.

- **Kung fu.** A term meaning "skill discipline," kung fu was originally used to describe any practice requiring skill. In the nineteenth century, it came to be applied to martial arts in general, as well as to mind/body exercise. It is sometimes used to refer to specific Chinese styles supposedly developed centuries ago at China's famous Shaolin monastery.

- **T'ai chi chuan.** A soft style developed from mind/body fitness exercises. It means "supreme ultimate fist."
- **Pa kua.** One of the more recent techniques to be developed in China. It is based on ideas about mind/body harmony derived from the *I Ching* and takes its name from the pa kua, or eight trigrams, used in divination.
- **Jujitsu.** The oldest martial arts form of Japan, originating among the samurai, jujitsu means "gentleness technique," referring to the fact that it is intended for self-defense without weapons. It includes numerous styles involving hand striking, kicking, throws, and choke holds.
- **Judo.** A style derived from jujitsu founded in 1882 by Jigoro Kano and taught at the Kokodan center, which remains famous for judo performance and instruction. Judo means "gentleness way."
- **Karate.** One of the most popular and well-known of all Eastern martial arts forms, karate was introduced into Japan by an Okinawan named Gichin Funakoshi. Karate is alternately said to mean "Chinese hand" or "empty hand." After World War II, Funakoshi was hired by the U.S. Air Force to teach karate to servicemen.
- **Tae kwon do.** Korean form based on the combination of several styles, which were unified by presidential decree after the Korean War.
- **Aikido.** Self-defense system designed as a means of evasive action. There are no blows or painful holds in aikido. Instead, the style relies on turning out of the way of attack and controlling attackers by twisting their wrists.
- **Ninjutsu.** Ninjas were hired spies and assassins of Japan's Shogun era who dressed in black and used weapons that made no noise and were easily concealed. They have been wildly romanticized, as well as lampooned, in the West.

Karma Dogma

If one studies the arts of the warrior without following the true Way, his heart will be drawn by the hope of reputation and profit.

—*Tengugeijutsuron* (*Treatise on the Tengu Art of Fighting,* 1730)

Legends of the Art

The history of the Eastern martial arts is an important part of their mystique. To enhance this mystique, many martial arts buffs stress the long and rich legacy of their tradition. Some claim that it goes back to China's ancient Shang Dynasty, around

2000 B.C.E. or even earlier, or that it was practiced in India around the same time before spreading to China. In other words, people who are deeply into martial arts tend to make a strong association between its development and the growth and spread of Eastern thinking itself. They suggest that martial arts and philosophy have always gone hand in hand.

Grand masters and other teachers of many different martial arts styles sometimes trace their heritage back through lines of discipleship, much as Buddhist and Hindu sages have done. Some, of course, really have inherited a rich legacy of skill and understanding from their teachers. How far back these legacies extend, however, is subject to debate. Tied in with this question of how old martial arts traditions are is the question of whether they were ever actually used in battle, as opposed to competition and performance.

Martial Monks

One of the most widely told legends about the origin of martial arts says they were brought to China by the Buddhist sage, Bodhidharma, who arrived from India and settled at the Shaolin Monastery. Bodhidharma, as you may remember from Chapter 12, "Flesh on the Bones," is credited as the founder of Ch'an (Zen) Buddhism, which emphasizes meditation. According to the story, the monks at Shaolin spent so much time meditating that their bodies became weak. Bodhidharma taught the monks strengthening exercises to maintain their health.

Lotus Lore

Interest in the Shaolin temple has been sparked in recent years by the Hong Kong film, *Shao Lin Temple* (1982), starring kung fu master Jet Lee in his debut role as a seventeenth-century fighting monk. The movie generated so much interest in the temple that it prompted renovations to meet the growing numbers of tourists. The movie was equally beneficial to Jet Lee's acting career. He is now one of China's biggest stars and went on to do many more films, including several others that draw on the Shaolin legend. He is becoming well-known in the West and appeared in the Hollywood film, *Lethal Weapon 4*. Even so, he currently lags behind martial arts star Jackie Chan in notoriety among Westerners.

Some believe this was the origin of Shaolin kung fu, a system of exercises that developed into a martial arts style. Just when and how kung fu grew from a method of exercise into a martial arts system isn't known. There's very little historical documentation of the subject, but the Shaolin monks are depicted as martial artists in a nineteenth-century Chinese novel called *Shaolin Yen Yi,* or the *Historical Drama of Shaolin,* by Shao Yu-sheng.

The Shaolin mystique is fueled by the fact that, in China, popular rebellions against the government were sometimes supported, and even led, by Buddhist monks who participated in the fighting. It's tempting to imagine these monks as skilled martial arts practitioners, kicking and flipping against government corruption. In fact, many books and movies depict just this scenario. Shaolin is also the monastery where "Grasshopper" got his philosophical and martial arts training in the 1970s TV show *Kung Fu,* starring David Carradine.

Shaolin has become a popular tourist attraction, both because of the legends surrounding the fighting monks and because it is reputedly the site of the origin of Zen Buddhism. Shaolin kung fu has become one of the most popular forms of martial arts in the West, with thousands of students who practice it as a means of self-defense, as a form of beneficial exercise, and as an approach to Zen-based philosophy.

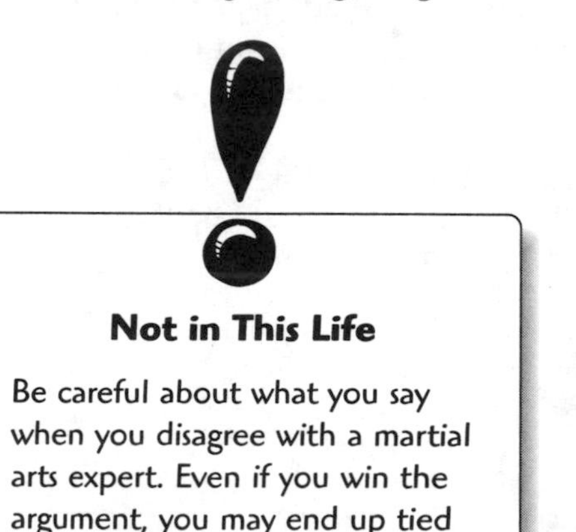

Not in This Life

Be careful about what you say when you disagree with a martial arts expert. Even if you win the argument, you may end up tied in a knot!

Other sources contributing to the martial arts legend and mystique include the many secret societies that have long been a feature of life in China, along with their secret symbols, rituals, and initiation practices. Some of these societies have been involved with underground political movements which sometimes erupted in fighting. So, like the fighting Buddhist monk, the underground secret-society martial artist is another popular figure in the ongoing legends of the East.

Mysterious Past

Several factors contribute to the uncertainty surrounding the history of the development of martial arts. If rebel monks and secret societies did use kung fu and other styles in combat, there are few reliable historical records that say so. It may be, as many martial arts buffs claim, that records were lost, destroyed, or simply never kept as a result of the underground nature of the groups who trained and fought.

On the other hand, the martial arts forms that first gained wide popularity in this century apparently developed out of Japanese jujitsu in the nineteenth century, which has been most visible as a formal and competitive tradition, rather than as a military tactic used in actual warfare. It's possible that other styles had formal and competitive origins, too, despite the appeal of imagining otherwise.

But martial arts fans argue that few styles were developed merely for show; most started as a practical necessity during times when weapons were outlawed. Forbidden from arming themselves, people refined techniques of hand-to-hand combat in order to protect themselves from thugs and robbers.

Another confusing aspect of martial arts history is that it's hard to say for certain just where exercise systems like t'ai chi and ch'i kung—which are geared toward mind/body health—become styles of martial arts. T'ai chi exercises can be applied to self-defense. In fact, t'ai chi, which means "supreme ultimate," when used as a means of self-defense, is known as t'ai chi chuan, which means "supreme ultimate fist."

Some martial arts buffs suggest that t'ai chi and t'ai chi chuan developed together at the same time. It's likely, however, that t'ai chi chuan developed out of t'ai chi in the twentieth century in the wake of the tremendous popularity of other martial arts forms, such as judo and karate. But because there are no hard and fast distinctions between t'ai chi and t'ai chi chuan, it's easy to confuse their histories.

Film Fighting

Ever since the end of World War II, martial arts and martial arts movies have fed one another's popularity. Because martial arts require constant control, they are ideal for staged fights, making them look realistic and exciting without endangering the participants. Modified judo techniques have been used in many war films of the forties and fifties. James Bond and other spy movies have made extensive use of martial arts sequences. TV action shows of the sixties, like *The Avengers* and *The Green Hornet,* made campy use of martial artistry.

The Green Hornet, in fact, was the breakthrough show of the most famous martial arts actor ever—Bruce Lee. Lee played the Green Hornet's high-kicking assistant Kato in this series before moving on to star in feature-length martial arts action films. In fact, he defined the genre with his charisma and technique.

Lee's most famous movie is the Hollywood blockbuster *Enter the Dragon* (1973). Here he plays a special undercover British agent who uses his skills to battle drug traffickers. This was his last completed film before his untimely death shortly before its release, and it made him a legend. Some say Lee was killed by foul means by enemies who were envious of his success in show business.

Lotus Lore

Many legends surround the life and untimely death of martial artist and film actor Bruce Lee. Some say he was killed by an esoteric karate chop called the vibrating palm, designed to cause death after a delay of several months or years. Others say he was done in by the death touch, a deadly pressure point known only to a few adepts. Some say influential Japanese martial artists were resentful of Lee's fame because Lee is Chinese. Others say that the Chinese monks of Shaolin were angry at Lee for revealing some of their ancient secrets.

The Least You Need to Know

- *The Art of War* by Sun Tzu is perhaps the world's best-known military treatise. It is still consulted today by corporate executives in search of competitive strategies.
- The samurai were warrior-administrators of Japan who served under warlords and practiced bushido, the way of the warrior, emphasizing personal honor and cultivation.
- Martial arts as we know them stem largely from training and conditioning techniques developed by the samurai during times of peace.
- Martial arts styles may be internal or external, hard or soft, linear or circular.
- Legends surrounding the history of martial arts center around fighting monks at the Shaolin monastery and secret societies in China.

Chapter 29

Rx East

In This Chapter

- Eastern medicine and philosophy
- The limits and drawbacks of Western medicine
- Acupuncture and acupressure
- Herbal remedies
- Yoga and interior cleansing

Despite the spectacular achievements Western science has made in the field of medicine, the sad truth is that Western medicine cannot do everything. In fact, in limiting their focus on specific treatments for specific illnesses, the drug and health care industries in the West often seem set up to reinforce unhealthy lifestyles. As a result, Westerners are constantly on watch for alternative medicine to go with alternative lifestyles. Of the many increasingly popular alternative approaches, many of the most popular come from the East.

And, again, despite its great achievements, Western medicine alone cannot provide effective treatment for everything. In focusing solely on physiological problems, spiritual solutions get overlooked. Many in search of mental and spiritual therapy for their health problems turn to Eastern mind/body approaches.

Eastern medical approaches aren't always reliable from a scientific point of view, and controversy abounds on the subject of the efficacy of various alternative treatments. Despite the bickering, there is real value in much that the East has to offer in the way of medical treatments and, perhaps more important, in attitudes about health. In fact, Eastern and Western approaches are increasingly practiced together in many parts of the world to the benefit of all concerned. It seems the best approach to personal health is to consult with a doctor while taking responsibility for your own lifestyle and attitude.

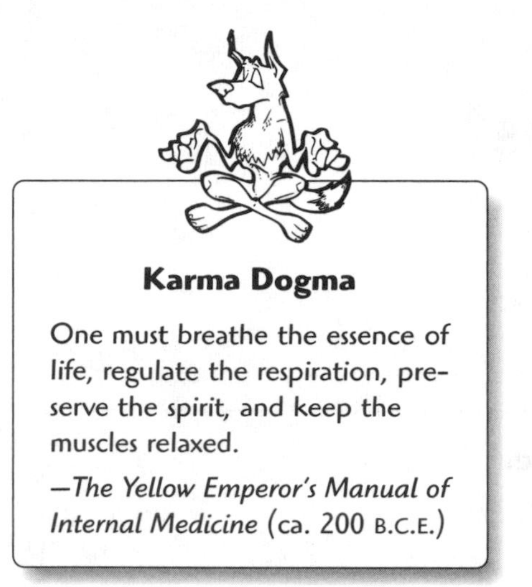

Karma Dogma

One must breathe the essence of life, regulate the respiration, preserve the spirit, and keep the muscles relaxed.

—*The Yellow Emperor's Manual of Internal Medicine* (ca. 200 B.C.E.)

Wide View

Eastern medicine is based on an approach to health that sharply differs from that of the West. Just as Eastern philosophy does not limit itself to the intellect in its conception of wisdom, Eastern medicine does not limit itself to the physical body in its conception of health. The body is just one aspect of a complex reality that includes many interpenetrating systems. When the body is sick, the whole set of relationships may be out of balance. As a result, you need to see the big picture if you want to know how to be cured. This big picture includes body, mind, spirit, and social relationships, all of which can be important factors in personal health.

Tunnel Vision

Western medicine tends to isolate different parts of the body, different processes and functions, and different diseases and symptoms in order to identify and treat health problems. Regarding the body as a machine made up of independent working parts, Western medicine singles out trouble spots in order to treat them directly. If there's a tumor, cut out the tumor. If there's a virus, kill the virus. If there's a system that isn't functioning properly, administer a drug that will correct the problem. If there's a dysfunctional organ, replace it with one that works.

There's no doubt that, in general, Western medicine is tremendously effective in curing illnesses and saving lives. In fact, there's nothing in the deepest wisdom of the East to suggest that it isn't a good idea to see a physician trained in the arts of Western medicine when you think there's something wrong with your health. Yet most Western doctors will admit that Western medicine is far from perfect. As you may know from experience, there's lots of room for improvement in Western health care!

What You Don't Know Can Hurt You

In particular, the traditional Western attitude to health—based on isolating the condition and treating it directly—can tend to lead to two interrelated problems.

The first problem stems from the wait-until-something-goes-wrong-and-then-get-help attitude. Some people trust Western medicine so much that they don't think enough about whether they lead a healthy lifestyle. People with poor habits sometimes assume that nothing's wrong as long as they don't actually feel sick. Then, when they do feel sick, they leave it up to their doctors to fix them up. The doctor is likely to treat only the isolated symptom of a larger health threat.

In recent years, Western health-care experts have started promoting the importance of preventive medicine. Most people realize that unhealthy lifestyles are a major long-term source of illness. The litany has become familiar these days: Inadequate exercise; too much fat, sugar, and salt in the diet; and emotional stress lead to disease. These diseases are actually much easier to treat before they become noticeable—by improving your lifestyle.

Preventive medicine has been a basic idea in Eastern thought for centuries and ties in with the Taoist conception of well-timed action. By acting in harmony with the circumstances, you save yourself a lot of trouble that could become almost impossible to deal with in late stages. This applies not only to physical health, but also to emotional and social well-being. Fixing problems is good, but avoiding them is better.

Not in This Life

Don't rely on your doctor for everything related to your personal health. You need to get involved, too. On the other hand, don't try any risky self-healing techniques without getting competent medical advice first!

Another problem that is too common in the West is side-effect syndrome. In aggressively treating a particular problem, Western cures often create new problems. Many drugs are addictive, toxic, or harmful in combination with other drugs. Some even interfere with the body's natural ability to heal itself.

Side effects can occur on many levels. Excessive, nonselective use of antibiotics to treat just about every minor ailment caused by a bug can breed stronger, more resistant strains of disease. Perhaps the worst side effect of all is that over-reliance on quick-fix medicine encourages unhealthy lifestyles and attitudes.

Unhealthy Habits

The problems of Western medicine are not merely shortcomings in medical science, but result from ingrained habits and attitudes toward health that science alone cannot fix. These bad habits include lifestyle problems, and they are worsened by the multibillion-dollar drug industry's attempts to encourage the use of medication for every imaginable ailment. Many Westerners are so quick to medicate themselves on feeling even minor discomfort that they lose touch with their own bodies. This can lead to increased dependence on "relief," which can stand in the way of a focus on health.

Office-itis

Imagine this nightmare scenario: You work in an office. Sometimes you're under lots of pressure. Other times, you go through the day nearly stupefied with boredom. You need to be at your desk almost all the time, so you rarely get any exercise. (Sound familiar?) You find that eating throughout the day helps calm you down and makes it easier to stay in your chair for long periods of time. Besides, it's something you can do at your cubicle besides work. (If you practiced qigong [ch'i kung] by your desk during your coffee break, people would think you'd lost your marbles, but no one thinks anything about it if you eat half a dozen donuts in the morning before going to lunch!)

Of course, because you eat when you're not really hungry, you need lots of salt, sugar, and fat in your food to make it more appetizing. After all, the most readily available snack foods are all like this anyway. Often, the excess food makes you drowsy, so you drink coffee throughout the day to stay awake, despite the fact that it makes you even more tense than you would be otherwise. Over the years, you build up a high tolerance for caffeine, so you have to drink more of it in an attempt to counteract the effects of your surging and crashing blood sugar levels.

Lotus Lore

Tea, which, like coffee, contains caffeine, is widely considered a healthfully stimulating beverage in the East. Legend has it that Bodhidharma, the founder of Zen Buddhism, advocated tea drinking to help his monks stay awake during meditation! In an elaboration of this legend, it is said that Bodhidharma once fell asleep while meditating and, in a pique of self-loathing, cut off his own eyelids to ensure he would never make the same mistake again. His disembodied eyelids took root and sprouted into the first tea plant. Ever since, tea has been keeping people from nodding off at the wrong time.

Stress, lack of exercise, and bad diet gradually take their toll, and you begin to suffer from headaches, back problems, and digestive problems. You medicate yourself with pain relievers, antacids and other medicines that make it harder for you to feel what's going on with your body. Meanwhile, because you drink so much coffee and get so little exercise, you have a hard time sleeping, so you take sleeping pills at night before bed.

Situation Normal

It never occurs to you that anything about your life is out of the ordinary. After all, millions of Americans live essentially the same way you do. You are bombarded every day with ads on TV and the radio for the medications you use, together with many you don't use—although you suspect they might help, since you tend to feel under the weather! Meanwhile, while you take medications to avoid feeling bad, your physical condition progressively worsens. Your heart becomes weak from stress and inactivity. Your blood fills with more and more cholesterol, and your arteries harden and become clogged with fat. Although you are overweight, your diet is lacking in fresh fruits and vegetables, and, as a result, you are at risk for many kinds of cancer.

Because you believe medical science can work miracles, you avoid worrying about your health. You figure if something goes wrong, your doctor can fix it. In fact, chances are that he can. Many kinds of cancer can be successfully treated with surgery and chemotherapy, while bypass surgery can help alleviate even the most serious heart disease. But, of course, not even medical science can cure every severe case.

Sadly, many Americans have had to face drastic treatments for serious medical problems stemming from the tendency to regard health strictly as the business of doctors, nurses, and pharmacists, rather than as a larger mind/body/lifestyle/environment situation. This is not to say that Eastern philosophy offers easy solutions to Western woes. Lifestyles, after all, are hard to change, especially when your livelihood depends on them. But the good news is that Eastern ideas—and many common-sense Western ideas consistent with Eastern thought—are gaining recognition. Health consciousness seems to be increasing in the West as holistic and preventive approaches are gaining ground.

Karma Dogma

An ounce of prevention is worth a pound of cure.

—Western saying

Nonprescription Treatments

Eastern philosophy is very much concerned with finding the right way to live one's life, so it should come as no surprise that many Westerners who recognize the important connection between health and lifestyle are interested in Eastern medicine. Eastern medicine draws on many sources and incorporates many influences. These include Taoist alchemy, five elements correspondences, yin-yang polarity, qigong (ch'i kung), yoga, and herbal remedies. The influences that have had the greatest impact in the West are yoga and qigong, herbal remedies from China, and Chinese acupuncture.

Balance of Power

Many Eastern ideas about diet and exercise are intended to promote spiritual as well as physical health. This is true of qigong and yoga, which are often practiced in the West for their physical health benefits, but grew originally out of concern for spiritual well-being. In fact, the sharp distinction between physical and spiritual health tends to be fuzzier in the East, where mind, body, and spirit are often thought to be interrelated.

Lotus Lore

In Chinese Taoism, the concern with health traditionally coincides closely with magical and religious belief. The Taoist cult of immortality generated a strong interest in discovering recipes and techniques to promote long life, including controlled breathing exercises, esoteric sexual practices, and alchemical concoctions (some of which had a strongly adverse effect on health). Several Taoist religious sects have taken shape around charismatic faith healers who acquired followings through feats of medical magic. The famous Yellow Turban Rebellion of the second century had its origins in the activity of one such faith healing sect.

Traditional attitudes toward health in China and India tend to regard the body as a system made up of both spiritual and physical forces, which correspond to physical and spiritual forces in nature. In other words, the microcosm of the human body corresponds to the macrocosm of the universe. In China, this idea has been developed into the five elements theory. Earth, air, water, fire, and metal are said to combine to form all things in the body and in the cosmos. Appropriate balance among the five elements results in natural harmony and physical health. (See Chapter 19, "Tao and Forever," for more on the five elements.)

This doesn't mean that you're supposed to eat wood, metal, fire, and dirt to keep your body in a state of natural balance! Instead, these elements correspond to various things that can be eaten, including foods and herbs. In fact, many herbal remedies in China have been introduced over the centuries to restore natural balance to the body. Some have been found to have pharmaceutical value and continue to be taken, even by people who don't believe in the five elements theory. Several Chinese herbs have become extremely popular as health products in the West, most notably astragalus, gingko biloba, ginseng, and dong quai (Angelica Senensis).

In the course of the development of Chinese medicine the five elements theory has been combined with other theories and beliefs concerning the body. Perhaps the most important concept from traditional Chinese medicine is *chi*. The word chi has many meanings, including breath and energy. It is often translated into English as life force. It is a vital power said to travel through all parts of the body. A proper balance of chi is necessary for good health. Not enough chi in an area results in a yin condition in that place. Too much chi results in a yang condition.

Chi can get out of balance in various parts of the body when its flow becomes blocked through stress, inactivity, or other causes. The practice of qigong developed largely as a means of increasing the free flow of chi throughout the body. Controlled breathing is another technique for improving the flow of chi. Still another means of increasing chi flow is acupuncture, a traditional medical technique of China that has become one of the most widely respected alternatives and supplements to Western medicine.

Not in This Life

Not all herbal remedies really work beyond exerting a placebo effect. For many touted herbs, including the ever-popular ginseng, scientific tests have failed to disclose any positive effects. On the other hand, some herbal remedies can be beneficial. Tests show that gingko biloba, for example, has evidently exerted a positive influence on some Alzheimer's patients.

Under the Needle

Acupuncture is based on the idea that chi flows along pathways throughout the body called meridians. A whole system of meridians, known to experienced acupuncture practitioners, crisscrosses the body. These meridians are located just under the skin, so they can be influenced by the accurate insertion of fine needles. These needles can open up blockages in chi flow to enable it to reach depleted areas or drain off excess chi that has accumulated where it shouldn't.

Meridians are thought to be governed by various organs of the body. Organs also govern other body parts and bodily processes. For example, the kidneys are said to govern blood, bones, joints, hair, and even willpower. Thus, ailments of different organs, as well as dysfunctions related to those organs, can be treated by acupuncture of their respective meridians. In addition, certain points on the body are said to correspond with other body parts. For example, the ear is thought to correspond to the whole body, so that acupuncture points located in the ear can produce effects throughout the body. Many detailed maps of meridians and of acupuncture points have been developed to facilitate study of the art.

The effects of the acupuncture needles can be altered by slight changes in the depth of insertion and in the width of the needles. More than one needle may sometimes be inserted into a single point where necessary. In addition, the effect of the needles can be enhanced by the traditional technique of applying burning mugwort to the head of the needle. This heats the entire needle and increases the stimulus at the point of insertion. This heating technique is known as moxibustion (moxa is another name for mugwort). Many acupuncturists now apply low voltage electrical current instead of burning mugwort to produce a similar effect.

Acupuncture has spread throughout the world and increased in popularity in the West since the 1970s, yet it remains a controversial practice. Many studies have suggested, however, that it can be an effective course of treatment (acupuncture is usually administered several times over the course of days, weeks, or months), especially for muscular pain caused by bruises, sprains, strain, and stress, and for pinched nerves. In China, acupuncture has been used as a form of local anaesthetic. Studies have also suggested that acupuncture may be effective in treating drug addiction.

Lotus Lore

Many surgical procedures in Chinese hospitals have been performed with much less reliance on general anesthesia than there is in the West. Instead, the Chinese use combinations of local anesthetics and acupuncture. In addition, Chinese patients are sometimes trained to gain mental control over their breathing and their sensitivity to pain prior to an operation, thus enabling them to remain conscious while undergoing surgery. Acupuncture has been used as an anesthetic in Chinese hospitals during thyroid operations, cataract operations, and in mitral valve surgery. A Chinese source has claimed that a qigong master successfully tranquilized numerous patients during surgery merely by directing a flow of chi from his fingers to a spot on their foreheads from a distance of several inches!

Although there is little scientific evidence to support the theory of chi flow and meridians that traditionally account for acupuncture practice, some practitioners believe that acupuncture works by triggering the release of endorphins, chemicals produced by the body that alleviate pain. Electrical stimulus sometimes used to replace moxibustion may also have a relaxing effect. In any case, acupuncture has become so widely accepted that many insurance companies are now willing to subsidize acupuncture treatment.

A therapeutic art closely related to acupuncture is acupressure, or *shiatzu,* a massage technique based on meridian theory that uses many of the same pressure points used in acupuncture. The idea is that by exerting pressure on these points, the flow of chi can be beneficially influenced. Many shiatzu pressure techniques can be self administered. In fact, some may have been developed by martial artists interested in healing themselves after sustaining injuries in combat.

Healthy Postures

Like China, India has its own ancient medical traditions, some of which continue to influence health practice today. Some concepts from ancient Indian medical thinking are remarkably similar to Chinese ideas. Just as Chinese tradition recommends maintaining physical balance through the five elements correspondence theory, Indian tradition recognizes the importance of balance among the three gunas—characteristics that make up the body as well as the things in nature. Balance among the gunas can be maintained through a proper diet.

In addition, traditional Indian medicine includes ideas that resemble concepts in Chinese meridian theory. The body contains pathways, or channels, that guide the flow of energy, or *prana,* from place to place. Prana is a word that can mean life, breath, or vital force. As a life force, the flow of prana can be enhanced by proper diet and yoga.

Orient Expressions

Shiatzu is a form of acupressure—the art of pressing and massaging acupressure points in order to improve the flow of chi. **Prana** is a Sanskrit word for "life force" or "vital energy," which is supposed to flow through the body along various channels.

Deep Cleaning

Of all India's traditional health practices, yoga has exerted the deepest influence on the West. The branch of yoga most closely concerned with physical health is hatha-yoga, an approach that recommends many techniques for promoting health, strength, and cleanliness. In hatha-yoga, bodily cleanliness is considered an important aspect of spiritual discipline as well as of physical health.

Hatha-yogic hygiene techniques include cleaning the body inside and out. Interior cleaning, as you may imagine, isn't always easy, but the purpose of hatha-yoga is not to do things the easy way. One cleaning technique for the digestive tract is to swallow large quantities of air and force it down into the intestines so that it comes out as flatulence!

An even more drastic approach is to swallow one end of a length of cloth or rope and pass it gradually through the whole digestive tract. This takes days and is done while fasting. Hatha-yogis also practice self-induced vomiting and enemas. The sinuses may also be cleaned by passing a rope or cloth through the nostrils and out the mouth or by flushing the nostrils out with water.

Body of Knowledge

In fact, few of the interior cleansing techniques of hatha-yoga have caught on in the West in a big way. Most Western yoga practitioners are content to limit themselves to the strengthening and flexibility exercises. Many of these are said to be good for the interior organs as well as the muscles, nerves, joints, and bodily functions. Repeated and controlled muscle contractions and bodily postures can serve to massage internal organs. Controlled breathing can also exert healthful pressure on various parts of the body.

Karma Dogma

The body is the lord's temple.

—Yogic saying

One great potential health benefit of yoga goes beyond the particular effects of the various postures and exercises. Since yoga is a practice that improves bodily control and awareness, yogic discipline helps people get in touch with their own bodies so they are better able to avoid unhealthy things and to recognize that something is wrong. In fact, it may be that the greatest value of Eastern medicine in general lies not so much in specific cures and treatments, but in its recognition of the value of balance, harmony, interconnectedness, and disease prevention. Fortunately, this recognition has been growing among Westerners.

The Least You Need to Know

- Excessive reliance on the power of Western medicine can make people ignore the importance of a healthy lifestyle.
- While Western medicine tends to isolate sources of disease, Eastern approaches tend to see disease in relation to the larger physical, mental, and spiritual environment.
- Eastern approaches to health most popular in the West include herbal remedies, yoga, qigong, and acupuncture.
- Acupuncture appears to be most effective in treating muscle and nerve pain and as a supplementary anesthetic.
- In addition to its many specific techniques intended to promote strength and cleanliness, yoga tends to contribute to body awareness.

Chapter 30

The Art of Wisdom

In This Chapter

- Eastern art and philosophy
- Hindu art and image worship
- Buddhist shrines and statues
- Tantric art and inner development
- Zen art and spontaneity

There's a close bond in many Eastern cultures between art and philosophy. In fact, partly because of the emphasis in Eastern thought away from dogmatic, formulaic teachings, art serves as an important reminder that wisdom must be experienced first-hand. Of course, art does not contain ultimate wisdom any more than mere words do. But, because art is capable of awakening feelings and ideas without words, it can point the way beyond ordinary ways of thinking toward a more profound awareness of existence.

This awareness is different for different people and cultures. So it's a good thing that there are art forms and attitudes toward artistic creation to help bring about and reflect awareness in different ways. Mahayana Buddhists say that there are different kinds of teaching for different kinds of people. The same could be said about art and its philosophical applications in the East, where the way you experience art depends not only on who you are, but on where you are on your journey to enlightenment.

Art is especially important in many Hindu and Buddhist sects as an expression of religious and philosophical attitudes. Hindu and Buddhist art traditions developed side by side in India for many years, influencing one another. And as Buddhism spread beyond India, Buddhist art developed in new ways.

Turn to Stone

India has produced some of the most spectacular religious art on the planet. This art is based on rich Hindu traditions and draws on philosophical teachings and religious myths. Statues representing gods and spirits, often carved out of stone, were erected in ancient Hindu temples that served as centers for worship and ritual. Sculpted images may have served as visual aids for sermons and lessons. And, of course, they contribute a special aura to places of worship.

Lotus Lore

Christian missionaries arriving in India in the nineteenth century looked upon the "image worship" practiced by many Hindu sects as vain and superstitious. The images seemed bizarre, with their many heads, hands, and eyes, their provocative sexuality, and combinations of human and animal features. Westerners tended to see Hindu religious art as uncivilized, probably because they failed to appreciate the role of divine images in Hindu religious worship. Actually, not all Indians wholly approved of the use of religious images. Shankara, the famous Vedanta philosopher, said they were useful only to those with an inferior capacity for wisdom. The response of some Indian philosophers to Western views was that worshiping Christ on the cross was the same as image worship!

Graven Images

Hindus have always responded to religious imagery in a variety of ways. For some, concentrating on religious images in meditation provides a means of stilling and focusing the mind, much like chanting a mantra or concentrating mental energy on a particular part of the body. For others, the images and the divine figures and myths they represent depict a cosmic, transcendent reality capable of permeating the world of physical existence. For still others, religious images point the way, not to a transcendent reality, but to a transcendent awareness of this reality.

In general, however, Hindu art is intended to lead the individual beyond his or her particular situation to an understanding of larger cosmic forces. This may involve gradual personal development as the individual progresses from a narrow belief in the image as divinity to an appreciation of the symbolic nature of the image, which leads, ultimately, to a wider awareness of the pervasiveness of the divine throughout the cosmos. Thus Hindu art not only means different things to different people, it can mean different things to the same person at different times.

Stock Figures

Traditional Hindu religious art is highly conventional, adhering closely to established motifs. Although it is often beautifully and painstakingly crafted, the emphasis tends to be placed as much on the meaning of the symbolism as on the beauty of the form. An elaborate iconography has developed in India over the centuries, incorporating elements of a common set of mythic traditions that make it possible to identify the divine figures being represented. Vishnu, for example, is often depicted with a disk, or chakra, in his hand, representing the wheel of dharma. He may be standing with one foot raised, symbolizing his ability to make great strides forward.

Shiva has matted hair denoting his accomplishments in yogic exercise. He often has a cobra wound around his neck or body. Ganesh is easiest to recognize of all divine Hindu figures; he's the one with the head of an elephant. He is always shown with one of his tusks broken. (They say he broke it off to use as a pen to write the words of scripture.) Another striking figure is Kali, the goddess of destruction, who wears a necklace of severed heads and has blood dripping from her mouth. She often has a third eye in the middle of her forehead, signifying spiritual knowledge. And she is standing on the prostrate body of her husband, Shiva!

Not in This Life

Aside from a few special cases like Ganesh, the elephant-headed god, you won't get far identifying statues of Hindu deities by their facial characteristics. For the most part, their faces aren't that distinctive. Instead, you'll need to look at what they are carrying and wearing to figure out who they are.

Standard motifs associated with the various divine beings indicate their powers and aspects, and allude to myths that are told about them. These divine characteristics can be interpreted on many levels. They can be taken to represent attributes of the gods themselves or of larger forces at work connecting physical reality to the cosmos. In other words, those who worship images may see them not just as representations of the gods, but as depictions and embodiments of cosmic power. Worship can be seen as a way of understanding, as well as tapping into, this power.

Religious imagery may symbolize wisdom, strength, compassion, prosperity, the union of opposites, victory over evil, and many other aspects of life, portraying them in such a way as to present the human condition in a cosmic setting. In universalizing aspects of human existence, religious art can help people project their awareness of their own lives outside themselves and help them see the big picture. For example, one way of understanding the horrific image of Kali, the goddess of destruction, is to see her as providing a way of coming to terms with tragedy and mastering the suffering it causes. Kali helps people visualize suffering and death in cosmic terms. This, in turn, can help people cope with their own tragedies more easily.

A Show of Hands

Because the significance of divine figures needs to be represented in visual terms, statues and paintings of these figures are often crowded with symbols. These include characteristic physical traits, items of clothing, implements, and plants and animals. In fact, many Hindu gods have so many cosmic attributes, they need extra hands to carry them around. At any rate, this is one way of accounting for the extra arms and hands attached to so many Hindu deities.

Lotus Lore

Not all divine Hindu symbolism is produced by artists. Some of it occurs in nature. A famous example of natural divine symbolism is the salagrama. Salagramas are fossilized snail shells found in Indian river beds. They are often worn smooth by the river and exhibit beautiful spiral shapes said to represent the chakra of Vishnu. (Vishnu's chakra is, simultaneously, an aspect of his body, the wheel of dharma, and the disk of the sun.) The various shapes of the salagramas represent different incarnations of the god. As manifestations of Vishnu, salagramas are highly prized religious objects and are often collected in temples as objects of worship.

Hindu gods may be shown with two, four, six, or more arms and hands. Although these multiarmed deities would be great at directing traffic, the extra limbs usually signify divine powers and attributes. The extra hands, in addition to coming in handy for carrying cosmic attributes, are good for forming mudras, the symbolic hand gestures used in ritual and meditation.

Ganesh is often depicted with many arms. In one, he carries a hatchet with which to chop away at false teaching. Another carries an elephant goad as a spur to truth. A third carries a rope used to restrain the passions.

Shiva uses an extra hand to carry a flame representing wisdom. He also carries a drum symbolizing the creative power of sound.

Kali holds a sword representing enlightenment in one arm. In another, she holds a severed head representing death. A third arm carries a bowl symbolizing generosity.

Interestingly, extra arms are said to suggest passionate aspects of the gods. The same gods may also be represented in Hindu art with only two arms, symbolizing self-control.

Buddha Beauty

Just as Buddhist thought is closely related to Hindu thinking, Buddhist and Hindu art are interconnected. In fact, some scholars have suggested that Hindu art developed largely as a response to Buddhist art, rather than the other way around. It seems that most Hindu art dates from the time after the arrival of the Buddha, whose life and teachings were soon memorialized in the form of shrines and statues throughout India and beyond. Buddhist art got a big lift during the third century B.C.E., thanks to the support of the Buddhist Emperor, Asoka.

Not in This Life

Scholars disagree about the origins of and relationship between Hindu and Buddhist sculpture. Some say Hindu religious sculpture did not develop until after Buddhist sculpture paved the way. Others say Hindu sculpture predates Buddhist sculpture, but was generally done in wood, rather than stone, and has since decayed in the tropical Indian climate.

Stupa-fied

One of the earliest forms of Buddhist art is an architectural design—the *stupa*. A stupa is a large, dome-shaped shrine where relics are kept. Emerging out of the dome is a pillar representing the axis of the world. Many stupas are decorated with elaborate relief carvings depicting events told in the Buddhist jataka tales (tales about the Buddha's previous incarnations in animal form). Pilgrims show devotion at stupas outdoors by slowly circling their facades.

Despite the beautiful relief carvings around the outside of many stupas, they are considered more important for the holy relics enshrined within. Though many are grand, elaborate, stone structures, the first stupas were patterned after Hindu burial mounds. As stupas moved east and were adapted to local building styles, they were erected in the form of pagodas—square instead of round and multileveled.

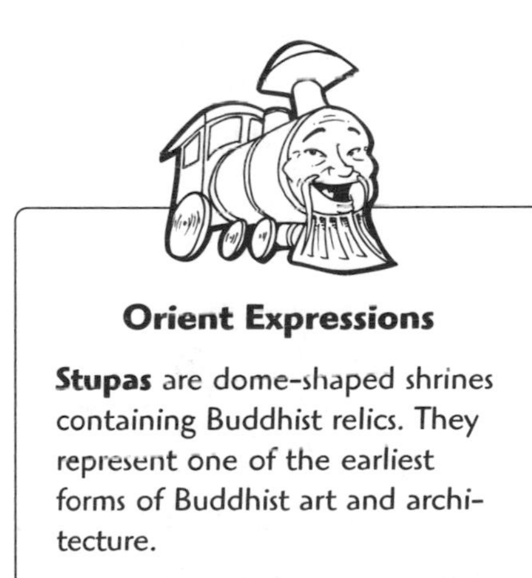

Orient Expressions

Stupas are dome-shaped shrines containing Buddhist relics. They represent one of the earliest forms of Buddhist art and architecture.

Stone Still

Buddha statues were carved as shrines, which have been visited by traveling pilgrims, local monks, and devotees since at least as far back as 200 B.C.E. Although worship of religious figures is not consistent with the original teachings of the Buddha, carved representations of the Buddha serve as objects of devotion as well as memorials to the Enlightened One.

Statues of the Buddha tend to be simpler—less crowded with symbolism—than statues of Hindu Gods; nevertheless, many symbolic features are incorporated in them. Carvings in statue and in relief depict events of Buddha's life, especially his birth, his enlightenment, his teaching, and his death. He is often shown meditating, sometimes in serene contentment, sometimes as an emaciated ascetic. He usually has a raised knob on the top of his head, symbolizing his attainment of wisdom. His hands often form mudras representing blessing, concentration, or peace. Sometimes he is shown stretching a hand to the Earth, calling on the Earth to witness his enlightenment, and representing his resistance of the temptations of the evil seducer, Maya.

Ultimate Art

As Buddhism spread, Buddhist art began to take on diverse characteristics and to develop various philosophical applications. Art and philosophy have an especially close relationship in Tantric Buddhism practiced in Tibet. Tantric art is used to promote spiritual development in ways suited to the particular needs of different people. It does so by triggering psychological responses that can be worked through in the process of attaining spiritual insight.

Scrolling Up

Tantric Buddhists consider their traditional art forms manifestations of ultimate being. Tantric art does not depict ultimate reality—though it is filled with representations of divine beings in idealized realms. Instead, it embodies ultimate reality within the understanding of those who encounter it. When ultimate reality is understood with the help of art, it can be experienced more easily in everyday life. Art, then, can help the individual work through the limitations of his or her own mind that pose obstacles to absolute existence.

Orient Expressions

Thangkas are scroll paintings of Tibetan Tantric Buddhism representing enlightened beings. The term comes from a Tibetan word for record. The purpose of thangkas, however, is not historical record-keeping but inner knowledge and enlightenment.

Chapter 13, "The Diamond Path," which is about Tibetan Buddhism, goes over the importance of Tantric symbolism as a means of achieving enlightenment. It mentions the use of mandalas—geometric designs, often beautiful and elaborate—which represent spiritual maps of the self and of the cosmos. Another important Tantric art form is the *thangka*. Thangkas are paintings, usually on pieces of silk cloth, depicting enlightened beings and divine figures. Thangkas may also depict mandalas and written mantras.

Thangkas were rolled up and carried from place to place by traveling monks, who used them in teaching. They have come to be used as tools for dealing with psychological barriers to enlightenment. Reflecting on thangkas, especially under the guidance of a teacher, provides a way of understanding existence from the perspective of an enlightened being.

In fact, many thangkas represent enlightened beings—Buddhas, Boddhisattvas, and gurus. These thangkas serve the dual purpose of recording the identity and succession of enlightened beings and of providing a source of psychological refuge and release for those who reflect on them. Tantric Buddhists believe that those who take refuge in the enlightened beings depicted in thangkas can free themselves from other kinds of psychological dependencies.

Scroll Models

Other figures depicted in thangkas are known as *yidams* and *dharmapalas*. Yidams are personal deities representing aspects of the psychological makeup of each individual. They help people understand their own natures in positive terms so they can make productive use of their personal tendencies. Dharmapalas are guardian spirits. Their role is to provide protection against false teaching and confusion.

Yidams can be either angry and fearsome or mild and peaceful. Angry yidams are not intended to inspire fear or hatred, but to eliminate doubt and foster courage. Many wear crowns made of skulls that represent emotional obstacles to be overcome. They may also wear capes made of human or animal skins. Tiger skin stands for courage, elephant skin stands for strength, and human skin stands for compassion.

Orient Expressions

Yidams are tutelary (personal) deities commonly represented on Tibetan Buddhist thangkas. **Dharmapalas** are guardians of Tibetan Buddhist teaching.

Peaceful yidams, in contrast, inspire openness and tranquility. In addition, various yidams are grouped into different "Buddha families." As a result, identifying with one's personal yidam can provide an understanding for relating to Tantric culture as a whole. In this way, Tibetan Buddhists can fit in, even as they are pursuing their goal of enlightenment.

Yidams can be male or female. Male and female yidams are often depicted together locked in sexual embrace. This symbolic sexual union is called *yab-yum,* which means "father-mother." It represents the merging of opposites and the interplay and simultaneity of the planes of samsara and nirvana.

Dharmapalas, or guardians of dharma, are said to embody powers that can be assimilated and controlled by those who look to them. In addition to serving as protectors of the teachings of Buddhism, some of them are also Tibetan national deities. Whereas most of the divine figures depicted in Tibetan thangkas have their cultural origins in India, some of the dharmapalas were originally Tibetan gods who were converted to Buddhism.

Zen and the Art of Art

Thangkas were not traditionally made by Buddhist monks, but by specialized craftspeople. Although they are intended to be beautiful as well as symbolically meaningful, the purpose of creating them is not to display the personality of the artist. The same can be said of traditional Hindu religious art and, in fact, of religious art in general. The genius of the individual artist is usually considered less important than the religious significance of the image.

While traditional Hindu and Tibetan Buddhist art is both religious and philosophical, the art of Zen Buddhism tends not to be religious in the same sense. It places emphasis on the spontaneous act of creation and the state of mind of the artist. Zen art is not based on an established, highly formalized symbolic tradition, but reflects the Zen attitude of the artist.

Lotus Lore

A famous anecdote about a well-known Japanese potter reveals something of the Zen approach to art. The potter was commissioned to make some pottery for an important occasion and felt that his professional reputation was on the line. So he committed the fatal mistake of Zen—he tried too hard. In attempting to make the pottery as hard and fine as he possibly could, he overheated it in the kiln, and it cracked. With the important occasion at hand, the potter couldn't start all over, so he fixed the pottery by melting gold into the cracks. The pots turned out to be the finest and most highly prized pieces he had ever made, in part because they expressed perfectly the tensions involved in their creation.

Serendipity

The Zen attitude toward life is that it should be lived by letting things happen. This is essentially the Zen attitude toward artistic creation as well. It is applied toward painting, poetry, pottery, and calligraphy (the art of handwriting). This attitude has been so influential in China and Japan that it has been adopted at various times by large portions of society, not just by Zen Buddhists.

In fact, in China and Japan, artistic ability was considered an important expression of a gentleman's nature. Scholars, soldiers, and monks were often expected to be able to paint, play music, and write poetry along with their other pursuits. This focus on artistic ability incorporates Zen beliefs with Confucian and Taoist ideas about personal and natural behavior. An aspect of the approach is that it is a mistake to specialize—to place all your energy into one activity. The goal of life should not be so narrow, but should include an appreciation of nature, the arts, and human feelings.

Just as you should not control life by attempting to be perfectly skilled in a single profession, you should not exert too much control over your artistic creations. Rather than trying to make them look a certain way, you should allow them to take shape naturally, in response to your mood and the larger situation. In this way, it becomes possible to capture the essence or spirit of a thing, or a moment in art, as opposed to its mere appearance or assertion. It is considered better in much Japanese and Chinese painting, for example, to depict elusive, hard-to-pin-down qualities of a subject than to represent things realistically. The best way to do this is by taking a natural, effortless approach—to let things happen.

Famous Last Words

Perhaps the most important Zen-inspired artistic medium is poetry. Zen poems were influenced by koans—the sayings and word puzzles used by Zen monks to trigger awareness and enlightenment. In addition, Zen monks traditionally wrote poems to describe enlightenment experiences. This kind of poem helped demonstrate and memorialize the attainment of enlightenment, showing how existence can be understood in a new way, from the perspective of newly opened eyes, so to speak. Monks also wrote poems intended to capture their state of mind at the moment just before death. Like enlightenment poems, death poems look past ordinary, conventional ways of understanding experience.

Zen tradition stands behind the well-known Japanese poetic form—the haiku. A haiku is a very brief poem that often describes an image or experience in a way that conveys profound insight. Although the form developed over the course of centuries, it crystallized in the seventeenth century in the writings of the famous poet Basho (1643–1694). The point of haiku is to capture the essence of an experience as briefly and plainly as possible, so that it resonates within the awareness of the reader. It usually takes the form of three lines, the first of five syllables, the second of seven, and the third of five again. The form remains in use today, not only among Japanese poets, but also poets around the world.

Karma Dogma

Disturbing the stillness of an ancient pond
A frog jumped into the water
—a deep resonance.
—Haiku by Basho

Perhaps the most famous haiku ever written is the one printed here as a bit of "karma dogma." As your mind resonates with the profundities stirred up by Basho's frog, it's time to bring this book to a close. If you want to deepen your awareness still further, take a look at the appendixes on the following pages: Appendix A, "Terms of En-seerment," is a glossary. Appendix B, "Guru's Who's Who," lists and describes famous figures in Eastern thought. And Appendix C, "It Is Written," is a list of books for further reading.

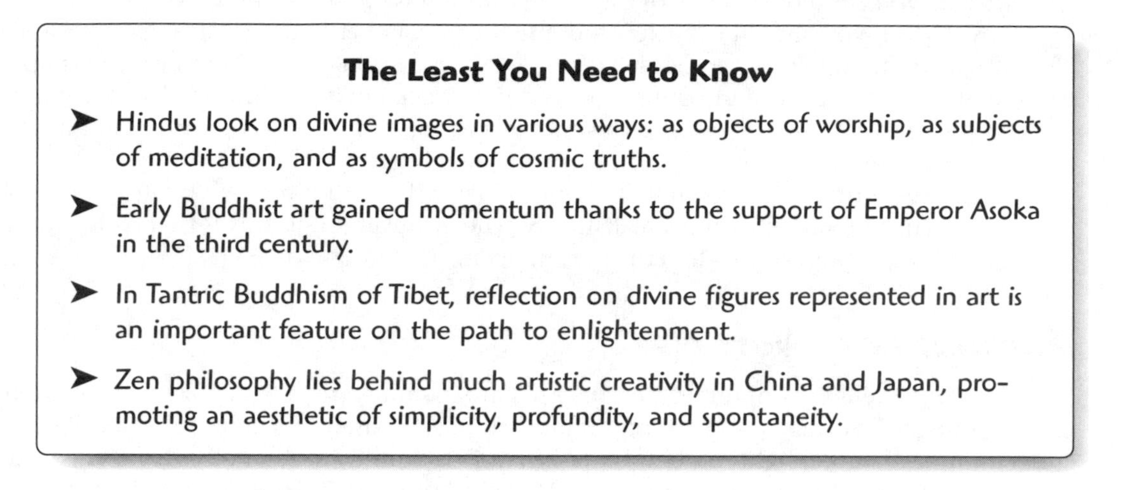

The Least You Need to Know

- Hindus look on divine images in various ways: as objects of worship, as subjects of meditation, and as symbols of cosmic truths.
- Early Buddhist art gained momentum thanks to the support of Emperor Asoka in the third century.
- In Tantric Buddhism of Tibet, reflection on divine figures represented in art is an important feature on the path to enlightenment.
- Zen philosophy lies behind much artistic creativity in China and Japan, promoting an aesthetic of simplicity, profundity, and spontaneity.

Terms of En-seer-ment

Here's a glossary of important Sanskrit, Chinese, and Japanese philosophical terms.

Adrishta According to the Vaisheshika system, Adrishta is an unseen power that causes and directs the course of existence. It is closely related to the principle of karma and associated with God by some philosophers.

ahankara According to Sankhya philosophy, ahankara is consciousness of individuality, which evolves from buddhi and gives rise to the senses.

ahimsa The moral principle of respect for life in Hindu and Buddhist philosophy. This principle has been practiced in many forms, including vegetarianism and nonviolent resistance.

Alaya-vijnana "Storehouse consciousness," the concept of Yogacara Buddhist philosophy that says mind is the only reality where distinctions disappear and existence may be understood in its "suchness."

arhat A Theraveadin Buddhist who has achieved enlightenment and will be released from the cycle of samsara at death.

asceticism The practice of self-denial, usually for the sake of spiritual development, asceticism can be found as part of many religious and philosophical traditions. Ascetic practices include celibacy, fasting, self-induced sleep deprivation, and the rejection of material comforts in general.

ashram The four stages of life—studying, householding, forest-dwelling, and renouncing—recommended by Manu's Dharmashastra. An ashram is also the retreat or hermitage of a guru or spiritual seeker.

Atman In Hinduism, the universal self, the absolute knower. It is the source of cosmic experience, uniting all consciousness.

avatar An appearance on Earth of a deity, usually Vishnu, in human or animal form. Vishnu is often said to have 10 avatars, including Krishna. The avatars appear on Earth during times when evil predominates in order to restore righteousness.

bardo In Tibetan Buddhism, bardo is a transitional state, especially the state of the dying and recently dead soul on its way to rebirth or nirvana.

bhakti Devotion. It represents the pursuit of enlightenment through the adoration of God. The importance of bhakti within Hinduism was galvanized through the Bhagavad-Gita.

bhog The practice in Hindu ritual of providing the gods with pleasurable things, including food, music, and adornment. It is a way of sharing the fruits of human labor and divine providence.

Brahman Transcendent, absolute reality in Hindu thought.

Brahmin A member of the priestly caste in traditional Hindu society.

Buddhi In Sankhya philosophy, cosmic intelligence as it exists in individuals.

bushi Members of the Japanese warrior class who followed a strict code of honor known as **bushido,** or way of the warrior.

castes Traditional social divisions in Indian society consisting of the brahmins, the kshatriyas, the vaisyas, and the sudras. The word "caste" is not originally Indian, but comes from the Portuguese word "casta," meaning race or breed.

chakras Or chakradds, chakras are lotus-shaped energy centers of the mystic body recognized by yogic philosophy.

ch'ang The five chief Confucian virtues, according to Tung Chung-shu.

ch'eng The Chinese word for sincerity, which is an important Confucian virtue that can be developed by imitating the beneficial nature of heaven.

chi The Chinese word for breath that also means life force or energy. It is the matter or substance of all things that take shape through the influence of li.

chih The Confucian virtue of wisdom.

ch'ing The propensity of feelings and desires, which Tung Chung-shu associated with the yin principle.

citta Sanskrit (Hindu) for "consciousness." The term can be used to refer to spirituality and to reason. When the citta is polluted, you are filled with erroneous ideas about life. When it is purified, you understand things clearly.

Darsanas The main philosophical schools in India. They include six orthodox systems and three unorthodox schools. The term comes from a word meaning "sight."

dharma Sanskrit for "duty," dharma is an important concept in many systems of Indian philosophy. In Buddhism, **dharma** is Buddhist teaching and **dharmas** are qualities of existence. By joining together into temporary compounds, they give form to reality.

dharmapalas Divine guardians of Tibetan Buddhist teaching.

dhyana Sanskrit word often translated as "meditation." Early Chinese Buddhists called it Ch'an, and it became the name of an important school of Chinese Buddhism which spread to Japan where the school is called Zen and the dhyana meditation is called **zazen.**

Diamond Path Vajrayana, the form of Buddhism originated in Tibet.

fang hsien tao Meaning "the way of recipes and immortality," fang hsien tao is Chinese alchemy, the art of discovering the secrets of immortality by means of chemical experiments.

Feng Shui Literally "wind and water," Feng Shui is the ancient art of Chinese geomancy, or earth divination, used to identify the best sites for buildings and graves. It has recently become a trendy design concept.

fu Chinese for "return," fu is the Taoist principle of balance or equilibrium. All extremes return to a state of balance with their opposites.

hsing The human potential for good as described by Tung Chung-shu, who associated it with the yang principle.

I Ho Chuan The Society of Righteous Fists, better known to the West as the "Boxers," a group of militant nationalists who terrorized Westerners and Western sympathizers in China at the turn of the twentieth century.

Ishvara Means "Lord" and is used to refer to a concept that resembles the Judeo-Christian and Islamic idea of God—that is, an all-powerful being who cares about human beings in a more or less personal way. In India, those who believe in the supremacy of Brahma, Vishnu, or Shiva may address their particular god as Ishvara.

jen The Confucian concept of humanity, involving compassion for others. The word also means human being and, more particularly, a gentleman.

kami The gods of shinto, the native religion of Japan.

kang The cords in the mesh of a net used by Tung Chung-shu to refer to the three most important human relationships: parent/child, husband/wife, and ruler/subject.

kang-ch'ang The virtuous life involving both personal goodness and social ethics.

karma The ongoing influence of past actions on the future. It carries over from past lives into present and future incarnations. **Prarabda-karma** is the influence of past actions on your present life; **sanchita-karma** is the influence of past actions on future lives; **agami-karma** is the influence of present actions on future lives.

koan A story, verse, riddle, or question that is traditionally used in Zen to test and train monks. Ideally, a koan produces the experience of satori, or enlightenment, either after it has been contemplated over a period of time or else all of a sudden. The term is from the Chinese word kung-an, which means case.

kundalini yoga A form of yoga that attempts to awaken the kundalini—cosmic energy in the form of a coiled snake residing at the base of the spine—so that it rises through the **chakras**, or lotus-shaped energy centers of the mystic body.

kung fu (**gong fu** in Pinyin) The general term used in China for mind/body discipline. It literally means "skillful practice."

lama A high-ranking Tibetan Buddhist monk, such as those in charge of monasteries. The highest-ranking is the Dalai Lama, the spiritual leader of Tibet.

li The Chinese word for ritual. It also refers to the rules of proper conduct and good manners. As a Neo-Confucianist term, it means "ultimate principle," which was thought to determine the nature of all things.

mahat In Sankhya philosophy, mahat is cosmic intellect, which is the first aspect of nature to evolve.

mahatma A term of honor and respect accorded a great person in India, most notably Mahatma Gandhi. It is also a title given by Theosophists to spiritual adepts who are supposed to have enlightenment and superhuman powers.

mandalas Elaborate circular designs that represent the self and the cosmos.

mantras Words and syllables used in meditation.

maya The illusory reality of everyday experience. Belief that maya is real prevents us from experiencing unity with Brahman and Atman.

moksha Release from the human condition that prevents union with Brahman and Atman. It is what happens to you when you experience enlightenment.

mondo Question-and-answer exchanges between a Zen master and a pupil. Mondo stories are often considered **koans,** since they illustrate the nature of Zen.

mudras Hand gestures whose symbols facilitate the concentration and flow of energy.

Namo Amida Butsu or **nembutsu** Meaning "Praise be to Amida Buddha," nembutsu is the prayer uttered in Japan by Pure Land (Shin) Buddhists who want to be reborn in the Pure Land.

nirvana The Buddhist state of enlightenment roughly equivalent to the Hindu concept of moksha. Whereas moksha means "release," nirvana means "extinguishing," which refers to the extinguishing of desires and the ego.

padarthas Analytical categories describing objects of experience. Different philosophical schools recognize different groups of padarthas and sometimes interpret the same padarthas differently.

panca-makara "The five M's"—earthly pleasures forbidden to most monks and ascetics but used in left-handed Tantric ritual to achieve a heightened spiritual condition.

Pinyin Romanization system One of the most commonly used systems for transliterating written Chinese into the Roman alphabet.

prakriti Physical nature, according to Sankhya philosophy. It is opposed to purusa, or consciousness.

pramanas Criteria or proofs of the validity of knowledge, important for the logical aspects of Indian philosophy. Different philosophical schools recognize different pramanas and emphasize similar pramanas to varying degrees.

prana Sanskrit for life force or vital energy, prana flows through the body along various channels.

pratityasamutpada Has been translated as "dependent arising," "conditioned arising," "dependent origination," and "interdependent cooperation." It is the Buddhist principle of causality and explains why all things are conditioned and impermanent.

pu In traditional Chinese lore, pu is a category of foods that are thought to strengthen the body or provide a special source of energy.

p'u Taoist term for a simple, unassuming attitude. It is often translated literally as "uncarved block," meaning lumber that has not had its rough edges smoothed off.

purusa Pure universal consciousness. According to Sankhya philosophy, existence evolves out of the interaction of purusa and prakriti.

qigong (ch'i kung in Wade-Giles) The technique of Chinese mind-body exercise.

sacred cow A Western expression used to refer to an idea that gets undeserved respect. It stems from the veneration of cows among Hindus, which British colonialists considered irrational.

samurais Japanese knights or warrior-administrators who formed the top layer of the **bushi**, or warrior class in Japan.

samsara The cycle of birth and death that accounts for our physical existence. It is the idea of reincarnation as explained in the Upanishads.

sangha The Buddhist community, originally the order of nuns and monks that embraced Buddhism from the beginning. The sangha is considered one of the Three Jewels of Buddhism, together with the Buddha himself and Buddhist teachings.

san ts'ung An expression used in imperial China that literally means "three times obedient." It described the social predicament of women who were expected to obey their fathers, husbands, and sons.

satori The Japanese, Zen Buddhist term for enlightenment. This may come as the result of dedicated, disciplined effort or in a sudden, spontaneous revelation.

satyagraha The philosophy of adhering to the truth advanced by Mahatma Gandhi. Truth adherence underlies Gandhi's commitment to nonviolent resistance, as well as his belief that all people contain aspects of divinity.

sheng A sage, one of the most highly venerated figures of China's Classical Period. Not simply a wise man, the sage was also virtuous and capable of taking the reins of government.

shiatzu A form of acupressure—the art of pressing and massaging acupressure points in order to improve the flow of chi.

shoguns Japanese warlords who ruled in Japan from the twelfth to the nineteenth centuries.

shunyata Void or emptiness, shunyata is a term used by Nagarjuna to explain the underlying reality of all things and the failure of conceptualization to convey the truth.

skandhas Groups or aggregates that constitute the various aspects of human existence and experience. They are **rupa** (body), **vedana** (feelings), **sanna** (perception), **samskara** (predisposition), and **vijnana** (consciousness). They are temporary conditions, showing that the self, which is based on them, has no essence. **Rupa** is the physical skandha. The others are **nama**, or mental.

stupas Dome-shaped shrines containing Buddhist relics. They represent one of the earliest forms of Buddhist art and architecture.

syad-vada The "maybe theory" of Jaina philosophy which says reality is too complex to be described adequately by any single statement. Thus, conflicting statements can be valid simultaneously, provided they are made from distinct points of view.

t'ai chi Chinese term meaning "Supreme Ultimate," it is made up of yin and yang and determines the nature of things. It is also a well-known form of kung fu.

Tao A Chinese term usually translated as "the Way." It includes the way of heaven, of nature, and of humanity.

Tao Chia Contemplative, or philosophical, Taoism, studied and practiced as a down-to-earth yet mystic way of life.

Tao Chiao Magic, or religious, Taoism, practiced in hopes of attaining immortality and divine blessing.

tathata The mahayana concept of "suchness." It refers to reality as it really is, apart from distinctions imposed by the ego-centered mind. One who sees reality in this way is a **tathagata,** "one who has gone thus." Tathagata is a term that is used to describe the Buddha.

te The power of the Tao. It is the principle that enables things to be what they are and is expressed differently by each individual living thing.

thangkas Scroll paintings of Tibetan Tantric Buddhism representing enlightened beings. The term comes from a Tibetan word for record. The purpose of thangkas, however, is not historical record-keeping, but inner knowledge and enlightenment.

Tzu An honorary title applied to many famous Chinese philosophers, including Kung Fu Tzu, the philosopher whose name has been Latinized as Confucius.

Vajrayana The Diamond Path, the form of Buddhism originated in Tibet.

varnas The four castes in the traditional caste system of India. They are the brahmins, the kshatriyas, the vaisyas, and the sudras. The word varna also means color, which reinforces the theory that the original caste system reflects racial differences between white Aryans from the North and the brown city-dwellers they invaded.

Wade-Giles Romanization system One of the most commonly used systems for transliterating written Chinese into the Roman alphabet.

wu wei The Taoist principle of effortlessness or inaction. By adopting wu wei, the Taoist sage accomplishes things without encountering resistance.

yab-yum The union of the divine male and female principles in Tibetan Tantric Buddhism. It represents the nonduality of nirvana and samsara.

yi The Confucian concept of righteousness, involving just and appropriate behavior.

yidams Tutelary (personal) deities commonly represented on Tibetan Buddhist thangkas.

yin and **yang** The passive and active principles of the universe, recognized by most schools of Chinese philosophy. The interplay of yin and yang are perpetually in flux, giving shape to the changing world.

yung The Confucian virtue of fortitude.

Guru's Who's Who

Here's an annotated list of some of the more famous names in Eastern thought:

Arjuna A prince whose story is told in the Bhagavad-Gita. He is on the verge of leading troops into battle but is reluctant to do so since the enemy forces are those of his uncle, so that, win or lose, large numbers of his relatives will be slain.

Asanga Together with his brother Vasubandhu, a founder of the Yogacara, or "mind-only" school of Buddhist philosophy.

Asoka (264–226 B.C.E.) Emperor of India who converted to Buddhism around the middle of the third century B.C.E. Asoka was the grandson of Emperor Chandragupta, who founded the Mauryan dynasty in the wake of the invasion of India by Alexander the Great.

A. C. Bhaktivedanta Swami Prabhupada Devotee of Krishna who founded the Hare Krishna movement in the United States.

Bodhidharma The twenty-eighth Buddhist patriarch, who brought Buddhism to China in 520 C.E. in the form of Ch'an, or Zen.

Brihaspati Philosopher who lived around 600 B.C.E. and founded the Carvaka school.

Caitanya (sixteenth century) A bhakti revivalist leader who spread Krishna worship throughout Eastern India. Caitanya taught that Krishna is both transcendent and personal—a timeless, absolute being that still has personal qualities and characteristics. He founded a long line of disciples that includes A. C. Bhaktivedanta, the founder of the Hare Krishna movement.

Chih-k'ai (538–597) Founder of the school of Buddhism known as T'ien T'ai (or Tendai in Japan), which means "heavenly terrace," named after the mountain where Chih-k'ai taught.

Chu Hsi (1130–1200) Neo-Confucian philosopher who brought together the separate currents of Buddhism, Taoism, and Confucianism into a way of thinking that generations of Chinese after him continued to accept.

Chuang Tzu (369–286 B.C.E.) Author of the *Chuang-tzu,* a favorite Taoist text among intellectuals who enjoy its rich imaginative qualities. The *Chuang-tzu* is generally more concerned with spiritual matters and less concerned with political affairs than the *Tao Te Ching.*

Confucius, or **K'ung Fu Tzu** (551–479 B.C.E.) Teacher and philosopher whose teachings became the ideological underpinning of the Chinese Empire.

Dharmakara Famous Boddhisattva who became Amitaba Buddha, the Buddha of infinite light and life.

Dogen (1200–1253) Japanese Buddhist master who founded the Soto School of Zen Buddhism in 1227.

Eisai (1141–1215) Japanese Buddhist master who founded the Rinzai school of Zen Buddhism in 1191.

Mohandas Mahatma Gandhi (1869–1948) Indian philosopher and political leader who galvanized his countrymen into nonviolent resistance of British rule, helping India achieve independence.

Gautama (ca. 150 B.C.E.) Founder of the Nyaya school of Indian philosophy. This school is predominantly concerned with logic.

Aurobindo Ghose (1892–1959) Philosopher of the Indian Renaissance who incorporated Western ideas into his thinking.

Siddhartha Gotama Shakyamuni Buddha The founder of Buddhism who lived during the sixth century B.C.E.

Han Fei Tzu (?–233 B.C.E.) Leading Legalist philosopher of China who opposed Confucian ideals as impractical.

Hsun Tzu (ca. 300–240 B.C.E.) Confucian philosopher who stressed learning and personal cultivation as antidotes for evil human tendencies.

Jaimini (ca. 300 C.E.) Legendary Indian sage said to have founded Mimamsa philosophy.

Kanada (ca. 300 C.E.) Founder of the Vaisheshika school of Indian philosophy. His name means "atom eater."

Kapila Legendary founder of the Sankhya School of Indian philosophy.

Kashyapa Disciple of Buddha who smiled when Buddha held up a flower. It was supposedly through him that Zen Buddhism was transmitted.

Krishna An avatar, or incarnation, of the god Vishnu.

Lao Tzu The legendary founder of Taoism supposed to have written the *Tao Te Ching* around 600 B.C.E. Scholars say, however, that the book may have been written by several authors as late as 250 B.C.E.

Lieh Tzu Author of a Taoist text called the *Lieh-tzu,* written around 300 B.C.E. This work is more accepting of Confucian philosophy than other Taoist works.

Madhva Thirteenth-century Indian sage who advanced the Vedanta philosophy of dualism, regarding Brahman and Atman as separate.

Maharishi Mahesh Yogi Founder of Transcendental Meditation (TM), popular in the United States from the 1960s through the 1980s.

Mahavira Teacher and religious leader who founded Jaina around 600 B.C.E., although Jains trace their origins even further back, regarding Mahavira as the last of 24 tirthankaras—legendary teachers said to have achieved complete freedom from worldly desires.

Malunkyaputta Legendary Buddhist monk who had doubts about the Buddha's knowledge and demanded categorical answers to questions about the world, eternity, infinity, the soul, reincarnation, and other metaphysical issues. An account of his debate with the Buddha is provided in a Buddhist sermon called "Questions Which Tend Not to Edification."

Mani Middle Eastern sage and visionary of the third century C.E. and founder of Manicheism.

Manu Legendary sage to whom is attributed an important code of laws. He is said to be the first human and to have descended from the gods.

Mencius, or **Meng Tzu** (ca. 370–290 B.C.E.) Confucian philosopher who taught that human nature is inherently good.

Mo Tzu (ca. 480–380 B.C.E.) Founder of Mohism, the Chinese philosophy of universal brotherly love.

Nagarjuna Founder of the Buddhist philosophical school of Madhyamika sometime around the second century C.E.

Guru Nanak Teacher and holy man of the fifteenth century who founded Sikhism. Nanak was originally Hindu but was influenced by Islam before developing his own beliefs.

Patanjali Sage who formulated yoga as a school of philosophy around 300 B.C.E.

Sarvepalli Radhakrishnan (1888–1975) Philosopher, scholar, and president of India from 1962 to 1967.

Sri Ramakrishna (1836–1886) Hindu holy man who espoused the common value of all religious teachings.

Ramanuja Twelfth-century Indian sage who advanced the Vedanta philosophy of qualified nondualism.

Ram Mohun Roy (1772–1833) Philosopher and Indian nationalist who founded the Brahmo Samaj, or Brahma Society.

Saicho (767–822) Japanese monk who introduced T'ien T'ai Buddhism to Japan, where it became known as Tendai.

Samkara Ninth-century Indian sage who advanced the Vedanta philosophy of nondualism, which says that all distinctions are finally illusory.

Dayanda Sarasvati (1824–1883) Brahmin who founded the Arya Samaj (Society of Aryans), an Indian nationalist group that advocated the Vedas as an answer for India's problems.

Shinran Shonin (1173–1263) Champion of the faith of Pure Land Buddhism in Japan, where it is known as Shin in his memory.

Shiva vengeful and destructive. Brahma balances these two opposing principles. Vishnu is regarded by Vishnuists as Ishvara, the Lord of all being. The universe is his breath, which he will reassimilate by inhaling. Then he will exhale again and recreate the world.

Tung Chung-shu (ca. 180–100 B.C.E.) Influential minister and scholar who first proposed the examination system of imperial China and who interpreted the Six Classics of Confucianism as a prophecy of the Han Dynasty.

Tzu-ssu Grandson of Confucius who is supposed to have written the *Doctrine of the Mean,* a famous classic and one of the Four Books of Confucian scholarship.

Vasubandu Together with his brother Asanga, founded the Yogacara, or "mind-only" school of Buddhist philosophy.

Vishnu Hindu god who originated during the Vedic period as a minor solar deity, but who rose in importance in the following centuries. Vishnu is a key member of the divine Hindu triad, the trimurti, including Brahma and Shiva. Vishnu is good and merciful and preserves the universe. In the Bhagavad-Gita, as well as other sources, Vishnu is associated with Brahman, or absolute being.

Swami Vivekananda (1863–1902) Indian spiritual philosopher who spread the teachings of Sri Ramakrishna regarding all religions as acceptable paths to the truth.

Vyasa Indian sage credited with founding Vedantic philosophy.

Wang Yang-ming (1472–1529) Neo-Confucian philosopher who emphasized the concept of Universal Mind.

Yang Chu A Taoist recluse who probably lived around 350 or 400 B.C.E. He is thought to have been pessimistic and fatalistic, with an every-man-for-himself attitude. His philosophy is described in the Taoist writings of Lieh Tzu.

It Is Written

Here's a list of books on Eastern philosophy for further reading.

Billington, Ray. *Understanding Eastern Philosophy*. London: Routledge, 1997.

Capra, Fritjof. *The Tao of Physics*. Shambala Publications, 1976.

Damodara, K. *Indian Thought: A Critical Survey*. New York: Asia Publishing, 1967.

Dharma Publishing Staff. *Ways of Enlightenment: Buddhist Studies at Nyingma Institute*. Berkeley: Dharma Publishing, 1993.

Eliade, Mircea, and Willard R. Trask, trans. *Yoga: Immortality and Freedom*. Princeton University Press, 1969.

Epstein, Mark. *Thoughts Without a Thinker*. New York: Basic Books, 1995.

Evans-Wentz, W. Y., ed. *The Tibetan Book of the Dead*. Oxford University Press, 1960.

Harris, Marvin. *Cannibals and Kings*. New York: Random House, 1977.

Huang, Chichung, trans. *The Analects of Confucius*. Oxford University Press, 1997.

Legge, James. *The Four Books: Confucian Analects, The Great Learning, The Doctrine of the Mean, and the Works of Mencius*. Shanghai, 1923, reprinted New York: Paragon Books, 1966.

Radhakrishnan, Sarvepalli, and Charles A. Moore, eds. *A Source Book in Indian Philosophy*. Princeton University Press, 1957.

Stryk, Lucien, ed. *World of the Buddha: A Reader*. New York: Doubleday, 1968.

Suzuki, D. T. *Manual of Zen Buddhism*. New York: Grove Press, 1960.

Watts, Alan. *The Way of Zen*. New York: Pantheon, 1957.

Wilhelm, Richard, and Cary F. Baynes, trans. *The I Ching, or Book of Changes.* Princeton University Press, 1961.

Wu, John C. H., trans. *Tao Te Ching of Lao Tzu.* New York: St. John's University Press, 1961.

Yu-Lan, Fung, and Derk Bodde, trans. *A History of Chinese Philosophy* (two volumes). Princeton: Princeton University Press, 1953.

Index

A

B

C

D

E

F

G

H

I

J

K

L

N

O

P

Q–R

S

T

U

V

W–X

Y

Z